ICONS
of the
CENTURY

ICONS
of the
CENTURY

Giorgio Taborelli

Icons of the Century
by Giorgio Taborelli

First English language edition
for the United States, its
possessions, and Canada
published by Barron's Educational Series,
Inc., 1999.

All inquiries should be addressed to:
Barron's Educational Series, Inc.
250 Wireless Boulevard
Hauppauge, NY 11788
http://www.barronseduc.com

Library of Congress Catalog Card No.:
99-64029
International Standard Book No.:
0-7641-5201-7

Translated from the Italian by Rosanna M.
Giammanco Frongia, Ph.D.

Printed and bound in Spain by Artes Gráficas Toledo, S.A.
D.L. TO: 1390 - 1999

9 8 7 6 5 4 3 2 1

TABLE OF CONTENTS

Introduction

Our intent in writing this book was to give the readers a sense of the twentieth century and its history, by walking them through a portrait gallery of one hundred personalities, much like icons of saints embodying the virtues, values, and strengths the world has loved, feared, and respected most.

Men and women, kings and generals, dictators and magnates, scientists and screen stars, inventors and forerunners, artists, ghosts, objects, children, and feast days of many nations walk down these pages like so many heroes and heroines of this century. They each represent something unique, whether good or evil, that earned a place in the fascinating ambiguity of history and in the imagination of billions of men and women.

It was our intent to tell you about these personalities in a concise manner; and treating them like icons, we introduced them in portraits, medallions, and images, along with the written word.

Passion was our companion in this work, because the myths that we and our forebears have encountered are the heritage of the author as well as the reader, the photographer as well as the observer who looks at the photographs today. It is a living heritage, for we are permeated with these myths, submerged in the trends they noted, began, and symbolized.

In retrospect, we can say that we worked during happy years. The Americas are at peace. Europe is no longer the bloodied battleground of major powers, and its formidable Eastern and Western dictatorships have fallen. The former Communist countries are in the throes of a crisis that signals their rebirth. The loss of permanent jobs, a source of anxiety for so many families, no longer happens in the welfare vacuum that characterized the turn of the century. Many former third world colonies—so named when the first world started to revolve around Washington and the second around Moscow—have developed influential economic systems of their own. Devastating pandemics such as tuberculosis and syphilis have been defeated, if not totally wiped out. And although the plunder and destruction of the biosphere continues, at least now the world is aware of the gravity of the situation, many seek the technology to remedy it, and some even genuinely intend to stop it. This was a century of deadly violence, but also one where the need for justice and the value of human beings were recognized by all.

We can pause and reflect by looking at the icons in the following pages, illuminated by the hundreds of illustrations in this book.

What is a century? How long does it last? It is one hundred solar years beginning either on a set day or with the end of the previous century. And where does a century exist? In every part of the world. These oft-repeated answers have been given since mankind first decided to record history by dividing it into centuries, in addition to measuring days, weeks, months, years, even hours with uniform regularity. The word "century" (from the Latin *centum*, one hundred) has other meanings as well. For example, it means "epoch": "the century of Leo X" which was once thought to be "the Renaissance," lasted only from 1513 to 1521 in Rome and Florence. And "of the century"—secular (from the Latin *saeculum*)—also means "of the world": for exam-

ple, Leo X's secular name was Giovanni de' Medici, son of Lorenzo the Magnificent. As for Dante, the "future century" was the eternity that would follow the end of the world.

But which world? There is one world that began on the day mistakenly presumed to be the day Christ was born. There is another world which, according to the ancient Hebrews, began—and here the chronology is really off the mark—with the beginning of the world. Finally, there is the Muslim world, which began in September of the year 622 of the Christian era, when Mohammed left Mecca for the city that was to become Medina. Yet today Jews, Muslims, and everyone else use the Christian calendar in all secular matters. This is the time used by the stock exchanges of the world.

Which world lived in this twentieth century? For the first time in the history of humanity, all of the Earth and even more. Gradually, over the years, all men and women entered the "Christian" world that began to prevail from the seventeenth century on. Today there are no longer separate worlds, except maybe for a few frightened "savages" left in the heart of Malaysia or in the Amazon forest, and they also are fated to succumb. The few surviving Australian aborigines left the stone age several decades ago and now wear jeans. And we did walk on the moon.

For good and for evil, the Earth has become one. This is why we feel justified in wanting to devote a book to the personalities that achieved fame in this century, because they can be everyone's icons, reaching all corners of the world.

Giorgio Taborelli

The world seen through metamorphoses

by Aldo Grasso

Icons, myths, and the media

An icon is a form of temporary earthly immortality; there are roads in life that from the beginning place man before this type of immortality, which albeit uncertain or unlikely, is already a real possibility: these are the roads taken by artists and entertainers, those who succeed in having their type, their essence, accepted. Which means being able to freeze the real with something unique that suspends its continuous change.

Icons are a myth of today, a fragment of eternity inserted in the feverish tale of our uncertain condition. The word derives from the Greek *eikón*, which means image, and originally referred to the sacred effigies in eastern Christian Churches. Later, computer science gave the word a more mundane, less spectacular, symbolic meaning, and toned down the rhetoric of myth. For the task of the icon is to replace an individual's traits, purifying them and endowing them with a clarity that is not one of explanation, but the aura of finality.

Icons make up an ideal, exclusive catalogue that opens the doors to the best of worlds. An image, it is also the ceremonial hallowing of that image. The death of Diana Spencer and her funeral allowed us to follow "live" the explosion of a myth and the consecration of an icon, in television time. A case of tragic unpredictability becoming eternity thanks to a media event.

Icons live in our substantial being, and we in theirs: no longer banished to heaven, on the border with humanity, the icon has entered our homes and is even ready to vanish at the first breeze, to be replaced by other icons, in a never-ending metamorphosis.

Diana's iconic story

Diana was the first princess who belonged wholly to the world of the media, instead of the world of fairy tales. As in fairy tales, her story had a tragic ending, more so because this was a fairy tale told by the media. Even more poignantly, it all began with the marriage of the century, royal nuptials celebrated as a spectacle for an audience of eight hundred million viewers. Imperial tradition, *raison d'État,* and sacred ceremony were the prototype for televised events. After that day in July 1981 a sort of curse befell the life of the princess: disagreements with her husband, secret affairs, tapped telephones, stolen photographs, the ongoing violation of her privacy became the controlling features of her not very happy life. A sort of media quandary plagued Diana: her husband did not like all the attention the media bestowed on her, and so neglected her; to attract his attention, she punished herself. First a lovely, elegant, radiant young woman and then a failed queen, Diana was the darling of the magazines, and soon became their prisoner. She was the most coveted of prey. The exasperation that molded her life found a tragic epilogue in Paris: the photo hunt ended once and for all. To die in a tangle of cars

Ancient copy of the Russian icon *Mother of God of Theodore.* This icon was believed to be particularly miraculous, tied as it was to the warrior saint Theodore of Stratilate and the city of Kostroma, to Prince Basil (brother of Alexander Nevsky), and to the Romanovs' accession to the throne.

July 17, 1994, Los Angeles. Dunga's penalty kick. Brazil beat Italy and once again won the Soccer World Cup.

1982, Monaco. Prince Rainier of Monaco follows the coffin of his wife Grace Kelly, who died in a car accident. With him are two of their three children: Crown Prince Albert and Princess Caroline.

trying to escape the paparazzi: this was the wildest paradox of the media's ruthless, brutal pursuit. To die in order to become a myth, an icon.

Thus, a funeral became the greatest television event of all time, more than the conquest of space, a great celebration, or a sports competition. Mourning becomes TV. Diana had already broken the audience record on her wedding day, which had been suitably staged for the cameras and had chipped the coolness of the Royal Family. Her good-bye was transfigured into the TV event of all events. While the World Soccer Games in 1994 were seen by two billion viewers and the 1996 Atlanta Olympics were followed in 170 countries, for Diana the BBC provided direct coverage to 187 countries and taped cover-

1933. Hedy Lamarr bare-breasted in the film *Ecstasy*, directed by Gustav Machaty. For many years, the film was considered a symbol of Hollywood's eroticism, and Miss Lamarr's husband tried in vain to buy up all copies of the film.

July 19, 1996, Atlanta. Olympic Games opening ceremony, on the centennial of the first modern Olympics.

1946. Rita Hayworth and her famous glove in *Gilda*, directed by Charles Vidor. The screen glove became the ghost of an erotic fetish.

age to 45 more; it used 200 cameras, and the number of viewers broke the record.

TV has shown funerals of other eminent individuals: John F. Kennedy in 1963, his brother Robert in 1968, Pope Paul VI in 1978, Grace Kelly in 1982 (one of Diana's first incarnations). Each one of these left an indelible mark on television. For Robert Kennedy, the true funeral procession was the train that traveled from New York to Washington, the tracks lined with mourners. For Pope Paul VI, the cameras aimed with their shots to unite the "high" of the shuttered balconies and jalousies with the "low" of St. Peter's Square, the heavenly and the earthly locked in St. Peter's amphitheater. For Diana, the BBC chose to use a sports event style: high-angle shots and shots from the side of the street, at carriage level. A clean, sharp, essential style with lap dissolves, very slow zooms, no close-ups of the royal family.

The crowds who attended Diana's funeral showed great respect, with sparse applause (something extraordinary) limited to Pavarotti, the Queen, and the Queen Mother. Her brother's stirring eulogy received an ovation. Elton John sang *Candle in the Wind* and everyone shivered. An extraordinary media ceremony where the subject was canonized, the live consecration of a myth, was followed in real time all over the world. Of course, only time will tell if the myth will hold up or if it will be forgotten as quickly as it was generated. We should not forget the paradox of this fable: Diana, pop star and new age diva, was a victim of her own fame; she lived the last years of her life as the object of everyone's morbid curiosity—our lusting eye was that of the paparazzi—until the supreme sacrifice.

The icon fetish: Gilda's glove

While the television eye is like a universal artificial aid that allows the icon to be hailed "under everyone's eyes," Hollywood still remains the great forge of modern myth-making, because only film has been successful in breathing life into the ghosts of the psyche.

An icon is an Event, it is a substance of this world that manifests itself in a continuous process; while the star is an Idea, the icon is something fixed, and belongs to the world of concepts.

"Man's oldest dream, and the cruelest, is to make a ghost come alive. Now, the cinema allows us to come closer, as never before, and with frightening immediacy, to this dream. In the movies ghosts do come alive, but like a strip of exposed celluloid or figures moving on a white screen, they do not quite exist and cannot quite be grasped or defined. It is the quasi non-existence and supra-existence of these ghosts that seals their perfection and power. For what is Rita's glove in *Gilda?* An object (such as we might find in a museum of the moving image), the fetishist ghost *par excellence* (think of Max Klinger's glove etchings!), a shared hallucination experienced in a dark movie theater by millions who are strangers to each other, who do not care to know each other, and who communicate only through this silent image.

"The sum of these three elements? At the very least, a stretching of the myth. And I mean this in a literal sense: sooner or later we must understand that movie stars are like the heavenly stars, like Andromeda, the Pleiades, and other classical mythological figures. Only by acknowledging such shared celestial and fantastic origin can we hope to understand what sets Sunset Boulevard apart from Olympus, and the distance separating the two." (Roberto Calasso)

Then also, movie stars are creatures of aesthetics, of acting, not of faith. They are poised at the edge between bravura and seductiveness, awareness and illusion; for this reason, even a glove, a fetish can, in a gesture of metonymy, become an icon. A glove replaces a face, the most celebrated of faces.

"Garbo's appellation of *Divine* was undoubtedly meant to convey not so much a superlative state of beauty as the essence of her bodily person, descended from a heaven where things have an exceedingly clear, sharp form. . . .

"Garbo's face exemplified that fragile moment when cinema stands poised to extract an existential beauty from an essential beauty, the archetype moving to yield to the seductiveness of corruptible faces, the clear, carnal essence on the verge of giving way to the poem of woman." (Roland Barthes)

Glove and face, accessory and countenance: the myth precedes each gesture, it is the invisible lining that moves with it; the icon is the presence of the divine through an image that wears itself out, that may be replaced, like the signs of writing.

The long stellar liturgy

The heaven of Hollywood stars is one of sovereign, motionless beauty that absorbs, understands, and coats everything in glossy enamel.

"Made into heroes and divine beings, stars are not simply objects to be admired: they are objects of worship. Around them the beginnings of a religion are born. This religion spreads far and wide, so that no moviegoer can claim to be totally immune from its call. Standing out in the movie throngs is the tribe of relic bearers who are consecrated to worship: they are the fanatics, the fans.

"The preponderance of women endows the star system with a feminine character . . . In today's society, a woman is a more mystical subject, and object, than man. By her very nature, she is more star-like than man. . . ." (Edgar Morin)

As we witness life converting into spectacle, icons form a heaven, a cosmography that includes the largest constellation ever explored;

An almost unrecognizable Greta Garbo, in her last years. The Divine has been reduced to an old, withered, unfeminine woman.

1954. A dance scene from *A Star Is Born*, directed by George Cukor, starring Judy Garland (1922–1969), who began her acting career as a teenager. The film tells of the rise and fall of a Hollywood star, a life in many respects similar to Garland's.

1973. Romy Schneider in *Ludwig*, directed by Luchino Visconti, in the role of Elizabeth of Austria, wife of Emperor Francis Joseph. Elizabeth was born Duchess of Bavaria. Romy Schneider interpreted the romantic role of the princess in a slew of Austrian B-movies, and she became identified with the lovely Sissi.

the media reports the stars' movement on charts and reintroduces the only mythological system of our times. The icon completes the media transformation of the star. It generates a kind of metamorphic knowledge, confined to the mind, where taking part in the life of the star is a pathos that mysteriously turns the participants into identical stereotypes. A participation propelled by an inexhaustible force, manifesting gracefully and shrewdly as a psychological device: that of identification.

"While the star shines of her own light, the actor shines only by virtue of acting, and the light he sheds lasts only that long. On the contrary, the star continues to glow even after the film is over, since the film is merely a moment—albeit an important one—of her expo-

sure to the public eye . . . When he acts, the actor is unrecognizable as an individual: art for him is a mode of being that is pretending. But the star does not need to perform because she is always herself, the boundary between being and pretending vanishes because she always pretends, never stopping to remove her mask . . . The beam of light projected on the star—on the stage and in real life—shines on a body that reflects light and radiates it; the viewer lets himself be penetrated by this light in the exalting viewing of the film. To exist, a star need not break up into characters, because what makes her stand out is her capacity of distilling many characters into one: herself." (Adriano Aprà)

Thus, after the star the icon, which is the image of a world of endless, aimless change that desires only itself. The icon is the media's creation, a luminous, weightless shadow that collides with us.

Finale

The icon is a star that ends up on the Internet, having given up her solitary life. In meeting one we meet them all. It is an infatuation that already includes the good-bye, the hypocrisy of leave-taking, the faraway look. It is mythical rather than myth.

"What characterizes myth is its pure, unsullied occurrence, its total obviousness, its lack of self-awareness. The mythical, on the other hand, comes complete with instructions: it wants to explain itself, to tell its history." (Stefano Bartezzaghi)

Is it fair to say that today's media creates only myths to be seen up close, myths followed by talk shows? And that their memory is a tired catalogue that bows to the hierarchical preeminence of the die (the cast, the copy, the reproduction) where the newest is the most ancient? An event means that the media project what they are showing as something unique. They interrupt everyday routine, the regular schedule, to allow the audience to witness a great occasion, covered in a reverential but calculating tone. In so doing, they leave a special mark in the collective memory: an icon. Thus icons are mental landscapes, at once threatening and amiable ghosts that no one can claim to have invented, which we encounter over and over again, as they patiently wait to be recognized. Icons are a sequence of ghosts that allow us to keep on living inside that enduring ghost we used to call life.

1962. Joan Crawford and Bette Davis in *Whatever Happened to Baby Jane?,* directed by Robert Aldrich. This film brutally plays up the different talents and styles of two stars, mercilessly shown in their physical decline, as sunset myths, devastated icons.

From 1961 to 1983 Sean Connery (b. 1930) starred in six James Bond movies as Secret Agent 007. The audience identified the Scottish actor with the movie character to such an extent that it was years before he was offered other parts.

Juliette Gréco, a favorite performer in French night clubs right after World War II. Her long, smooth, dark tresses, her black pants and vest, her heavy make up made her the icon of the "existentialist" generation of the 1950s.

1901

QUEEN VICTORIA

GUSTAV MAHLER

ENRICO CARUSO

HEIHACHIRO TOGO

SIGMUND FREUD

PAUL CÉZANNE

RUDYARD KIPLING

HENRY FORD

GUGLIELMO MARCONI

MARIE CURIE

The nineteenth century had shown the Western world remote parts of the Earth through daring expeditions and explorations that brought back reports, drawings, and photographs for all to see. It had divided the Earth into two parts: the "civilized" West and the rest, with the second subjected to the first. In this view, everything that changed the world for the better was the work, property, and privilege of Western men, who felt superior to the rest, because they set down laws—often by prearrangement among themselves—and dominated the world economy through science, technology, industry, and the capitalist system of production. They also did not hesitate to go to war to seize territories and subjugate whole populations as they saw fit, and usually won. At the end of the nineteenth century, Western man possessed more food, better tools, more efficient weapons, and a more rational organization than anyone else. He was highly inquisitive, a risk-

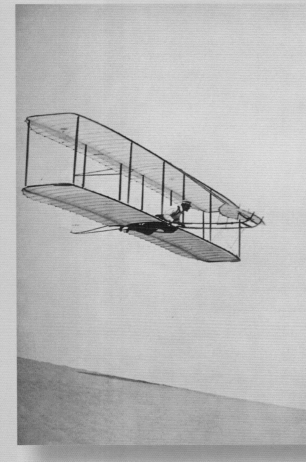

taker, and a gambler. Western man experimented,

climbed the highest mountains, flew over the

Earth. He was individualistic yet a good discipli-

narian, he had values, and he had faith in Chris-

tianity and his country. Patriotic and proud, he

believed he had a mission: to teach others to think

like him. Western man was committed to social

progress and thought everyone had the potential

to achieve it. Western man's society was more or

less modern, having abolished slavery. His cities had many buildings, large ports, engine-powered

metal ships, and linking railroads. His written and spoken word traveled instantly to enormous dis-

tances over cables. His most important philosophies were pragmatism—the belief that concepts

are valid only insofar as they are useful to action, and positivism—which held that philosophy is

no more than a synthesis of the sciences and that the Darwinian concept of evolution must also

be applied to the moral sciences. All these ideas engendered faith in progress, a faith that

remained unshaken for half a century, well into the mid-1950s.

October 10, 1902. Wilbur Wright (1867–1912), inventor of the heavier than air air-craft, together with his brother Orville (1871–1948), flying a biplane glider on the empty beach of Kitty Hawk, North Carolina. The first flight of an engine-powered plane took place the following year.

On January 27, 1901 Giuseppe Verdi died in a Milan hotel. He was probably the most popular composer of the nineteenth century. For Italy it was a day of national mourning, and everywhere opera lovers felt the death of "the swan of Busseto" as an irreparable loss. The old century segued into the new bringing with it many legacies.

In 1903 in Great Britain, Emmeline Pankhurst founded the movement whose aim was to secure for women the right to vote ("suf-

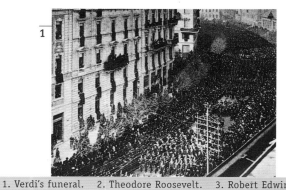

the internal affairs of neighboring countries. In 1903, Roosevelt organized a near revolution in Colombia, taking a piece of its territory from which the Republic of Panama was created. Panama, in turn, deeded to the United States the land where the canal joining the Atlantic and Pacific oceans was dug. The canal was inaugurated in 1915 and was to remain under U.S.

1. Verdi's funeral.   2. Theodore Roosevelt.   3. Robert Edwin Peary.   4. Rasputin.   5. A Hollywood *Merry Widow*.

military occupation until 1999.

As is clear from later decades, this was the century of the United States. Some of the greatest explorers were also American, such as Robert Edwin Peary (1856–1920), who demonstrated that Greenland is an island and in 1909 was the first to reach the North Pole.

Another rising power, the Japanese Empire, lay in the Pacific Ocean. In the Meiji era it fought China and Russia in short,

frage"). In 1908, 129 immigrant women workers died in a fire in a New York garment "sweatshop," the Triangle Shirtwaist Company. In remembrance, March 8th is celebrated as International Women's Day.

In 1904 Theodore Roosevelt (1858–1919), U.S. President from 1901 to 1908, proclaimed the right of his country to intervene in

THE BELLE ÉPOQUE LIVED ITS LAST, GREAT PERIOD. BIG INDUSTRY CELEBRATED ITS SUCCESSES AND MARRIED INTO ARISTOCRACY. ART NOUVEAU WAS THE NEW ART, AT ONCE A DESIGN, A STYLE, A TASTE. NEW ARTISTS PRODUCED NEW AVANT-GARDE ART: FAUVISM AND CUBISM. SEA BATHING BECAME POPULAR. CINEMA CAME INTO ITS OWN.

bloody wars leading to the annexation of the kingdom of Korea and several Chinese territories. In 1906 Roosevelt received the Nobel Peace Prize for his efforts to broker peace between Japan and Russia. On a different note, tradition was still held in high esteem everywhere, thus there was a bustle of court life in the many royal capitals. In addition to two imperial palaces, the Romanovs

5

had eight palaces for the widowed empress and assorted Grand Dukes. Tokyo had nine palaces for various members of the imperial family.

In the meantime, the Serb and Portuguese kings were killed in separate anarchist attacks. The

throne of the czar was also in peril, as the ambiguous shadow of Grigori Yefimovich Rasputin (1871–1916), a faith-healing monk, hovered over the imperial palaces. Nicholas II (1868–1918), czar since 1894, and his wife Alexandra had turned to Rasputin in the hope he could cure their son, crown prince Alexis, who was born with hemophilia in 1904.

In 1905, in the port of Odessa the sailors of the battleship *Potemkin* ignited revolution, forcing the czar to establish a Parliament.

6. The battleship *Potemkin*.　7. Pope Pius X.　8. Haakon VII of Norway.

That same year the kingdom of Norway was reborn, with a Danish king, Haakon VII (1872–1957).

7

1905 was also the year of *The Merry Widow*, an operetta by Franz Lehár (1870–1948) that made fun of a small, bankrupt Balkan court.

In 1903 Pope Leo XIII (Vincenzo G. Pecci, born 1810, crowned pope in 1878) died. In his encyclical *Rerum novarum* he had attempted to find a Catholic answer to the Socialists' demands for social jus-

tice. He was succeeded by Pius X (1835–1914), who was proclaimed a saint soon after his death; in the encyclical *Pascendi* this pope condemned modernism, a current of innovative thinking that was coursing through the Catholic laity, and with which some bishops sympathized. Although the pope was no longer a king, there still existed some monarchies that were believed to be sacred. The Japanese *mikado*, for example, was held

8

to be the direct descendant of a goddess; and several Islamic princes, called *shereef*, claimed to be direct descendants of the Prophet Mohammed; in the Himalayas several sovereigns were believed to be reincarnations of the Buddha or of holy lamas. The Dharma Radya, Prince of Bhutan, was believed to represent Buddha, and the Turkish

sultan was still the caliph of Islam. In the meantime, Louis Blériot (1872–1936) flew over the English Channel on July 25, 1909, proving that the airplane was a serious means of transportation.

An intense revolution took place in the arts, and a tenth muse was born with the cinema. In 1909, Maria Montessori (1870–1952) published *The Montessori Method*. While Freud was preoccupied with infantile sexuality, Montessori

10

9. Lisbon. Death of Carlos I and Dom Luiz.　10. Maria Montessori.

9

suggested that instead of doll houses we should build kindergartens designed for children and we should attend to the development of children's mental, motor, and sensorial faculties.

The great discovery of this century was the child: a subject, not an object, of education and learning. Women also became full-fledged political subjects, above and beyond their roles as wives, mothers, housekeepers, and nurses.

QUEEN VICTORIA

The Victorian Age died with her

Alexandrina Victoria was born in 1819 to Duke Edward of Kent and Victoria of Saxe-Saalfeld-Coburg. At the age of one she lost her father. In 1837 she lost her uncle William IV, whom she succeeded because her cousin, Charlotte, had died young, making a widower of her husband, Leopold of Saxe-Saalfeld-Coburg, since 1831 king of the newly formed kingdom of the Belgians. Leopold and the Duchess of Kent found a husband for young Victoria: he was close kin, three months younger than Victoria, extremely handsome, intelligent, poor but hardworking: it was Albert of Saxe-Coburg and Gotha. Albert took English citizenship and married Victoria in 1840. The couple had nine children. In 1857 the queen declared him prince consort, although he had been involved in his wife's decision-making since their wedding day. Albert died in 1861, after which the queen retired to Windsor Castle and made only rare public appearances; she wore mourning until her death. In 1877 her beloved prime minister Disraeli made her Empress of India. Queen Victoria died in 1901.

and geographic exploration. The majestic Zambezi River Falls in Africa were named after the queen by David Livingston (1813–1873) in 1855. Three years later, John Hanning Speke named a large African lake (26,286 square miles) and the part of the Nile into which it flows after her. A large desert in Western Australia and several other places, including part of Antarctica, were named after the queen.

EUROPE'S GRANDMOTHER. Victoria had eight children. She was the grandmother of Kaiser William II (son of her firstborn daughter who had married Frederick III) and of Alfonso XIII, king of Spain, who married Victoria Eugenia of Battenberg, a child of Victoria's youngest daughter. Her son, Edward VII, was brother-in-law to Czar Alexander III (they married two sisters, daughters of King Christian IX of Denmark) and to George I, king of Greece.

NO MORE HANNOVER. William IV of the House of Brunswick-Luneburg, male successor to George I, was king of Great Britain, Ireland, and Hannover. At his death, the kingdom of Hannover went to another of Victoria's uncles, Duke Ernest August of Cumberland, since female succession was not allowed by Hannover. Therefore, England lost its foothold in Germany. Queen Victoria's children and grandchildren bore her husband's name of Saxe-Coburg until World War I, when they changed their name to Windsor.

VICTORIA AND GEOGRAPHY. The Victorian era was the apogee of British power

PRIME MINISTERS. During her reign, Queen Victoria appointed capable statesmen. She was close to two of them: Lord Melbourne and Benjamin Disraeli (1804–1881); she named the latter Count of Beaconsfield. The queen had changing relationships with the other prime ministers, such as Sir Robert Peel (1788–1850), Lord John Russell (1792–1878), Lord Henry Palmerston (1784–1865) and finally, William Ewart Gladstone (1809–1898).

16

DECORUM

Perhaps Victoria was not a great queen. Sensual but not warm-hearted, capable of strong dislikes, indifferent to culture and the arts, she often obstructed her prime ministers and was averse to novelty. Authoritarian, she did not allow infractions to etiquette. As a widow she hid behind a haughty reserve, not at all gracious or discrete. She had passionately loved her husband and had failed to protect her rebellious son, heir Edward VII (1841–1910) from a harsh education. At her husband's death she found comfort in his reputation as a prudent, dedicated, self-sacrificing prince, who cared about the happiness of his subjects, even the most humble. As a widow, Victoria made respectability and decorum, two bourgeois values, a true religion. No waste, few ceremonies, no parties, no indiscretions, no public statements, no superfluous activities. She maintained a strict control over the morality of the royal children and the court, and punished improper behavior with removal from the court or threatening silences. For 64 years Victoria was queen of the greatest world power and she imposed her rules of behavior on the upper classes, replacing the libertine, eccentric habits of her uncle George IV (1762–1830) with respectability at all costs, reticence, and silent suffering. "Virtues" that, taken all together, are called decorum and ruled the upper crust until the end of World War II.

| 6

| 8

| 10

01 1902 1903 1904 1905 1906 1907 1908 1909 1910 **1901** 1902 1903 1904 1905 1906 1907 190 1905 1906 190

| 9

| 7

| 5

1. Bertha Muller, *Queen Victoria*, 1900.
2. John E. Millais, *Portrait of Benjamin Disraeli*. Disraeli, who headed the "new" Tories, was prime minister in 1868 and 1874–1880.
3. Windsor Castle, the queen's residence in her last years. According to persistent rumors, it was here that she secretly married a commoner from her retinue.
4. Franz X. Winterhalter, *Portrait of Queen Victoria*.
5. E. H. Landseer, *Queen Victoria and Prince Albert*.
6. A view of the Parliament building at Westminster, built almost completely during Queen Victoria's reign, and largely rebuilt after 1945.
7. Victoria Falls, Zambezi River.
8. Badge of Knight Commander of the Order of the Indian Empire, which belonged to the Maharajah of Patiala. Spink & Son Jewelers, London.
9. Natives on the shores of Lake Victoria.
10. A court reception in the first years of Queen Victoria's reign

"Disraeli had launched the idea that the queen should take on the title of Empress of the Indies. Victoria . . . urged her prime minister to implement his proposal."

Lytton Strachey, *Queen Victoria*

GUSTAV MAHLER

Completed the *Fifth Symphony*

Gustav Mahler was born in Kalištĕ, Bohemia, in 1860 to a family of modest Jewish merchants. He studied music at the Vienna Conservatory, where one of his teachers was Anton Bruckner (1824–1896). Among the highlights of his career as orchestra conductor were Bad Hall, Lower Austria (1880), Ljubljana (1882), the German Theater in Prague (1885–1886), Leipzig (1886–1888), where he filled in for the great Arthur Nikisch (1855–1922), the Royal Opera, Budapest (1988–1891), the Hamburg Municipal Theater (1891–1897), and the Vienna Court Opera (1897) where he remained for ten years, giving life to that theater's golden age. From 1898 to 1900 he also directed the Vienna Philharmonic Orchestra. In 1907 he was in New York to direct the Metropolitan Opera Orchestra and, starting in 1909, the Philharmonic Orchestra. He returned to Vienna, near death, in 1911. Mahler was one of the greatest conductors of all time; for him, to conduct meant to recreate a musical work. He introduced contemporary music to the repertory: his own and that of Richard Strauss (1864–1949). He was a source of inspiration for the new Viennese school, encouraging Arnold Schoenberg (1874–1951). Mahler spearheaded a Mozart renaissance and with Alfred Roller revolutionized and modernized opera stage production.

LADY LUCK. Mahler the conductor was relegated to the limbo of the greatest maestros of the end of the century. However, Mahler the composer was practically ignored due to the difficulty in performing his scores, their alleged lack of balance, their corruption and disintegration of the classical form and, finally, because he was made "obsolete" by musical developments after World War I (the twelve-tone revolution, Stravinsky's neoclassicism). Mahler's rediscovery and the rise of the Mahler cult took place after World War II, when his music appeared for what it is: the greatest interpreter of the unresolved complexities of our time.

THE SYMPHONIES. In addition to those already mentioned, Mahler composed the *First Symphony in D Major* (1884–1888); the *Second Symphony in C Minor* (1888–1894) for soprano, contralto, chorus and orchestra; the *Fourth Symphony in G Major* (1899–1900) for soprano and orchestra, which includes the well-known third movement, the marvelous *Fifth Symphony in C-Sharp Minor* (1901–1902); the *Sixth Symphony in A Minor* (1903–1904); the splendid *Seventh Symphony in E Minor* (1905); the *Ninth Symphony in D Major* (1908–1909); and the unfinished *Tenth Symphony in F-Sharp Major.*

JEWISH CULTURE. Mahler was Jewish, like Schoenberg, Freud, Wittgenstein, Einstein, and Kafka. Jews had long been an integral part of Western European culture. At the time of the French Revolution, they acquired civil rights, irrespective of their economic status. Thus Jews were no longer outsiders, and their culture was recognized as a precious, irreplaceable element of Western civilization. Apart from this, there was in Mahler an added element of tormented, deeply grieving experience. He was apparently the model who inspired Thomas Mann (1875–1955) to write *Death in Venice* (1913), a tale of people and love in a city disintegrating in the undeclared cholera epidemic.

TITANISM

Mahler had a rich, complex, original personality. As a composer, with his powerful music and wealth of nuances, he was one of the best interpreters of the final crisis of the post-Romantic period, of decadentism and of the nihilist angst so deeply expressed by Friedrich Nietzsche (1844–1900) in the 1880s. Another Nietzschean element, the "will to power," is aesthetically expressed in the titanic quality of works such as the Eighth Symphony in E-Flat Major (1906), which Mahler wrote for double orchestra (one with brass instruments), two mixed choruses (one a children's choir), and eight solo singers; or like the Third Symphony in D Major, (1893–1896) composed for orchestra, female chorus, children's choir, and contralto that lasts two hours. But even the extraordinary Das Lied von der Erde (The Song of the Earth,

1908) for contralto, tenor and orchestra, almost a touching lieder oratorio, and the Kindertotenlieder (Songs on the Deaths of Children, 1901–1904) are tense with a heightened melody and color that expresses the same symphonic titanism even in their more reduced orchestration and dimensions. The final crisis of the musical tradition extending from Bach to Bruckner is also expressed in the lilting irony, the raw sarcasm of so many passages in Mahler's music, along with a new use of phrasings and modes taken from popular as well as Jewish and Eastern music, no longer recreated in traditional academic forms, but inserted in jarring conflict with the most refined achievements of Western music. Thus Mahler's music paints for us, as a final metaphor, the last, immense effort of Samson defeated.

1907 1908 1910 1901 **1902** 1903 1904 1905 ... 1905 1906 190

1. Vienna, the Court Opera Theater, in a photo from the early part of the century.

2. Gustav Mahler's famous bust by François-Auguste Rodin.

3. Arnold Schoenberg in a 1924 portrait by Oskar Kokoschka. Schoenberg created the twelve-tone (dodecaphonic) system in the 1920s.

4. Mahler and Richard Strauss in Graz in 1906 for the premiere of Strauss's *Salome*.

5. A card by Alfred Roller depicting Fasolt, a character in Wagner's *Das Rheingold,* 1905.

6. Interior of the New York Metropolitan Opera House in the first years of the century. Gustav Mahler and Arturo Toscanini, who directed the Metropolitan orchestra, greatly contributed to its myth.

7. Alma and Gustav Mahler in Basel for a performance of the *Second Symphony,* which was held in the Cathedral.

8. Portrait of Anton Bruckner.

9. Detail of the entrance to the Secession in Vienna (1897–1898), one of the best-known works of architect Joseph Olbrich (1867–1908). The second verse of the inscription reads: Art and Freedom.

"When someone pointed out to him that he was performing a piece . . . in a different, nontraditional way, he would reply: 'That's what I do! What passes for tradition is usually sloppiness.'"
Alma Mahler in *Gustav Mahler*

ENRICO CARUSO

Sang in New York

The most famous tenor of the first half of the century was born in Naples in 1873 to a very poor family. As a boy, Caruso sang in the streets and in church. He was noticed and was given lessons by Lamperti and Concone, two respected local teachers, and by Vincenzo Lombardi, a conductor. Caruso debuted at the Teatro Nuevo of Naples; he was successful right away in 1895 in the role of Turiddu in Mascagni's *Cavalleria rusticana.* Caruso then triumphed at the Teatro Lirico of Milan in Cilea's *L'Arlesiana,* and his career took off: the fame of his miraculous

voice brought him to St. Petersburg, to Milan's La Scala under maestro Toscanini (who did not care for him much), to the Colón Theater in Buenos Aires, and finally, to the New York Metropolitan Opera, where he performed regularly from 1903 to 1920. The lyricism of Nemorino (*L'Elisir d'Amore*), Don Ottavio (*Don Giovanni*), Lionello (*Marta*), Faust (*Faust* by Gounod), the overpowering, carnal passion of Cavaradossi (*Tosca*), Canio (*I Pagliacci*), Dick (*La Fanciulla del west*), Loris (*Fedora*), the nobility of Verdi's heroes such as Manrico (*Il Trovatore*), the Duke of Mantua (*Rigoletto*), Radames (*Aida*), found a formidable interpreter in Enrico Caruso for the range, color, tone, and balance of his voice. He died young in 1921 in Naples.

TOSCANINI. Arturo Toscanini (1867–1957) was a cellist and orchestra conductor. His career took off in 1898 when he became musical director of Milan's La Scala Theater; he became an international star when he began his collaboration with the New York Metropolitan Opera in 1908, to which he added much luster. Toscanini is considered the greatest Italian opera conductor of our century, and caused a near revolution when he abolished the encores, the cuts, and the arbitrary embellishments not written in the score. He was feared by the singers, because he did not let them indulge in the virtuoso feats of volume, length (held notes), and pitch (high notes) that made the most popular tenors and sopranos famous.

THE GRAMOPHONE. In 1888 Emil Berliner, a German immigrant to the United

States, invented the first modern gramophone; in 1892 the first records appeared, reproduced from a single master. Thanks to these spring-powered gramophones, we can have an idea of the voice and the art of the best lyrical singers of this part of the century.

A GRAND LIFE. Grand hotels, expensive automobiles, precious rings, extensive first-class travel on ocean liners, appearances at the most celebrated restaurants, casinos, spa resorts, beaches. This was the lifestyle of the great opera singer. When motion pictures added sound, an even larger audience was able to enjoy their voices and their figures (which were often ungainly).

TENOR

Caruso was the highest paid of his contemporaries worldwide. Although not formally educated, Caruso loved art and collected paintings, bronzes, furniture, and medals. Were he alive today, he probably would not be tempted by the orgy of badly sung kitsch to which some declining golden voices succumb. Caruso wrote a modest Singing Method. He was a warm man, and a powerful professional. Although a tenor voice is the rarest of voices, he was able to forge himself into a myth at a time when other great tenors abounded, and to remain so even when other exceptional voices appeared on the scene, up to this day.

Caruso's greatest rivals were the virtuoso Angelo Masini (1844–1926), the Verdi tenor Francesco Tamagno (1850–1905), the elegant Fernando De Lucia (1860–1925). Later tenors were

Giovanni Zenatello (1876–1949), who introduced the summer season at the Verona Arena, Bernardo De Muro (1881–1955), Aureliano Pertile (1885–1952), who was Toscanini's favorite, Giovanni Martinelli (1885–1969), the sophisticated Tito Schipa (1888–1965), Beniamino Gigli (1890–1957), one of the loveliest tenor voice of the century, and Giacomo Lauri Volpi (1893–1979), who had great technique and power. The dates of birth of these tenors give an idea of the abundance of good voices in the first half of the century, and the list is by no means complete. Some of these singers had long careers, including in the United States, and helped to introduce Italian opera to the world and make it popular, because opera tells of intense love stories, and the tenor interprets the passionate, sincere lover.

1. The exterior of the old New York Metropolitan Opera House at the turn of the century.
2. November 13, 1911. Enrico Caruso in the heroic role of Radames, in Verdi's *Aida*, with Arturo Toscanini conducting.
3. 1911, New York, Metropolitan Opera House. *La Fanciulla del west* by Puccini, with Caruso in the role of Dick Johnson.
4. Art Nouveau style gramophone by the French company Pathé, 1905. Very few records are left of Caruso that give a genuine idea of what his voice was like.
5. 1913. Caruso steps into his Lancia car.
6. 1903. Caruso in the role of Cavaradossi in *Tosca* by Puccini, staged at the New York Metropolitan Opera.
7. 1902. A poster by Adolfo Hohenstein for the La Scala premiere of *Germania*, with music by Alberto Franchetti and libretto by Luigi Illica. Caruso created the role of the student Federico.
8. Caruso was much applauded in his role of Canio in *I Pagliacci* by Leoncavallo, at the Metropolitan.
9. Caruso and his family on an ocean liner during one of his Atlantic crossings.

"*At the center of the Italian vocal style is always* bel canto. *The high notes sung by Caruso, Gigli, Di Stefano or Pavarotti . . . release a vital force that German singers do not possess.*"
Wolfgang Sawallisch, *My Life with Music*

HEIHACHIRO TOGO

Blocked the Russian ports on the Pacific

Heihachiro Togo was born in 1847 in the province of Kagoshima, on the island of Kyushu, Japan, to a family of the lesser Japanese nobility. He joined the Navy at age 18. Emperor Mutsuhito (on the throne from 1867 to 1912) had abolished the *shogunate* in 1868, transferred the court to Yedo (Tokyo), reestablished imperial government and abolished feudalism (1869), when in 1871 Togo was sent to study in Great Britain at the glorious Royal Naval College. In 1873, he was at the Greenwich Sailors' House. In 1878 Togo returned home as a highly trained officer. During the Sino-Japanese war for control of the kingdom of Korea, Togo was captain of the cruiser *Naniwa*. Rear admiral in 1895, vice admiral in 1900, he became admiral in 1904. He either sank or blocked the Russian Pacific fleet at Port Arthur in Manchuria and in Vladivostock. As Navy Chief of Staff in 1905, on May 27–28 Togo destroyed the weary Russian Baltic fleet (which had sailed by way of the Suez Canal), in the Strait of Tsushima near Korea. Togo was made count in 1909, fleet admiral in 1912, and a teacher to Emperor Hirohito. He died in 1934.

908 1909 1910 1901 1902 1903 **1904** 1905 1906 1907

1

2

1901 1902 1903 **1904** 1905 1906 1907 1908

4

HERO. ". . . The meaning of the word *togo* [*hero* in Venetian dialect] . . . is derived from the name of the admiral who led the Japanese fleet during the 1904–1905 Russian-Japanese war" wrote a reader to a Venetian magazine in 1998. At the time of the events, newspapers all over the world were full of images illustrating the events of this very popular Japanese officer.

GOD. The Marquis, later Prince, Ito Hirobumi, was the true author of the 1885 Oath and Constitution and the force behind the speedy modernization of Japan (1868–1893). The emperor followed this principle: "To strengthen the foundation of our imperial policy we shall seek knowledge in all parts of the world." Science, technology, what today we would call Western "management science" were learned and adopted by the Japanese to serve their "imperial policy." The empire hired about five thousand Western experts, appointing many of them to official posts. However, nothing changed in the country's social structures and values. Prince Ito, for example, wrote that "the emperor is heaven on earth, sacred and divine." It was not simply an expression, but an article of faith.

SEEDS OF CONFLICT. The first treaty signed on an equal basis by Japan and a Western power was an 1895 treaty between Japan and the United Kingdom. The taking of California by the United States made the latter a power in the Pacific. The problem of Korea's independence, a country that for centuries had been contested by China and Japan, then by Russia and Japan, was to become an issue in Chinese, USSR, and U.S. relations.

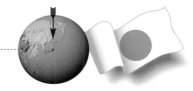

SAMURAI

"Oh, how I would like to make this country second to none, by adopting the good and rejecting the bad."

From a poem by Emperor Mutsuhito

The Russians lost both the sea and land war against Japan for control of Manchuria and Korea. Baron General Nogi set siege to Port Arthur, which surrendered in the first days of 1905. Between February 24–March 10, 1905, Nogi's forces and those of Marquis Marshal Oyama routed the Russian forces (which were superior) in the Battle of Mukden: 700,000 soldiers fought each other. With the Treaty of Portsmouth, Japan received Korea, which it annexed in 1910, and in practice Manchuria was opened to Japan. This caused an enormous stir in Europe, since for the first time in history a Far Eastern country had humiliated a large European empire.

To Japan, however, the peace that had been brokered by President

5

8

901 1902 1903 **1904** 1905 1906 1907 1908 1909 1910 1901 1902 1903   1910 1901 190

6

1. 1904–1905. Japanese soldiers seize the Russian base at Port Arthur.
2. An official portrait of Admiral Togo in European dress uniform.
3. Heihachiro Togo on board the warship *Nikasa*.
4. 1905, Tokyo. Imperial Princess Iwakura, president of the Patriotic Women's Association, welcomes Alice Roosevelt, daughter of the U.S. president, at the Shinbashi Railroad Station.
5. A frame from *Ran* (1985), a film by Akira Kurosawa, a brilliant rendering of the long and fierce Japanese Middle Ages.
6. The *Mikado* Mutsuhito (1852–1912) *Meiji Tenno*, which means "Emperor of the time of lights" (1867–1912), founder of modern Japan, wearing the European uniform of chief of the imperial armies.
7. 1906. Prince Ito Hirobumi, Japanese resident general in Korea, with a Korean puppet prince.
8. A popular Japanese print of a naval battle.
9. 1906. Illustration by Achille Beltrame for *La Domenica del Corriere*. Russian soldiers returning home from Manchuria attack railroad stations looking for food.

7

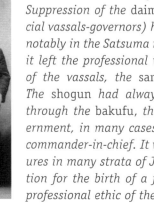

Roosevelt seemed too biased in favor of Russia. This discontent had the effect of rallying the nation around its emperor, even more than Japan's 1895 victory over China. The shogun *system had almost fallen on its own since the last* shogun *had no male heirs. Suppression of the* daimyo (the large provincial vassals-governors) had met with hostility, notably in the Satsuma rebellion, also because it left the professional warriors at the service of the vassals, the samurai, without a role. The shogun *had always exercised his power through the* bakufu, *that is, the military government, in many cases practically disappearing behind the figure of a commander-in-chief. It was this pervasive presence of strong military figures in many strata of Japanese society that provided a cultural foundation for the birth of a formidable armed force that deployed the fierce professional ethic of the* samurai.

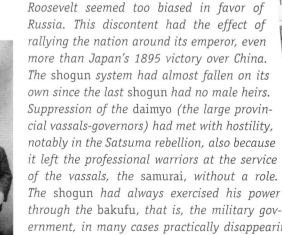

9

SIGMUND FREUD

Published *Three Essays on Sexual Theory*

igmund Freud (Pribor, Moravia, 1856–London, 1939) was born to a family of modest Jewish merchants who moved to Vienna in 1860. Freud lived there until 1938, when anti-Semitism forced him to expatriate to London. He completed a degree in medicine in 1881 and qualified as a university professor in 1885. Freud married in 1886 and in the same year opened an office for the treatment of neuroses. Toward 1900, he began to develop the theory of psychoanalysis. Essentially, the theory holds that every human action is inscribed with unconscious motivations,

urges, and forces. Psychoanalysis, the science of human subjects, attempts to describe this psychic world; the interpretation of dreams identifies its mechanisms, its logic, and the pleasure principles that guide and control them. Together with his colleagues and students, Freud systematized and extended psychoanalytic discoveries. The psychoanalytic movement branched out to Europe and the Americas where other, often conflicting, trends and schools were developed. Thus a new conception of mankind was born that revolutionized the human sciences and penetrated the arts, the mentality, and the vocabulary of even the man in the street.

DREI ABHANDLUNGEN ZUR
SEXUALTHEORIE

VON
PROF. DR. SIGM. FREUD
IN WIEN

439591-R

LEIPZIG UND WIEN
FRANZ DEUTICKE
1905

901 1902 1903 1904 **1905** 1906 1907 1908 1909 1910 1901 1902 19   03 1904 **1905** 1906 1907 1908 1909 1910

PRECURSORS. Jean-Martin Charcot (1825–1893) at the Salpêtrière Clinic in Paris was the director of the most authoritative Center of Psychiatric Studies. He was one of the founders of in-depth psychology. He highlighted the affective quality of some neurological illnesses and considered hysteria to be a type of neurosis.

JOSEPH BREUER (1842–1925), an Austrian, was associated with Freud from 1880 to 1895, and published

with him *Studies into Hysteria* (1895). A hypnotherapist, he invented the "cathartic method" which induced patients to verbally describe past traumatic events. It was a step toward Freud's method of free association of ideas.

HERETICS. Several disciples and colleagues of Freud came to criticize his ideas and took different paths. Among

them, Alfred Adler (1870–1937) in 1911 and Carl Gustav Jung (1875–1961) in 1914. They were followed later on by Erich Fromm (1900–1980), Otto Rank (1884–1939) in 1924–1926, and Wilhelm Reich (1897–1957) in 1927. Heretics but not apostates.

THE WRITINGS. Over the years, many of Freud's publications have been high-

lighted or set aside by scholars of various currents. Essential reading: *The Interpretation of Dreams,* 1900; *Psychopathology of Daily Life,* 1901; *Three Essays on Sexual Theory,* 1905; *Totem and Taboo,* 1912–1913; *Metapsychology,* 1915–1917; *Beyond the Pleasure Principle,* 1920; *Introduction to the Study of Psychoanalysis,* 1915–1917, 1932. Freud's letters are also of great interest.

PSYCHOANALYSIS

Psychoanalysis is a science that aims to understand the human being through his subjective psychic processes, which condition human cognitive experience. According to Freud, the new science has three interdependent aspects: it is a process that investigates psychic processes; from that, it develops a method to treat neuroses and related disorders (psychotherapy); it also develops psychological information that in turn is fashioned into a science (psychoanalysis). The individual so analyzed is the subject of the research, which seeks to gain access to the unconscious where the Id (libido, sexual drives) resides, and to discover why it was repressed. Through the benign, neutral assistance of a psychoanalyst and by interpreting dreams and the free association of ideas, the subject releases ideal and affective manifestations that take shape on the conscious surface of the Ego.

Through various stages, the major one being "transference" (the emotions felt by

the patient toward the psychoanalyst), treatment can slowly overcome the infantile amnesia produced by the Ego's defense mechanisms. Of these, the most important is repression, an unconscious process by which the individual removes from his consciousness the representations related to drives, which are mostly sexual. Thus, with the help of the psychoanalyst, the patient can recognize and accept the contents and processes of his unconscious psychic life and eliminate his inner conflicts.

7

8

3 1904 **1905** 1906 1907 1908 1909 1910 1901 1902 1903 1904 **1905** 1906 1907 1908 1909 1910 1901 1902 1903 1904 **1905** 1906 1 1903 1904

10

9

"Psychoanalysis is a medical practice which aims to treat given states of neurosis through psychological techniques."

Freud, "The Psychological Interest," 1913,
in *Interest in Psychoanalysis*

1. The Imperial Pavilion (Kaiser-Pavilion) of the Vienna subway at Schoenbrunn. It was one of several stations designed in 1894–1897 by Otto Wagner (1841–1918).
2. Sigmund Freud at the height of his powers.
3. 1913. Freud on a mountain vacation with his daughter Anna, who also became a psychoanalyst.

4. 1905. Frontispiece to the first edition of *Three Essays on Sexual Theory*. Franz Deuticke, Leipzig-Vienna.
5. 1900. Karl Feiertag, *The Wurstelprater Puppet Theater*. A snapshot of Viennese life.
6. Statue of a guardian forefather. Baluba art.
7. 1922, Vienna. Freud, Sándor Ferenczi, Sachs and, standing, Otto Rank, Karl Abraham, Eitingon, and

Ernest Jones, the biographer of the master.
8. 1457–1458. Piero della Francesca, *The Dream of Constantine*. Medieval thought held that dreams, as in this example, could also be premonitory.
9. 1962. Montgomery Clift in the sensitive role of Freud in *Freud,* directed by John Huston.
10. Cover of the 1893 *Almanach de Gotha,* the 130th annual issue.

PAUL CÉZANNE
Died after sowing the seeds of an art revolution

Paul Cézanne was born in Aix-en-Provence, the son of a banker, in 1839. In 1861 he often traveled to Paris where he would visit the Louvre museum to study El Greco, Caravaggio, and Velázquez. At home he sometimes worked in his father's bank, and often went back to Paris. Among the contemporary artists he admired were Delacroix, Daumier, and Gustave Courbet (1819–1877). He painted like a self-taught, dilettante artist.

In Paris, Cézanne liked to frequent the Café Guerbois, where many artists liked to meet. In 1871–1872 he was at L'Estaque; between 1872 and 1877, in Pontoise and Anvers-sur-Oise where he painted Provençal landscapes and the Île-de-France. Starting in 1866 he began to submit some of

his works to the Paris Salon, which refused them. He also exhibited at the Nadar Atelier in Paris, a gallery that handled impressionist paintings. Cézanne also traveled briefly to Holland and Belgium. He again exhibited his paintings at the Salon in 1877 and 1882, and in 1889 and 1890 in Brussels. When he showed his work at the Ambroise Vollard Gallery in 1895, the *Temps* wrote that he was unknown to the public. He died in 1906.

CAFÉ GUERBOIS. Much of what the nineteenth century gave to the West in the areas of politics and culture was born in the Paris cafés, among agitated discussions, passions, grudges, nights of drinking, praises, and curses around a guardian deity. At the Café Guerbois sat Zola who had achieved fame by 1867. The impressionist painters gathered 'round him, including the brilliant Claude Monet (1840–1926), Cézanne, and many others. Cézanne broke off his friendship with Zola in 1886, after the

author, in his novel *The Work*, created the figure of Lautier, an unhappy, failed genius of a painter.

SOLID IMPRESSIONISM. Cézanne found himself at ease with the impressionists; however, he was not interested in capturing on canvas the colors vibrating in the light of an instant. He wanted to "solidify" their art. He was looking for a "local tone," for the "geological nature" of a landscape. As an artist he did not care to give form

to his impressions. Impressionism was a revolution in nineteenth-century painting. Cézanne was like a yeast that leavened twentieth-century art.

CITY WITH REVOLUTION. Cézanne was not the provincial enamored of Paris. He did not paint the city. He preferred to paint Mont Sainte-Victoire near Aix, L'Estaque in the Gulf of Marseilles, or *The Bathers* as robust nymphs in a pyramid of bare trees against a city of cubes and cylinders. His was a silent

revolution. When, for example, in 1871 the Commune uprising broke out in Paris, Cézanne left the city. Unlike Manet, he did not care for sensational events: the barricades, the violence, or the repression that sent thousands to their death or to prison (among them, Courbet).

A SEARCHING ART

Artists try to create works that did not exist before, thus producing novel representations of the world and of art. Some artists, however, are bolder and more talented than others. By dint of reflection, experiments, and natural talent they find forms of expression that go beyond tradition, that were not conceived before, that are full of thought and beauty.

Cézanne's work was of this nature. He was not appreciated, not even toward the end of his life, because he had been confused with impressionists who were already known. When, however, van Gogh and Gauguin met him in Arles in 1888, they found in him the teacher post-impressionists were already looking for.

Cézanne's painting is solid, drawn with color, on the mar-

1. Cezanne, *View of L'Estaque and If Castle*, 1883–1885.

2. Inside the Café Guerbois, Paris, in an 1869 drawing by Manet.

3. Cézanne, *Self-Portrait with Rose Background*, detail, 1875.

4. The handsome intellectual face of Camille Pissarro in a photo from the 1890s.

5. Édouard Manet, *Civil War*, 1871.

6. Cézanne, *Mont Sainte-Victoire Seen from Bibémus*, ca. 1897.

7. Cézanne, *Madame Cézanne in a Yellow Armchair*, 1893–1895. Cézanne's portraits are also studied by twentieth-century artists.

8. Cézanne, *Portrait of Ambroise Vollard*, 1899.

9. Georges Braque, *The Aqueduct at L'Estaque*, 1908. In his transition from Fauvism to Cubism, Braque was influenced by Cézanne's research and choice of subject.

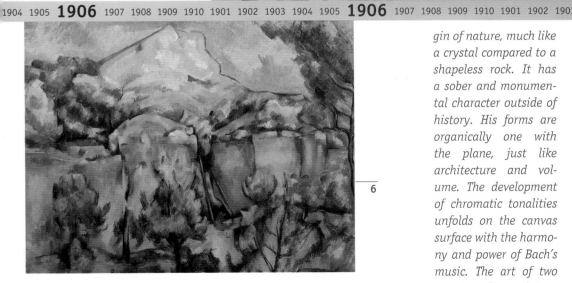

1904 1905 **1906** 1907 1908 1909 1910 1901 1902 1903 1904 1905 **1906** 1907 1908 1909 1910 1901 1902 1903 1902 1903 190

gin of nature, much like a crystal compared to a shapeless rock. It has a sober and monumental character outside of history. His forms are organically one with the plane, just like architecture and volume. The development of chromatic tonalities unfolds on the canvas surface with the harmony and power of Bach's music. The art of two avant-garde painters, Matisse (for color) and Picasso (for structure), is rooted in its experimental stage in Cézanne. The research done by the master of Aix, a bourgeois who was incapable of being a revolutionary, was done by sheer work: in order to continue painting, he even missed his mother's funeral. Today we can say that Cézanne resembles two other painters, Paolo Uccello and Masaccio, who created the foundation of Renaissance figurative art between 1420 and 1450.

"Sometimes I imagine colors as if they were . . . living ideas, beings of pure reason with which to communicate. Nature is not on the surface, it is deep down . . ."

Paul Cézanne

RUDYARD KIPLING
Received the Nobel Prize for literature

Rudyard Kipling was born in Bombay, India in 1865, the son of an Englishman who was director of the museum and art school of Lahore, Punjab. He spent his early childhood in India, and studied in England. In 1886 he published his first collection of verses; the following year, his first collection of short stories. In 1887–1889, Kipling was assistant managing editor of *The Pioneer* in Allahabad, Uttar Pradesh. The newspaper sent him to England by way of Japan, San Francisco, and New York; he wrote accounts of his travels in letters to *The Pioneer* that were later collected in *From Sea to Sea* (1899). In 1891 he published *Life's Handicap,* a large collection of short stories. In 1892 he married and lived with his wife in Vermont until 1896. These were important years, in which he published *The Jungle Book* and *The Second Jungle Book,* and the *Seven Seas* poems. In the winter of 1897–1898 Kipling was in South Africa where he was active on behalf of imperialism; in 1900, as a reporter, he witnessed the battle of Karree Siding against the Boers. Kipling's best novel, *Kim,* was published in 1901. In 1903 his book of verses, *The Five Nations,* was published; it included "The Recessional," a poem written for the anniversary of Queen Victoria's death. In 1907 Kipling was awarded the Nobel Prize for literature. During World War I the "imperial poet" was very active in working against the Germans. Kipling died in 1936.

1904 1905 1906 **1907** 1908 1909 1910 1901 1902 1903 1904 1905 1906

WHITE MAN'S BURDEN. Kipling sang the praises of the English nation, the English system, and the hierarchical order, of dutiful service for the good of the whole. He believed that the "chosen race" had the duty to civilize the inferior races; this was "the white man's burden." To better do so, Kipling believed, the white man invented the locomotive, the automobile, and the wireless telephone, of which Kipling wrote with a rough soldier's language full of technical expressions.

RACISM. As early as 1929, Helmut von Gerlach, an eminent scholar, had written: "We cannot state that the pure Nordic race is the bearer of everything that we call German culture." It was the French diplomat Joseph-Arthur, Count of Gobineau (1816–1882) who had first introduced the concept of race, on which he discoursed seriously in his *Essay on the Inequality of the Human Races* (1853–1855 and 1884). In the essay he affirmed the primacy of the "Aryan race" and of its Germanic element. For many years, it was even claimed that the primacy of Greek culture was due to the Dorian people who had descended from the North and were true proto-Germans.

POPULARITY. Although chauvinistic and anti-German, Kipling was immensely

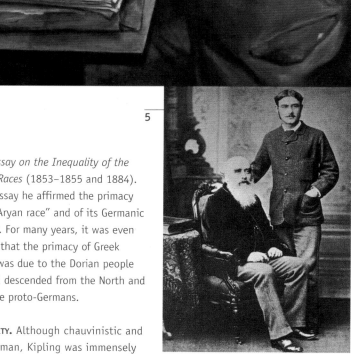

A NEW EXOTICISM

"Even today there are English citizens who are slow to understand that the barbarians were educated by the state, from birth, to live on thievery and homicide."

Rudyard Kipling about the Germans, in *Germany*

Kipling grew up in India, the son of an artist who was to illustrate his works; from the time he was born he was immersed in Indian nature and culture. His heroes were colonial service functionaries and officers who led both English and native troops in the defense of the empire, thousands of miles away from their motherland. They waged war, they won, and were honored as knights and crusaders of the queen. But India was not a strange land to Kipling, it was an English dominion, and master that he was, Kipling observed places, sculptures, and temples, invented benevolent ape-kings or elephant-gods and wolf-children, and described the savagery of the Thugs—the sect of stranglers who worshipped the Goddess Kali. Over time, he came to love the empire. He sang the praises of English soldiers who defeated the Boers with blood and tears, but also of the Dutch settlers who claimed autonomy in the territories they had conquered and farmed. Later, this feeling of English imperial greatness will become prejudice against non-Britons, in particular the Germans.

1907 1908 1909 1910 1901 1902 1903 1904 1905 1906 **1907** 1908 1909 1910 190   1906 **1907**

1. Frontispiece of *Wee Willie Winkie,* short story by Kipling, 1888.
2. A Boer gunner waits for the English to attack during the last battle of the Boer War (1899–1902), which was fought at Elands Laagte.
3. Cover of *The Recessional,* a patriotic poem Kipling offered in 1914 to the British soldiers leaving for the front.
4. Philip Burne-Jones, *Portrait of Rudyard Kipling,* 1899.
5. Kipling with his father, a respected art historian and illustrator.
6. Errol Flynn (1909–1959) in the part of the heroic spy in *Kim,* a successful film directed by Victor Saville (1950).
7. A view of the eighteenth-century Badshahi Masjid Mosque in Lahore, the garden city in the Pakistani Punjab.
8. A frame from *The Jungle Book* animated film (Wolfgang Reitherman, 1967), which marked a return to the more classic Disney style.
9. Cover of an old MacMillan edition of *The Jungle Book.*

popular in Europe and America until mid-century. His ideals of domestic and international order founded upon the primacy of the white race and his virile, heroic feelings were for a long time shared by the lower middle classes. Besides, every Western country had its Kipling, though often not as good as the original.

Thankfully, our century has forgotten the obtuseness of Kipling's racial views, but not the figure of the innocent wolf-child of The Jungle Book, *Mowgli, a new, exotic Parsifal, or of Kim, the orphan of the English sergeant who grew up among English spies and Indian gurus and learned to boldly serve king and country.*

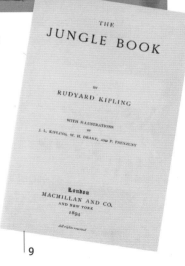

THE
JUNGLE BOOK

BY

RUDYARD KIPLING

WITH ILLUSTRATIONS
BY
J. L. KIPLING, W. H. DRAKE, AND P. FRENZENY

London
MACMILLAN AND CO.
AND NEW YORK
1894

All rights reserved

HENRY FORD

Built the Model T

Henry Ford was born to a modest family on July 30, 1863, in the Michigan countryside. At 17 he was already a factory worker in Detroit. In his free time he built a gasoline-powered car. In 1899 he founded the Detroit Automobile Company, which he left three years later to build a car, the 4-cylinder, 80 HP 999, which he raced in several competitions and won. With the money from the prizes and other capital, Henry Ford founded the Ford Motor Company in 1903. He was the sole owner of the company, together with his son Edsel. From 1906 to 1908 Ford improved on the design of the Model T car, 15 million of which had been produced by May 26, 1927, when it was replaced by the Model A.

Ford was the most popular entrepreneur of his age. He started from the utopian idea that the automobile, then a recreational hobby of the rich, would become a vehicle for all, thus guaranteeing mobility and freedom to the common man. To this end, the car had to be light, powerful, strong, simple, and inexpensive to buy and to maintain: thus was born the Model T. Ford was an innovator: in materials (he was the first U.S. manufacturer to use vanadium steel), in production systems, and in developing a structure of interrelated companies. He was a merciless businessman. In 1926 his conglomerate was the biggest in the world, with 200,000 employees.

By January 1937 he had already built 25 million cars.

4

1

Uno dei maggiori successi della Fiera di Milano

la Nuova Ford

FORD ITALIANA — SOC AN · TRIESTE

3

2

TAYLORISM. The theoretician of work organization in the industrial era was Frederick W. Taylor (1856–1915), an American metallurgical engineer. Taylor was intent, first of all, on improving machine performance, then on increasing work output by eliminating superfluous movements and waste of time, creating a functional relationship between worker and machine that would become one element in the production process and perfectly complement the machine itself.

PROTEST FILMS. Taylorism and Fordism were targeted by films decrying the condition of man subjected to machines. This protest produced masterpieces such as *Metropolis*, 1927, directed by Fritz Lang (1890–1975), *A nous la liberté,* 1931, directed by René Clair (1898–1981), and *Modern Times,* 1936, directed by Charlie Chaplin.

1929. In January, before the New York Stock Exchange crashed, the U.S. National Automobile Chamber of Commerce reported that there were 31,778,203 automobiles in the world, and that the United States had one car for every 4.9 inhabitants (21,291,719 cars).

WAR. On March 1, 1941, Ford built the first Jeep, using a Studebaker patent. In the summer of that year the company began the production of airplanes, and in the fall of armored tanks and bomber planes. From 1942 to 1945 the U.S. government forbade Ford to manufacture cars and ordered the company to produce only war vehicles. When his son Edsel died, Henry returned to lead the conglomerate. On September 21, 1945 he retired to private life, leaving his grandson Henry II at the helm. Ford died in Dearborn, Michigan, in April, 1947.

FORDISM

Ford plants were organized around a strict Taylorist system. The excellent quality-to-price ratio and the incredible commercial success of the Model T were due to the assembly line process that Ford perfected in almost maniacal fashion. This process of mass production yielded a higher volume of production, a shortening of the work hours needed for each car, a reduction in cost of production (due in part to the "scientific" exploitation of machinery), a reduction in price, and an increase in salaries. An enemy of bank borrowing, Ford self-financed his companies, reinvesting the profits and organizing a "vertical" production system (he owned mines from which he extracted iron and coal, mercury and manganese, along with whole forests, railroads, and ships) which he then used to diversify his products: after the car, he manufactured Fordson tractors, all-metal Stout planes, tires, and so on. Ford reasoned that the assembly phase could be located in different geographic locations; therefore, he opened 35 branches throughout the United States and 25 abroad. These plants received finished pieces ready for assembly.

At the end of the 1920s, Ford also began to decentralize the production of components, following a cost-saving plan that also took into account the local cost of raw materials and labor, tax laws and transportation costs, from raw materials to delivery of the finished product. This entire system was called "Fordism." For generations, it was followed by entrepreneurs the world over, who also liked to imitate Ford in the generosity he exhibited toward "his" employees and society at large: for example, the trip he took in Europe in 1915 in a vain effort to secure peace.

1. Young Henry Ford on the four horsepower "Quadricycle" he built in 1896.

2. Henry Ford in the countryside. He liked to be alone when he needed to reflect and make important decisions.

3. Ford advertisement in an April 1930 issue of *L'Illustrazione Italiana,* a popular Italian magazine.

4. From left: Thomas Edison, naturalist John Burroughs, Henry Ford, and the famous tire manufacturer Harvey Firestone on the wheel of an old mill.

5. A 1928 Ford trimotor plane used by Admiral Richard E. Byrd (1888–1957) to fly over the South Pole in 1929. Three years earlier, Byrd had flown over the North Pole.

6. A frame of "Charlot" at work in *Modern Times* (1936), one of Charlie Chaplin's strongest social protest films.

7. A 1927 Model T Ford in all its glory, the pride of the automobile industry.

8. The Henry Ford Museum and Greenfield Village in Dearborn, Michigan. A not-for-profit private learning institution, it is endowed by the Ford Foundation and the group's companies.

9. One of the first assembly lines for car production.

> *"At first the automobile was considered a nuisance, because it made a lot of noise and frightened the horses . . . finally, I had to carry a chain with me so I could fasten it to a street light every time I had to leave it."*
> Henry Ford

GUGLIELMO MARCONI

Awarded the Nobel Prize for physics

Guglielmo Marconi was the son of a Bologna, Italy, landowner and Annie Jameson, an Irish girl from an established family. He was born in 1874. He did not attend regular school. As a child he was fixated on electrology (as early electronics was then called) and as a teenager intuited that it was possible to send messages, which could be received at a distance, using electromagnetic waves, which had been discovered by the German physicist Heinrich R. Hertz (1857–1894). In the summer of 1895, near Bologna, Marconi succeeded in transmitting the three dots of the letter S (in Morse code) about one mile, although there was a hill between the transmitting device and the receiving device. No one had yet discovered that although transmitted in a straight line, Hertzian waves are reflected by the ionosphere; thus they can transmit a message to the other side of the world at the speed of light, through a succession of reflections.

In 1897, with English financing, Marconi founded the first of a number of companies, of which he owned the majority stake, to exploit his inventions. He also invented other devices. On December 12, 1901, he was able to transmit radiotelegraphic signals from Cornwall, England, to Saint John's, Newfoundland in Canada. John A. Fleming (1849–1945), an Englishman, invented the thermionic valve (diode), ushering in the age of radio.

1

04 1905 1906 1907 1908 **1909** 1910 1901 1902

2

3

1901 1902 1903 1904 1905 1906 1907

4

INVENTOR. Like Thomas Alva Edison (1847–1931), who perfected the telephone and invented the phonograph and the light bulb, Marconi represents the inventor type, heir to the tradition of artisan innovation and alchemist research, which was the source of modern experimental science. In the past, the inventor produced the wondrous machine, the clever contrivance. In our century he produces the industrial patent.

BOSS. Marconi patented his inventions and those of his assistants in every country, and trained and hired out wireless radiotelegraph operators. Many companies tried to compete with him, not always by respectable means. It is still common opinion today that had the *Titanic* been equipped with Marconi's wireless telegraph equipment and operators, there would have been fewer victims.

FAME. Marconi was perhaps more English than Italian thanks to the language he spoke, his friends, and the financing he received. The Italian government rejected his invention on the grounds that "it was not sound for telecommunication purposes." Years later, however, he did receive some help from the king of Italy, who in 1914 made him a senator, and later a marquis. The Fas-

cist Party, which Marconi joined, flaunted him as the living example of "Italian genius." Marconi became a member of the Grand Fascist Council and president of the Italian Academy and the National Research Council. He died in Rome in 1937.

PROPAGANDA. More than the printing press, the radio was all-pervasive. In

addition to affecting pronunciation and coining and diffusing words, the radio revolutionized the art of advertising and propaganda, giving them an all-encompassing presence. The radio invented the sponsor, a company that pays for a program, a serialized novel, or a concert, and in return is allowed to advertise its products during the broadcast.

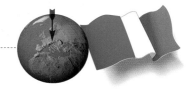

THE RADIO

Wireless, or radio, telephony developed in the 1920s from the possibility of transmitting and receiving sound at a distance. The revolution engendered by this invention was possibly of even greater import than the one wrought by television, for thanks to a portable device, everyone could listen in real time, in their home, at the office, while traveling anywhere, to all kinds of programs or information, from a weather report to the news, from music to poetry readings, from actors to heads of state giving their speeches. Family, friends, travelers, all gathered around the radio. Peace and war erupted over the radio. People listened to programs in foreign languages, to news, culture, and music from other countries, whether friend or foe. The isolation of hamlets that could not be reached by road was forever ended. The farmer became less of a farmer, the mountain man less so. New industries sprouted up for the radio, new newspapers, new types of shows and entertainment businesses. Legal issues arose about their use. Rulers could create propaganda that could reach everyone directly. Finally, radio enthusiasts could talk at great distances, even broadcast or receive messages that could save human lives.

"In the history of science . . . no other inventor . . . remained in the forefront of the development of his inventions and personally managed its major applications all over the world."

Luigi Solari, manager, Compagnia Marconi Italia, ca. 1932

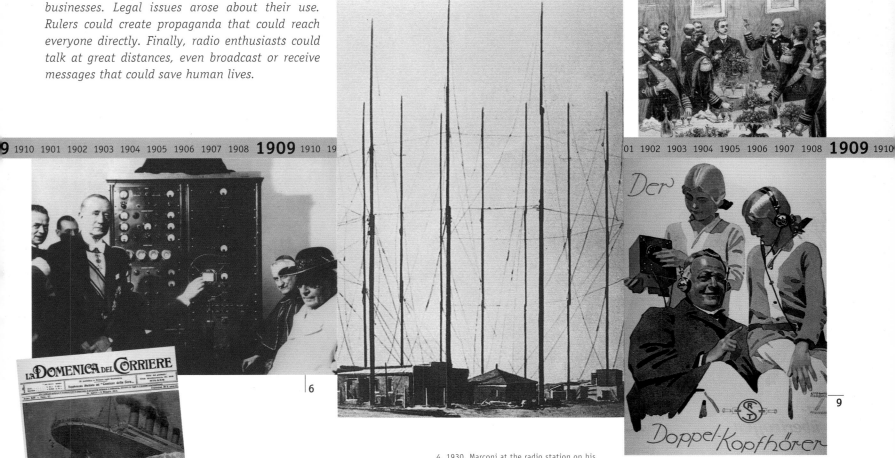

1. View of Villa Grifone in Pontecchio, Italy, where Marconi made his radio telegraph experiments in 1895.
2. Young Marconi with his great invention, the wireless telegraph.
3. 1931. Marconi speaks with Mussolini, the head of government, at the opening of the first Congress of Nuclear Physics organized by the Volta Foundation at the Italian Academy.

4. 1930. Marconi at the radio station on his yacht *Elettra*.
5. The tragedy of the *Titanic* (April 14–15, 1912) in an illustration from *Domenica del Corriere*.
6. In the presence of Pope Pius XI, on February 13, 1933 Marconi activates the first radio service between the Vatican and the papal villa at Castel Gandolfo.
7. The Poldhu station in Cornwall, England, from

which in 1901 Marconi transmitted signals to St. John's, Newfoundland, Canada.
8. Banquet honoring Marconi on the royal ship *Carlo Alberto*, anchored at La Spezia in 1902.
9. L. Hohlwein, a German poster advertising a Doppel-Kopfhörer radio headset, in the 1920s and 1930s.

MARIE CURIE
First woman scientist to achieve world fame

Maria Sklodowska was born in Warsaw in 1867, then part of the Russian Empire. At 16 she completed high school, earning a gold medal. She registered at an underground university that often changed locations because at the time it was a crime to teach in Polish. Maria later worked as a private tutor to support a sister who was studying at the Sorbonne University in Paris, where women were accepted as students. In 1891 she joined her sister in Paris, where she attended the Sorbonne, obtaining a chemistry degree in 1893 and a mathematics degree in 1894.

It was at this time that she met and married Pierre Curie (1859–1906). Their

first child, Irène, was born in 1897. Marie qualified for her university teaching position with a dissertation on the rays emitted by uranium. In the storage room of the School of Physics, with her husband she studied the emission of rays, to which they gave the name of radioactivity. In 1903 they won the Nobel Prize for physics (together with Henri Becquerel—1852–1908) for the discovery of spontaneous radioactivity. In 1904 their second daughter, Eva, was born, and Pierre was given a chair at the Sorbonne. He died two years later, and Marie took his place at the Sorbonne. In 1907 she was able to identify the atomic mass of metallic radium, demonstrating that it was a new element. In 1911 she was awarded, alone, the Nobel Prize for chemistry.

1

1906 1907 1908 1909 **1910** 1901 1902 1903 1904 19

2

4

3

OTHER DISCOVERIES. The Curies also discovered radioactivity "induced" by radioactive elements in the bodies next to them, and formulated the hypothesis of "radioactive transmutation," the transformation by decay of one radioactive element into another.

HEROISM. The amount of work done by the Curies, especially by the unassuming Marie, was vast. They lacked adequate equipment or laboratory sites, until, after Pierre's death, Marie became a world celebrity. The handling of radioactive substances made both of them seriously ill. Pierre died in an automobile accident, Marie of radioactive poisoning in 1934. Both refused to patent their research, thus refusing to exploit their research techniques for personal gain.

PATRIOTISM. A proud Polish patriot, Marie was also devoted to France. During World War I she organized the radiology department for the Military Health Corps, equipped with x-ray machines, on mobile ambulance units. After publication of the *Radium* review, the new element began to be used therapeutically by a group of French scientists, based on an article by Becquerel and Curie, who believed in 1901 that radiation could cure tumors.

FAMILY AND SCHOOL. "It is possible that radioactivity could become extremely dangerous in the hands of criminals," Pierre Curie said when he received the Nobel Prize. Against this risk stood the moral stature of Pierre and Marie Curie. In her last years Marie, her hands covered with sores, trained new generations of students in the hard discipline of experimental research. First among them, her daughter Irène and son-in-law Frédéric Joliot-Curie who discovered artificial radioactivity and jointly received the 1935 Nobel Prize for chemistry. Frédéric was a leader of the French Resistance during World War II.

RADIOACTIVITY

Becquerel, who came from an illustrious family of French Academy members, formulated the hypothesis that the fluorescence emitted by uranium salts that were exposed to sunlight was a phenomenon analogous to the production of X rays. He found that after exposing the salts and then covering them with black paper, they still made an impression on a photographic plate and, later, that the impression occurred even without any exposure to sunlight. This showed that the salts' radiation was independent of any other triggering rays. Marie identified a method for analyzing (including quantitative analysis) these rays; together with her husband, she demonstrated that radioactivity was proportional to the quantity of uranium: it was an "atomic" (today we would say "nuclear") property. In

a brilliant intuitive leap, Marie decided to also investigate uranium ores found in nature, and discovered that they had a specific action that was even higher than that of contained uranium.

After years of hard work, together with Pierre, and after grinding and purifying an enormous quantity of pitchblende (a specific residue of the glass coloring industry), she succeeded in isolating a new element, 400 times more radioactive than uranium. The Academy of Sciences called it "polonium" in her honor.

5

6

"Every moment of her life Marie felt she was at the service of society and her deep modesty was never replaced by conceit. She was tormented by a continuing sensitivity to social injustice."

Albert Einstein, *Memoirs of the Difficult Years* (1935)

1909 **1910** 1901 1902 1903 1904 1905 1906 1907 1908 1909 **1910** 1901 1902 1903 1904 1905 1906 1907 1908 1909 **1910** 190 07 1908 190

7

8

9

1. Frédéric Joliot-Curie, Pierre and Marie's son-in-law. Frédéric and his wife Irène received the Nobel Prize for chemistry in 1935.
2. Instruments used by Marie Curie for her experiments at the Radium Institute in Paris.

3. A touching portrait of Madame Curie at work.
4. The mill Marie Curie used to crush pitchblende. Enormous quantities were needed to extract minute quantities of radium.
5. 1896. The Curies in their laboratory.

6. Madame Curie's desk at the Radium Institute.
7. School of Physics, Paris. The storage room that became the Curies' first laboratory.

8. Henri Becquerel, 1903 Nobel Prize winner, in his uniform of a member of the French Academy.
9. 1898. Madame Curie's work notebook.

As a result of the wars fought in the twentieth century, Europe lost the world hegemony it had gained in the preceding 400 years. The main issues that preoccupied the Old World in this decade were the size of the German Empire, the rapid decline of the Turkish Empire, and the crises in the Russian and Habsburg monarchies. The vast Russian Empire not only suffered a frightening shortage of capital accumulation, but also a dearth of leadership in its ruling classes. To aggravate the problem, Russia's peasant masses lived in abject poverty. Nevertheless, the dull and vengeful Nicholas II pursued a "great power" policy that created difficulties for him even in foreign affairs.

Elsewhere, the union of the Austrian Empire and the kingdoms of Hungary and Bohemia, with Slovenia, Croatia, and Bosnia-Herzegovina, was undermined by the different levels of development of the various provinces and the ill feeling between the three dominant ethnic groups—German, Magyar,

and Slav—that made up the empire. Emperor Franz Josef was incapable of promoting or accepting change. The ongoing crisis in the Turkish Empire extended to three con-

An Italian position during the 1911–1912 Libyan war. After the war, Turkey transferred sovereignty of the two countries to Italy, but was resisted by the Senusyia Islamic Brotherhood, which was harshly repressed and defeated only in 1934. After World War II, the Grand Senussi became king of Libya.

tinents, since the Turks had sovereignty or quasi-sovereignty over provinces and principalities located in Europe and Africa and over Asian dominions where Arab nationalism was on the rise. The ruling class was small and inadequate, the court backward. The expansion of the modern German Empire, the last of the great powers to come into being, led to war with France and England for hegemony in Europe.

Harbingers of war occurred in June 1911 when, in violation of existing pacts, the French seized Morocco; two months later, the Germans ordered their gunboat *Panther* to the port of Agadir. Then, in September, Italy took advantage of the situation by seizing Cyrenaica and Turkish Tripolitania (Libya), in a 1911–1912 war where airplanes and poison gas were used for the first time. The Moroccan affair was concluded with treaties that granted minor concessions to the Germans and the French and prepared public opinion for war.

WORLD WAR I CHANGED THE LIVES OF MANY. THE RETURNING VETERANS, YOUNG MEN FOR THE MOST PART, NOW CHALLENGED AUTHORITARIANISM. WOMEN WHO HAD BEEN LEFT TO BE THE FAMILY BREADWINNERS NOW REVEALED "MASCULINE" TRAITS. MEN FROM SMALL TOWNS AND RURAL AREAS WHO HAD BEEN SENT TO THE FRONT IN FARAWAY LANDS CAME BACK WITH A CHANGED VISION OF THE WORLD.

In 1911 a lawsuit begun in 1906 ended with a ruling that Standard Oil Company (owned by John D. Rockefeller, 1839–1937) was guilty of monopoly practices; the company was broken up into 34 separate companies (among them, Exxon, Amoco, and Mobil). For the same reason another large company, American Tobacco, was broken up into 16 companies. The United States, a strong believer in free-trade capitalism, seemed not to be aware of the ultimate consequence of that doctrine: that some companies get bigger at the expense of others.

The motor vehicle and the airplane became widely used means of transportation, and their terrible effectiveness was put to work in war. In 1912 the French engineer Alexandre-Gustave Eiffel (1832–1923) set up the first laboratory for aerodynamic research. Bertha Krupp (1886–1957) and her husband Gustav von Bohlen (1870–1950) owned a steel empire in Germany's Ruhr region, which included steelworks and weapon factories.

In China, Sun Wen, known as Sun Yat-sen (1866–1925), the founder of the Republican Party, deposed the child emperor of the Manchurian dynasty (1644–1912), and was proclaimed president of the Republic of China.

In 1912 the "unsinkable" ocean liner *Titanic* sank during its maiden crossing, after hitting an iceberg, a tragedy that was to remain in the collective consciousness of this century.

In 1917, three young Portuguese shepherds saw a mystical apparition: Our Lady of Fatima. The site of the apparition became a pilgrimage destination.

In 1918 the Women's International Council crowned the struggle of the English suffragettes by winning for United Kingdom women the right to vote. Two years later, an amendment to the United States Constitution

1. Alexandre-Gustave Eiffel (in top hat). 2. Sun Yat-sen. 3. Women's International Council. 4. Vasl

officially marked the beginning of Prohibition.

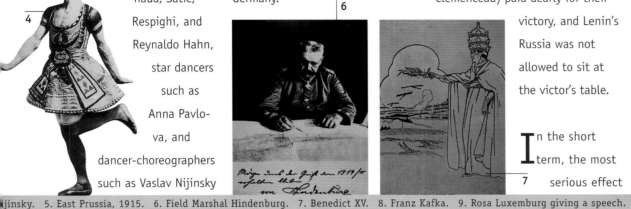

Diaghilev's Ballets Russes brought to the West barbarian echoes, Cubist and Fauve stage sets, exotic worlds, luxury and sensuality, with music by Stravinsky, Prokofiev, De Falla, Debussy, Poulenc, Milhaud, Satie, Respighi, and Reynaldo Hahn, star dancers such as Anna Pavlova, and dancer-choreographers such as Vaslav Nijinsky

(1890–1950) and Fokine. Europe was on the verge of momentous changes in other ways as well.

On June 28, 1914, in Sarajevo, a Serb nationalist killed Archduke Franz Ferdinand, heir to the Habsburg throne. A month later, Austria invaded the Kingdom of Serbia, Russia mobilized its army, Germany declared war on Russia and France, and invaded neutral Belgium, and the United Kingdom jumped into the fray against Germany. One by one, Belgium, Serbia, Italy, Romania, the United States, and Japan joined the war, along with Russia, which later withdrew in 1917. Bulgaria and Turkey joined on the side of Austria-Hungary and Germany.

Austria-Hungary and Germany had some success in Russia, under General von Hindenburg and thanks also to the Bolshevik revolution. In 1918 the German, Austrian, and Turkish Empires were defeated and destroyed.

World War I cost 10 million dead and 20 million wounded; it brought famine and general devastation and wasted vast resources. The peace treaties signed between 1919 and 1923 with Germany, Austria, Bulgaria, Hungary, and Turkey changed the world's political geography forever, as new states were born and the dominions and colonies of the defeated empires partitioned. The losing countries were branded so strongly with the mark of the victors that their economies and morale were devastated. The war also adversely affected those countries, such as Italy, whose war effort had been greater than their resources allowed. Even the United Kingdom and France (under the indomitable Clemenceau) paid dearly for their victory, and Lenin's Russia was not allowed to sit at the victor's table.

In the short term, the most serious effect

of the war was that right-wing dictatorships took root in Europe; in the middle term, World War II; and in the long term, the Arab question, arising out of the partitioning of Turkey and the abolition of the Ottoman caliphate, whose influence had extended as far as India.

The senselessness of World War I suggested the desperate, grotesque allegories of Franz Kafka (1883–1924); in 1916 he published *The Metamorphosis*. In 1917, it brought Pope Benedict XV (Giacomo della Chiesa, 1854–1922, pope since 1914) to strongly condemn the war's "useless slaughter;" and it brought jail time for conscientious objection to Lord Bertrand Russell (1872–1970), the English mathematician and philosopher who spoke out against war all his life.

The mutiny of the German fleet and the Communist revolutions in Bavaria and Hungary are events pointing to a Europe that was in search of a new identity.

jinsky. 5. East Prussia, 1915. 6. Field Marshal Hindenburg. 7. Benedict XV. 8. Franz Kafka. 9. Rosa Luxemburg giving a speech. 10. Clemenceau, in an oil portrait by Manet.

FILIPPO MARINETTI

Prophet of Futurism

Filippo Tommaso Marinetti was born in 1876 to a family of wealthy Italian merchants in Alexandria, Egypt. He completed the baccalaureate in Paris and received a law degree from the University of Genoa, Italy. His first literary prize was the "Samedis populaires" by Sarah Bernhardt (1844–1923), for his *Les vieux marins* (*The Old Sailors*) in free verse. He thus made his entry in the Parisian literary salons, and his collection of poems *Destruction* (1904) confirmed him as a daring, fertile poet. In 1905 in Milan, he founded *Poesia* (*Poetry*), which was both a poetry review and a publishing house. In 1909 his *Le roi Bombance* (*The Feasting King*), a satirical play on Marxist democracy, was staged in Paris. In the same year, he published the first manifesto of Futurism in the French newspaper *Le Figaro* and a novel, *Mafarka il futurista* (*Mafarka the Futurist*). In 1912, it was the turn of the *Technical*

Manifesto of Futurist Literature; in 1914, the "words-in-freedom" collection *Zang Tumb Tuuum*. In 1929 Mussolini made him a member of the Italian Academy and the national secretary of the Writers' Union; later, he was appointed president of the Italian Encyclopedia Institute. Thus the revolutionary artist became an establishment figure. Fifty years after his death (1944), the critics still do not consider him a great author; not so, however, the historians of culture.

F. T. MARINETTI
FUTURISTA

ZANG TUMB TUUUM

ADRIANOPOLI   OTTOBRE 1912

PAROLE IN LIBERTÁ

EDIZIONI FUTURISTE
DI "POESIA"
Corso Venezia, 61 - MILANO
1914

MOCKERY. An iconoclastic spirit along the lines of Alfred Jarry (1873–1907) pervaded Marinetti when he wrote *Les Dieux s'en vont, D'Annunzio reste* (*The Gods Leave, D'Annunzio Stays*, 1908), or the poems of *Le Monoplan du Pape* (*The Pope's Monoplane*, 1912). But there is an element of threat in his *Spagna veloce e toro futurista* (*Fast Spain and Futurist Bull*) or his prose work *L'alcova d'acciaio* (*The Steel*

Alcove). Marinetti's replies to his critics were good-humored and juvenile but could also turn fierce.

POLITICS. Dynamic Marinetti became an early ally of the Fascist "revolution." Wounded as a volunteer in World War I where he received several medals, in the post-war period Marinetti led the Futurists in a "struggle to preserve victory." He founded the Arditi Associa-

tion, a group of volunteer veterans who had favored hand-to-hand combat. In 1929 he was elected to the Italian Parliament, the Fascist candidate with the highest number of votes after Mussolini.

ART. Like Sergey Diaghilev (1872–1929), the all-powerful impresario of the new ballet form, Marinetti was the international engine behind the first

and second (1929) Futurist wave. The leading Futurist writers in Italy were Corrado Govoni and Aldo Palazzeschi; in Russia, Velimir Khlebnikov and Vladimir Mayakovski. The more important painters were Umberto Boccioni (1882–1916); Giacomo Balla (1871–1958), Gino Severini (1883–1966), Carlo Carrà (1881–1966), and several Russian artists known for their unusual "radialism."

AVANT-GARDE MOVEMENTS

1. Cover of *Zang Tumb Tuuum, Free Words* by Marinetti, part of a futuristic series published by Poesia, Milan, 1914.

2. Rouzena Zatkova, *Portrait of Marinetti*, ca. 1920. Marinetti's personality attracted Slav intellectuals.

3. Marinetti and his wife in a portrait by Ghitta Carell, well-known 1920s photographer.

4. Umberto Boccioni, *A Futurist Evening*, 1911. In the drawing, the black figures on the stage behind the orchestra are, from left, Boccioni, Balilla, Pratella, Filippo T. Marinetti, Carlo Carrà and, seen from the back, composer and painter Luigi Russolo. In the center, the brawl.

5. Tato. *Flying in a spiral over the Coliseum (Spiralata)*, ca. 1930. Sky writing was the last expression of Futurism in painting.

6. Léon Bakst (1866–1924), *Portrait of Sergey Diaghilev*, 1904–1906.

7. Enrico Prampolini (1894–1956), *Portrait of Marinetti*, plastic composition, 1924–1925.

8. Umberto Boccioni, *States of Mind I: Goodbyes*, 1911.

9. Giacomo Balla, *Girl running on a balcony*, 1912.

The twentieth century stands out in the history of culture for a number of movements that broke off from traditional expression. In the figurative arts, the most important of these, in the years from 1905 to 1916, were: Die Brücke, the Fauves, Cubism, Der Blaue Reiter, Orphism, Suprematism, Constructivism, Dadaism. In music, it was the Second Vienna School, the symbolic, anti-naturalist theater of Adolphe Appia and Edward Gordon Craig, Isadora Duncan's free dance, and Diaghilev's Ballets Russes. At the center of these innovations was the symbolist poet Guillaume Apollinaire (1880–1918), who was both a critic and a prophet of avant-garde art. Futurism, however, rather than concentrating on issues of form, preoccupied itself with technical possibilities, with the relationship between the aesthetic product, society, the city, technology, and machines (the automobile, the airplane, sky writing; an effective example was the project for a rail-

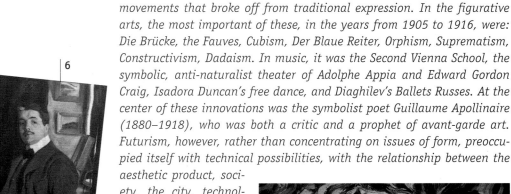

1918 1919 1920 **1911** 1912 1913 1914 1915 1916 1917 1918

road-airport station by Antonio Sant'Elia, who in 1914 authored the Manifesto of Futurist Architecture). *In opposition to the static analysis of Cubism, Futurism proposed an aesthetic analysis of dynamics, in an explosion of colors. It proposed and accepted all expressive forms in a series of "Futurist evenings" that were meant to provoke and embarrass the audience. Marinetti preached that the new aesthetics should be part of everyday life, possibly influencing Chanel. In 1932, Marinetti and Fillia even published* La cucina futurista *(Futurist Cooking). Futurism held that war had the effect of renewing society. In 1915 Marinetti published* Guerra, sola igiene del mondo *(War, the Only Hygiene of the World); in 1919, a collection of poems,* Otto anime in una bomba *(Eight Souls in One Bomb). Thus Futurism had affinities with the absolutist avant-garde movements that arose after World War II.*

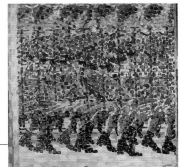

41

TARZAN
The Ape Man fights evil

William Burroughs was an American novelist of the beat generation, born two years after Tarzan, who criticized society through his innovative style and a crude form of satire. Edgar Rice Burroughs (1875–1950), another American novelist, also criticized society but used a different language, in effect creating a character, Tarzan, who was to become internationally famous. Rather than moaning about the failings of Western civilization, E. R. Burroughs left it behind and made good triumphant in a fantasy world, partly inspired by the forest of James Fenimore Cooper (1789–1851) and Kipling's India. In 1912 his *Tarzan of the Apes*, first published as a serial, was the first in long series of novels, short stories, and screenplays. The last story in the series, *Tarzan and the Foreign Legion*, was written after World War II. The protagonist of these works is a white adult male whose family drowned at sea and who was raised by apes. A number of other characters are developed, along with the setting: Tarzan's companion, Jane; Cheeta the ape; their young son; friendly elephants, natives (mostly Africans) from the nearby village, and evil Western men intent on plundering the wealth of the innocent natives, all set in the jungle and in mysterious local cultures that echo ancient Egypt and are cruel, sybaritic, and perverse.

17 1918 1919   1915 1916 1917 1918 1919 1920 1911 **1912** 1913 1914 1915 1916 1917 1918 1919 1920 19

1

2

5

3

4

LUCK. Tarzan was the subject of cartoons, comic strips, advertising, illustrated short stories, plays, radio programs, TV series, and, especially, films. In 1935–1936 the author became also the producer of two Tarzan films. Tarzan first appeared in the movies in 1918. Over the years, he was interpreted by Elmo Lincoln, G. Pollar, P. Dempsey Tabler, J. Y. F. Miller, Johnny Weissmuller, Buster Crabbe, Herman Brix (later known as Bruce Bennett), Glenn Morris, Lex Barker, Gordon Scott, Denny Miller, Jock Mahoney, Mike Henry, Ron Ely, Christopher Lambert.

"ME TARZAN. YOU JANE." This immortal phrase was spoken by Johnny Weissmuller (1904–1984), the first talking Tarzan and the greatest of them all. A swimmer of Austrian heritage, Olympic swimming champion in 1924 and 1928, he signed a contract with MGM and in 1932 starred in *Tarzan, the Ape Man,* directed by Van Dyke, the first of a dozen or so movies, the last of which, *Tarzan and the Mermaids,* directed by Florey, was made in 1948. Until 1942, Jane Porter was interpreted by the enchanting Maureen O'Sullivan

42

In the film—Greystoke: The Legend of Tarzan, Lord of the Apes (1984), Tarzan returns to the aristocratic estate in Europe that belonged to his ancestors. Terrified by the lack of sensitivity of Western culture and science, he rejects modernity. Thus we discover the feeling that moved readers and audiences all over the world and animated Tarzan the character. Unlike Mowgli, the wolf-child of Kipling's The Jungle Book, *Tarzan is not the good native who lives in a natural condition and magically communicates with wild animals, learning their culture. On the contrary, he is a white man who has rejected shoes, weapons, money, private property, the vices of contemporary society. He is a gatherer, not a hunter; he lives with a woman whom he loves, but without lust; he lives with a child, but instead of a father, he is more like an older brother of the same animal species who worries about the child's present, not his future; he lives*

1. Weissmuller yelling, in a frame from *Tarzan Finds a Son!*, directed by R. Thorpe, 1939.
2. Johnny Weissmuller with Cheeta and Maureen O'Sullivan in *Tarzan, the Ape Man,* directed by W. S. van Dyke II, 1932.
3. Weissmuller and the "wild men" in *Tarzan Escapes,* directed by Richard Thorpe, 1936.
4. Elmo Lincoln in *Tarzan of the Apes*, 1918. Jane was interpreted by Enid Markey.

5. Lex Barker atop his trusted elephant in *Tarzan's Magic Fountain,* directed by Lee Sholem, 1948.
6. Cover of an old Italian collection of stories by Burroughs, with Tarzan as protagonist.
7. Johnny Weissmuller swinging on his vine in *Tarzan Finds a Son!,* directed by Richard Thorpe, 1939.
8. Tray with Coca-Cola advertising from the 1940s with pictures of Maureen O'Sullivan and Johnny Weissmuller in swimsuits.
9. Drawing by Burne Hogarth for an American cartoon from the late 1930s, with Tarzan as protagonist.

1911 **191** 16 1917 1918 1919 1920 1911 **1912** 1913 1914 1915   1919 1920 191

with an ape whom he treats as a friend from a like species; he uses healing remedies taught him by the apes; he seeks and secures the help of "wise" animals; in case of need, he returns the favor as a peer. Tarzan stays away from everything that "modern man" has corrupted, such as the city. He freely, happily uses his athletic body, his mind, his human senses. All children would like to live his adventures; men would like to avoid the frustrations of modernity; and women love his body and his kindness.

(Mia Farrow's mother), a fresh, unaffected ingenue who aptly filled the role of Tarzan's companion. Weissmuller starred in several Tarzan films for MGM, and later for RKO.

MEANWHILE, Burroughs published *Under the Moons of Mars*. The *Titanic* sank: 1,513 dead. Another Balkan war broke out for control of Turkish Macedonia, which was coveted by Serbia, Greece, and Bulgaria. Twenty eight countries competed in the fifth modern Olympics in Stockholm.

"We are tired of looking at society, at sex, at allegorical and historical films. It's a relief to watch an extraordinary story of a hero who was kidnapped by apes as a child and raised by them . . ."
Theatre Magazine, 1918, on Elmo Lincoln's *Tarzan of the Apes*

COCO CHANEL

Invented the twentieth-century woman

Gabrielle Chanel was born in 1883 in a poor people's shelter in Saumur, the natural child of peddlers. As a young girl she lived in Moulins and learned about chic by observing the aristocratic officers of the 10th Cavalry and the fashionable people of nearby Vichy. "Little Coco" worked as a counter girl and a dressmaker's apprentice, but she dreamed of being a vaudeville star. Unable to afford costly dresses, she opted for a provoking simplicity, dressing like Colette's character Claudine. Chanel became the lover of Étienne Balsan, a textile businessman. She became an excellent horsewoman and enjoyed fox hunting. At one of these events in Pau she met Arthur "Boy" Capel, an Englishman who was in the coal business, and he became her new lover; they set up house in Paris.

Chanel started designing and selling hats. Boy lent her money so she could open a hat-maker's shop at 21 Rue Cambon, on the mezzanine floor, where she also sold knit shirts, similar to the ones Boy wore when playing polo, except that she sold them to ladies. In May 1912 the *Journal des modes* printed the photograph of an actress wearing a Chanel hat. In the summer of 1913, Boy financed the opening of a second boutique in Deauville, where Chanel sold high-neck, sailor-style sweaters and jersey and flannel items to women. Reminiscing, Chanel commented: "In those years, everyone wanted to meet me . . . I invented a fashion: the stylist as star."

1

2

3

4

NEW WOMAN. Boni de Castellane, the champagne king, said: "Women have disappeared; all we are left with are boys dressed by Chanel." Aldous Huxley wrote that Coco's woman was "lithe and tubular like a boa constrictor." At the end of World War I, *Vogue* wrote: "Everything she does is news: the quilted coat . . . even her studied tan."

ARCHITECTURE. Coco had a sure taste for color and small ornaments. Her greatness, however, resided in inventing a new feminine body: the "little black dress," the raincoat, the svelte winter coat, the soft hat to be folded and stored in a travel bag, long pants with low, masculine heels, the short skirt, a low waist, the dress slightly longer in the back, the extra-size knit sweater. Chanel's woman is athletic, slim, at ease, superbly elegant, a woman to take seriously, a woman who is self-possessed.

IN THE LIMELIGHT. With Chanel the great tailor became a high society character. She financed Diaghilev and supported Stravinsky, who was also her friend. In 1939, Coco closed her fashion house. She stayed in Nazi-occupied Paris and was later accused of collaborating with the Nazis. After Paris was liberated, she hung the following notice in her shop window: "Free perfume for G.I.s."

THE "LITTLE CHANEL"

1. Chanel, in her atelier before a show, uses scissors to alter a jacket.
2. 1959. A classic Chanel suit.
3. Entrance of the Ritz Hotel in Place Vendôme, Paris. For many years it was Miss Chanel's residence.
4. 1913. A comfortable, sporty knit ensemble by Chanel.
5. Ca. 1930. Coco Chanel in top and pants, with her dog Gigot at La Pausa, her country house in Southern France.

6. 1916. Chanel clothes from *Vogue* magazine.
7. Jean Cocteau (1889–1963). *Portrait of Coco Chanel*, ca. 1933. Cocteau was a novelist, poet, playwright, painter, and film director who influenced twentieth-century French culture. He was a friend of Chanel and loved her novelty and vigor.
8. Chanel No. 5's classic bottle, created by Coco Chanel in 1921. Profits from the perfume products have always been much higher than those from Chanel fashions.

Summer 1914. Will the Germans take Paris? Unsure, society ladies fled to Deauville. Diane de Rothschild, who had a disagreement with her tailor, introduced Chanel's creations to the cream of society. Moreover, ladies needed new, comfortable dresses to wear when they volunteered in the military hospitals. Once they were convinced that Paris would not fall, they returned to their city mansions. Austerity was the perfect opportunity for the Chanel style to come into its own, for she did away with girdles and corsets, so women could be natural; and the fear of bombs (and of running to the shelters) decreed the triumph of another Chanel invention: lady's pajamas.

> **"**Fashion is in the sky, the streets, fashion has to do with ideas, the way in which we live, the events surrounding us. **"**
> Coco Chanel

COMEBACK. In 1953, at the age of seventy, Coco Chanel reopened her Rue Cambon fashion house, except that now fashion belonged to men such as Dior. Chanel had told Dior: "I love you, but you dress women as if they were armchairs:" At her first show Paris mourned the fact that there was nothing new, it was Chanel's eternal style. But the collection had enormous success in the United States, where her creations stood for simplicity, the architecture of the body, eternal freshness, true chic. When she died in Paris in January 1971, Chanel was hailed as one of the greatest fashion designers.

After the war, Chanel opened a house in Biarritz, on the Atlantic coast near Spain, where the Spanish noblewomen turned Coco into Madrid's fashionable dressmaker. In Paris, she moved her shop from 21 to 31 Rue Cambon, a six-story building. Now wealthy, she repaid Boy's loans. Her friends included Stravinsky, Satie, Diaghilev, Picasso, Matisse, Cocteau, Radiguet, Colette, Paul Morand, and Misia Sert. Boy got married. Her heart dried out, no longer open to love. By then, Mademoiselle Chanel had created what came to be known as the Chanel style, symbolized by the "little Chanel": a small 2-piece suit with short jacket and short skirt, masterfully cut shoulders, unusual fabrics, a few refined buttons, and elegant trimmings around the neck and the jacket's borders.

WILLIAM II

Plunged Germany into World War I

On November 17, 1887, old King William I entrusted his grandson William with a sort of viceroy's power, given that the Crown Prince Frederick (1831–1888) was dying of throat cancer. In fact, Frederick III was king for only three months and was succeeded by his son William, born in 1859 to him and his wife Victoria, a daughter of Queen Victoria of England. William was born with a paralyzed left arm. He did not do well at school. In 1881 he married Augusta Schleswig-Holstein-Sonderburg. While William I had entrusted Prussia and the German Empire to the capable hands of Chancellor Bismarck, William II wanted to both reign and govern. He proclaimed to the people that he was king by divine right, and persuaded Marshal Moltke to resign, followed in March 1890 by Bismarck, the "iron chancellor." In the meantime he embarked on several diplomatic trips: in 1888 he visited Czar Alexander III, Oscar II of Sweden, and Christian IX of Denmark. Returning to Kiel he crossed Germany and paid a visit to Emperor Franz Josef in Vienna, Humbert I in Italy, and Pope Leo XIII in Rome. In 1889 he received the king of Italy and the emperors of Austria and Russia. In London he paid a visit to Queen Victoria; in Istanbul to Abdul Hamid; in Monza to King Humbert I; again to Emperor Franz Josef in the Tyrol. Everywhere he gave endless, self-aggrandizing speeches. He wanted to soften the anti-Socialist and anti-clerical laws passed by Bismarck, but he picked weak chancellors, and fell into the trap of World War I.

1 — BERLIN — Reichstagsgebäude

2

3

4

and Trieste. The rash interest shown in the Maghreb disgusted France, which had not forgotten the 1870–1871 defeat and the loss of Alsace and part of Lorraine.

COLONIES. William II expanded the German colonial empire. The presence of the German navy on the seas was one reason for the conflict with Great Britain.

ALLIANCES. The emperor's activism, his tactless words, the grandiose land and sea maneuvers, as well as conflicts of interest destroyed the system of alliances Bismarck had put into place.

German initiatives in the Turkish territories worried Russia. Industrial competition and the sympathy shown to the South African Boers frightened the United Kingdom. Loyalty to Austria disappointed Italy, which was seeking to take over the South Tyrol (with Bolzano/Bozen) and the cities of Trent

DEFEAT. In November 1918, a revolution broke out in defeated Germany. On the 28th, the emperor resigned in favor of his son Frederick William, to no avail. He then fled to Holland where he lived secluded in Doorn Castle and wrote his memoirs. He died in 1941, almost forgotten, at the zenith of Hitler's power.

5

GERMAN *LEBENSRAUM*

Germany was the last of the major European countries to develop a strong, modern state. It succeeded thanks to the great Otto Eduard Leopold, Prince von Bismarck, Count von Bismarck-Schönhausen (1815–1898), who was president of the Royal Prussian Council. Bismarck was assisted by Chief of Staff Count Helmuth von Moltke (1800–1891), who was responsible for the quick, victorious wars against Denmark (1864), Austria (1866), and France (1870), which persuaded the German kings to recognize William I of Prussia (1797–1888) as Emperor of Germany. The German state was expanded further by Hitler when he annexed Austria, the Sudetenland, and other smaller regions. Previously, since the Middle Ages, there had been large German migrations to the Baltic territories, to the Volga, and later, to the United States.

In this nationalistic century, the idea took shape in Germany that

1917 1918 1919 1920 1911 1912 1913 **1914** 1915 1916 1917 1918 1919 1920 1911 19   1915 1916 19

all Germans must be included in a German state. This ambition went hand in hand with the impressive development of German literature since the eighteenth century, the military status Germany achieved under Frederick II of Prussia (1712–1786), industrial power, and, in general, with the strong German economy starting in the nineteenth century. William II of Hohenzollern believed he was heir to Charlemagne and Frederick II the Great. He wanted to win for "his" people a "living space" (Lebensraum) through politics (for which he had no talent) and if need be,

through war, for which he was as inept as his Chief of Staff Helmuth Johannes von Moltke (1848–1916), the nephew of the earlier von Moltke. Appointed commander-in-chief at the outbreak of World War I, Moltke was out of office already in September 14, 1914.

1. The Reichstag Building in early twentieth-century Berlin.
2. 1895. Crown Prince Frederick William of Hohenzollern greets his father William II on the field.
3. 1914. William II and Empress Augusta Victoria of Schleswig-Holstein-Sonderburg at the inauguration of the North Sea canal on the River Elbe.
4. William II and Mohammed V in Istanbul. Germany supplied Turkey with financial aid and technical personnel.
5. Vittorio M. Corcos, *Portrait of William II King of Prussia and Emperor of Germany*, detail, 1904.

6. Emperor William II studying the operations map, between Chief of Staff Erich Ludendorff (1864–1937) and Paul von Beneckendorff von Hindenburg (1847–1934).
7. Ca. 1914. Color lithograph with stamps of the Samoa Islands, a German colony in the Pacific Ocean.
8. A German soldier looking through a periscope from a trench.
9. 1908. William II at the left of Austrian Emperor Franz Josef during a military parade in Vienna. Germany, Austria, and Italy were united by the Triple Alliance, created in 1882.

"The day of Austro-Hungarian mobilization, whatever the reason, will also be the day of German mobilization."
William II

WOODROW WILSON

Led the United States through World War I

Thomas Woodrow Wilson was born in 1856 in Staunton, Virginia, to a family of Scottish origin and Presbyterian faith. He received a refined education: Princeton B.A., law degree from the University of Virginia, a Ph.D. in history and politics from Johns Hopkins in 1886. The following year he married Ellen L. Axson; they had three daughters. Wilson taught jurisprudence and political economy at Princeton, and was a history and constitutional scholar. In 1902 he was elected president of Princeton University. At age 54 he left academia, having been elected governor of New Jersey.

As governor, Wilson distinguished himself by fighting cronyism and corruption. His fight against unscrupulous business dealings gained for him the 1912 Democratic presidential

nomination, and he won. He then set out to submit to Congress a large number of new bills regulating customs, banks, currency, the administration, and trusts. Opposed to "dollar diplomacy," on October 27, 1913, Wilson announced that the United States would not acquire any land at the expense of its neighbors. In 1914 he offered to mediate peace between Germany, France, and the United Kingdom. In 1915 he was financing the Entente's war effort.

920 1911 1912   9 1920 1911 1912 1913 1914 **1915** 1916 1917 1918 1919 1920 1911 1912 1913 1914 **1915** 1916 1917 1918 1919 1920

THE GAZETTE TIMES.

Founded July 29, 1786
Largest 2-Cent Circulation in Pennsylvania
The Weather Fair

TWO CENTS A COPY.   ••••••   PITTSBURGH, FRIDAY MORNING, NOVEMBER 10, 1916.   TEN CENTS A WEEK.

PRESIDENT WILSON IS RE-ELECTED

UTOPIA. Wilson conceded to France and the United Kingdom many points in order to establish the League of Nations, which was to be a forum for the resolution of conflicts and a guarantee of peace in the world. However, upon returning home and submitting the Versailles Treaty to Congress on July 14, 1919, he met with hostility, especially to the League of Nations. During a promotional campaign in the Midwestern and Western states, Wilson suffered a stroke and became semi-paralyzed. From then until the end of his second term, in 1921, his wife and a small White House clique

"His charm and good manners notwithstanding, Wilson was still a strange combination of college professor not used to being contradicted, and Presbyterian pastor unable to question the divine truth by which he was always inspired."

Gore Vidal, *Idem*

that refused to have the president declared incompetent took over for him. He died on February 3, 1924.

LEAGUE OF NATIONS. The League became a reality on January 20, 1920, and went into a fatal crisis at the outbreak

of World War II; it died officially in 1946. The League included the countries that won World War I and 13 neutral states; Germany joined in 1926, the USSR in 1934. In 1933 Germany and Japan left the League; in 1937 it was Italy's turn. It had as

many as 58 member states. Without the United States among its members, and dominated by the major European nations, the League had no real effectiveness or power.

HEIR. Wilson dreamed of ensuring a lasting peace by applying the "principle of equity to all peoples, all nationalities" along with the "right of everyone to live in equal conditions of freedom and security, one next to the other, be they strong or weak." Franklin D. Roosevelt, refined and educated like Wilson, but less professorial and more capable, became Wilson's true successor.

INTERNATIONAL ORDER

In 1914 Wilson conceived a Pan-American Pact of "reciprocal guarantees to independence and territorial integrity" that was not signed due to the outbreak of World War I. Wilson negotiated tirelessly with the United Kingdom, urging an end to its naval blockade, and with Germany, urging an end to its submarine warfare. He proclaimed U.S. neutrality, yet supplied arms to the Entente powers, initiating strong relations with the United Kingdom, which was later to become a U.S. base of operations in Europe. Wilson's sympathy went to the Entente and to Belgium, which had been invaded by surprise, yet in 1916 he was still offering to mediate for peace, while continuing to finance the English-French war effort. In April 1917 he took the United States to war and in January 1918 enunciated his principles for peace in "Fourteen Points," which were more ethical than political. The allies pledged to respect them.

From a military standpoint, U.S. intervention was not decisive with respect to the war's outcome; however, from the point of view of war materiel, weapons, and financing it was crucial, and it hastened the defeat of the central powers, which were reduced to poverty by the war effort. Against the advice of his staff, Wilson decided to join the 1918 peace conference held in Versailles, near Paris. Ignoring the complexity and the history of problems and relations in Europe and the Mediterranean, he found himself outdone by two masters of the political and diplomatic arts: Georges Clemenceau (1841–1929) and David Lloyd George (1863–1945), French and British prime ministers respectively, who turned the peace negotiations into French and English acts of revenge against Germany, Turkey, and Austria, as well as Italy, a lesser ally that had dared to try to join the circle of great powers.

8

3 1914 **1915** 1916 1917 1918 1919 1920 1

1915 1916 1917 1918 1919 1920 1911 1912 1913 19

5

I WANT YOU
FOR U.S. ARMY
NEAREST RECRUITING STATION

7

9

6

1. A view of the Capitol Building Great Rotunda, Washington, D.C., seat of the U.S. Congress.
2. William Horpen. *Portrait of Th. W. Wilson*. Detail, 1919.
3. November 10, 1916. Pittsburgh's *The Gazette Times* announces President Wilson's reelection.
4. April 2, 1917. Wilson announces to Congress that the United States has joined the war on the side of the Entente.
5. 1913. Outgoing President William Howard Taft and President Elect Wilson at a parade.
6. The six great powers of the League of Nations at Geneva's Bavaria Restaurant. Caricature by Derso and Kelen, 1928.
7. U.S. poster for 1917 military recruiting.
8. 1918. Propaganda for the home front. John J. Pershing (1860–1948) was Commander-in-Chief of U.S. forces in Europe.
9. 1919. Passing through Milan, Wilson greets the crowd.

Published *The Foundation of the General Theory of Relativity*

The most famous of German scientists was born to a liberal Jewish family in Ulm, Switzerland in 1879. On the second try he passed the acceptance exam for the Federal Polytechnic Academy of Zurich, where he exhibited a penchant for solitary meditation. In 1902, thanks to the recommendation of friends, he was hired by the Bern Patent Office, which left him plenty of time for thinking and writing scientific articles.

Einstein graduated in 1905 and married his schoolmate Mileva Maric. They had two children. When they separated, Einstein gave her the money from the Nobel Prize for physics he had won in 1921. In 1909 Einstein was teaching at Zurich University; in 1911 he received tenure at the German University in Prague and met Elizabeth of Belgium at a Solvay Council; she was to be his friend all his life. In 1913, still a Swiss citizen, he became a member of the Prussian Academy and director of the Kaiser Wilhelm Institute of Berlin. In 1914 he began work on the general theory of relativity. His publications made him increasingly popular, and he loved to play the genius in public. In 1933 the atmosphere in Germany had become oppressive; therefore, Einstein emigrated to the United States, where he taught at the Institute for Advanced Studies at Princeton University. He worked and lived there until his death in 1955.

920 1911 1912   919 1920 1911 1912 1913 1914 1915 **1916** 1917 1918 1919 1920 1911

GENERAL RELATIVITY. General relativity extends the principle of relativity to include motion that is neither uniform nor rectilinear. It is clear that two accelerating systems are not equivalent with respect to each other. For example, for an observer in a free-falling elevator, the force of gravity effectively disappears.

BEYOND NEWTON. Einstein postulated that gravity could be reduced to a modification of the curvature of space. For Newton's action at a distance he substituted curvature of the space-time continuum. Einstein's theory projects the equivalence of the gravitational field and the frame of reference in accelerated motion; thus we can conceive of the presence of stellar masses modifying space into a non-Euclidean structure and, if matter and energy are equivalent, we can attribute to the energy of light a property of mass: that of being attracted to another mass.

PHOTONS. With respect to the emission of electrons by a metal subjected to light radiation (photoelectric effect), in order to justify the occurrence of the phenomenon also in the presence of weak radiation having a certain frequency (the "threshold" frequency), but not in the presence of extremely intense radiation that has a lower frequency, Einstein postulated that light consists of energy particles—called photons—and that the emission of an electron depends upon its interaction with even just one photon; therefore, emission does not occur even in the presence of multiple-photon radiation, if the frequency is very low.

ATOMIC BOMB. Although a pacifist, upon the urgings of Enrico Fermi and Leo Szilard, Einstein advised Roosevelt to finance studies to produce the atomic bomb. Later, he stated that he would never have done so if he had known the Nazis were so far behind in their atomic research.

RELATIVITY

In 1905 Einstein published three brilliant works. The first, On a Heuristic Viewpoint Concerning the Production and Transformation of Light, communicates the discovery of light quanta and the interpretation of the photoelectric effect. The second, On the Motion—Required by the Molecular Kinetic Theory of Heat—of Small Particles Suspended in a Stationary Quiet Liquid, showed that atoms really exist. The third, On the Electrodynamics of Moving Bodies, contained the special theory of relativity. These works on different subjects illustrate well Einstein's unusual mind: they are revolutionary, bold, and use mathematically simple models and an iron logic rooted in experience.

Einstein postulated that the speed of light is a constant, independent of the motion relative to an observer. The constancy of the speed of light leads to a negation of the absolute nature of the concept of simultaneity of events; not just that, but from now on the concept of space and time as separate entities must vanish, while the union of the two continues to have a real existence. The effect of the theory of "special relativity," which asserts the constancy of the speed of light and the invariability of physical laws, with respect to any frame of reference (as long as it is inertial, that is, in uniform, rectilinear motion), leads to the conclusion that there is a maximum speed for transmitting signals and that the law of conservation of mass must be replaced by mass-energy conservation, since mass can become energy.

1. Einstein in Palm Springs, California, with his second wife, Elsa.
2. Portrait of young Einstein lecturing.
3. Albert Einstein when he lived in Berlin. He was already famous and popular with the intellectuals who enlivened the city's cultural life.
4. 1933. Einstein with Princeton colleagues, wearing academic robes.
5. Einstein welcomed by a crowd in New York. The scientist was very popular, especially among Democrats and pacifists, and not only in the United States.

6. Einstein during his daily, solitary walk on the campus of Princeton University.
7. December 1934. Einstein holds a lesson at the Carnegie School of Technology, at Pittsburgh's Carnegie-Mellon University.
8. Einstein's first wife and colleague, Mileva Maric, with their son Hans Albert. Einstein had no great loves or friendships.
9. Group photo of the 1911 Solvay Council meeting, attended by the leading physicists of the time. Einstein is the second from the right.

"When, in political life, faith in the omnipotence of brute force takes hold, this force takes on a life of its own and turns out to be stronger than the men who believed they could use it as a tool."
Albert Einstein, upon receiving the 1948 United World Prize

Instigated the Arab uprising against the Turks

Thomas Edward Lawrence was born in 1888 in Wales. He grew up believing in the Victorian myth of the empire. In 1910–1914 he worked at the British Museum excavation in Karkemish on the Euphrates River, and later studied the architecture of the crusaders in the Middle East. At the outbreak of World War I he enlisted in the British secret service and was sent to Egypt; from there he was sent to Hejaz where he became intimate with the family of the Mecca *shereefs*.

Lawrence was the motivational force and instigator of Prince Faysal's Bedouin guerrilla war against the Turks. Lawrence pushed the Turks north of Arabia while the English were maneuvering in Palestine. Faysal and Lawrence were able to reach Damascus before the English. Until 1922 Lawrence had a post at the Colonial Office. Meanwhile, the English and the French had divided the Middle East between them in the Sykes-Picot agreement (1916); in their Balfour declaration (1917) they also had promised to carve a "national Jewish homeland" in Palestine. Feeling that the Arab rebirth had been betrayed, Lawrence left the service.

| 1914 | 1915 | 1916 | **1917** | 1918 | 1919 | 1920 | 1911 | 1912 | 1913 | | 1919 | 1920 | 1911 | 1912 | 1913 | 1914 |

1

2

COLUMBIA PICTURES presents THE SAM SPIEGEL · DAVID LEAN Production of

LAWRENCE OF ARABIA

WINNER OF 7 ACADEMY AWARDS
BEST PICTURE OF THE YEAR

Starring
**ALEC GUINNESS · ANTHONY QUINN · JACK HAWKINS · JOSE FERRER
ANTHONY QUAYLE · CLAUDE RAINS · ARTHUR KENNEDY** Screenplay by **ROBERT BOLT**
OMAR SHARIF as 'ALI' introducing **PETER O'TOOLE** as 'LAWRENCE' Produced by **SAM SPIEGEL** Directed by **DAVID LEAN**
A HORIZON BRITISH PRODUCTION in **TECHNICOLOR**

3

4

5

> *"This is the man I had come to seek in Arabia, the chief who would ensure the full success of the struggle."*
>
> Thomas E. Lawrence, *The Seven Pillars of Wisdom*

SEVEN PILLARS. *Revolt in the Desert*, published in 1927, is a distillation of Lawrence's thought and experience about his adventures in Arabia. In 1936, *The Seven Pillars of Wisdom* was published posthumously, although it was already well-known because underground copies had been circulating for years. Lawrence wrote of everything in that book, except his disappointment. The book immediately became an international best-seller because of its perfect fusion of war chronicle and reflections on Arab thought, especially on the wisdom of the nomadic tribes, which is permeated by fatalism, abandoning oneself to the will of God.

SHEREEFS. Arabs call Mohammed's descendants "shereefs." Husayn ibn Ali (1856–1931) was the *shereef* custodian of Mecca and Medina. A member of the al-Fatat secret society of Damascus and a Nationalist, in 1915 the *shereef* obtained from the English commissioner in Egypt, Henry MacMahon, a pledge that England would recognize an Islamic state; he thus proclaimed himself King of Hejaz, but the title was wrested from him by Abd al-Aziz ibn Saud in

ADVENTURE

Lawrence was a good scholar and archeologist of Eastern civilization, though not a model soldier. Having been sent to supervise English interests in the Middle East, he allowed himself to be seduced by the desert people; their patriarchal customs; their intimate relationship with the splendid, harsh environment; their struggle to resurrect their great past. He possessed the courage of a great soldier, being bold but not reckless, and the ability to think and carry through impossible, miraculous plans such as the seizure of Aqaba, deep in the Persian Gulf between Sinai and Hejaz.

Lawrence was a frugal, solitary, incorruptible young man. He loved adventure, not for its own sake, but in the service of a great ideal, in an immense natural and human landscape. Obedience was not his forte. His career progressed rapidly: he was already a lieutenant colonel at the age of 30, and could have become the governor of an English colony. But to be great, an adventurer must have honor and consistency. Lawrence of Arabia—this is what the world called him—could not betray the Arab cause, not even to serve his own king. For this reason he chose to withdraw, change his name, and disappear.

6

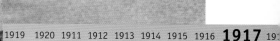

9

17 1918 1919 1920 1911 1912 1913 1914 1915 1916 **1917** 1918 1919 1920

1919 1920 1911 1912 1913 1914 1915 1916 **1917** 19

7

8

1924. Faysal, the son of Husayn, reigned with his descendants in Iraq (1921–1958). His brother Abdallah's descendants still reign in Jordan.

THE LEGEND. Lawrence of Arabia was a popular legend in the 1920s. *The Sheik* and *The Son of the Sheik,* played by Valentino, are echoes of that legend. In the 1930s *The Seven Pillars of Wisdom,* translated into many languages,

sold millions of copies. In 1962 David Lean directed *Lawrence of Arabia*, an English spectacular, thus bringing back the myth. The film immediately became a cult classic.

HISTORY. The press took a continuing interest in Lawrence. Old and new stories continued to appear. Some discovered the identity of his natural father; some claimed that Lawrence's

fatal motorcycle accident was in fact suicide. Serious historiography, however, did not accord him much space. Ira Lapidus of the University of California at Berkeley, in his monumental *History of Islamic Societies*, devoted one third of a line to him.

1. 1918. Harry Chase, photograph of Lawrence. In their reports, war correspondents such as Chase spoke of Lawrence as a hero.
2. Bedouins in Saudi Arabia. The nomadic tribes were the most effective allies of Shereef Husayn of Mecca and his children in the fight to free Syria from the Turks.
3. 1962. A poster for *Lawrence of Arabia,* directed by David Lean. The film's soundtrack was an instant success and is still popular.
4. Trans-Jordan. Group photo with, from left, Lawrence, Prince Abdullah, and General Allenby, British commander in the Middle East.
5. Lawrence of Arabia sitting to the right of Prince Faysal on the Orion bridge, right before the Paris Conference.
6. *Krak des Chevaliers* in Homs, the splendid crusaders' fortress inside the Kingdom of Jerusalem.
7. Omar Sharif (Faysal) and Peter O'Toole (Lawrence) in *Lawrence of Arabia.*
8. Thomas E. Lawrence wearing the costume of a Bedouin notable.
9. Lawrence (O'Toole) sabotaging the Middle Eastern Turkish railroad.

LENIN

Established Bolshevik power in Russia

Ilya Ulyanov, a school inspector, had five children, and all of them became revolutionaries. Lenin, born in 1870, graduated from high school (he studied at home) with the highest marks in the whole empire. He studied law in Kazan starting in 1887, but was expelled because of his Marxist beliefs. He obtained his law degree in 1891 in St. Petersburg, studying on his own, and began to practice law. He was arrested and exiled to Siberia. In the summer of 1900, Lenin left Russia for Munich. With Georgiy Plekhanov

(1857–1918, a Marxist who had led the Mensheviks since 1903) and others, Lenin founded "Iskra" (the spark). In October 1905, he returned underground to St. Petersburg. Unlike the Mensheviks, Lenin and the Bolsheviks believed that an armed struggle was necessary to defeat the czar. In 1907 he left Russia again. When World War I erupted, Lenin was in Poland. In March 1917 the revolution caught fire in Russia, and the German Secret Service allowed Lenin to return home. Together with Leon Trotsky (1879–1940) Lenin led the October Revolution, which on November 7 defeated the government of Aleksander Kerensky (1881–1970). The supreme originator of Communism ruled until 1923; he died in 1924.

1

912 1913 1914 1915 1916 1917 **1918** 1919 1920 1911 1912 1913

1913 1914 1915 1916 1917 **1918** 1919 1920 1911 1912

4

2

3

5

THE COMRADES. Vladimir Ulyanov, alias Nikolai Lenin, had a capable team to assist him: in addition to Trotsky, there were eminent figures such as Mikhail Tukhachevsky (1893–1937) who organized the Red Army. For a brief period, the painter and stage designer Alexander Benois (1870–1960) was superintendent of museums.

HEALTH. Lenin wore himself out in his work. He was tormented by rheumatism, arthritis, and heart disease. He was weakened by narrow escapes, deprivation, worries, and attempts on his life, being severely wounded in one such attempt on August 30, 1918. Beginning in

May 1922, Lenin suffered several strokes. Half paralyzed, he moved with his faithful wife to Gorky (now Nizhny Novgorod) where he died on January 21, 1924. Embalmed, his body was displayed in a mausoleum built below the Kremlin wall in Moscow.

THE MYTH. Lenin's successors acquired legitimacy by stoking the myth of Lenin: father of the country, inventor of the dictatorship of the proletariat ruled by a single-party system (and by those who control the party). St. Petersburg, the old capital, changed its name to the Russified Petrograd, then Leningrad, and so it stayed until the Communist Party collapsed. It

is now St. Petersburg again. Monuments to Lenin sprouted like mushrooms all over the Soviet Union and in Communist countries all over the world.

CULTURE. Lenin began a gigantic work on behalf of culture. Alphabets for oral languages were developed. Medieval structures were abolished. The khan of Khiva and the emir of

COMMUNISM

Lenin led the implementation of Marxist Communism. He was a rabble-rouser, a philosopher, and a statesman who made hard decisions and created similarly harsh institutions. He adapted Marxism, theoretically and thoroughly, to the backwardness of Russian society (the 1926–1932 edition of Lenin's writings consists of 31 volumes). At first, Lenin concentrated power in the class councils (the Soviets), creating Soviets of workers, soldiers, peasants, students, etc. He crushed the Mensheviks and other moderate

Socialists. He had Czar Nicholas II, his wife, and children executed by a firing squad. In March 1918 he withdrew Russia from the war, since the Western democratic countries were financing the czarist generals (the "White Russians"). He then entrusted the command of the civil war to the capable Trotsky; immense grain requisitions were ordered, and the circulation of currency was suspended. In March 1921, peace with Poland signaled the end of the civil war as well. To combat the traditional power of the clergy, Lenin propounded and organized atheism. On March 6, 1919, he founded the Third International (known as the Comintern) to spread the Communist revolution to other countries.

The centralization of power took the life out of the system of Soviets and committees. From 1921, the New Economic Policy (NEP) transferred to the state ownership of all industry and large-scale commerce. On December 30, 1922, the Union of Soviet Socialist Republics (USSR) was established. All power was now concentrated in the hands of the party's political office in Moscow, the new—and ancient—capital of the USSR. In these years Lenin set up the secret police, initiated the systematic persecution of cultural, ideological, and political enemies in the struggle for power, and created the gulags.

5 1916 1917 **1918** 1919 1920 1911 1912   1914 1915 1916 1917 **1918** 1919 1920 1911 1912 1913 1914 1915 1916 1917

7

9

"The transfer of power to the revolutionary proletariat . . . will mark the beginning of the struggle . . . for a stable peace that will cause less pain to humanity . . ."
Lenin, June 1917

Bukhara were demoted. Theaters, conservatories, libraries, universities, and hospitals became accessible to all. "Mansions are the people's property" wrote Lenin; however, the owners of Lopasnya House were allowed to remain in their home, since they were Pushkin's nephews and nieces.

1. 1897. Lenin among his comrades when they founded the Union for the Struggle of the Liberation of the Working Class, St. Petersburg.
2. 1902. Cover of the first edition of Lenin's *What Is To Be Done?* Published in Stuttgart.
3. Lenin in 1918.
4. Georgiy Plekhanov, leader of the Mensheviks and supporter of Aleksandr Kerensky's inept Social-Democratic government, which lasted from the February 1917 revolution to the October Bolshevik revolution.
5. 1918. Attempt on Lenin's life from a hagiographic painting of the time. Many capable Soviet artists illustrated in Socialist realist style the heroes, events, and myths of the Soviet regime, from the Baltic to the Pacific.

6. A portrait of Lenin, in a Mongolian propaganda poster.
7. An actor in the role of Lenin in October. *Ten Days that Shook the World,* directed by Sergey Eisenstein, 1927.

8. A crowd in front of the Lenin Mausoleum in Red Square, Moscow. The photo was taken many years ago.
9. Poster in several languages (and spelling errors) of the Third Communist International.

WALTER GROPIUS

Founded the *Bauhaus*

Walter Gropius was born to a family of architects in Berlin in 1883. He studied architecture, first in Munich, then in Berlin. From 1907 to 1910 he worked for Peter Behrens (1868–1940), a master of Secessionism (Central European art nouveau) and a design pioneer. Gropius opened his own architect's office and in 1911. He collaborated with the Werkbund (the German Artisans' League), and with Adolf Meyer (1881–1929) in designing the Werkbund offices at the Cologne Exposition (1914).

After World War I, Gropius created the Bauhaus of Weimar, which was at once a school of applied arts and an art academy. He developed a new theory of art education and called on excellent teachers to assist him. However, Weimar's citizens grew hostile to what they referred to as "Bolshevik" art. Gropius then built the faculty quarters (1925) and the new school building (1925–1926)

in Dessau. In 1928 he resigned his position as school director and opened an office in Berlin. During the Nazi period he moved to England. In 1937 he was teaching at Harvard University. In 1945 he founded The Architects Collaborative (the celebrated TAC) with a group of young architects. Gropius died in 1969. He is considered one of the great architects of our century.

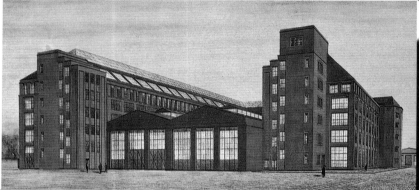

1

2

4

3

5

14 1915 1916 1917 1918 **1919** 1920 1911 1912 1913 1914 1915 1916 1917 1918 **1919** 1920 1911 1912 1913 1914 1915 1916 1917 1918 **1919** 1920 1911 1912 1913 1914

THE BAUHAUS TEACHERS. Architects: together with Gropius and Adolf Meyer, the brilliant Marcel Breuer and Hannes Meyer (1889–1954); the latter was Swiss and directed the Bauhaus from 1929–1930. Painters, graphic, and etching artists: Johannes Itten (1888–1967); Lyonel Feininger (1871–1956), who was American; Wassily Kandinsky (1866–1944), who was Russian; Paul Klee (1879–1940),

Swiss; Laszlo Moholy-Nagy (1895–1946), Hungarian, directed the New Bauhaus in Chicago in 1937; Josef Albers (1888–1976). Among sculptors, Oskar Schlemmer (1888–1943), who also painted; and Gerhardt Marks (1889–1891). Altogether, an impressive roster.

DESIGNER. The school's teachers and students contributed to the decoration

of the Dessau school building. The Dessau school was not as authoritarian as the other great German school of the time, the Frankfurt School for Social Research (1924–1933). The Dessau school moved to Paris in 1934 and from there to New York.

BUILDING. The Bauhaus aesthetic principle opposes the notion of symmetry and of the facade. In order to know a building one must go inside, walk through it and around it. Moreover, for the Bauhaus a building is a useful object, its beauty is essentially no

56

RATIONAL DESIGN

1. Bauhaus teachers. From left: Albers, Scheper, Muche, Moholy-Nagy, Bayer, Schmidt, Gropius, Breuer, Kandinsky, Klee, Feininger, Ms. Stolzl, Schlemmer.
2. Behrens, AEG Company factory in Berlin, 1909–1910.
3. Gropius and Meyer, Fagus factory at Alfeld-an-der-Leine, 1911, detail.
4. 1928. Gropius, photo by Hugo Erfurth.
5. Gropius, Meyer, Werner, Fagus factory, western entrance, 1910–1914.
6. Bauhaus class schedule, 1921–1922 winter semester.
7. The Dessau Bauhaus, seen from the southwest.
8. TAC, porcelain milk pot, 1969.
9. Gropius, Siemenstadt estate, detail. Berlin 1930.

The Bauhaus movement did not discover rationalism, which was already present in Meyer's work, in that of the brilliant Ludwig Mies van der Rohe (1886–1969), etc. However the Bauhaus made a decisive contribution to its acceptance, by establishing that the design process must be removed from tradition and that artistic creation is the joint result of craft and art. It was the Werkbund's goal to manufacture on an industrial scale quality products that would enhance the quality of life of the masses. Gropius believed that the aesthetic quality of a house or a utilitarian object has educational and moral import. The Bauhaus artists, as well as other masters from other countries, shared ethical and social concerns: for example, the Siemenstadt workers' quarters in Berlin were built

17 1918 **1919** 1920 1911 1912 1913 1914 1915 1916 1917 1918 **1919** 1920 1911 1912 19 **1919** 1920 1911 1912 1913 1914 1915 1916 1917

under the direction of Gropius in 1929; in 1927, the Weissenhof quarter was built in Stuttgart under Mies's direction and with the contribution of Le Corbusier, Behrens, and Gropius.

For the Bauhaus, an assembly-line production required a perfect model and material of adequate quality: this is why rationalism and project design are a crucial part of the manufacturing process. The courses given at the Bauhaus were rich and complex: they included technical courses on building materials and equipment. Theory courses included observation principles and techniques; a study of building materials and their theory; drafting theory and practice; theory of projection and building technology, in addition to production of designs and models for every type of object, and composition with theory of space and color. Generally, twentieth-century programs in architecture and design are based on this model.

different from that of a chair. Gropius studied at length the prefabrication of buildings, both the theoretical and practical aspects.

Color. For the Bauhaus, rationalism went hand in hand with color and poetry. Klee and Kandinsky taught at the Bauhaus, and Feininger

taught etching. Rationalism but with utopian vision. The students studied the theater of Erwin Piscator (1893–1966), a brilliant, innovative Marxist playwright. For political reasons the Bauhaus moved from Weimar to a Dessau suburb; it ended during the Nazi period and most of its teachers migrated to the United States.

"The final Bauhaus goal, however far away in the future it may be, is a unitary work of art where there is no boundary between monumental and decorative art."
Walter Gropius

MAHATMA GANDHI

Launched the first civil disobedience campaign

Mohandas Karamchand Gandhi, later called the "Great Soul" (Mahatma), was born in Poorbandar, India in 1869. He studied law in England. While living in South Africa, he became politically active in opposing discriminatory laws. Arrested and sent to prison, he was freed in Pretoria in January 1908. He then decided to pursue his struggle in India to liberate the Indian subcontinent. He became the leader of the Indian National Congress, which had been established in Bombay in 1885. He was to lead the party from 1919 until 1924, the eve of the first civil disobedience campaign, when he allied himself with the Khilafat, the Islamic movement, in fighting the English. The Muslim riots in Kanpur (1913 and 1931), Calcutta (1918), and Bombay (1929) signaled that a large minority was frightened by the threat of Hindu supremacy and offended by the peace conditions that had been forced on the Turkish sultan and caliph at the end of World War I.

Gandhi literally invented thousands of occasions for non-violent struggle, to convince Great Britain to leave India and to keep Indians united. He was opposed in this by Muhammad Ali Jinnah's Muslim League, which demanded the foundation of a Muslim state, Pakistan, in 1940. In 1947 George VI set aside the crown of India; thus the Indian Union and Pakistan were born. The following year, Gandhi was murdered by a Hindu fanatic.

1913 1914 1915 1916 1917 1918 1919 **1920** 1911 1912 1913 1914 1915 1916 1917

"Let me express my pleasure to you for this new India created by your charisma."
Nehru to Gandhi in the 1930s.

THREE PHASES. Gandhi's political strategy developed in three phases. From 1919 to 1924 the Hindus' alliance with the Muslims multiplied the mass effect of popular unrest. From 1929 to 1932, Gandhi undertook a number of long trips, to give life to the movement with his presence, such as the *satyagraha* march on Dandi to "liberate" salt, the trip to Europe in which he sought support, and his participation in the London round table that was to decide India's future. From

1942 to 1947 he engaged in a hard policy of collision with Great Britain under the slogan "Out of India."

DIGNITY. Gandhi traveled around the world and allowed himself to be photographed wearing the clothes of an Indian peasant; like a peasant, he traveled with a goat, milking it and living on the milk. When he was not working, he spun and wove, and prayed while walking. Cultivated, civilized Europe laughed at him. Little did anyone sus-

pect that twenty years after his death many young Europeans and Americans would seek out Gandhi's way.

CONGRESS. Gandhi's relationship with the great "number 2," Pandit Nehru, and the Indian National Congress was not always smooth. Gandhi was not enamored of subtle and crafty political maneuvers. He was in favor of suppressing the caste system, or at least of suppressing the caste of untouchable pariahs, and could not stand the

Congress's powerful conservative wing with its princes, Brahmins, and bankers. Gandhi himself came from a low caste of grocers.

WAR AND PROGRESS. The World Wars weakened the colonial powers that first needed to utilize the wealth reserves and manpower extracted from the colonies, and then had to answer to their colonial subjects who had learned to use European science and technology.

NONVIOLENCE

Gandhi believed that the hold the British had on India was made possible by the cooperation they received, whether willingly or not, from Indians of all classes. He believed that should that cooperation cease, the empire would crumble. In order to achieve this, 400 million Indians needed to be "roused" so as to create a controlled movement, based on a moral imperative that proceeded from a very simple principle, that of the "will to justice," or satyagraha. This will to justice had to be expressed in an unequivocal, yet peaceful, manner, through nonviolence. Civil disobedience, taught Gandhi, was one form of nonviolence: by that, he meant not only strikes or the refusal to pay taxes, but actions of passive resistance in which hundreds of thousands of Indians lay down across railroad tracks, millions of Indians marched to the salt works to appropriate salt for their use, or other peaceful demonstrations of dissent that ended in mass arrests.

Obviously, anti-British riots also erupted, such as the 1930 Chittagong riot and the Peshawar uprising, or the attack on the salt warehouse in Vitala; worst of all were the fratricidal urban battles between Hindus and Muslims. Yet, the voice and the figure that counted as much as an army was that of Gandhi: preaching justice and peace, praying silently and while surrounded by vast crowds, or fasting as a form of protest in a small room with a few disciples, with crowds upon crowds of people in other rooms, around the house, in the streets of the whole city, crowds all looking toward that small room where Gandhi was fasting.

7

8

920 1911 1912 1913 1914 1915 1916 1917 1918 1919 **1920** 1911 1912 1913 1914 1915 1916 1917 1918 1919 **1920** 1911 1912 1913 1914 919 192

5

9

6

1. Gandhi in his old age.
2. Gandhi in 1939 on a visit to a Calcutta prison.
3. Ca. 1942, Calcutta. Gandhi sitting calmly among the crowd.
4. 1931, Bombay. A wounded man is brought to safety during a protest that was harshly repressed by the colonial authorities, a frequent event at the time.
5. Gandhi (Ben Kingsley) among the crowds in the film by the same name, directed by Richard Attenborough, 1982.
6. His people gathered in prayer around the deceased Gandhi.
7. 1922. March protesting Gandhi's arrest.
8. Gandhi during the famous "salt march" through India.
9. Gandhi moves resolutely before the tamed British lions in a 1940s poster.

BENITO MUSSOLINI

TUTANKHAMEN

KEMAL ATATÜRK

GIACOMO PUCCINI

LOUIS ARMSTRONG

RUDOLPH VALENTINO

STALIN

CHIANG KAI-SHEK

ALEXANDER FLEMING

GRETA GARBO

According to the English historian Eric Hobsbawm, the twentieth century was "the bloodiest century in recorded history, for the magnitude, the frequency and the length of the wars strewn over it . . . and because it produced unprecedented human catastrophes, from the most severe famines, never before seen in history, to systematic genocide." Ten million dead and twenty million wounded, mostly combat-age men: this was the price paid in the 1914–1918 war for hegemony in Europe, which in 1914 still meant hegemony in the world. At the close of that war, Europe began its decline: from one third of the world's population, the continent's population shrank to one sixth. In the 1920s, "for a few moments" there were no wars, yet the system of international law continued to deteriorate. The good will of the League of Nations notwithstanding (the United States did not join the League; in fact, it refused to

sign the peace treaties President Wilson had dic-

tated), the law of the strongest continued to pre-

vail. Lack of respect for the law intensified,

compared to the progress made in the period

between the first abolition of torture (1740) and

Japan's war against Russia (1904–1905), which

began without a declaration of war. Marshal Jozef

Pilsudski in 1926 Poland, Admiral Miklós Horthy

in 1920 Hungary, Alexander I in 1929 Yugoslavia,

Mussolini in 1922 Italy, General Miguel Primo de

Rivera in 1923 Spain, all ushered in a period of right-wing dictatorships in Europe. There was a return

to random arrests, torture, political assassination. When, at the height of the Expressionist move-

ment, Friedrich Murnau (1889–1931) filmed *Nosferatu* (1922), in which Max Schreck plays an abom-

inable blood-sucking vampire, many read in that character both the unforgettable horror wrought by

World War I, and fear of the future (along with, at least in the West, a great yearning for fun).

The great problem Europe faced at the close of World War I was the conversion of industry from war to peace production. In 1921 a terrible famine struck Russia, and in the United Kingdom one million impoverished miners went on strike. There was an echo of this in *Lady Chatterley's Lover* (1928) by D. H. Lawrence (1885–1930), a hymn to physical inter-class love, according to the author the only way in which the neuroses of the century could be overcome.

Weimar Germany's economy was a disaster, as it was forced to pay unrealistically high war reparations

the Rapallo Conference, Walther Rathenau, owner of the AEG Company and Germany's foreign minister, was the first to recognize Soviet Russia. The German mark devalued at a galloping pace: in early June, a dollar was worth 74,500 marks. By the end of June it was worth 150,000 marks.

In Russia, the civil war came to a close: it had been financed by

3

1. Leon Trotsky. 2. Hirohito in ceremonial attire. 3. *Metropolis*, directed by Fritz Lang. 4. Sacco and Vanzetti, oil painting by B

THE 1920S WERE A CONTRADICTORY DECADE. AFFLUENCE CONTINUED TO GROW AT A MODERATE PACE IN THE WEST, ESPECIALLY FOR THE LOWER MIDDLE CLASS AND THE BOURGEOISIE. UNTIL 1929 THE GENERAL ECONOMY EXPANDED, BUT THIS DID NOT EQUATE WITH A GROWTH IN DEMOCRACY, ALTHOUGH, FOR EXAMPLE, TURKEY AND PERSIA—WHICH IMITATED THE FORMER—TRIED TO MODERNIZE THEIR COUNTRIES. AUTHORITARIAN RULE BECAME PERVASIVE. THERE WAS, HOWEVER, GREAT PROGRESS IN CULTURE AND LITERACY.

2

with which, in turn, the United Kingdom and France planned to repay the loans they had received from the United States. In addition to Lorraine and the Rhineland, other parts of Germany were occupied in order to force the Weimar Republic to pay up. At

Western powers that were owed huge sums by the czarist empire; on December 30, 1922, the Soviet Congress established the Union of Soviet Socialist Republics. Upon Lenin's death, a brutal war of succession ensued. Leon Trotsky, the War Commissioner largely responsible for Soviet victory, was expelled from the party and exiled in 1929; he would later be murdered on Stalin's orders in Mexico City in 1940. In 1928, the USSR initiated a five-year plan, the first example of a planned economy.

In the East, of all the winners of World War I, Japan was perhaps the country that profited most: it invaded China, taking advantage of that country's civil war. Hirohito,

the crown prince, visited Europe in 1921. Upon his return he was named regent for his incapacitated father Yoshihito, and he ascended the throne upon his father's death in 1926. India was shaken by independence riots. In Persia, Reza Khan seized power, dethroning the Cagiari Turkish dynasty (1794–1925). In Arabia, Abd al-Aziz III ibn Saud (1887–1953) established an authoritarian state, Saudi Arabia, in 1932. Even Muslim Northwest Africa was in a state of unrest, especially due to

the Rif rebellion in Morocco, which Abd el-Krim (1882–1963) waged against the Spanish and the French; in 1921 he proclaimed Morocco a republic; but in 1926 he surrendered to Marshal Pétain's vastly superior forces.

The United States went through an isolationist period. A decade-long economic boom raised the average standard of

living to exceptional levels and helped expand industry, so much so that the German film *Metropolis* (1926), directed by Fritz Lang (1890–1976) almost sounded as a warning. In it, a monopolizing tycoon is assisted by a scientist in enslaving a large city. There were other disquieting signals as well.

In 1925, Hitler published his racist and war-mongering plan, *Mein Kampf*. Franz Kafka's (1883–

1924) posthumous novel *The Trial* was published: it's an unfinished work about Everyman who is constantly in fear of being punished for an unnamed crime. In 1924, in Nevada, the gas chamber was used for the first time for capital executions. The following year, in Washington, a Ku Klux Klan rally was attended by 200,000 participants. In 1927, six years after their indictment for bank robbery and homicide, Nicola Sacco and Bartolomeo Vanzetti were put to death in Boston. They were anarchist Italian immigrants; half the world believed they were innocent.

In the area of customs and morals, the decade was known as the "roaring '20s" of jazz and the Charleston. In 1927, Mickey Mouse, the cartoon character created by Disney, made its appearance. And in 1930, the first Soccer World Cup was played. That same year saw the end of a civil war in Brazil, as

strongman Getulio Vargas took over the government. Meanwhile, in 1929 the New York Stock Exchange crashed, plunging the United States into a dire economic crisis.

There was great progress in technology: *Norge*, the dirigible developed by Umberto Nobile and Roald Amundsen (1872–1928), the first man to reach the South Pole, flew over the North Pole in 1926;

three years later, the *Graf Zeppelin*, a German dirigible, circled the world in just over twenty days; in London in 1926 John Baird introduced his invention: television.

In culture, this decade gave exceptionally rich fruits: James Joyce (1882–1941) *Ulysses*; Sigmund Freud (1856–1939) *Civilization and Its Discontents*; John Maynard Keynes (1883–1946) the foundations of a new economic science.

Shahn. 5. Out-of-work New Yorkers in 1930. 6. Getulio Vargas. 7. Dancing the Charleston in London. 8. The *Norge* flies over the North Pole. 9. John Maynard Keynes.

BENITO MUSSOLINI
Founded the National Fascist Party

The "Duce" (leader) of Fascism was born in 1883 in Romagna, northern Italy, to a blacksmith and an elementary school teacher. He graduated from Teachers' School, and absorbed Socialist, anarchist, and anti-clerical ideas. He joined the Socialist Party, becoming the leader of its revolutionary faction, and in 1912–1914 was editor of *Avanti!*, the party's newspaper. A skilled journalist, he founded another daily, *Il Popolo d'Italia*. In 1914, having taken a position in favor of Italy joining World War I, he was expelled from the party. The following year he founded the Revolutionary Action *Fascio*. On March 23, 1919 he founded the Combat *Fasci*, the advance guard of the National Fascist Party and embryo of the "Fascist revolution." Elected to Parliament in 1921, his Black Shirt militia goons clashed with Socialists, Catholic cooperative workers, anarchists, and farm hands. In 1922, Mussolini was appointed Prime Minister by Italy's king. He held this post until July 25, 1943, when he was sent into internal exile to the top of a mountain, from which the Führer rescued him. Hitler put him in charge of the Italian Social Republic, a short-lived, fictitious government that dissolved when Mussolini was executed on April 28, 1945 by Communist resistance fighters.

1

2

930 **1921**   1922 1923 1924 1925 1926 1927 1928 1929 1930 **1921** 1922 1923 1924 1925 1926 1927 1928 1929 1930

3

4

HIS WARS. When all is said and done, Fascism *was* Mussolini. In 1935–1936 he waged a brutal war to conquer Ethiopia so that he could feel equal to the great powers. In 1936–1939 he sent war materiel and volunteers to assist Franco in the Spanish Civil War. On June 10, 1940, he suddenly plunged Italy into the war although it was not a requirement of Italy's alliance pact with Germany. During the short-lived Social Republic, the Duce made every effort to send his soldiers to the front to fight alongside the Germans.

DUET. From 1922 to July 1943 when he betrayed Mussolini by arresting him in his home, King Victor-Emmanuel III (1869–1947), who had been king since 1900, was Mussolini's accomplice. He signed the coup d'état that revoked democratic safeguards, kept him in power even after the Fascists murdered Matteotti, a parliamentary deputy, appointed him First Imperial Marshal and his peer in the armed forces, signed the hideous racial laws and the declarations of war. In exchange, Victor-Emmanuel III became King of Albania and Emperor of Ethiopia, and even King of Croatia. In the end, the king fled to Brindisi with his son to escape the Germans.

THE CONCORDAT. On September 20, 1870, the House of Savoy, which had only recently become kings of Italy, took Rome by force from the pope. Instead of fleeing as some of his predecessors had done, the pope chose to become a recluse in the Vatican Palaces. Thus Catholic Italy was torn apart, as the pope forbade the faithful to exercise their rights as Italian citizens, such as running for office and voting. Fascism found the road to reconciliation and signed with the Vatican the Lateran Pacts on February 11, 1929. These pacts recognized the pope's sovereignty over Vatican City and made Catholicism the state religion.

FASCISM

There is common agreement that the entry "Fascism" in the Enciclopedia Italiana *that is signed by Mussolini, was mostly written by idealist philosopher Giovanni Gentile (1875–1944). It pompously reads: "Outside of history, man is nothing. Therefore Fascism stands against all individualistic abstractions, and has a materialistic base; it is against all utopias and all Jacobin innovations . . . . The Fascist state, which is a higher, more powerful form of human personality, is spiritual strength and subsumes in itself all the forms of man's intellectual life." Thus, man is free only insofar as he is part of the state. What does this mean in practice? That the state is corporate and merged with the Fascist Party (the only legal party)*

8

1. Mussolini swimming at sea. Many photos of the Duce's virile, handsome physique were disseminated throughout the media. In the same vein, another famous photo (possibly a photomontage), showed old Chairman Mao swimming in the Yangtze River.
2. 1920. Mussolini's Milan office when he was managing editor of *Il Popolo d'Italia*. The office served as a "Fascist den."
3. October 1922. A Fascist squad leaves Milan to march on Rome.
4. 1922, Rome. King Victor-Emmanuel III and Mussolini at the Victor-Emmanuel II Monument celebrating Italy's victory in World War I.

1923 1924 1925 1926 1927 1928 1929 1930 **1921** 1922 1923 1924 1925   22 1923 1924 1925 1926 1927 1928 1929 1930 **1921** 1922 19

and that the party is a "will to power."

The social benefits Fascism gave to Italy—such as the "English Saturday" (only half a day of work on Saturday), welfare aid to mothers and to children, free elementary education, the establishment of a pension system, and the creation of a national health care system— were simply ways in which the state expressed itself, just like the ban on strikes, the imperialistic war the regime waged in Africa, the obligation for teachers and magistrates to take an oath of loyalty to the regime (and so many did . . .).

As far as the rest of the regime's life is concerned, in the first years it was preoccupied with persecuting its political adversaries, which it did with merciless killings and suppression of civil liberties. There was also a kind of state economy, there were racist laws (Italians were forbidden to have sexual relations with the Empire's African natives, and anti-Semitic laws were passed based on the German model), and there was a strong alliance with powerful economic groups and with the Church, and a lot of corruption.

9

5. Hitler and Mussolini during the Führer's visit to Italy.
6. 1944. Mussolini and Marshal Rodolfo Graziani review a unit of the Italian Social Republic that had been trained in Germany.
7. October 28, 1940, Florence. Mussolini, his son-in-law, and Foreign Minister Galeazzo Ciano (whom he executed for treason in 1944) meeting with Joachim von Ribbentrop, Hitler's foreign minister.
8. 1939, Rome. The Duce speaking from his Piazza Venezia balcony to an "oceanic gathering."
9. 1939. A flag for the twentieth anniversary of the Combat *Fasci*.

"The Fascist State is a will to power and to domination."

Benito Mussolini, "Fascism" in
Enciclopedia Italiana, vol. XIV.

TUTANKHAMEN

Was brought back to light

On November 11, 1922 in Luxor, an archaeological expedition directed by the Egyptologist Howard Carter (1873–1939), identified the untouched tomb of Tutankhamen. Tutankhamen (1347–1339 B.C.) had succeeded Akhenaton, the heretical pharaoh. He was one of the children the pharaoh had fathered with a lesser wife, and had been placed on the throne together with his wife, daughter to the lovely royal wife Nefertiti. Akhenaton had attempted to under-mine the power of the clergy who served Amon and the other deities; he had changed the name of his kingdom to reflect that of Aten, the sun deity, which he had proclaimed to be his only god. He had abandoned Thebes, founding a new capital, Memphis. The reasons for Akhenaton's death are still uncertain, as are the reasons for the death of Tutankhamen, the young pharaoh, whose widow promptly remarried into royalty. Tutankhamen's mummy was found resting in his sarcophagus. The jewels, amulets, accessories, and votive statues, all were found intact.

1

4

2

3

THE ROYAL TOMBS. An ancient tomb robber confessed: "We opened the coffins and sarcophagi which contained the mummies, and we found the king's mummy. He was armed with two swords and had a large number of amulets and gold jewelry around the neck; his head was covered with a gold mask. This king's noble mummy was hidden under all the gold; his sarcophagus was encrusted with silver and gold, both inside and outside, and decorated with all kinds of precious stones . . . We also found the queen, and took everything we found on her, then we set fire to her sarcophagus. We also took their furnishings. We split into eight parts . . . the gold we had taken from these two deities."

A TIME OF CRISIS. As far as royal tombs go, and unlike the more ancient pyramids or those that were built after the 19th dynasty, Tutankhamen's tomb is not grandiose. It was probably built by Ay, his vizier. It has only a few rooms, none stately in size. The lively wall paintings are not of exceptional quality, and its contents were probably also modest, compared to the tombs of the great kings who had reigned for many years and had secur_ peaceful succession.

THE _ _ _ _ _ _ tomb was dug into rock in the _alley of Kings. It contained the sarcophagus that enclosed the royal mummy, a yellow quartzite

66

EGYPTOMANIA

Love for the exotic spread like wildfire throughout the West, beginning with Napoleon's 1798 expedition on the Nile. When, in 1822, Champollion succeeded in decoding the ancient Egyptian hieroglyphics carved on the Rosetta Stone, Egypt fever struck. Egyptian collections were formed in Cairo, Turin, Paris, London. The rituals of the Book of the Dead captivated the imagination of many people. In that context, the discovery of Tutankhamen's tomb triggered a kind of morbid curiosity, and an enthusiastic interest that is still alive today. The life of the boy king, threatened as it was by clerical plots and ambivalent military chiefs, the father's mysticism, and the ambition of sister brides and generals made up an adventurous, enthralling novel.

Egyptology became quite fashionable in the period between the two wars. The legend of the "pharaoh's curse," a revenge wrought on those who dared to desecrate Tutankhamen's tomb, was born. Films, novels, short stories were set in ancient Egypt, entwined in fanciful adventures with the present. Mika Waltari wrote The Egyptian (1945). Brilliant, exciting concordances were found between the Bible and ancient Egyptian history. In February–July 1967 Tutankhamen and His Time, a museum exhibition, attracted over a million visitors in Paris alone. It was certainly not the last exhibition to be dedicated to the treasures of the Nile.

"He crushed . . . disorder so that order was restored. He destroyed falsehood, and it is as if the world were created by him."

From the Restoration Stele found in the king's tomb

1922 1930 1921 19 1923 192 1925 1926 1927 1928 1929 1930 1921 19 1930 1921 192

monolith measuring 109 x 60 x 60 inches. The sarcophagus was placed inside three wooden coffins, one inside the other, lined in gold leaf, the outermost coffin measuring 211 x 143 x 143 inches. On the mummy, inside the bandages, and on the coffins were an impressive number of jewels and amulets, symbols, and inscriptions. There were statues of the "doubles" of the king's person, everything the god-king needed for the afterlife and everything that had been used in the prolonged funeral rites. Objects and statues were on a natural scale or in miniature. There were astonishing quantities of gold, silver, enamels, gems, precious woods, alabaster, and semiprecious stones.

1. Thebes, Valley of the Kings. On the right, on the road that was excavated, are the entrances to the tombs of Ramseses VI and Tutankhamen.
2. The funerary mask of Pharaoh Tutankhamen.
3 A statue of "ka" (one of the king's "doubles"), taken from the tomb of Tutankhamen.
4. Miniature gold sarcophagus of Tutankhamen, 15" in length.

5. Poster for the film The Mummy (1 ʃ ected by Karl Freund, interpreted by Boris ʃ 1969). Karloff was unforgettable i Frankenstein and was the greates horror films.
6. Detail of a fan with a relief showing the king on a chariot, hunting with the bow. Taken from the tomb of Tutankhamen.

7. Interior of Tutankhamen's tomb. Before reforming religion, one of his father's names—Amenophis IV—recalled the god Amon.
8. The opening of the "golden tabernacle doors" inside the king's tomb. The photographs of the Carnarvon expedition were used as models for the many film reconstructions of similar events.

Founded the Republic of Turkey

Atatürk, "Father of the Turks," was born in Salonika (now Thessaloniki, Greece) in 1881 to a treasury employee. In 1904 he graduated with the rank of captain from the General Staff State School and the same day was arrested for holding liberal views and exiled to Syria. In 1905, Atatürk established the Country and Freedom Society, which together with other reform groups succeeded in forcing Sultan Abdülhamit II (1842–1918) to return to the 1876 Constitution. In 1909, together with other military officers, he quelled a counter-revolution. In 1912 he was defending Cyrenaica from the Italians; he

returned home at the outbreak of the First Balkan War, which freed the European lands west of the Enez-Midye line from the Turkish Empire. In 1915, he defended the Gallipoli Peninsula, then Syria and Arabia. Promoted to general, he led the Syrian army units until the armistice was signed. While the political chiefs fled, Atatürk fought to prevent the Greeks from landing in Smyrna, and led the war of liberation. In the summer of 1919 he set down the principles of the national movement (which was to become the People's Republican Party) and was elected president of Anatolia's and European Turkey's representative committees. On December 27, 1919, now head of the Turkish state, he moved the capital to Ankara where he settled.

1

4

1930 1921 1922   28 1929 1930 1921 1922 **1923** 1924 1925 1926 1927 1928 1929 1930 1921

2

3

5

THE PARTY. Under the Turkish empire, all the land belonged by law to the sultan and all subjects were his servants. In practice, they were all state employees. Atatürk left untouched the authority enjoyed by administration employees and officials. He did make of his party a tool of modernization in the cities and, with much less success, in the countryside as well. He established the Ministry of Religious Affairs, abolished the *dervish* orders, turned some mosques that had formerly been Byzantine churches into museums,

and introduced the requirement of taking a family name.

THE TURKS. Feelings of Turkish national pride had faded when the empire stretched from Hungary and Transylvania to Albania and Mesopotamia, almost touched the Indus River, reached the Persian Gulf, and included Mediterranean Africa all the way to Morocco. As the empire gradually lost provinces, the Turks rediscovered their nationalism. The phenomenon of nationalism also spread in Europe, and there was a rebirth of the Arab movement as well. The Turkish peasants then became swayed by nationalist propa-

TURKISH MODERNISM

1. A view of Istanbul around 1910.
2. Mustafa Kemal Atatürk.
3. Atatürk's bedroom in the former imperial palace of Dolmabahçe in Istanbul, overlooking the Bosphorus.
4. Atatürk defends the Gallipoli Peninsula during World War I.
5. 1919. Atatürk seated with the delegates to the National Movement Congress in Sivas.
6. Atatürk's mausoleum in the city he made capital, Ankara.

7. Turkish banknotes with the likeness of Atatürk.
8. 1928. Atatürk during the national campaign to adopt the Latin alphabet.
9. Detail of the Mosque of Istanbul, formerly the Roman Byzantine Cathedral of Saint Sophia, which Atatürk turned into a museum.

After declaring an insurrection against Istanbul's government, on April 23, 1920, Atatürk called the National Assembly. He refused to acknowledge the Sèvres Treaty that had been imposed on the countries defeated in World War I. He reorganized the Turkish armed forces and settled pending international disputes about Cilicia and the Caucasus. The 1923 Lausanne Treaty recognized the full independence of Turkey. He then deposed the last sultan, Mehmet VI (1861–1926) and proclaimed the republic. Elected president in 1927, he was reelected in 1931.

Atatürk proceeded quickly with his program to modernize Turkey, creating a secular country and promoting the identity of the Turkish

"Kemal roused the Anatolian peasants from their inertia . . . through a war of liberation.**"**

J. Romein, *Il secolo nell'Asia* (*The Century in Asia*)

people; in this he was fulfilling the program of the Committee of Union and Progress. In 1924 he deposed the last caliph, Abdülmecit II, and proclaimed the end of the Ottoman caliphate. In 1924 he abolished polygamy and gave women the right to divorce. In 1925 he forbade men from wearing the fez, a Turkish head covering that harked back to the times of Mahmud II (1808–1839), and encouraged everyone to wear European-style clothes, although he did not forbid women to wear the veil. In 1928 he replaced Arabic script with the Latin alphabet and supported measures to remove Arab and Persian words from the Turkish language. He recognized equal rights to education and work for women, and in 1934–1935 granted them the right to vote and to hold office.

Atatürk became the object of a true personality cult. He died in 1938. Ankara is now a secular, modern capital, and Istanbul a metropolis where women are free to drive their cars and to frequent restaurants and theaters.

ganda, and Armenians and Smyrna's Greeks were the victims of brutal slaughters; nationalism also opened the way to the Kurdish problem, since Kurdistan is split between Turkey, Iraq, Syria, and Russia.

AN EXAMPLE. Atatürk's policies improved the economy, developing

industry, banks, and transportation, although at first Turkey relied on Soviet aid. Atatürk's was the first successful modernization of a Muslim country, inspiring Reza Khan in Persia, Bourghiba in Tunisia, Nasser in Egypt, and Senghor in Senegal, who all developed their countries in a more or less secular spirit.

GIACOMO PUCCINI
Died before finishing *Turandot*

The Puccinis moved from the mountains to the city of Lucca in Tuscany in the eighteenth century. Over several generations, the family included organists, composers, and teachers. Born in 1858, Giacomo Puccini was the fifth of seven children. Giacomo studied at the Pacini Institute and later attended Milan's Conservatory. Three years later he competed in a contest organized by the music publisher Sonzogno with a one-act opera, *Le Villi*, which, after being changed to a two-act work, successfully premiered in 1884 at the Dal Verme Theater in Milan. At this point, music publisher Giulio Ricordi (1840–1912) gave him a contract.

In 1889 his *Edgar* premiered at La Scala, Milan, but did not meet with much success. Success came with *Manon Lescaut*, first staged at the Regio Theater of Turin in 1893, followed by his three masterpieces (all with librettos by Luigi Illica and the excellent versifier Giuseppe Giacosa): *La Bohème* (1896, Regio Theater), *Tosca* (1900, Costanzi Theater of Rome), and *Madama Butterfly* (1904, La Scala). In 1910 the New York Metropolitan Opera staged the premiere of *La Fanciulla del west*. In 1917, *La Rondine* premiered at the Monte Carlo Opera House. The following year, it was time for three one-act operas: *Il Tabarro, Suor Angelica,* and *Gianni Schicchi,* which were first performed at the New York Metropolitan Opera House.

His last opera, *Turandot*, was never finished. Puccini died in 1924 in Brussels of throat cancer.

28 1929 1930 1921 1922   1 192   1929

1

2

3

4

CONFLICT. The "Vieni! Vieni!" aria Pinkerton sings to Butterfly, and her dreamy reply, admirably express the contrast between the urgency of male desire and the lingering nature of caressing, feminine sensuality. Rarely was music more immodest or an artist more adept at expressing this difference between man and woman.

OTHER WOMEN. In 1904 Puccini married Elvira Bonturi: they already had a child together. Since 1891 they had been living in a villa at Torre del Lago on the Tuscan coast. Puccini was a very sensual man and a demanding gourmet, a lover of wine and women. Since 1904 they had had a woman servant in the house, who took her life in 1908, a circumstance that was never satisfactorily explained and which marked forever Puccini's marriage. Elvira was accused of murder by the servant's family; at the trial she was found not guilty.

LYRIC OPERA

1998, Japan. Opening ceremony of the Winter Olympics. Before the world's TV cameras, a young woman in a kimono approaches the huge Olympic brazier and lights it with her blazing torch. In the silence the music of Madama Butterfly *issues forth: a language understood the world over, the language of Giacomo Puccini's lyric opera. Puccini's creative period lasted forty years, from 1884 to 1924. Though the critics continued to accuse him of superficiality, the criticism was unfounded, for more than once the public came away bewildered from the premiere of some of his works. Later, critics from outside of Italy stressed his international culture, his refined orchestration, the skillful expressive leaps of his compositions, the exceptional openness of his melodic line.*

Puccini the artist wanted at once to match the audience's inner taste, and to mold his creations to his own taste. His music expresses feeling, just like the music his father played on the organ of Lucca's Duomo. The public understands that somehow, his music projects a sacral tension, though the religion is that of love, and the suffering is that of Manon, Mimi, Tosca, Cio-Cio-San, Minnie, Sister Angelica, Liù. Italian opera reached its last high point with Puccini's Turandot, *a work exploring the mystery of woman. Franco Fornari, an eminent Italian psychoanalyst, devoted one of his last studies to it.*

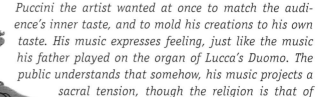

7

8

1922

MADAMA BUTTERFLY

1921 1922 1923 **1924** 1925 1926 1927 1928 1929 1930 1921 1922 1923 **1924** 1925 1926 1927 1928 1929 1930 1931

Far bene. Puccini worked slowly, going over every word, the plot and structure of the story with his libretto writers and even his music publisher, Ricordi. He detested redundancy. Questioning and tormented until he reached a decision, he was immovable after he made up his mind. He wrote beautiful, terse letters. He was humble when his works flopped. He rethought and reworked. He had an excellent knowledge of and respect for good language.

The public. Puccini wanted to make up for his poor childhood by living in high society. As a guest of Mahler at the Vienna Court Opera, he insisted on being introduced to an archduchess. He also enjoyed consorting with Lucca's comfortable country squires. Like Verdi, he greatly respected his audience.

6

9

1. A cocksure Puccini, with his hat high on the forehead, and the inevitable cigar.
2. Two silver cigarette cases. The covers depict a famous scene from Act III of *Bohème* and a florid Tosca.
3. A room in Giacomo Puccini's villa at Torre del Lago, Lucca. The piano and many other mementos are visible.
4. Photo of a stage set for *La Fanciulla del west*, from Puccini's time. He wrote the opera in 1910.
5. The manuscript for the finale of Act I of *Madama Butterfly*. After the fiasco at La Scala, Puccini rewrote it.

6. February 1904. A suggestive poster, a work of Adolph Hohenstein printed by the music publisher Ricordi, for the world premiere of *Madama Butterfly*.
7. April 1926. Statuette by Umberto Brunelleschi of Liù, the main character in *Turandot*. The opera was completed by Franco Alfano and had its world premiere at La Scala under the baton of Maestro Arturo Toscanini.
8. Ca. 1896. Some of *La Bohème*'s characters.
9. 1906. A poster by Hohenstein for *Tosca*.

"Oh divine beauty! Oh dream! Oh wonder! Give me victory! Give me love."
Calaf in *Turandot*, Act I.

LOUIS ARMSTRONG

Chose the trumpet and recorded with the Hot Five

Louis D. Armstrong was born around 1901 in Back o' Town, in New Orleans, to Mary Albert, a young girl, who was not married to his father, William Armstrong. Armstrong grew up poor amid drug peddlers and other ghetto denizens. At the age of seven he was already working for the Karnosfskys, Russian Jews who had a rag business and who gave him his first trumpet, a tin toy. As a child, Armstrong sang tenor in a quartet of friends who performed on street corners for pocket change. On New Year's Day, 1913, he fired a pistol into the air, was arrested and sent to the Colored Waifs' Home in New Orleans.

He was to learn music in the in-house orchestra. Armstrong took from many teachers, and this blend of influences gave complexity to his talent and variety to his embellishments, performance, and singing, bringing him fame. He played the cornet like no one before him. For a few years he played on river boats, before joining Joe "King" Oliver's Chicago band as second cornet. His second marriage was to Lillian Hardin, who was the band's elegant pianist and who later played in Fletcher Henderson's group, at the time New York's leading orchestra. In 1925 Armstrong returned to Chicago to play in Erskine Tate's orchestra. Between 1925 and 1928 he performed with the Hot Five, then the Hot Seven, recording 54 records that are masterworks of jazz.

SOLOIST. There is an Armstrong manuscript, *Cornet Shop Suey*, from 1928, which is completely written out from the introduction to the refrain, the theme, and the coda. Only the final repeat is left to improvisation. Often his solo performances were well rehearsed. Gunther Schuller wrote that in the late 1920s Armstrong considered "jazz solos not more or less embellished pop motifs, but a harmonic progression to be exploited with as much creative originality as possible."

STAR. Other musicians had greatly developed the polyphonic jazz style.

Starting in 1929, Armstrong became a national star. He took up singing again, first with a tenor voice which gradually became a baritone, and then the dark, broken, unique voice of the 1940s. Starting in 1932 he was in several films, but rarely as an actor.

EUROPE. Around 1932 Armstrong decided to embark on a long European tour, which he then repeated several times. In London he was given the nickname that was to make him famous, Satchmo, from "satchel mouth."

FREEDOM. American soldiers introduced

jazz to the European masses during World War II. Their jazz records became hot items. After the war, European kids used to dance to the sound of jazz in thousands of make-shift dance halls, with the music erupting from a record player or from a piano, at home, on terraces, in the squares and in the parks of the liberated cities. The sounds of Duke Ellington's orchestra, Satchmo's trumpet, his voice, and that of Ella Fitzgerald, Bessie and Mamie Smith, and the "divine" Billie Holiday (1915–1959), was the music of freedom and love.

JAZZ

Blues, Afro-Latin Caribbean rhythms, work songs, Protestant church hymns, Jewish songs, silly contemporary tunes, English and Irish dance music, gospels and spirituals, ragtime, a great and varied wealth of sources, a preponderance of wind instruments, an ancient feeling for rhythm, and percussion: all of this makes up jazz. In addition, it includes the oppression and misery into which emancipation had plunged many American blacks, isolating them next to other poor ethnic groups, in ghettos ripe with racial and social strife. Louis Armstrong was also influenced by French and Italian opera; some music critics compared his variations to those of opera singers such as Luisa Tetrazzini.

Jazz evolved from music for African-American social events, to dance music for everyone, then to concert music. Until World War II it was the music of American blacks and was played in a great variety of forms, by a great variety of instruments and voices, including orchestras and smaller groups, choruses and soloists, and went through several revolutions to which white artists also contributed. Not just "instinctive," jazz searches to express itself especially in solo variations, which are sometimes any-

thing but improvisations. When it distanced itself from its African-American roots and became part of the virtuoso mainstream, it became simply twentieth-century music.

1. Louis Armstrong (fourth from left) as second cornet in King Oliver's band. At the piano is Lillian Hardin, who later became Armstrong's second wife.
2. Louis Armstrong in concert.
3. An old aerial view of Saint Louis, the "gateway to the West." Its since demolished old slums, one of the cradles of blues and jazz, were later totally eclipsed by New Orleans.
4. Armstrong surrounded by fans and reporters.
5. A crowd welcoming Armstrong at a French railroad station. Paris became a center of European jazz.

6. Armstrong with the great vocalist Billie Holiday in Arthur Lubin's film, *New Orleans* (1947).
7. A view of Chicago skyscrapers built between 1923 and 1929.
8. Armstrong teaching a college class in jazz, a popular music course in the United States.
9. Armstrong with some of his musicians in G. Simonelli's film, *Saluti e baci (Hugs and Kisses)* filmed in Rome in 1953.

"There was a thrilling element of athletic competition in the maddening length of his notes and the extremely high notes to which he climbed with clear, vivid, pure sounds, like Scarlatti's harpsichord."
Massimo Mila commenting on Armstrong's 1933 concert in Turin, Italy

RUDOLPH VALENTINO

Filmed *Son of the Sheik* right before his death

Rudolph Valentino was born Rodolfo Guglielmi in 1895 in Castellaneta nelle Puglie, a large, poor farming town in Italy's heel, known for its almond syrup and a number of caves with astonishing stalactites. Like many other dirt-poor farm hands, eighteen-year-old Valentino emigrated to the United States. He was athletic, handsome, and a good dancer. He found work as a gardener, then became a professional tango dancer, and some say a gigolo. Many women, some of whom preferred to remain unnamed, opened doors for him. Soon he was in films, first as an extra, then as co-star (*A Society Sensation*, 1918) and star (*The Four Horsemen of the Apocalypse*, 1921). On both U.S. coasts, in South America, and in Europe the myth of Valentino quickly caught fire, producing a colossal box-office success. In 1921 he also filmed *The Sheik*, in 1922 *Blood and Sand* (in the remake, Tyrone Power (1914–1958) played the bull-

fighter Juan Gallardo), in 1924 *A Sainted Devil* and *Monsieur Beaucaire*, in 1925 *Cobra* and *The Eagle*, in 1926 *Son of the Sheik*. Valentino died suddenly in New York City after contracting pneumonia, of a perforated ulcer. He left no children. His fans were devastated, as were Hollywood's producers, who looked in vain for a successor.

Rodolfo Valentino e Doris Kenyon in " Monsieur Beaucai...

RUDOLPH VALENTI
'THE SON OF THE SHEI
a Sequel to The Sheik
with VILMA BANKY
John W. Considine, Jr. presents.
...RGE FITZMAURICE PRODUCTION

HIS WOMEN. It was rumored that Valentino's success with women was also due to his suave, non-macho personality, which contributed to break down a woman's "defenses." His film partners paled in comparison to him. Paramount always avoided pairing Valentino with actresses who might upstage him.

FOREVER WEEPING. For many years veiled women (the "Women in Black") brought flowers to his tomb. The anniversary of his death was celebrated by thousands of women at least until

World War II. In the 1950s a Broadway musical dedicated to Valentino caused a sensation. More recently, Nureyev interpreted Valentino in a biographical film, but surviving admirers judged the original to be far superior.

IMITATORS. Upon his death, the Hollywood producers who had Valentino under contract launched a world-wide contest to find a new Valentino. The winner, Italian Alberto Rabagliati, went to Hollywood but didn't make it. Back in Italy, he became a successful pop singer. The Valentino type was

later interpreted by other actors, such as Ramón Novarro, Cesar Romero, and Fernando Lamas.

MEANWHILE, a new agitated dance, the Charleston, became the international rage. *Wozzeck*, an opera by Alban Berg (1885–1935), premiered in Berlin.

The Austrian poet Rainer Maria Rilke (b. 1875) died without receiving a Nobel prize. In France and Germany, the film *Potemkin*, a masterpiece directed by Sergey Eisenstein (1898–1948) that glorified the failed 1905 Russian revolution, was banned from movie houses.

LATIN LOVER

Valentino was the first cinema "lover" to enjoy overwhelming success, as yet unmatched. Forty-thousand women followed his casket as the funeral procession wound its way down Broadway; some fans collapsed, others took their own lives, or stopped eating, but it would be wrong to attribute this outpouring of love to collective hysteria. In the critics' unanimous judgment, Valentino was a tireless, attentive, meticulous, and unassuming actor. The public and critics were also unanimous in their opinion of his exceptional beauty and photogenic ease. But there had to be something more to explain the raging success he had with women all over the world. Maybe it was because in a society mostly made up of coarse, unpolished men, farmers, factory workers, artisans, and lower-middle class working stiffs, Valentino's exceptional good looks and suave manners, his unique elegance of movement and feline intensity seemed magical.

Older women still tell of how he demanded to be royally dressed in his role of Juan Gallardo, how on the screen his character's eyes melted when he gazed into those of his beloved, how he approached her face in a kiss, how he moved his shoulders, enveloping the woman in his arms, holding her as she swooned. All this intense, dominating, tender body language seduced them. Thus was born the myth of the Latin lover, prince and peasant of demanding, single-minded passions.

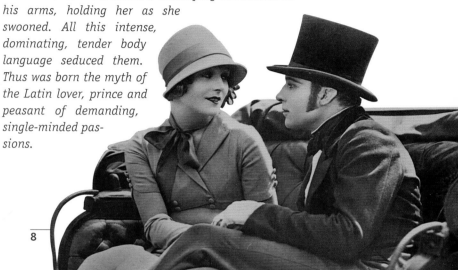

1928 1929 1930 1921 1922 1923 1924 1925 **1926** 1927 1928 1929 1930 1921 1922 1923 1924 1925 **1926** 1927 1928 1929 1930 1921 1922 1923 1924 1925 **1926** 1927 192

1. 1924. Rudolph Valentino and Doris Kenyon in *Monsieur Beaucaire*, directed by S. Olcott.

2. 1928. Valentino the Latin lover in a portrait by Evans.

3. 1924. Valentino and Helen d'Algy in *A Sainted Devil*, directed by J. Hanebery.

4. 1926. Poster for Valentino's last film, *Son of the Sheik*, directed by George Fitzmaurice, to which sound was added in 1938. Valentino played both the sheik and the son.

5. 1921. Valentino and Alice Terry in their famous tango in *The Four Horsemen of the Apocalypse*, directed by Rex Ingram.

6. Valentino's funeral in New York.

7. 1926, Italy. Illustration in *Domenica del Corriere* of a contest for Valentino's successor.

8. 1925. Valentino and Louise Dresser in *The Eagle*, directed by Clarence Brown.

9. 1971, Castellaneta, Italy. A fan brings flowers to Valentino's monument in the town where he was born.

" . . . Valentino: Arab sheik, Roman aristocrat, aviator, a god who died and was reborn transmuted into Osiris, Attis, and Dionysius, a hero of many battles . . . "

Edgar Morin, 1963

STALIN

Became dictator after defeating his rivals

Iosif Vissarionovich Dzhugashvili was born in Georgia in 1879 to a family of former serfs. His father, a blue-collar worker, died in 1890; his mother worked as a house maid. Iosif attended parochial school and later the seminary. In 1899 he was expelled for low grades. He found employment as a public servant for two years. In 1901–1902, Stalin, now nicknamed Koba, was already a local political boss. In 1902 he was arrested in the wake of the Batumi riots and escaped during his deportation to Siberia. He resumed underground political activity, and joined Lenin from the first days of Bolshevik activity. In 1907 he was one of Georgia's bosses, organizing "proletarian expropriations" to finance the party. In 1912, while in internal exile, he was elected to the party's nine-member executive board. By February 1917 he had changed his name to

Stalin, and was one of two Bolshevik bosses of Petrograd (now St. Petersburg). In 1922 Lenin appointed him to be his assistant and the secretary general of the Central Committee. He was Kamenev and Zinoviev's ally from 1922 to 1925. After replacing Lenin upon his death, Stalin stripped Trotsky of power. By 1927 all three rivals were defeated. He took his time having them killed, because he was already the *de facto* dictator.

1929 1930 192   1926 **1927** 1928 1929 1930 1921 1922 1923 192

5

THE SLAUGHTER. Leon Trotsky (b. 1879) was murdered in Mexico in 1940. The 1936–1938 purges left at least half a million dead. Marshal Mikhail Tukhachevsky (b. 1893) was tried and executed by a firing squad in 1937; the same fate befell Nikolay Bukharin (b. 1888) in 1938. Hundreds of thousands of small landowners, the *kulaks* who were opposed to the collectivization of farm land, were also victims. And the great 1932–1933 famine that was caused by the forced collectiviza-

tion resulted in the death by starvation of at least five million people, mostly peasants. For intellectuals, often the only way out was to take their own lives.

OMNISCIENT. There was no argument, no practical or theoretical problem, no issue in science, art, or culture on which Stalin did not write or speak, imposing his will. His *opera omnia* is vast and was made possible by the all-encompassing state bureaucracy and

the many state agencies Lenin had created, which Stalin expanded and enriched with discretionary powers.

PERSONALITY. The cult of Stalin's personality flooded the entire Soviet Union and its satellite countries, permeating all aspects of Soviet life. His name was given to schools, hospitals, factories, even cities. In photographs, "realist" paintings, posters, bas

reliefs, statues, drawings, and on stamps, the likeness of the dictator appeared everywhere.

STYLE. The style of Stalin's regime was at once bureaucratic, military, clerical, and Byzantine. There were endless secular processions carrying profane icons, of children, vehicles, airplanes, weaponry, athletes, farmers, workers, soldiers, airmen, sailors, all orches-

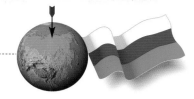

THE SOVIET EMPIRE

In 1944–1946 Sergey Eisenstein (1898–1948) filmed the first two parts of Ivan the Terrible. *The director was accused of giving "a false impression of history." Whether consciously or not, the director had painted the czar as a great statesman, troubled and merciless like Stalin. Having done away with his rivals, deported millions, murdered or imprisoned in gulags all those who could even remotely threaten him or his accomplices (themselves in turn, often killed and replaced); decimated the party and the army, Stalin imposed his economic and military policies on the Soviet Empire, which caused the death of* millions of people. He forced the dictatorship of the party on the country, and his own on the party. From 1936 on, Stalin was a despot more powerful than any czar. He was to remain so until his death in 1953.

Stalin's Soviet Empire extended without interruption from the Pacific Ocean to the Elbe River in East Germany, and included the northern Japanese islands, Mongolia, the Baltic republics, Bulgaria, Romania, Hungary, Czechoslovakia, and part of Germany. He exercised a sort of protectorate over Finland and Albania, and threatened the nationalist Communist regimes in Yugoslavia, China, Korea, and Vietnam. The czar of terror for dozens of satraps and puppet dictators, Stalin was a "Little Father" to hundreds of millions of people who depended on him for work, bread, education, sports, health care, recreation, even ideals: all men and all women were slaves at his mercy.

927 1928 1929 1930 1921 1922 1923 1924 1925 1926 **1927** 1928 1929 1930 1921 1922 1923 1924 1925 1926 **1927** 1928 1929 1930 1921 1922 1923 1924 1925 1926 **192**

1. February 1945. Conference of the Big Three at Yalta, Crimea. Churchill, Roosevelt, and Stalin divide up the world.
2. Soviet realism and Stalinist hagiography. Stalin depicted behind Lenin during a political meeting.
3. 1936. The execution of Kamenev and Zinoviev in an illustration by Achille Beltrame for *La Domenica del Corriere*.
4. 1917. A photographic portrait of young Stalin.
5. 1950s. Children offer flowers to their "Little Father."
6. Cult of personality in Mongolia. Stalin is depicted among local military and civilian leaders.

7. 1936, Moscow. Stalin with Georgi Dimitrov (1882–1949), from 1935 Secretary of the Third International and Bulgaria's premier after World War II.
8. May 1, 1937. Labor Day parade in Red Square, Moscow. On the steps of Lenin's mausoleum the marshals (among them Tukhachevsky) stand at attention; at the top is Stalin. With him, among others, are Khrushchev and Palmiro Togliatti, secretary of the Italian Communist Party.
9. Stalin, his daughter Svetlana and, in the center, Sergey Kirov, his designated successor, who died (most likely murdered) under mysterious circumstances.

trated in clever liturgies that weighted the effects and heightened them with music and song, marking all the nation's ceremonies and anniversaries. The meetings of the Supreme Soviet (which, at least indirectly, still held some power), and all other assemblies involved long-winded, hypnotizing rituals.

"*The proletariat needs the party not just to defeat the dictatorship, but even more, to safeguard the dictatorship, consolidating and extending it . . .***"**
Stalin, *On the Principles of Leninism*, university lectures held in April, 1924

CHIANG KAI-SHEK

Waged the first civil war against the Communists

Born in 1887 in a small town in Zhejiang, China, Chiang studied at the Military Academy and later at the Military Institute of Tokyo. A follower of Sun Yat-sen, who had founded the Republic of China, he joined the only party then in existence, the Kuomintang. Sun, who was preaching agrarian Socialism, feigned pro-Soviet leanings in order to obtain Russian aid for China. Thus he sent Chiang to Moscow to study that country's military organization and structure. From the 1911–1912 revolution, up to Chiang's flight to Taiwan (Formosa), China was divided up among different warlords and governments; from 1937 to August 1945 part of it was controlled by Japan. In this chaos, Chiang easily climbed the hierarchical ladder: he became chief of staff and commander-in-chief, executed a coup against the pro-Communist Kuomintang, and took the helm of Nanking's government and the now purged Kuomintang. From 1928 he was commander-in-chief in the war

against Mao's Communists; from 1938, commander-in-chief in the Kuomintang war against Japan and in alliance with the Communists. In 1946 he was reelected president and the civil war between Kuomintang Nationalists and Communists broke out anew. The Communists had a strong following among the peasants and were supported by the intellectuals and the factory workers in the larger cities. Although the United States sent massive aid to Chiang ($2,252 million from July 1946 to July 1947 alone), the Nationalist army was defeated and collapsed. In 1949 Chiang fled to the island of Taiwan where he established the Nationalist Republic of China under the protection of the United States. He was president until his death in 1975.

MANCHURIA. The last Chinese imperial dynasty was of Manchurian origin. When Japan occupied Manchuria, it set up a puppet state, Manchukuo (1932), whose nominal head of state was the last Chinese Emperor. Manchuria was occupied by the Soviets in 1945, and it was here that the final, decisive battles between Lin Piao's Communists and the Kuomintang forces took place in 1946–1948.

SHANGHAI. Chinese financial interests were allied with Chiang; however, they played with aplomb an unscrupulous game between the Peking and Nanking governments, the warlords that dominated the provinces, Japan and the Western powers that maintained important interests in the area. Corruption, which was endemic in the China of the mandarins, grew to such an extent that it even demoralized the Nationalist army.

MOSCOW. Stalin was not Mao's ally, and after the war he allowed Chiang to keep China's seat (with veto power) in the United Nations Security Council. The Soviet ambassador was the only diplomat to follow Chiang when the latter left Nanking and moved to Taiwan. When Japan surrendered, Moscow signed an alliance pact with Chiang that recognized his government as the only true government of China. Stalin did not believe in Mao's orthodox Leninist views, and was aware that Mao would never accept domination by the Soviet Union.

MILITARY DICTATORSHIPS

"With Chiang Kai-shek the Kuomintang developed into what it had been in embryo, another corrupted regime of landowners and warlords."

Eric J. Hobsbwam, *Ages of Extremes—the Short Twentieth Century 1914–1991*

Dictatorships were routine in the Roman Empire beginning in the second century A.D.; in Japan, dictatorship was hereditary beginning in the twelfth century; in Europe, Napoleon became the first modern dictator at the end of the eighteenth century. In our century, military dictatorships have been used to "modernize" countries with poor, backward populations and inept and corrupt (or absent) aristocratic or bureaucratic classes. In these countries, the military caste held the monopoly of "higher Western civilization" through their control of weaponry and the armed forces.

Every case is different. In countries where the Communist Party ruled,

926 1927 **1928** 1929 1930 1921 1922 1923 1924 1925

the party's "functional," Western-type structure used the military caste without trusting it; once securely in power, the party then dismissed the military or, as in the case of Stalin, decimated it. In Muslim countries, often the nationalist military succeeds in setting up a more or less "collective" dictatorship that sometimes can even propel the country toward some genuine progress. In black Africa, tribal enmity, ethnic hatred, and the military class often combine in an explosive mix. In Latin America, the alliance of military juntas and vast economic potentates—whether domestic or foreign—sometimes created harsh, brutal regimes. In the second half of this century in Latin America and in the Far East, monstrous alliances between the military and organized crime to produce and market drugs have introduced a type of criminal regime that sometimes breaks the country up among various warlords and drug lords. Everywhere, the example of military dictatorships teaches brutality and intolerance.

1. September 1945. Mao and Chiang toasting their joint victory over Japan.
2. 1939. Chiang arrives at the Kuomintang assembly that is to elect him President of the Executive Council.
3. Chiang as a young officer.
4. 1971, Taiwan. The president and his wife, Mei-ling Soong Chiang, review military and civilian authorities.
5. 1931. Chiang, on the steps and with the hat in his hands, at the close of the First Pan-China National Congress.
6. 1938. Under the walls of Nanking, Japanese soldiers execute Chinese prisoners.
7. Taiwan. Detail of a memorial to Chiang Kai-shek.
8. Japanese troops occupying Manchukuo.
9. Chiang and Nehru.

79

ALEXANDER FLEMING

Discovered penicillin

Alexander Fleming was born in Scotland in 1881. Unhappy with his job as a clerk, he turned to medicine, and was hired by the laboratory of St. Mary's Hospital in London, under the direction of Almroth Wright, a bacteriologist. Fleming studied antibacterial agents identifying, around 1921–1922, lysozyme, an enzyme found in organic tissues and liquids, such as tears, that has an antibacterial action. In 1928, Fleming observed that accidental contamination by a *Penicilium notatum* fungus of an agar plate seeded with staphylococci, caused the bacteria to rarefy more quickly the closer they were to the fungus, until they disappeared. Fleming observed the phenomenon and concluded that the *Penicilium* had produced an antibiotic substance that destroyed

the staphylococci. Having identified that substance, he called it penicillin and in 1929 published his findings. This discovery caused no stir until the outbreak of World War II, when Howard W. Florey (1898–1968), an Oxford physiologist, and the Jewish biochemist Ernst Chain (1906–1979) who had fled Germany in 1933, published a joint article on penicillin in 1940 in the medical journal *Lancet*. In 1941 Florey secured the support of the United States government for the industrial production of pure penicillin.

4

1

2

3

GLORY. The scientific community came to realize that Fleming had failed to grasp the implications of his 1928–1929 observations; it was only some ten years later that Florey, Heatley, and Chain succeeded in turning Fleming's discovery into a revolutionary drug; so it was only fair that Florey and Chain share the 1945 Nobel Prize for medicine. In 1944, King George VI knighted the Scottish scientist. At the close of his career Fleming was professor of bacteriology at the University of London. He died

in 1955, when already tens of millions of men, women, and children had cause to be grateful to him.

TUBERCULOSIS. In the late 1940s antibiotic therapy was able to defeat tuberculosis, which for centuries had sown death, especially among young people and children, and even more so among the poor and malnourished. Had they lived in the age of antibi-

otics, the heroines of *La Bohème* and *La Traviata* would not have died such a sad death. Now girls who may look pale and are toothpick-thin are no longer suspected of being afflicted with tuberculosis, which often was kept secret, as if it were something shameful.

LUES. The great shame, however, was to suffer from lues, which was heredi-

tary syphilis. Both lues and syphilis destroy the body and the mind, and great men have died from it. It became extremely virulent in Europe toward the end of the fifteenth century, and children born with lues were often terribly deformed. In advanced countries, antibiotics have succeeded in eradicating almost completely both syphilis and gonorrhea, another serious venereal disease.

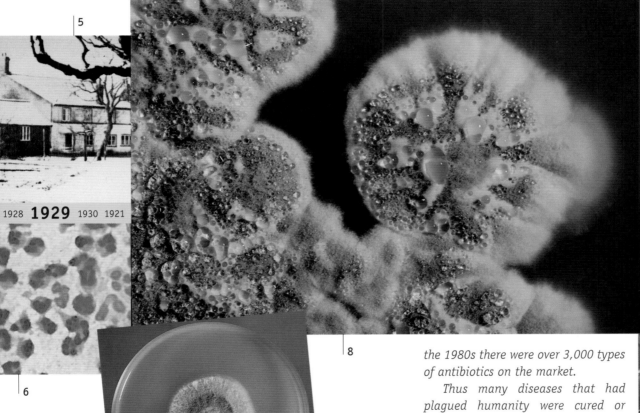

ANTIBIOTICS

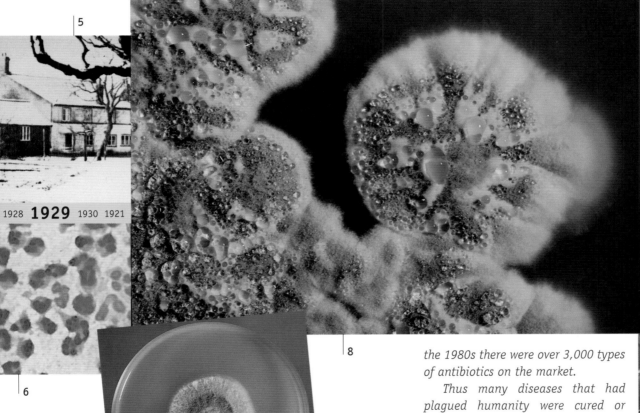

" . . . One of the most important medical discoveries of the century . . . "
Guinness Book of the 20th Century

The phenomenon of antibiosis, an antagonistic state among living agents, had been known for a long time in medicine, while the pharmacological virtues of spores and molds had been known for millennia. When the Oxford scientists picked up on Fleming's discovery in the context of their research on antibiotic substances, they were able to extract and purify penicillin, which they gave to Fleming for testing its therapeutic effects. A serious problem at the time was the high morbidity and mortality rates of war wounds. Penicillin produced by various types of Penicilium was found to be effective and non-toxic. In 1944 Selman A. Waksman (1888–1973, 1952 Nobel Prize), then doing research at Rutgers University, New Brunswick, New Jersey, was able to produce another antibiotic from Streptomyces griseus, for which industrial production began in 1946. Streptomycin was found to be effective against tuberculosis. In 1947 chloramphenicol was discovered; in 1949 aureomycin, then tetracycline. In the 1980s there were over 3,000 types of antibiotics on the market.

Thus many diseases that had plagued humanity were cured or defeated, such as septicemia, pneumonia, bronchial pneumonia, tuberculosis, diphtheria, typhoid and parathyphoid fever, tetanus, leprosy, bubonic plague, cholera, gonorrhea, syphilis, and so on. It seems very few microorganisms can withstand the attack of antibiotics. The semi-synthetic at first, and later totally synthetic production of antibiotics and their mass use in Western countries spurred the pharmaceutical industry to unthinkable growth.

1. The small laboratory where Fleming made his important discovery.
2. The Italian ocean liner *Vulcania*, turned into a hospital ship, photographed during World War II at anchor in Gibraltar.
3. Sir Alexander Fleming receives the 1945 Nobel Prize for medicine from King Gustav V of Sweden.
4. Young Fleming.
5. The building where Fleming's "small laboratory" was located.
6. Neisser's gonococcus (*Neisseria gonorrheae*) which causes gonorrhea and blennorrhagia, greatly enlarged.
7. *Penicilium notatum* on agar malt. The discovery of penicillin's antibiotic properties was the result of pure accident.
8. Detail of a *Penicilium notatum* culture, greatly enlarged.
9. Fleming photographed in the lab of St. Mary's Hospital in London.

GRETA GARBO

"Garbo Talks!"

Greta Lovisa Gustafsson was born to a poor family in Stockholm, Sweden in 1905. She graduated, majoring in drama, from the Royal Dramatic Theater School. In 1921 she was given a part in *Peter the Tramp*, a comedy by A. Petschler. Mauritz Stiller (1883–1928) invented a stage name for her and gave her the leading role in *The Atonement of Gösta Berling* (1924). The state-owned Universum Film Aktiengesellschaft called her to Berlin and gave her an important part in *The Joyless Street* (1925), directed by G. W. Pabst

(1885–1967). MGM took notice of Garbo and called her to Hollywood where she worked in about thirty films, the first two (1926, *Torrent, The Temptress*) under Stiller's direction. These were followed by *Flesh and the Devil, Love, Anna Karenina* (1927 [with the title *Love*] and again in 1935), *The Divine Woman, The Mysterious Lady, A Woman of Affairs, Wild Orchids, The Single Standard* and *The Kiss,* the last major silent movie. These were followed by *Anna Christie, Romance, Inspiration, Susan Lenox: Her Fall and Rise, Mata Hari, Grand Hotel, As You Desire Me,* and *Queen Christina* (1933). With this last film Garbo reached the apex of her career. These films were followed by *The Painted Veil, Camille,* and *Conquest* in 1937 and, two years later, by her first comedy, *Ninotchka.* Her last film, *Two-Faced Woman* (1941), MGM's attempt to Americanize the diva, was a flop. Greta Garbo retired to private life. She died in 1990.

MEN. MGM had a problem casting Garbo with partners who would be sufficiently attractive to the public. Garbo starred with John Gilbert (1897–1936) and Ramón Novarro (1899–1968), both imitators of Valentino; Lionel Barrymore (1878–1954), who belonged to the "royal family" of American theater and cinema; the capable Charles Boyer, the handsome Robert Taylor, the brilliant Melvyn Douglas. In her private life, after Stiller, Garbo had no other important men.

DIRECTORS. In addition to the two major directors already mentioned, Garbo made a film with George Cukor and her only comedy with Ernst Lubitsch (1892–1947). Other directors sometimes are mentioned only in connection with Garbo, such as George Fitzmaurice, Clarence Brown, Edmund Goulding, Fred Niblo. These names are not important to us today. Yet, perhaps Hollywood was made great not so much by brilliant directors and screenwriters, as by skilled artisans, especially in the years when many European filmmakers were fleeing the racial laws and World War II, migrating to the United States.

A NEW GARBO. Hollywood tried hard to create a new Garbo. Those that came closest to the diva were Bette Davis (1908–1989), the Swedish Ingrid Bergman (1915–1982), and Joan Crawford (1908–1977), who had played the role of the social-climbing secretary in *Grand Hotel*. But Garbo remained without peers.

MEANWHILE, Marlene Dietrich (c. 1901–1992) filmed *The Blue Angel* (1930) directed by Josef von Sternberg (1894–1969). Sir Arthur Conan Doyle (b.1859), Sherlock Holmes' creator, died. The Nazi parliamentarians appeared at the Reichstag in their uniforms. French-Argentinian Carlo Gardel was king of the tango.

GARBO "THE DIVINE"

1. Greta Garbo in *Anna Christie* (1930), directed by Clarence Brown.

2. Greta Garbo in a famous portrait by photographer Clarence Sinclair Bull.

3. Basil Rathbone, one of Hollywood's best "bad guys," Greta Garbo, and Fredric March (1897–1975) in *Anna Karenina*, directed by Clarence Brown (1935). The first Karenina film in which Garbo starred (*Love*, 1927) was directed by Edmund Goulding.

4. Poster for *The Temptress* (1926), directed by F. Niblo and M. Stiller, starring Garbo and Antonio Moreno.

5. 1925. Garbo with Mauritz Stiller on the ship that brought them to America.

6. Greta Garbo and Melvyn Douglas in *Ninotchka* (1939), directed by Ernst Lubitsch, a great German director and actor.

7. 1923. Greta Garbo when she was a model in Stockholm.

8. Greta Garbo in *Queen Christina* (1933), directed by Rouben Mamoulian.

9. Greta Garbo and John Gilbert in *A Woman of Affairs* (1929), directed by Clarence Brown.

There were other stars before Greta Garbo: Theda Bara (1890–1935), The Vamp; *Francesca Bertini (1892–1985); Mae West (1892–1980),* Sex; *Mary Pickford (1894–1979), nicknamed "America's Sweetheart"; Gloria Swanson; angelic Lillian Gish (1896–1993), a few others. But Greta Garbo was the only superstar, the divine, who overshadowed all the others that came before her and after her. Was she beautiful? No; she was* extremely *beautiful. She moved on her long feet with the strong, fluid elegance of a panther goddess. Her voice? It was divine. Her countenance? Divine. Her gestures? Divine. Her elegance, the way she carried herself, the noble, mobile expressions, the intensity in her eyes, and even her spiritual laughter, everything seemed divine to hundreds of millions of men and women all over the world. Was she divine? Undoubtedly she was.*

We must talk about Garbo in the past. Her figure stands out in the movies she made one after the other, but all we have are her films. Soon she refused to be photographed

9

1927 1928 1929 **1930** 1921 1922 1923 1924 1925 1926   22 1923 1924 1925 1926 1927 1928 1929   1927 1928

5

7

6

8

unless it was in relation to her work. She did not like to have the press attribute lovers to her and refused to marry and have children. She was as if possessed by the screen. When Garbo gave up acting with her beauty and dazzling talent intact, she went into hiding for almost half a century. Thus undocumented legends sprang up. For years newspapers would carry the sensational title "Garbo returns." But it never happened. Everyone thought that Garbo played the role of the divine star until her death, even without cameras and lights. For her public everywhere, the lonely queen of Sweden rose to heaven wearing the human smile of Ninotchka.

"*Garbo made her last film when she was thirty-five years old and in the full splendor of her beauty.*"
Richard Corliss, *Greta Garbo*

1931
1940
1941

CHARLIE CHAPLIN

BABY LINDBERGH

ADOLF HITLER

MAO DZEDONG

FRANKLIN D. ROOSEVELT

EDWARD VIII

PABLO PICASSO

FRANCISCO FRANCO

PIUS XII

WINSTON CHURCHILL

In the arts, next to newly developing avant-garde movements such as futurism, dadaism, surrealism, and abstract art, there was a general "return to order," an expressionist figurative art, sometimes with neo-Renaissance touches, while neoclassical music coexisted with popular music. Poetry flourished, especially in Spanish-speaking countries. The sufferings of daily life in these difficult years became powerful fiction themes. Some authors achieved fame, such as Hans Fallada (1893–1947) who wrote *Little Man, What Now?*, John Dos Passos (1896–1970), John Steinbeck (1902–1968) who wrote *Tortilla Flat* (1935) and *The Grapes of Wrath* (1939), and Erskine Caldwell (1903–1987), author of *God's Little Acre* (1933). But people preferred escapist literature and the police thriller became popular, giving birth to "immortal" detectives such as Commissioner Maigret (Georges Simenon, 1930), Nero Wolfe (Rex Stout, 1934), Lemmy Caution (H. Cheyney, 1936),

and Philip Marlowe (Ray-
mond Chandler, 1939). Murder became a popular
subject in films, along with
cops and robbers. Edward G.
Robinson (1893–1973), who

A frame from *Scarface*, based on a novel by
A. Trail, and directed by Howard Hawks
(1896–1977). The plot of the film is inspired by the Chicago gangs of the time.
Paul Muni (1897–1967) plays the lead role
of scarred criminal and boss Tony Camonte.

was "the first actor to rise from the Wall Street crash, and was the most callous, naked face of

the Great Depression" (C. Viviani), gave an awesome interpretation of boss Rico Bandello in *Little

Caesar* (1930) directed by Mervyn LeRoy; Paul Muni played an extraordinary criminal in *Scarface*

(1932), directed by Howard Hawks.

It could be said that the cinema was the protagonist of this decade. In America and Europe,
it mirrored the reality and dreams of an epoch, a mass art in which just about everyone col-

laborated: sophisticated writers, avant-garde musicians, brilliant set designers and tailors, actors

taken from the street and actors trained in studios or in the theater. Thanks also to the immigra-

tion of European Jews and freethinkers, Hollywood became a cosmopolitan cultural and artistic

center. With cinema, for the first time, the masses could determine the success of an art.

1931
1940

IN THE WEST THIS WAS THE DECADE
OF THE BOURGEOISIE—BOTH THE
MIDDLE AND UPPER CLASSES. IN THE
UNITED STATES THEY BOUGHT CARS,
HOUSEHOLD APPLIANCES, AND HOMES ON
THE INSTALLMENT PLAN. A BOURGEOIS
CLASS APPEARED EVEN IN RUSSIA.
DICTATORSHIPS MULTIPLIED THE
BUREAUCRATIC CLASSES. BUREAUCRATS
HAD EVERYTHING, EVEN WHEN THEY
POSSESSED NOTHING.

Film was the favorite art form of political and military propagandists, and dictatorships made savvy use of it. The best-known Soviet director, Sergey Eisenstein (1898–1948), gave voice to his country's pride in the film *Alexander Nevsky* (1938), with music by Sergey Prokofiev. The epic of Grand Duke Vladimir who in 1242 defeated the Teutonic knights in the battle of Lake Peipus was a metaphor for the twentieth-century wars between Russia and Germany.

In 1939, the grand, romantic *Gone with the Wind* was released. Directed by Victor Fleming and interpreted by Clark Gable and Vivien Leigh, it was a screen adaptation of Margaret Mitchell's novel of the same name. An authentic cinema myth the world over, it remained the leading box-office money-maker until 1975, and was repeatedly named as the most popular film of all time.

Starting in 1933, in only seven years Hitler's iron fist turned Germany into a dictatorship and Europe into a powder keg to which he set fire. In 1936 Germany reoccupied the Rhineland, in 1938 annexed Austria and the Sudetenland, in 1939 Czechoslovakia, then invaded Poland the same year. In the meantime, rabid anti-Semites disseminated a forged book that presumed to "document" the "International Jewish" conspiracy to conquer the world; it was entitled *The Protocols of the Learned Elders of Zion*. The 1938 Italian edition of this ignoble work, edited by Giovanni Preziosi, also attached a *List of 9,800 Jewish families* living in Italy.

Books, Jews, works of art. About 500 avant-garde works were collected and shown at Munich's Hofgarten in an exhibition that opened on June 19, 1937; in July, Hitler and Joseph

1. *Alexander Nevsky*.   2. 1933, Berlin. Books being burned.   3. Otto Dix (1891–1969).   4. The cover of *The Protocols of the Learne*

Goebbels, his propaganda minister, visited it. All told, two million visitors saw the exhibition, which was entitled *Degenerate Art*. Jewish artists were targeted.

Rearmament, an increasingly closer alliance with heavy industry, competent management, and the strict social order imposed by Hitler improved the German economy. Although the economic crisis of the early 1930s was worldwide, in Germany the standard of living rose. In 1938, following Hitler's design, the Volkswagen-werk was established, its mission being to manufacture "the people's car." Designed by engineer Ferdinand Porsche (1875–1951) and nicknamed the "Beetle," the Volkswagen was to be one of the most popular cars of all time.

In the second half of the 1930s President Roosevelt's social and economic policies gave a jolt to the U.S. economy. For the United States a period began in which it enjoyed a positive image abroad. This was the age of jazz; with the 1933 repeal of Prohibition, half the world learned to drink cocktails and whisky, and to imitate Hollywood. More than ever, Paris was the twentieth-century Athens. The members of international high society all knew each other, met, and socialized with each other on ocean liners such as the English *Queen Mary* and the French *Normandie*. Many people traveled to Paris to visit the Vincennes International Colonial Exposition where a copy of the Angkor temple had been erected.

In many Western European countries, Socialist governments were freely elected. In Sweden, starting in 1931, a long-lasting Socialist government was established. This happened in Norway also. The career of James Ramsay MacDonald (1866–1937) of the Labor Party, who was British Prime Minister in 1924 and again in 1929, then allied with both conservatives and liberals in coalition governments from 1931 to 1935, was very unusual. France's Socialist government was even more astonishing because of the economic power of that country and its international prestige. Léon Blum (1872–1950), the Socialist leader, reacting to the Nazi danger, signed a unity of action pact with the Communists and governed with them in the 1936–1937 Popular Front government.

Right-wing dictatorships, whether hidden behind kings or republican forms of government, appeared everywhere. Some brought their countries to war, some survived it. There were many others in addition to the famous trio of Mussolini, Hitler, and Franco: Antonio de Oliveira Salazar was Portugal's dictator until 1968; Léon Degrelle led Belgium's Rexists; Ante Pavelic, the Ustasi leader, was Croatia's dictator starting in 1941; General Ioannis Metaxas was a Greek dictator from 1936 to 1941; Monsignor Jozef Tiso headed Slovakia's puppet government from 1939 to 1944; Admiral Miklós Horthy de Nagy-bánya was Hungary's dictatorial regent from 1920 to 1944; Marshal Ion Antonescu was Romania's dictator from 1940 to 1944 with an "iron guard"; Marshal Jozef Pilsudski was *de facto* dictator of Poland from 1926 to 1935.

Arturo Toscanini (1867–1957) did not love the Europe of his time. In 1933 he refused to conduct at Bayreuth and moved to the United States; he conducted in New York until 1946. In 1939 Nobel Prize winner Enrico Fermi also found refuge in the United States.

Elders of Zion. 5. The Beetle in a parade. 6. The *Normandie*. 7. Léon Blum and other politicians. 8. Antonio de Oliveira Salazar. 9. Marshal Pilsudski. 10. Arturo Toscanini.

CHARLIE CHAPLIN

Directed *City Lights*

The man known as Charlie, Charlot, or Carlito was born to a family of vaudeville actors in London in 1889. His father died when he was five years old. As a child, Chaplin worked as an extra in circuses and night clubs. In 1910 he immigrated to the United States with his brother. In 1912 he was noticed by Mack Sennett (1880–1960), Keystone's artistic director and a scout of silent-cinema talents such as Buster Keaton (1896–1966) and Gloria Swanson (1898–1983). Chaplin made a large number of one-reelers; from 1914 on they were increasingly directed and scripted by him. In 1917 he was already famous in Hollywood. In 1918 he acted in *Shoulder Arms*; in 1921 he completed his first feature film, *The Kid*. In 1919 Chaplin and three other filmmakers founded United Artists, a film production house. In 1922 the FBI began to keep a record of his activities. He made *The Gold Rush* in 1925; *The Circus* in 1928; *City Lights* in 1931; and *Modern Times* in 1936. Although Chaplin composed the musical scores for his movies, he preferred not to add sound to them. In 1940, he made *The Great Dictator*, a fierce parody of Hitler and Mussolini. In 1947 he directed *Monsieur Verdoux* from an idea by Orson Welles (1915–1985). In 1952 he made *Limelight,* a bittersweet film for which he wrote the score; in it, Chaplin starred in the role of Keaton, a down-and-out actor. Suspected of being a Communist in the McCarthy years, he moved back to Europe, where he was knighted by Queen Elizabeth. He then settled in Switzerland with his young wife Oona and their small children, and directed only two more films. Chaplin died in 1977.

WOMEN. Chaplin was rumored to have been domineering with many of the women he loved. Two of the best-known were his wives, Paulette Goddard and Oona, daughter of playwright Eugene O'Neill (1888–1953) who was quite a few years younger than he was. He also had a great love affair with the actress Edna Purviance (1894–1958) who starred with him in *The Kid* and *Limelight.*

POLITICS. Chaplin's social consciousness developed out of his childhood poverty and the English tradition of political and labor struggles. As an orphan, he worked to support himself in a world of outcasts, whom he recreated in his role of Charlot. It was also rumored that his mother was Jewish; certainly, no other world-famous artist before the end of World War II had dared to satirize so scathingly, in *The Great Dictator,* anti-Semitism and dictatorships.

A MONSTER'S REASONS. Chaplin played the title role in his 1947 *Monsieur Verdoux*, about an unemployed banker who needed to support his son and paralyzed wife. To solve his financial problems he married then killed wealthy brides. The subject was taken from the life of Bluebeard (Henri-Désiré Landru, 1869–1922), the celebrated serial killer. But Verdoux was a bungler; he killed a dozen women in funny adventures and blunders. At the trial that was to sentence him to the guillotine, Verdoux's defense was that his victims were small change compared to the massacres caused by the powerful of this world. A moral the public at large did not appreciate.

LATE YEARS. In his later years, during the European period, Chaplin directed *A King in New York* (1957); several years later, *A Countess from Hong Kong* (1967) with Sophia Loren—films that are not masterpieces but still full of style.

POETIC COMEDY

1. 1918. Portrait of Charlie Chaplin.

2. Chaplin in *The Gold Rush*, one of his best loved films because of some irresistible gags, but not the best.

3. 1931. Poster for *City Lights*, a pathetic love story.

4. Chaplin with Jackie Coogan in *The Kid*. The choice of a child as a foil is original for a comic film; Coogan was one of the best child actors in the history of film.

5. 1912. In the foreground, Mack Sennett.

6. Charlie in *A Dog's Life*.

7. Poster for *The Great Dictator*. The film was released in Europe only after the war, and renewed Chaplin's popularity.

8. Poster for *Monsieur Verdoux*, the richest and most complete of Chaplin's films.

The comic act that was usually presented at the close of a show gave life to a successful genre for Hollywood, the Los Angeles suburb created in 1911 as a studio city. Max Linder (1883–1925), a Frenchman; Sennett's boys—Fatty Arbuckle, Chaplin, Buster Keaton, Stan Laurel (1890–1965) and Oliver Hardy (1892–1957) were among the most brilliant interpreters of this genre. Each had his own comic style: Fatty was the evil fat man; the handsome and unruffled Keaton created a moving situation comedy; Laurel and Hardy were complex comedians. Chaplin set his down-at-heel, hungry tramp in situations in which he was able to give something to those who were even more out of luck than he was. Charlie had dignity, nobility of feeling, the candor of the innocent and the courage to rebel, the gumption to steal for survival, and a sober bitterness that could thaw and turn to hope.

6

5

7

8

33 1934 1935 1936 1937 1938 1939 1940 **1931** 193 34   39 1940 **1931** 1932 1933 1934 1935 1936   31 1932 193

"Sound has spoiled the most ancient of the world's arts, the art of pantomime, and has canceled out the great beauty that is silence."
Charlie Chaplin

Some critics did not like Chaplin's pathetic roles, rooted as they were in the sentimentalism of popular theater and complacency toward the audience. Yet Charlie was able to wed the comical with feelings in his relationships with a puppy (A Dog's Life, 1918), with a street urchin, with a blind flower seller, with soldiers and trench mates, and to move us with a fresh, poetic laugh. His laughter is filled with the historical consciousness of abandonment, misery, pain, and social injustice. Film—which is our century's popular art par excellence—became, with Charlie Chaplin, great, absolute art.

89

BABY LINDBERGH

Kidnapped and killed

Charles Augustus Lindbergh Jr. was the firstborn of Air Force Colonel Charles Augustus Lindbergh and his heiress wife Anne Spencer Morrow. He was born on June 22, 1930. The family lived in a large house in Hopewell, New Jersey, with maids and a nurse. On the evening of March 20, 1932, at about 8 P.M., the nurse put the baby to bed. Two hours later she went to check on his sleep: the baby was gone. The only strange noise, which the father heard around 9 P.M., sounded like an orange crate being moved in the kitchen. On a window sill was an envelope with a note asking for $50,000 in ransom (later increased to $70,000). The note was written in capital letters, with the kind of spelling errors a German speaker not fluent in English might make. The investigation was headed by State Police Colonel H. Norman Schwarzkopf (father of the U.S. commander in the 1991 Gulf War). As evidence was uncovered, a conflict arose between the police, Lindbergh, and his attorney. Due to the father's notoriety, the kidnapping became an affair of state. Although the $50,000 ransom was paid, on May 12 the baby's lifeless body was found near the Lindbergh property.

HERO. Charles Lindbergh (1902–1974) became a national hero, a celebrity when on May 20–21, 1927 he flew the single-engine *Spirit of St. Louis* in the first solo non-stop New York–Paris transoceanic flight—3,640 miles—in 33 hours and 30 minutes. A crowd of over four million people greeted him upon his return to New York. After Baby Charles's tragedy, Lindbergh had other children. Later, he moved with his family to Europe in an effort to escape notoriety. He was criticized by the Roosevelt Administration for his non-interventionist position. After the war, President Eisenhower reappointed him to the Air Force Reserve with the rank of brigadier general.

TRIAL. An illegal German immigrant, carpenter Bruno Richard Hauptmann (1899–1936), was tried for the kidnapping of Baby Lindbergh and sentenced to the electric chair. He had a robbery and burglary record. The trial was intensely covered by the press worldwide. Even today, several Internet sites are dedicated to this event. As a result of the kidnapping, the U.S. Congress passed the "Lindbergh Law," making kidnapping a federal crime. However, doubts still remain about Hauptmann's guilt.

FROM FISCH TO FISHY. Confronted with the evidence of the ransom money that was found in his attic, Hauptmann promptly replied that he had earned the money from his fur-selling business with compatriot Isidor Fisch. From then on, "something fishy" meant something suspicious.

CHILDREN

"Scalpers sold reserved trial tickets for up to 500 dollars each. All types of celebrities wanted to assist, desirous of showing off their elegance: among them, Douglas Fairbanks, Ginger Rogers . . . even Jack Dempsey."

Gregory Egan, *Media Circus*

Louis XIII, who ascended the throne of France at the age of nine following his father's murder, as a child slept between his governess and her husband, in a narrow bed. If this is how a child king was treated, we can only guess at the lack of consideration and respect a common child suffered in pre-Revolutionary France. Things did not change much with the Enlightenment. Infant mortality remained high, and children counted as persons only when they were sufficiently grown to either work or serve as pawns in the family's social strategy. The millions who died in World War I and the 1918 "Spanish flu" epidemic, coupled with a generally more refined mentality, the result of improved living standards, meant that children were more highly valued as individuals. This may be one explanation for the commotion the kidnapping provoked in the West.

Important thinkers such as philosopher John Dewey (1859–1952),

1. 1927. Charles Lindbergh next to *The Spirit of St. Louis* at Roosevelt Field (Long Island, New York), the airport from which he departed for the transoceanic flight.

2. 1931. Little Lindbergh on his first birthday.

3. Anne Morrow with baby Charles.

4. May 1927. The crowds surround Lindbergh's single-engine plane at London's Croydon Airport.

5. Bruno Hauptmann, sentenced to death for the kidnapping and murder of Baby Lindbergh.

6. 1990. A school for young photographic models. In the United States, children's beauty contests, which award large prizes, are common.

7. Artist Bruno Munari.

8. A frame from *Lassie Come Home* (1943), directed by Fred M. Wilcox. The Scottish sheep dog Pal (progenitor of the Lassie family, active in films until 1978), Tom Drake, and Elizabeth Taylor (b. 1932), a child actress who went on to become a great star.

9. Psychiatrist Bruno Bettelheim.

6

7

9 1940 1931 **1932** 1933 1934 1935 1936 1937 1938 1939 1940 1931 **1932** 1933 1934 1935 1936 1937 1938 1939 1940 1931 **1932** 1933 1934 1935 1936 1937 1938 1939

5

Rudolf Steiner (1861–1925), Giovanni Gentile (1875–1944), Maria Montessori (1870–1952) and psychologist Jean Piaget (1896–1980) became interested in learning, education, and schools. Developmental psychology was born. Other scholars such as Anna Freud (Sigmund Freud's daughter) and Princess Marie Bonaparte studied child psychoanalysis. In the United States, Bruno Bettelheim founded an Orthogenic School for psychotic children. Bruno Munari (1907–1998), a well-known artist and designer, devoted part of his activity to teaching artistic expression to children. Great musicians such as Lorin Maazel and Bruno Maderna (1920–1973) began their careers as child prodigies, like many actors. Last but not least, children became a large market for a growing number of manufacturing industries.

8

9

ADOLF HITLER

Appointed Chancellor of Germany

Adolf Hitler was born in Braunau, Austria, in April 1889, the son of a customs officer. He attended a vocational high school in Linz, and found work in Vienna as an assistant decorator. In 1912 he moved to Munich. When World War I broke out Hitler enlisted as a volunteer. In 1918 both Austria and Germany suffered defeat and lost territories. While the German Parliament, meeting in Weimar, was giving the country a democratic constitution, in Munich Hitler was founding the National Socialist German Workers Party. In the midst of a stormy climate of unrest and financial ruin, the center was impotent, and the right became stronger. In 1923 Hitler attempted a coup; in 1924 he was sentenced but pardoned. He subsequently gave the party a military organization, setting up attack squads (SA, 1921) and defense squads (SS, 1925). Hitler received extensive financing from industry, and enjoyed some success in the 1930 elections, which waned in 1932, when he was defeated by Hindenburg in the presidential elections. Hindenburg then appointed Hitler Chancellor on January 30, 1933. On March 5th, Hitler was confirmed by the electorate. Thus began Hitler's dictatorship, and the march toward a war that was to end on April 30, 1945 with his suicide.

37 1938 1939 1940 1931 1932 **1933** 1934 1935 1936 1937 1938 1939 1940 1931

1 1932 **1933** 1934 1935 1936

1

2

3

INTERNAL ENEMIES. During his regime Hitler had few enemies, because most of them either went into exile or were murdered. The Christian churches were for the most part silent. There were two failed attempts on Hitler's life: by von Schlabrendorff in 1943 and by von Stauffenberg in 1944. A purge followed.

OUTSIDE ENEMIES. Practically all of highbrow international culture hated Nazism and was revolted by the Führer's style. All the Communist and Socialist countries and movements hated him, and the hatred was reciprocal. So did democrats worldwide, and all strong democracies, cautious politicians, conservatives, and liberals. And, of course, Zionists.

FRIENDS. Mussolini was Hitler's friend for many years; friends also included the Archbishop of Vienna and other prelates, right-wing dictators, especially from Latin America, the Great Mufti of Jerusalem, and other religious and political leaders from English and French colonies.

Also friends were a few great artists, such as the French author Louis-Ferdinand Céline (1894–1961) and the poet Ezra Pound (1885–1972). Many were convinced that humankind had to cross a veritable hell: the 21–24 million dead (in Europe alone) left by World War II in order to deserve a better future.

NAZISM

The "soul" of Nazism were the "Brown Shirts" (SA), squads that were set up in 1921, led in 1930 by Ernst Röhm, and abolished by Hitler in the bloodshed of the "night of the long knives" (June 30, 1934). Hitler himself had written its program in 1925 in Mein Kampf. The "action" of Nazism resided in the SS, which Himmler led in 1929. Starting in 1935, when German racial laws revoked the German citizenship of "non-Aryan" individuals, SS troops led the plunder, expulsion from society, and final extermination of six million Jews and of an estimated two million gypsies, political enemies, freethinkers, handicapped, and homosexuals.

In addition to anti-Semitism, the written principles of Nazism included a military, corporate restructuring of society, the nationalization of large businesses with employee profit-sharing plans, abolition of real estate speculation and of the stock exchange, and direct state control of financial markets. Furthermore, a new state-mandated physiology, psychology, and pedagogy would ensure the genetic health of all Germans: strong bodies, civic and sexual morality, a healthy culture and art.

In foreign policy, Hitler's Third Reich (which Hitler expected to last a thousand years), had to secure a Lebensraum ("living space" for Germany) extending, ideally, from the Spain of the Visigoths, the Italy of the Longobards, and the France of the Franks, to the cities the Vikings had originally founded in Russia in the ninth century, such as, for example, Moscow.

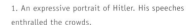

6

9

1

5

7

8

" *Do not be swayed, and maintain self-control up to the end: power will fall into our hands by itself.* **"**
Hitler to the SA, December 2, 1931

ACCOMPLICES. Mussolini and the king of Italy; Rudolf Hess (1894–1987) his designated successor, who was sentenced to life imprisonment at the Nuremberg: trial organized by the victorious Allies; Josef Goebbels (1897–May 1, 1945), propaganda minister whom the Führer had appointed chancellor in his last will, and who committed suicide after killing his family; Hermann Goering (1893–1946), who created the Gestapo and committed suicide just a few hours before he was to be hanged in Nuremberg; Adolf Eichmann (1906–1962), who was executed by the Israelis for his leadership role in the Jewish genocide. And, as in all dictatorships, many others, famous and obscure alike.

1. An expressive portrait of Hitler. His speeches enthralled the crowds.
2. 1933, Berlin. A cheering crowd surrounds Hitler upon his being appointed chancellor by Hindenburg, the German president who had distinguished himself in World War I.
3. Hitler admiring a model of the "Beetle," the people's car he wanted built.
4. Himmler and Hess sitting to the right of Hitler. Rudolf Hess, who was Hitler's favorite and his probable successor, flew to England (where he was detained) in 1941, apparently to engage in peace negotiations.
5. 1930. Hitler and young Brown Shirts in Munich's Brown House.
6. 1934. An illustration from *Kladderadatsch*: Germany, depicted as a lovely "Aryan" woman, confides in Hitler.
7. Hitler has conquered Paris. Here, with the Eiffel Tower in the background.
8. Hitler out on a walk with Eva Braun, the simple, trusting woman whom he later married, shortly before committing suicide with her.
9. July 20, 1944. Mussolini and Hitler in the place where an attempt was made on Hitler's life, in the German general headquarters. Hitler survived the assault, and in revenge decimated the military elite, including General Rommel.

MAO DZEDONG

Guided his people on the Long March to Shensi

Mao Dzedong was born in Hunan province in 1893, to a family of small land-owning farmers. He received his diploma from Ch'ang-sha Teacher's College, and in 1918 was working in the library of Beijing University. He became active in politics and journalism, and in 1920 joined the Marxist movement. In 1921 Shanghai, he was among the founders of the Chinese Communist Party. Mao believed that in order to succeed in China, the revolution had to be nationwide. In 1925 he joined the Kuomintang and became involved in studying peasant issues. He became convinced that to be successful, a revolution had to have the support of the peasant masses. This was a fundamental principle of Maoism, which conflicted with Lenin's and Stalin's theories.

In 1927 Chiang Kai-shek began his repression of the revolutionary movement, causing Mao to leave the Kuomintang. Demanding the expropriation of large land holdings, Mao led the Hunan revolution, which failed; he was against the Communist Party's line, which favored an urban

1

revolution. Cast aside, he began to organize the peasant masses into a military structure. He became president of the Kiangsi Soviet Republic, and Chiang unleashed repressive forces against him. In October 1934, Mao was forced to lead his army to safety in a 6,000 mile march through the continent to Yenan in Shensi, Northwest China. The march had a powerful, revolutionary propaganda effect among the masses in the regions it crossed. Thus Mao saved the party from the policies of Li Lisan, the party chief.

5

31 1932   **1934** 1935 1936 1937 1938 1939 1940 1931 1932 1933 **1934** 1935 1936 1937 1938 1939 1940 1931

2

3

4

CHANGING COURSE. At the time the People's Republic was proclaimed, China consisted of 3.63 million square miles of medieval society, still shackled to a pre-industrial agricultural economy and a patriarchal village structure. To this vast, slow, proudly conservative nation the "great helmsman" strove to give dynamism and modernity with a series of "course changes": the national liberation war fought by the peasants, the "four-class bloc" (workers, farmers, lower-

middle class, nationalist bourgeoisie), the "people's democratic dictatorship," the "campaign of letting a hundred flowers bloom," the "great leap forward" made possible by volunteer work, the "second revolution" (1955–1965) waged against the party itself by the "Red Guards," the "cultural revolution" of 1965 accomplished through a "triple alliance" of soldiers, militant Maoists and Red

Guards, and the suspension of most of the party membership.

A FRIEND. While Mao tried to change China, Zhou Enlai (1897–1976), who was at Mao's side uninterruptedly from 1935, negotiated the alliance with the Kuomintang, was foreign minister (1949–1958) and then prime minister until his death. Born in a Mandarin family, with an international culture,

Zhou Enlai was the statesman who governed the country amid all the confusion, and brought it closer to the West.

THE END. The People's Army always sided with Mao. Defense Minister Lin Piao (1908–1971) attempted a

94

THE LONG MARCH

The Long March to Yenan was a heroic sacrifice. Stalin's position toward Chinese Communism was ambivalent: he was pleased because it threatened the capitalist interests of Western countries in the Orient; but he was also wary because for centuries China had been a region into which the Russian Empire had wanted to expand, and because Maoism was predicated on agriculture and the countryside, unlike Leninism, which was rooted in industrialization and city workers. For these reasons, Russia did not provide aid to the Yenan march, while Chiang's war against Mao was financed by the United States. The principles of the Long March could be summarized thus: egalitarianism, thriftiness, self-

1. A portrait of the young Mao.

2. A grateful people rally around Mao during the march to Yenan.

3. The route of the Long March followed by Mao and his men, 1934–1936.

4. 1947. Mao speaks at the 7th Chinese Communist Party Congress, held in Yenan. At his side is Zhou Enlai.

5. 1966, Cultural Revolution. Mao's little "Red Book" is distributed to the Red Guards. Mao attacked Confucian culture claiming it was responsible for China's backwardness. Scholars, museums, libraries were the victims of the Red Guards.

6. 1966, Bejing. Mao reviews a Red Guard parade.

7. August 1992, Rostock. During an anti-racist protest, Mao is still the hero of the leftist youth.

8. Bejing. A protest in Tiananmen Square, several years after Mao's death.

9. Souvenirs on sale in a Moscow tourist store. They include busts of Marx, Lenin, Mao, and Ho Chi Minh.

6

1934 1935 1936 1937 1938 1939 1940 1931 1932 1933 **1934** 1935 1936 1937 1938 19

3 **193**

9

8

7

restraint, communitarianism, a merging of civilian and military society and of theory with action, an enhancement of peasant and popular culture in the name of Chinese purity and against city culture, considered a Western corrupting influence. Years later, in China and elsewhere among left-oriented people, the Long March became a metaphor for resistance in difficult times and for a movement toward successive, painful approximations to the ideals of Communism. This symbolic Long March was also meant to include an understanding between Communists and the Kuomintang in resisting the brutal Japanese occupation of China (1937–1945) and, later, the war between the Communist Party (led by Mao) and the Kuomintang (led by Chiang) (1946–1949), which lasted until the nationalist forces fled to the island of Taiwan, and the People's Republic of China was proclaimed on the mainland on October 1, 1949.

coup and died in mysterious circumstances. Later, around the elderly dictator sprang the "gang of four" headed by Mao's second wife, Chiang Ching. The Shangai group was composed of fierce Maoist intellectuals; when Mao died on September 9, 1976, they tried to seize power, but failed.

"*The true weapon that will bring us victory are the help of the people and the alliance with the peasants.***"**

Wood-cut slogan popular during the Long March.

FRANKLIN D. ROOSEVELT

Began the second phase of New Deal reforms

Franklin D. Roosevelt, the son of James Roosevelt and Sarah Delano, was born January 30, 1882 in Hyde Park, New York. Rich, handsome, and good-hearted, he was educated by private tutors. In 1905 he married Eleanor Roosevelt, the niece of Republican President Theodore Roosevelt (1858–1919) and a distant relative. After a short time spent in law practice, Roosevelt entered politics. He was Assistant Secretary of the Navy in 1913 under Wilson. In 1920 he was candidate for vice president. In 1921 Roosevelt was struck with polio-myelitis and lost the use of his legs. Governor of New York State in 1928, he reacted to the Great Depression with vast social programs. In 1932 Roosevelt was elected president on his New Deal plat-form, and reelected in 1936, 1940, and 1944.

In 1933 FDR initiated the "hundred |2

days" of reforms; in 1935 he opened a new phase of the reforms. On October 5, 1937 he spoke strongly against aggressive dictator-ships; in 1939 he reaffirmed his country's neutrality and invited Germany and Italy to choose peace. In 1940, while financing his country's weapons buildup, he pledged economic assistance and war materiel to Great Britain. In 1941, in the wake of Japan's sudden attack on the naval base at Pearl Harbor, Hawaii, on December 7, the United States entered the fray. Roosevelt died of a cerebral hemorrhage on April 12, 1945.

1

3

"The first freedom is freedom of expression, anywhere in the world. The second freedom is freedom for everyone to worship their God in their own way . . ."

Franklin D. Roosevelt

4

WAR. Both proconsuls appointed to lead the war effort were American: Eisenhower in the West and MacArthur in the East. Only the Soviets were left autonomy of command. The war's political direction was firmly in the president's hands. It was Roosevelt who, together with Churchill, decided on the 1943 Allied landing in Sicily, the January 1944 landing in Anzio, Italy, and the June 6 landing in

Normandy, France. At the Teheran Con-ference of December 1943, together with Churchill and Stalin, Roosevelt sketched Asia's future. In February 1945 at Yalta, the Crimea, Roosevelt and the two Allies split the world. Some say he gave too large a piece of the pie to Stalin, and Stalin took it.

HEGEMONY. Roosevelt decided to launch the research program that was to lead

to the making of the atomic bomb and the surrender of Japan. The two atomic bombs dropped after his death by his successor, President Truman, came to symbolize U.S. superiority. However, it was Roosevelt who had made it clear, albeit without arrogance, that the United States was the first country of the world. This heritage was not dispersed by a return to isolationism, as had happened after Wilson's presi-

dency, although until Kennedy, the presidents that succeeded FDR lacked his breadth of vision for a vast political program of moral substance.

THE FINAL FREEDOM. Said Roosevelt: "The final freedom is freedom from fear . . . to reduce armaments until . . . no other nation may attack its neighbor. . . ." Utopia, or a political message for the new millennium?

THE NEW DEAL

The third freedom Franklin Delano Roosevelt affirmed in a famous speech is not a freedom one traditionally associates with the United States: "The third freedom is freedom from want . . . economic agreements that will ensure a healthy and peaceful life to the citizens of every nation." This idea was premised on the studies of an aristocratic English economist, John Maynard Keynes (1883–1946), who was a favorite of the "brain trust" with which the president surrounded himself. Keynes argued that in cases where actual demand is insufficient to use up all available resources, the state may intervene by increasing public expenditure—although it will cause a deficit—since by doing so it will spur production and generate purchasing power.

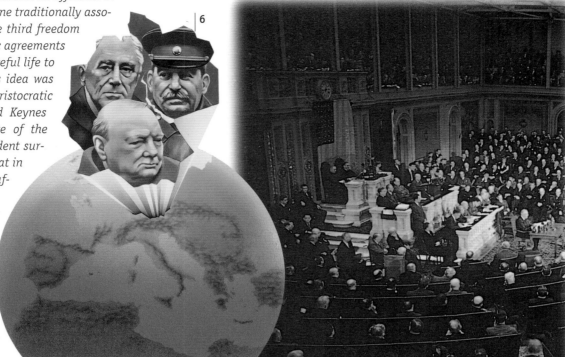

1940 1931 1932 1933 1934 **1935** 1936 1937 1938 1939 1940 1931 1932 1933 1934 **1935** 1936 1937 1938 1939 1940 1931 1932 1933

This concept was heretical to American free-market proponents since state intervention was believed to threaten free enterprise, open the doors to Socialism, and lead to a rethinking of traditional American protectionist policies.

Roosevelt's limited form of "Socialism" was not welcomed by the Left, which the president allowed great freedom of expression and which accused him of compromise. It was not welcomed by the moderates, because the president did not rein in the communists and was friendly to Stalin. Above all, it was not welcomed by the Right, which rejected all forms of government intervention and criticized Roosevelt's easy friendship with intellectuals and artists and Eleanor's feminism and philanthropic work. Federal assistance to the unemployed, the artists, the homeless, farmers about to be evicted from their land after losing their crops, and direct aid to workers displaced by the 1929 crisis, instead of to businesses, as well as a strict control over the economic cycle, were all policies of a strong president who favored a strong federal government, but they offended the American tradition of state autonomy.

1. 1942. Eleanor Roosevelt sitting with soldiers at a White House event.
2. Roosevelt in a 1942 photograph.
3. 1942. A U.S. tank factory. World War II brought enormous profits to U.S. industry and agriculture.
4. 1944. U.S. fleet with aircraft carriers in the Pacific.
5. 1935. Ben Shahn poster for the Resettlement Administration program that assisted failing farmers.
6. An eloquent illustration: the heads of Roosevelt, Stalin, and Churchill on the Earth's globe.
7. 1939, World's Fair, New York. The Finnish pavilion designed by Alvar Aalto.
8. April 1939, New York. Construction on the World's Fair grounds, which was to celebrate the success of the New Deal.
9. 1945, Washington, D.C. President Roosevelt speaking to Congress after the Yalta Conference.

EDWARD VIII
The King who abdicated for love

Edward (1894–1972) was born in Richmond, Surrey, on June 23, the son of the Duke of York and Victoria Mary of Teck. In 1910 his father took the throne as George V, and Edward became Prince of Wales. He traveled on extensive goodwill tours. In 1929, he visited the mines hit by the Great Depression and expressed his deep solidarity with the miners. The night of January 20, 1936, upon his father's death, he became Edward VIII, King of the United Kingdom of Great Britain and Ireland and of the Dominions as well as Emperor of India. He then went on a cruise in the Mediterranean in the summer.

In early December, the British press, following the U.S. media, finally broke its silence: the king intended to marry Wallis Warfield Simpson, an American who had divorced her second husband, Ernest

Aldrich Simpson, in October. On December 4th, the British government announced in Parliament that it would forbid the king from marrying "that woman." On December 10th, Edward abdicated in favor of his brother, the Duke of York; the following day he made a personal radio announcement to the country. Then he left England.

" . . . I have found it impossible to carry on the heavy burden of responsibility and to discharge the duties of king as I would wish to do, without the help and support of the woman I love. "

From the radio announcement to the country
by the Duke of Windsor.

AFTER THE FALL. Edward VIII abdicated and took the title of Duke of Windsor. He married Wallis Warfield Simpson on June 3, 1937: she became "Her Grace the Duchess," never "Her Royal Highness." After the abdication, Edward had hoped for a political role, which was never granted to him. His friend Winston Churchill, however, managed to have him appointed governor to the Bahamas (1940–1945). It was rumored that the Duke was sympathetic to the Germans. Once the war was over, the couple animated society life in Paris and New York. On his death, Edward received the honors of a royal duke in London; on that occasion, his widow was given permission to cross the Channel.

THE ROYAL HOUSE. Brunswick-Luneburg, founded by Ugo Marquis of Este around 1000; Dukes of Brunswick, 1235; Electors of Hannover, 1692; Kings of England by heredity through Elizabeth Stuart, 1706; Kings of Hannover, 1814–1866; Emperors of the Indies, 1877. In 1917, the house changed its name to Windsor.

THE KING'S ENEMIES. As king, Edward VIII was also head of the Church of England

HEART AND CROWN

Love and crown were often in conflict once Edward's great-grandmother, Queen Victoria, set the trend at court for a sober, bourgeois lifestyle. This meant a prince could no longer have a "favorite" and should marry a "suitable woman" at the "right age." The rules for princesses were even stricter. Anyone who broke them came to a sad end. In 1900, Crown Prince Franz Ferdinand (1863–1914) married a little-known Czech countess, Sophie Chotek, against all opposition; his uncle the Emperor made the unwelcome bride a princess and then Duchess of Hohenberg, but excluded her and her three children from the imperial family; the couple died in the Sarajevo assassination. Alexander I of Serbia (1876–1903), who became king in 1889, took as a lover Draga Masin, a widow who was ten years his senior. They married in 1895; eight years later, they were both murdered by the military, along with the king's greedy in-laws. In 1918 Carol II of Romania (1893–1953) wed a commoner, Miss Lambrino, in a morganatic marriage; the mar-

riage was annulled in 1921 and he married Elena of Greece. King in 1930, he abdicated in 1940. Of all his misdeeds, the people never forgave him his greedy lover, Magda Lupescu. History also censured Leopold III (1901–1983), King of the Belgians. De facto king between 1934 and 1951, a widower as a result of a strange car accident, he took as a lover Mary-Lilian Baels, the daughter of a fishmonger, whom he married and raised to the title of Princess de Rethy. The people never liked her and he was forced to abdicate. In its harsh wisdom, perhaps the British government avoided a worse fate for Edward VIII.

and Defender of the Faith. The bishops declared that a marriage between the king and a twice-divorced woman was unthinkable. All the "right-thinking" aristocracy judged his marriage with an American adventuress to be utterly unacceptable.

THE TWO-HEADED ICON. For romantics, the abdication of Edward VIII was the love

story of the century, but the malicious claimed that he drank too much and that she had an unsavory past. Yet for almost forty years, the Duke and Duchess of Windsor, with or without their dogs, in evening dress or on the tennis court, were the image of love that overcomes all obstacles.

MEANWHILE, 1936 was the year of the

Berlin Olympics: African-American athlete Jesse Owens (1913–1980) won the 100 m, 200 m, relay, and long-jump medals, to Hitler's great displeasure. The Civil War broke out in Spain (1936–1939). King Fouad of Egypt (b. 1868), Spanish poet Federigo Garcia Lorca (b. 1898) and Rudyard Kipling (b. 1865), the poet of the British Empire, all died in 1936.

1. A 1913 photo: King George V, Queen Mary of Teck and children Edward and Mary. During World War I, George V changed the family name Saxe-Coburg-Gotha inherited from his grandfather Prince Consort Albert, to the English name of Windsor.

2. Edward photographed by Cecil Beaton on his wedding day. Edward was considered the world's most elegant man.

3. The Duke and Duchess of Windsor with their dogs in 1954 onboard the *Queen Elizabeth*. Of his brother who became king, Edward said in his abdication speech: ". . . he also has the unequaled good fortune . . . which has not been granted to me . . . of having a happy home, a wife and children."

4. Prince Edward visiting a British factory.

5. Sea Bird, winner of the 1965 "Grand Prix de l'Arc de Triomphe," an event dear to the Windsors.

6. Wallis Warfield Simpson photographed in 1937 by Cecil Beaton. She is wearing her engagement ring: platinum, with a 40-carat emerald by Cartier.

7. May 12, 1937, London. The gala coach taking George VI, former Duke of York, and his beloved wife Elizabeth, a Scottish noblewoman, to the Coronation.

8. May 31, 1972. The R.A.F. guard standing vigil over the coffin of the Duke of Windsor in Benson Church.

9. June 3, 1937. A castle near Tours in France. The Duke and Duchess of Windsor photographed by Cecil Beaton on their wedding day.

10. A postage stamp from the brief reign of Edward VIII.

7

6

8

9

5

36 1937 1938 1939 1940 1931 1932 1933 1934 1935 **1936** 1937 1938 1939 1940

1940 1931 1932 1933 1934 1935 **1936** 1937 19

1ᴰ
POSTAGE

10

PABLO PICASSO

Painted *Guernica*

Pablo Ruyz y Picasso was born in 1881 in Malaga, the son of an art and design teacher who taught him at home. In 1895 he moved with his family to Barcelona, in whose artistic environment he matured. Starting in 1900 he traveled often to Paris, where he took up residence in 1904, making the city his new home. In his later years, Picasso moved to the French Riviera, where he died in 1973, acclaimed as the greatest artist of the twentieth century. Art critics have already divided his work into periods. Starting with the turn of the century, they are: the blue period, followed by the rose period and by primitivism; starting in 1907, Cubism, followed by the analytical and synthetic periods; in the 1920s Picasso reverted to the

figurative style and the classical period and, finally, the "Picasso style."

Picasso interacted with the people that counted: the art dealers Vollard and Kahnweiler, Leo and Gertrude Stein; the precursors anointed by the great Paris exhibitions such as Toulouse-Lautrec, Gauguin, van Gogh, Seurat, and Cézanne; the leading painters of his time such as Matisse and van Dongen, Braque, Soutine, and Gris. He was renowned as well for his intellectual appetites, for his expressive force, for the talent and energy he applied to refashioning other artists' ideas into his own.

1

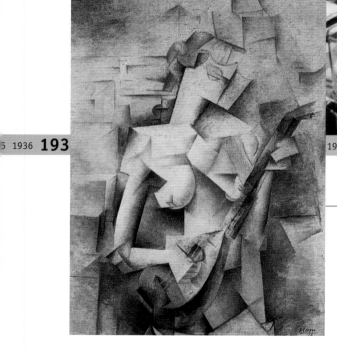

2

4

5

3

5

1938 1939 1930 1931 1932 1933 1934 1935 1936 **1937** 1938 19

5 1936 **193**

TIRELESS. Although ranking lists are foolish, many claim that Picasso, Henri Matisse (1869–1954), and Wassily Kandinsky (1866–1944) were this century's greatest painters. For many, Picasso is the best among them. He was certainly a tirelessly productive painter, sculptor, graphic artist, ceramicist, and decorator. None of his works are superficial, weak, or lacking in talent. For the masses, Picasso, or the Picasso style, embodied twentieth-century art. His style had a profound influence on the decorative arts, including textile printing for clothing and upholstery.

WOMEN. From a young age, Picasso loved many women who were usually faithful companions. He had many children and many friends. He was a passionate man, and his passion (even during the period of his friendship with Dali and his assent to surrealism), was reflected in his work all his life. In his last years he worked on *The Model and the Painter* series, a clearly passionate work. It has often been said that Picasso was a force of nature.

SPANISHNESS. A grand master of the Paris School, part Italian (on his mother's side, as his mother's Ligurian family name, which he chose as his own, attests), Picasso had Spain in his soul. Not so much for the homage he paid to Velásquez (he also took from Delacroix), or the themes of the

ART AND PROPAGANDA

In 1937 the small Basque town of Guernica was razed to the ground in a bombardment by the Nazis, who were allied with Franco during the Spanish Civil War. While few in Europe took notice of the Italian bombs falling on Ethiopia, the bombing of Guernica was seen as the first truly modern act of war. The slaughter terrified the patriotic, albeit non-political, Picasso, who went on to create the extraordinary Guernica painting. The language of this work is "Picassian": throats are thrown wide open by screams, and the animals, men, and women are torn apart by bombs in a forceful and vivid style. In 1944 Picasso joined the Spanish Communist Party, and after the war became known for his peace doves and his efforts on behalf of the internationalist and pacifist propaganda promoted by the Soviet Union. This collaboration continued until Stalin's death.

It was the Bolshevik Revolution that discovered the influence poets and artists could have on the masses through their art. Fascism imitated them, and major intellectuals committed themselves to working for dictators. This was especially true of film directors, as the Fascist regimes subsidized their efforts. The Nazi regime, which came later, was favored by renowned architects. Slowly, however, even the most brutal dictatorships bureaucratized. Often, major artists withdrew; sometimes, overwhelmed by their collapsing illusions, they committed suicide or were interned in concentration camps and gulags. An army of artisans took their place. In the palaces of Soviet power, every staircase, every hall, every lobby still exhibits the sculpted or painted faces and symbols of the party, the army, and the revolution's leaders.

86 **1937** 1938 1939 1930 1931 1932 1933 193

> *" When all is said and done,
> what is most frightening to a painter is
> the empty canvas. Painting is stronger than me,
> it makes me do what it wants. "*
>
> Pablo Picasso

bullfight, the bull, and the matador (his *Minotaur* is a famous etching), as for his faithfulness to the form and structure of Catalonia's and Castile's landscape and to a commanding, decisively male, magnificently expressive language.

1. 1952. Picasso with "bread" hands. Photo by Robert Doisneau, taken at Picasso's La Galloise villa in Vallauris (France).
2. Picasso, *Girl with Mandolin*, 1910. Oil on canvas.
3. Picasso, *The Guitar Player*, 1912. India ink and colored chalk on paper.
4. Picasso, *Seated Woman Drying Her Foot*, 1921. Pastel on paper.

5. Picasso, sketch for *The Three-Cornered Hat* by De Falla and Massine, 1919.
6. Picasso, *Minotaur*, 1935. Etching.
7. Picasso, *Guernica*, 1937. Tempera on canvas. This version of the painting is in the Casón del Buen Retiro of Madrid. Another version is at the Museum of Modern Art in New York. Exhibited in 1938 in London and later in New York, where

it paved the way for the great 1940 exhibition that turned Picasso into the painter of the century.
8. Picasso, *Owl with a Woman's Head*, 1953. Ceramic. Picasso's pottery creations have strong shapes and decorations.
9. Picasso, *Boy with Lobster*, 1941. Oil on canvas.

FRANCISCO FRANCO
Led the Nationalists to victory

4

Francisco Franco Bahamonde was born in 1892 in Galicia, Spain. In 1910 he graduated from the Infantry Academy. In 1912 he volunteered in the Regular Native Army in Melilla, Morocco; in 1920, still in Morocco, he fought against the anti-colonial guerrilla leader Abd el-Krim (1882–1963), defeating him in a decisive battle. In 1928 he was director of the General Military Academy. In 1934 he quelled the Asturian miners' uprising, and was rewarded with a promotion to Chief of the General Staff.

After the 1936 Popular Front victory, Franco was sent to an obscure command in the Canary Islands. Moroccan-based troops then rose against the government; Franco joined them. Made Generalissimo (Commander-in-Chief) on September 1, 1936 and head of state of the Nationalist regime on October 1st of the same year, Franco ferried the colonial soldiers to Spain on an Italian-German air bridge, and inflexibly led the right-wing forces in the war against the Republicans. On April 1, 1939 the civil war was over, and Franco was to remain dictator of Spain until his death in 1975, when, as he had decreed, power passed on to the king.

2

34 1935 1936 1937 **1938** 1939 1940 1931 1932 1933 1934 1935 19   31 1932 1933 1934 1935 1936 1937 **1938** 1939 1940 1931 1932 1933 1934 1

1

"You must sacrifice every thought, every ideology for the good of the nation and for the serenity of our fatherland.**"**
Franco speaking to the General Military Academy of Saragossa, 1931.

THE FALANGE. The Spanish Falange was a Fascist movement founded in 1933 by José A. Primo de Rivera, who was shot by a Republican firing squad in 1936; he was the son of General Miguel Primo de Rivera (1870–1930), to whom Alfonso XIII had entrusted the dictatorship following the 1923 coup, and whom he had removed in 1930. The only legal Spanish party since 1939, the Falange's principles were anti-Communist, nationalist, and corporate, with a sprinkling of weak Socialist demagoguery. The party declined after Franco's death, as it did not receive a role in the transfer of power to the king.

BLOOD. A dress rehearsal for World War II, the Spanish Civil War was among the most brutal in this century. There was horrible infighting among the Republicans, while Stalin refused to send help; priests, monks, friars were massacred, sacred statues and treasures destroyed in the war against the reactionary Catholic Church that owned extensive landed estates. The help tendered by foreign intellectuals and artists was noble but largely ineffective. Franco's forces advanced on "Red" cities and regions with exceptional brutality. The Nazi and Fascist air forces and artillery caused veritable slaughters.

NOT JUST THE GARROTE. After winning the war, Francoist repression continued with a series of executions that were carried out with the neck-breaking garrote until the 1960s. Essentially, however, the government became moderate. Franco kept the Falangists' thirst for revenge under control, ruled the Church by directly appointing the bishops, flattered the reactionary aristocracy while shrinking its power base, encouraged the new urban capitalism and ignored demonstrations in favor of regional autonomy. While waiting for the old tyrant to die, Spain progressed and began to smile.

FRANQUISMO

The tradition of military pronunciamientos originated in nineteenth-century Spain, during the war the monarchy and the upper crust waged against reform-minded officers and Liberals. The Moroccan pronunciamiento rebelled against the Popular Front government that was dominated by Liberal and Socialist forces, with strong radical (Communist and Anarchic) minorities. The military received crucial assistance from the Falange. In leading the civil war, Franco was able to impose the army upon the Falange. Cold and systematic, he conquered territory inch by inch, placing it under military rule and creating a personal dictatorship. In general, the democratic countries did not support the Republicans, since they were suspected of Communism, therefore they only allowed volunteers to join the Republican government's forces (notably, the 2,800-strong U.S. Lincoln Battalion). On the other hand, Italy and Germany's aid to Franco's army helped turn the war around in Franco's favor.

Franco supported the Axis by signing an anti-Comintern (thus anti-Soviet) pact in 1939; however, at the Hendaye meeting with Hitler (1940) and the Bordighera meeting with Mussolini (1941) he refused to grant them access to the Spanish bases from which they would have attacked Gibraltar. Thus he was able to keep Spain out of World War II. In 1942 however, he did allow Blue Division volunteers to fight the Soviet Army. Although in the 1945 and 1947 Constitutional papers Franco proclaimed Spain a "Catholic and social" country, he deprived the Falange Party of power and proclaimed himself head of state and regent for life, and established a Council to assist him. His refusal to enter the war on the side of the Axis and his anti-Communist stance won for Spain economic and military treaties with the United States in 1953 and acceptance, in 1955, into the United Nations, thus erasing the 1946 condemnation of Francoist Spain.

1. August 1936, Tocina near Seville. Falangist soldiers lining "Reds" up against a wall before shooting them.
2. Francisco Franco in his mature years.
3. *Aidez l'Espagne*, 1937, anti-Franco poster by Joán Miró (1893–1983). The best Spanish artists and intellectuals, including those of conservative bent, were for the most part against Franco's mutiny. As a result, many expatriated.
4. October 25, 1938. Final gathering of the International Brigades volunteers near Barcelona.
5. 1937. Guernica razed to the ground after being bombed by the Condor Legion.
6. The Fascist Air Force dropping bombs on Madrid.
7. Toledo. Robert Capa, photograph of a militiaman struck by machine-gun fire on a tree.
8. 1964, Madrid. Franco and, at his right, Juan Carlos de Borbón, the son of the Count de Barcelona, pretender to the throne; they are reviewing a parade celebrating the 25th anniversary of Franco's victory.
9. A 1939 Spanish calendar.

PIUS XII

Was crowned Pope

The son of a Vatican Council attorney on whom the pope had bestowed the title of marquis, Eugenio Pacelli was born in Rome in 1876. Ordained a priest in 1899, he began his career in the Curia. For several years he taught law in the Papal Academy of Noble Clergy, and in 1914 was appointed secretary of the Congregation on Church Affairs. Made titular archbishop of Sardi in 1917, he became nuncio to Munich and in 1920 nuncio to Berlin. He was the craftsman of the Vatican's treaties with Bavaria (1924) and Prussia (1929). Pope Pius XI made Pacelli a cardinal and in 1930 Secretary of State, treating Pacelli as his successor.

Elected pope on March 2, 1939, Pacelli took the name of Pius XII. After appointing Cardinal Luigi Maglione to be his Secretary of State, he did not appoint a successor at Maglione's death in 1944; similarly, he left many vacancies in the College of Cardinals (making appointments only in 1945

and 1952) and in the top Vatican hierarchy. In 1950, a Holy Year, he pronounced the dogma of Mary's Assumption into Heaven (immediately after her death, and before the final judgment). He also proclaimed two Marian years by sending copies of a "Pilgrim Mary" statuette to all parishes. He sanctified Pope Pius X and Maria Goretti, the latter a young martyred girl. Pius XII died in 1958, after a long illness.

"Pius XII was even involved in staging his contacts with the crowds, and made an effort to manage his image in a consistent way."
Andrea Riccardi, *Governo e "profezia" nel pontificato di Pio XII* (*Government and "Prophecy" in the Papacy of Pius XII*)

TRADITION. According to Pius XII, priests were expected to stay close to their churches, not become "worker priests." Theology was immutable: his 1950 encyclical *Humani generis* rejected all new theological ideas. Strong in his infallibility, the pope proclaimed the dogma of the Assumption, which was criticized by other Christian churches. Sexual morality was unchangeable: the pope was against divorce, contraceptives, cohabitation without marriage. As in the days when the Church was a state, his nephews were made princes. And the papal court was untouchable.

CHARITY. In his official acts from 1939 to 1941, Pius XII insisted repeatedly on disarmament, on the right of nations to their sovereignty, on the right of universal freedom, and first and foremost, freedom for the Church.

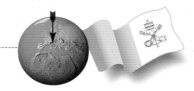

CHARISMA

Tall and slim, an extremely elegant polyglot, a consummate expert in the structure of power and the value of form, cautious, almost inaccessible, after the death of Cardinal Maglione Pius XII personally ruled the Church and Catholicism. Lacking in-depth theological training, he listened to Father Cordovani, a Dominican who died in 1950, and to conservative Cardinal Ottaviani for their opinions on these matters. Shy, eager to please, very slow in arriving at decisions, the pope avoided as much as possible face-to-face meetings, even reducing the number of "secret," periodic and "scheduled" meetings with the heads of congregations and the bishops. He refused to be subjected to pressure. The office of State Secretary became under him a sort of Prime Ministry, except that he himself was the Prime Minister. For routine matters he relied on Monsignor Montini (who later became Paul VI), who was open to reforms; for unusual matters on Monsignor Tardini, who belonged to the Roman Curia's conservative group.

No decision could be made in the Church without his explicit consent. Pius XII spoke out on all themes that might somehow be related to the Catholic faith, expressing his views from his residence window, on the radio (after expanding the Vatican radio station), in television broadcasts, in documentaries. All the world followed with interest his image: dressed in white, his eyes enlarged by spectacles, carried on the throne or the gestatory chair, amid ceremonial fans, Swiss Guards, noblemen, palatine guards, the red and purple capes of the cardinals, the court dignitaries, Pius XII embodied a majestic charisma that was popular worldwide.

8 | 9

36 1937 1938 **1939** 1940 1931 1932 1933 1

1938 **1939** 1940 1931 1932 1933 1934 1935 1936 1

He strengthened Catholic charity agencies, and acted very often and effectively, sometimes in secret, on behalf of prisoners, sentenced criminals, anti-Fascists, anti-Nazis, endangered Jews, and victims of bombings.

NAZIS AND COMMUNISTS. There is no text by Pius XII explicitly passing judgment on the Nazi or Fascist regimes, or Franco's dictatorship, not even for their most heinous crimes. After the war, however, the pope expressed his anti-Communism with very harsh words and deeds, to the point of excommunicating all Communists and their sympathizers. The Church was

active in politics, aiding the Catholic parties in word and deed.

DECLINE. Pius XII's extended illness was distressing for him and for the Church as well. Old, sick, isolated, he was at the mercy of the clique that had formed around him: his governess, his relatives, his physician, a few cardinals, and court dignitaries.

1. Pius XII in the splendor of the papal court.
2. The "Pilgrim Madonna" in a Roman house in June 1954.
3. An official photograph of Pius XII wearing the papal tiara.
4. 1939. A postcard with a portrait of the newly elected Pius XII.
5. 1955. Pius XII strolling alone in the Vatican gardens. According to rumors, the pope was prone to visions.
6. December 1939. The Vatican's official publication, *L'Osservatore Romano*, reporting on Pius XII's exceptional visit to Italian King Victor-Emmanuel III at the Quirinale palace, which until 1870 had been the popes' official residence.
7. Pius XII, on the throne, places the biretta on a recently appointed cardinal. The Consistory (an assembly of all cardinals headed by the pope), ruled the Church jointly with Pius XII to the full extent of the absolute powers granted to it by Pius IX at the 1870 Council Vatican I.
8. 1943, Rome. Pius XII on one of his rare outings visits Rome's bombed quarters.
9. Pius XII near his canaries' cage.

WINSTON CHURCHILL

Led the British Empire during World War II

Winston Leonard Spencer Churchill was born in 1874 and received his education first at Harrow, then at the Royal Military College at Sandhurst. Starting in 1900, he was a member of the House of Commons. First Lord of the Admiralty (the equivalent of Navy Secretary), from 1911–1915, in 1915 he conceived the disastrous Gallipoli campaign against the Turkish Empire. He fought on the French front. Having lost his Commons seat in 1922, he regained it in 1924 and once again became a government minister (Chancellor of the Exchequer). From 1929 to 1939 his political career seemed to be over. He spoke out against the Soviets, the Nazis, and the pacifists.

Appointed once more, on September 3, 1939, to head the Royal Navy, on May 10, 1940 he became Prime Minister in a coalition government. Churchill made it clear to the United States and the USSR that they had no choice but to join in the war. On June 4, 1945 he declared the British Labor Party's vision incompatible with democracy; a month later, England voted the Labor Party into power, thus excluding him from the end-of-the-war celebrations and the peace negotiations. Again Prime Minister from 1951 to 1955, Churchill died in 1965.

1940

FAMILY. Churchill had a sympathetic wife and children who were criticized. He came from an illustrious family founded by John, First Duke of Malborough (1650–1722), a greedy politician and military man who had wedded a maid much beloved by Anne, the last Stuart queen. Winston Churchill's father, Lord Randolph—a politician who followed Disraeli—was a younger brother of the Seventh Duke of Marlborough; Churchill's mother was American.

AUTHOR. Like his "rival" Charles de Gaulle, Churchill was a powerful speaker and a copious writer. Among his best-known works are *The World Crisis*, on World War I (4 volumes, 1923–1929), *Marlborough* (4 volumes, 1932–1938), and *The Second World War* (6 volumes, 1948–1953). In 1953, this great statesman received the Nobel Prize for literature.

SUMMIT. Throughout World War II, frequent personal meetings among the major Allies were a necessity. At the time, these summits were called conferences. Participants were President Roosevelt (and, after April 12, 1945, President Truman [1884–1972]), the British Prime Minister, and Stalin, Secretary of the Soviet Communist Party. Also a major ally, certainly in a moral sense, was de Gaulle, France's leader in exile. At the Teheran (November 1943), Yalta (February 1945), and Potsdam (July 1945)

HOLDING THE LINE!

BLOOD, SWEAT, AND TEARS

Courageous, strong, and as indomitable as a lion, well versed in history and geography, a war and economics expert, slightly eccentric, Sir Winston Churchill had an impressive memory and was obstinate in his ideas. A champion of the British Empire, he hated Communism and Socialism, he hated parvenus such as Hitler, and did not love the Germans. At the onset of World War I, Churchill was 40 years old and First Lord of the Admiralty. His love of country, his devotion to the good King George VI and to the glory of England knew no bounds. He was tireless in war. Although he slept in the morning, in the afternoon and evening he accomplished an incredible amount of work. He was the soul of the World War II

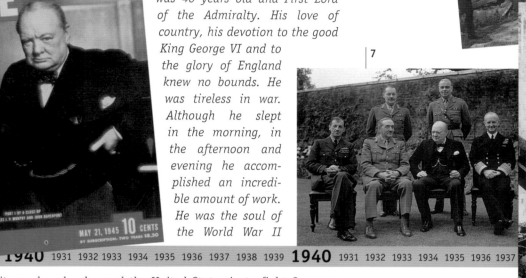

1937 1938 1939 **1940** 1931 1932 1933 1934 1935 1936 1937 1938 1939 **1940** 1931 1932 1933 1934 1935 1936 1937   1931 1932 19

alliance: it was he who dragged the United States in to fight Germany and Japan, the countries that posed threats to the British Empire. Wherever his mind and his example were needed, he was there. He convinced the Allied leaders and their peoples that the ordeal would be terrible, but victory would be theirs, no matter what the cost.

Churchill had a most gracious sense of honor; without batting an eyelid, he yielded the command of operations to Eisenhower in Europe and to Douglas MacArthur (1880–1964) in the Pacific. Paraphrasing Kipling, he promised blood and tears, honor and victory. Half the world was moved when the English voters cast him aside because they needed the Labor Party's social policies. Unable to surrender, in his masterful speeches in Fulton, Missouri (March 1946) and Zurich (September 1946) he coined the term "iron curtain" and called for the overthrow of Stalin's Communism. He did not realize that he had led his country into an undertaking from which Russia would emerge a great power, and that Great Britain would begin to decline.

"*We must win, because without victory there is no life. I have nothing to offer but blood, tears, toil and sweat. If required, for years; if required, alone.* **"**
Winston Churchill

conferences, these men forged strategies and divided up the world.

PAINTER. Like Hitler, and a little better than him, Churchill loved to paint. After World War II he sometimes took summer vacations on the Italian lakes. He was by then a living legend. People stared at him from afar. He would smoke a cigar, read, paint at his easel. It was rumored that he actually came to Italy to look for Mussolini's lost papers, to whom he had written letters that it was best to forget. In the meantime, he sampled the local cuisine.

1. 1913. Winston Leonard Spencer Churchill during his period as First Lord of the Admiralty, the equivalent of Secretary of the Navy.
2. Lord Randolph Spencer Churchill, Winston's father. He was an influential politician, and the younger brother of the Seventh Duke of Marlborough.
3. May 1944. King George VI, with Churchill at his side on the right, receives the prime ministers of the Commonwealth countries.
4. Sir Godfrey Kneller, *Portrait of the First Duke of Marlborough* (John Churchill), the rapacious politician and general.

5. 1942. Henry Guignon, poster of Churchill as a pugnacious British bulldog.
6. Churchill on one of the covers *Life* devoted to him.
7. July 1945, London. Churchill at No. 10 Downing Street with his General Staff.
8. July 17, 1945, Berlin. After visiting it, Churchill leaves Hitler's bunker, which had been built underneath the Reich's Chancellery.
9. May 11, 1941, London. Churchill inspects the ruins of Parliament after a German air attack.

ERWIN ROMMEL

WERNHER VON BRAUN

WALT DISNEY

ANNE FRANK

HO CHI MINH

RITA HAYWORTH

CHARLES DE GAULLE

LE CORBUSIER

KONRAD ADENAUER

DWIGHT EISENHOWER

No world event ever caused as much mourning as the war that was fought between September 1, 1939, when Nazi troops invaded Poland, and September 2, 1945, when Japan surrendered. With the exception of the Americas, all the other inhabited continents were theaters of war, Europe and Asia in particular. Men from all continents were called to arms. It was a horrendous blood bath: between 12 and 15 million dead in the Soviet Union alone; about 7 million Germans dead, 450,000 Britons and the same number of Italians, 300,000 United States military, 260,000 French. In the countries where the war raged, civilian deaths sometimes outnumbered military casualties. Dreadful wounds and mutilations, the ravages of hunger, and the hardships suffered in concentration camps continued to cause deaths for years after the war. The slaughter was tremendous in the Pacific also, among Japanese and Chinese, and other populations enslaved for

"reasons of war." The British Commonwealth

July 25, 1946. "Experimental" explosion

states and other Far Eastern countries all suf-

of an atomic bomb, launched by a U.S.

fered huge losses as they fought invading

bomber on Bikini Atoll in the Marshall

armies. Entire populations were slaughtered in

Islands. Atomic experiments were con-

cold blood for ethnic or cultural reasons,

ducted without precautions, not even

beginning with the genocide of the Jews and

for military and scientific observers.

the Gypsies. The final attacks on Hiroshima

and Nagasaki on August 6 and 9, 1945, did

not open the way to a quiet peace, but to a new terror, that of the atomic bomb, and to a war of

spies and scientists, of resources wasted in building a bomb that was tested in the stratosphere,

underground, and even under the sea, as at Bikini Atoll.

In a March 5, 1946 speech delivered at Westminster College (Fulton, Missouri), Winston Churchill said that the Soviet Union was hidden behind an "iron curtain," and that it was the

world's number one enemy of freedom. He claimed that free countries were morally bound to join

in the Cold War. In 1949 the Communists seized power in China, and the Soviet Union secured the

atomic bomb. In our century, more than one generation grew up under these frightful shadows.

The pact signed in August 1939 by Joachim von Ribbentrop (1893–1946) and Vyacheslav Molotov (1890–1986), Hitler's and Stalin's defense ministers respectively, guaranteed Germany's expansion to the east. While it is true that Hitler began World War II by invading Poland the following month, that country was split in October of the same year with the USSR, which the following year took over Latvia, Estonia, and Lithuania. In the meantime, the Germans overran Belgium, Norway, and Denmark; they conquered France and in 1941 invaded

1. Sleeping in Stalingrad. 2. Monte Cassino, before and after the Allied bombing. 3. Allied landing in Normandy. 4. Attack on Ber

echoed in the east: without declaring war, Japan bombed Pearl Harbor. The following February it captured Singapore, in March the Philippines, and then it swarmed over the Pacific archipelagos. The Axis powers, the weakness of the Fascist armies notwithstanding, prevailed everywhere until Field Marshal Bernard Montgomery (1887–1976) prevailed against the Italian and German armies at El Alamein and took Tripoli and

Yugoslavia, Greece, and Crete. 1941 was a fateful year. Without declaring war, Hitler invaded the USSR on June 22; on October 19 Moscow was in danger of being captured, and Stalin had lost vast territories, whole industries, sources of raw materials and food staples. On December 7 of the same year, Hitler's madness was

Tunisia (1943) as the Allies landed in Algeria and Morocco. The Axis' first irreparable debacle occurred in Russia. On September 3, 1942 the massive battle of Stalingrad began, led by Giorgiy Zhukov (1896–1974); the Red Army forced Field Marshal von Paulus to surrender in February 1943.

In July 1943 the Allies landed in Sicily. In a coup, King Victor-Emmanuel III deposed Mussolini;

CHILDREN, THE YOUNG, WOMEN, THE ELDERLY. NEVER DID SUCH A FEROCIOUS AND VAST MARTYRDOM BEFALL SO MANY INNOCENTS. HUNGER, THIRST, COLD, VIOLENCE, TERROR, THIEVERY, DESTRUCTION: THE POPULATIONS OF ENTIRE NATIONS SUFFERED. THOSE INDIVIDUALS WHO WERE IN COMBAT AREAS AND FOUND THEMSELVES ALIVE AFTER THE WAR, WERE HEROES.

together with his inept generals the king created the conditions for splitting Italy between the Germans and the Allies, with two puppet governments. Casualties of war also included precious works of art and historical artifacts. In Italy, the Germans had blocked the Allies' advance at Monte Cassino, so the Allies bombed the medieval abbey,

gary, and advanced into Germany and Austria. Tito's Communist resistance fighters liberated Yugoslavia, and the Greek Communist resistance began a civil war against the royalist forces. In April 1945 the Red Army took Berlin by storm. The Reichstag building was set on fire. On April 30 Hitler took his own life. Two days earlier, Mussolini had been executed by the Italian resistance. At Yalta, Roosevelt and Stalin divided the world between them. The strong understanding among the United States, the Soviet Union, and the United Kingdom,

USSR, United Kingdom, France, and China, and each of them has veto power.

The Pacific war was won by the Allies when the United States dropped atomic bombs on Hiroshima and Nagasaki.

The international military courts set up by the victors brought to trial the defeated German and Japanese leaders.

Robert Brasillach, sentenced to death in 1945, stated: "I lived in Germany. I loved the country. I hoped for its victory because of some of its principles." Enrico Fermi (1901–1954) who in 1942 created the atomic battery, opening the way to the atomic bomb, was devastated. In Italy, neorealist film was born.

In 1947, the "New Look" fashion

5 | 6 | 8 | 10

eichstag. 5. USSR propaganda. 6. President Truman. 7. Hiroshima after the atomic attack. 8. Goering in Nuremberg. 9. Scientist Enrico Fermi. 10. Boy, girl, and Lambretta motor scooter.

home of the Order of Saint Benedict, razing it.

7

On June 6, 1944 ("D-Day") 6,700 ships, 14,600 fighter and bomber planes, and 86 Allied divisions launched an attack on the European continent from the sea. The Normandy landing was successful, and the new French front closed the German army between two pincers. On August 25 Paris was liberated.

The Red Army occupied Poland, Romania, Bulgaria, and Hun-

which had been so heavily publicized, was already shaky.

The Yalta conferees also resolved to establish the United Nations. However, the San Francisco Charter that set up the U.N. during Harry Truman's presidency was not based on democratic principles: in the Security Council, 5 of the 11 seats are permanent and belong to the victors of World War II: the United States,

The Nuremberg court tried the German leaders. In October 1946 it sentenced 12 of them to capital punishment. Hermann Goering committed suicide shortly before his execution could take place. On December 23, 1948 the Tokyo court ruled that all the Japanese governments after 1928 were responsible for the war.

The disasters wrought by the war also affected the world of culture. The French writer

9

launched by Christian Dior required a lot of fabric. General George C. Marshall, U.S. Secretary of State, proposed the Marshall Aid Plan for Europe. In 1948, the Olympic Games were held in London. In 1949, the North Atlantic Treaty Organization (NATO) was born, and the Cold War was already raging. In 1950, war broke out in Korea. It was a time of reconstruction and Cold War. In Europe tiny motor scooters were becoming popular.

ERWIN ROMMEL
Led the war against the Allies in North Africa

Erwin Johannes Rommel was born to a modest Heidenheim family in 1891. A career officer, during World War I he received an Iron Cross first-degree for his conduct in the battle of Caporetto on the Italian front. He joined the Nazis and in 1939 was entrusted with the command of Hitler's headquarters. The following May, he headed an armored division. Advancing 50 miles on Cambrai, he captured 100 tanks and took 10,000 Allied prisoners. In 1941 he was sent with only a modest number of troops to Libya to aid the Italian army, which was on the brink of losing to the English forces. In March he launched an offensive and advanced up to the Nile delta; in the spring of 1942 he was at El Alamein. Here he was repulsed

by Montgomery's crushing forces. He left the command with the rank of general in March 1943. In May the Axis capitulated in Africa. From July 25 to September 8, 1943 he led the German forces in Northern Italy. In November he was sent to France to inspect German defense works along the English Channel coast. In January 1944 he was commander against the feared Anglo-American landing in Normandy. With insufficient men and equipment, and bound to follow Hitler's senseless orders, he was unable to repel the Allies. Wounded by a fighter plane attack on July 17, 1944, he was sent home to recuperate. He committed suicide on October 14.

1

45 1946 1947 1948 1949 1950 **1941** 1942 1943 1944 1945 1946 1947 1948 1949 1950 **1941** 1942 1943 1944 1945 1946 1947 19

3

4

PATTON. During the invasion of Sicily (July–August 1943) and later in the 1944–1945 French campaign, another general distinguished himself for his masterful, fast use of tanks. It was U.S. General George S. Patton (1885–1945), who was also known for his arrogance and self-boasting.

AOSTA. The Germans lost their African Empire in World War I, while the Italians, who at one time held Eritrea, Somalia, and Libya, subjugated Ethiopia (1935–1936) in a war that depleted their already inadequate war resources. Leading the Italian troops in Eastern Africa during the war was Amedeo of Savoy, Duke of Aosta; in 1941 he was crushed by superior English forces and died a prisoner a short while later. On the Amba Alaji after the last, futile resistance, he received the military salute from the

enemy who honored his courage. Like Rommel, he was heroic but ran out of luck.

SUICIDE. While Rommel did not participate in any plot to kill Hitler, he did conspire with the German commander in France to block the Führer and his faithful retinue and depose him, and then to engage the German armed forces in direct negotiations with the

Allies. The plot was discovered. On October 14, 1944, Generals Burgdorf and Maisel went to Rommel's house near Ulm and presented him with an ultimatum: suffer a court martial, or drink the poison they had brought with them, thus guaranteeing that his family would escape reprisal. He received the state funeral accorded to a hero, which was attended by his widow and son.

"The first twenty-four hours of the invasion will be decisive. The Reich's future is in your hands. "
Erwin Rommel speaking to his soldiers, a few days before D-Day, the Allied landing in Normandy.

A GENERAL WITHOUT BLEMISH

1. November 1917. Italian troops during the Caporetto retreat.

2. Erwin Rommel.

3. April 1941. Rommel inspects the positions gained after the battle of Sollum on the Egyptian front.

4. 1944. Marshal Rommel, commander of the B troops sent by Hitler to defend France, in Normandy. He is talking with General Meindl.

5. 1944. Rommel and Dönitz in Normandy inspect the defense works along the Channel coast. Admiral Karl Dönitz, who headed the Navy, succeeded Hitler as chancellor and signed Germany's surrender on May 9, 1945.

5

Together with young de Gaulle, as a young officer Rommel advocated the use of armored formations to advance quickly into enemy territory to immediately cut the enemy forces in two and split their command centers. Commanding the Axis forces in Mediterranean Africa was especially risky. Hitler deemed it less important than his planned advance from the east to block the Suez Canal, which would have cut off an irreplaceable source of English power. Taking advantage of the momentary superiority over Field Marshal Archibald Wavell, Rommel advanced from Italian Libya to within about 90 miles of Alexandria, Egypt. He was blocked at El Alamein, while the new English Commander Bernard Montgomery (1887–1976) gathered men and equipment and the British Navy controlled the Mediterranean. Rommel lost the epic battle of El Alamein (October 24–November 4, 1942); hounded by the English, his forces withdrew, lost Libya, and retrenched in Tunisia.

To preserve the Reich's honor, Hitler withdrew his heroic commander from the African front before the Allies could force him to surrender. In an effort to soften Wavell's defeat

8

1942 1943 1944 1945 1946 1947 1948 1949 1950 **1941** 1942 1943 1944 1945 1946 1947 1948

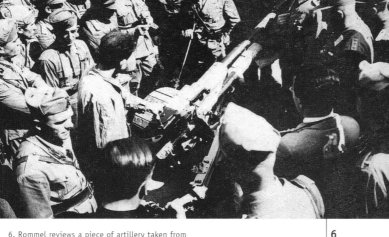

6. Rommel reviews a piece of artillery taken from the enemy.

7. 1942. Bernard Montgomery, commander of the British 8th Army, follows the battle of El Alamein.

8. Von Witzleben testifying at the trial held for the July 20, 1944 attempt on Hitler's life.

9. The wrecked car in which Rommel was riding on July 17, 1944. He suffered skull fractures from machine-gun fire.

6

7

9

and magnify this victory, English propaganda helped create the legend of the German general. It was said that, unlike Hitler's high command, he had predicted the Allies landing in Normandy (June 6–7, 1944). He was portrayed as a victim of the Nazi regime. Neither too ambitious nor self-centered, worshipped by his men, Rommel is still today the embodiment of the fearless twentieth-century general.

WERNHER VON BRAUN

Built the A4 rocket

Wernher von Braun was born in 1912 in Wirsitz, Germany (now Wyrzysk, in Poland), the son of Baron Magnus, a Prussian Junker and agriculture minister. For his confirmation he received from his mother a small telescope, his introduction to the extraterrestrial universe. In 1927 Wernher sent his first theoretical work—about a liquid-fuel rocket—to Hermann Oberth, because two years earlier he had read an essay by that scientist on the feasibility of building a rocket that could overcome the Earth's gravity field. In 1929 he met Oberth, who was then building a rocket for Fritz Lang's film *Frau im Mond* (*Woman in the Moon*). He joined a group of Oberth's students. In 1931 their liquid-fueled Mirak reached an altitude of 1,000 feet. Colonel K. E. Becker, a professor at Friedrich Wilhelm University and

chief of the Reichswehr ordinance department, took note of this success. The Reichswehr financed the group's research (albeit in violation of the Versailles Treaty), and moved the group to a secret forest site. In 1932, von Braun graduated from the Technische Hochschule and upon Becker's advice perfected his theoretical background at the university, where among his excellent teachers was the great Werner Heisenberg (1901–1976, Nobel Prize for physics in 1932). In 1934 von Braun defended his dissertation on liquid-fuel rockets. The dissertation was immediately declared a state secret.

MISSILE SCIENCE. Von Braun's unique contribution to the invention of the missile was to the liquid-fuel missile, whose major problem was the optimum ratio of the useful load weight to the missile's range (the distance measured on a plane between the launching point and the point of arrival). Liquid-fuel missiles usually employed two types of fuels—a combustible and an oxidant—to achieve combustion, stored in separate tanks and mixed in a separate chamber. In general, von Braun's missiles were propelled by an inertial guidance sys-

tem. He also built remote-controlled missiles such as the Wasserfell produced by the Germans during the war.

NEBEL. In June 1934, Rudolf Nebel, a brilliant scientist and von Braun's classmate, was arrested. He was accused of being a pacifist, of belonging to the Pan-Earth Association founded by Einstein, and of having a non-"Aryan" wife. Most importantly, Nebel had refused to work for the Reichswehr. All his patents were confiscated, thus depriving Germany of important knowledge.

ROCKETS OR MISSILES

In November 1934, on an island in the North Sea, two A2 rockets nicknamed Max and Moritz were launched to a height of 6,600 feet. When the Luftwaffe decided to build a secret missile center, von Braun chose the Peenemünde plain along the Baltic Sea. In 1937, an A3 rocket with a 110 lb. load reached an altitude of 72,000 feet. In 1942, an A4 flying at a speed of 4,500 ft/sec. (5 times the speed of sound), reached an altitude of 270,000 feet, falling 125 miles from the launch site. On September 8, 1944, at 6:43 P.M. an A4 hit Chiswich, a London suburb. It came to be known as a V2. By the end of October, 32,000 prisoners conscripted from the concentration camps worked feverishly in the underground laboratories of Peenemünde. Over thirty rockets were launched every day. In December, von Braun was decorated with the Knight's Cross with swords.

On May 12, 1945 von Braun surrendered to U.S. troops. The following year, first in Texas then in Alabama, von Braun

was a consultant to the launches of 100 V2s that had been salvaged and refurbished. On August 20, 1953, the Redstone, the first U.S. missile, was launched from Cape Canaveral, Florida. After the success in 1960 of the Jupiter C, von Braun was promoted to director of the Alabama NASA Center. In July 1969 his Saturn V launched into space the American astronauts who were the first men to land on the moon. In 1972, at the conclusion of the Apollo program, von Braun left NASA for private industry. He died in the United States in 1977.

7

9

1950 194

49 1950 1941 **1942** 1943

946 1947 1948 1949

6

8

"My country lost two world wars. Now I want to be on the side of the victors."
Wernher von Braun, May 12, 1945

A BECOMES V. The first missiles von Braun invented, the A2, A3, A4, became sadly known as the V1 and V2 once they were armed. The V1 was equipped with an air-motor, which took in the outside air it needed for combustion. The first German missiles were fueled with oxygen and alcohol. The V2 was especially dangerous because it was launched without a fixed launching pad, from mobile units that were easily disguised.

PURGED. In 1953 von Braun was

pressing for the Orbiter program that was planning to launch a 4.4 lb. satellite into orbit. However, he was removed from the program and the U.S. Navy was given the task of perfecting the missile (a Vanguard). On October 4, 1957 the Soviets sent a *Sputnik* into orbit; on December 6, the Vanguard's launch failed. To resolve the worst prestige crisis since the war, the U.S. government recalled von Braun, whose team then built the Jupiter C. Finally, in 1958, the Jupiter C sent the Explorer I into orbit.

1. Wernher von Braun with a model of one of his projects.
2. 1943, French coast. A V1 base. Workers are preparing to launch a rocket.
3. 1944. A V2 reached London's sky. Photo from *Signal*, a 1944 bilingual magazine.
4. 1943, London. Buildings destroyed by a V1.
5. May 1943, Germany. Von Braun, in civilian clothes, among a group of officers as they watch an experimental V1 launch.

6. 1944, Dutch coast. A V2 ready for launching.
7. 1968. *Explorer*, a small U.S. artificial satellite. It was launched into orbit by Jupiter C.
8. 1969. A Saturn V photographed at the NASA launch base, ready for lift-off.
9. The great German physicist Werner Heisenberg (1901–1976), 1932 Nobel recipient; in 1927 he formulated the principle of indeterminacy.

WALT DISNEY

Made *Saludos Amigos*

Walter Elias Disney was born in 1901 in Chicago to a family of farmers. He was already working while attending a city high school. An advertising graphic artist, he opened an animation studio in Kansas City. In 1923, with his brother Roy, he founded the Disney Brothers Studios where the *Alice Comedies* series was created. In 1924, his *Oswald the Lucky Rabbit* ushered in the famous "O" style, rounded and characterized by well-defined, closed shapes. In 1928, Mickey Mouse made his appearance in the *Gallopin' Gaucho* short, and became the first character to reach full development. Mickey Mouse had a companion, Minnie, whom he was not interested in romancing, but rather in saving from the frightful, gigantic Pegleg; later on, beginning in 1932, he would also save her from their surreal friend Goofy. Another character, Donald Duck, was born and achieved maturity between 1934

1

and 1937. Donald Duck was later flanked by a series of supporting characters, a whole family of ducks. Between 1934 and 1937, Disney created *Snow White and the Seven Dwarfs*, his first full-length animated feature. In 1940, during the war, he moved the studios to Burbank, and produced *Fantasia*, a full-length animated musical film made up of different episodes. *Bambi* was created in 1942; *Saludos Amigos* (1943), and *The Three Caballeros* (1945), following a publicity tour throughout Latin America.

4

3

2

5

MICKEY MOUSE AND DONALD DUCK. Quick, all angles and circles, Mickey Mouse was at first a comic character. Later, he became less angular and turned into a paladin of noble, stereotypical endeavors, thus embodying idealized American virtues; for a long time he was a first-rate private detective. Dressed only from the waist up, chattering away with a rounded beak shaped like a prominent mouth, Donald Duck was lazy, aggressive, the

eternal loser and, as such, immensely congenial to many.

FULL-LENGTH FILMS. 1940, *Pinocchio*. 1941, *Dumbo*. 1942, *Bambi*. 1950, *Cinderella*. 1951, *Alice in Wonderland*. 1953, *Peter Pan*. 1955, *Lady and the Tramp*. 1959, *Sleeping Beauty*. 1961, *101 Dalmatians*. 1963, *The Sword in the Stone*. 1967, *The Jungle Book*, Walt Disney's last film, on which he worked before his death in 1966.

Among the films with real actors, *Mary Poppins* (1964), starring Julie Andrews and Dick van Dyke, is unforgettable.

DOCUMENTARIES. *Bambi* narrated the life of a deer, from its birth to young adulthood. The animals' anthropomorphism is contained, and men are por-

trayed as cruel hunters. The interest in nature in its "as is" state, in reality transfigured by a vision at once determinist and anthropocentric, exploded in the post-war years with documentaries such as *The Island of the Seals* (1949), *The Valley of the Beavers* (1950), and *The Living Desert* (1953).

116

THE CARTOONIST

Animated cartoons already existed; however, it was Disney who made them into an artistic genre that he developed with great formal skill. He was an iron-willed talent scout and coordinator, as well as a film director and producer. After 1953, through Buena Vista, he also became the distributor of his own works. He created characters and surrounded them with complete environments, along with a series of supporting characters and stories, thanks also to teams that collaborated for many years and to massive investments ($1.5 million for Snow White alone). He focused on just a few products, adequately paid his staff and artists, required his artists to attend art school, and patented technical inventions. He was a tireless color

1942 **1943** 1944 1945 1946 1947 1948 1949 1950 1941 1942 **1943** 1944 1945 1946 1947 1948 1949 1950 1941 1942 **1943** 1944 1945 1946 1947 1948 1949 1950 1941 1

and sound-track editor, put the finishing touches to the scripts, and created whole hierarchies of characters from the protagonists to the supporting characters and the extras. He also devised a marketing system that targeted each character, story, environment, and message to a specific audience, trying to avoid disappointing the other audiences. He created stories for children of all ages, but not just for them.

Walt Disney's inexhaustible imagination was the result of systematizing that of his assistants. He was a master at "blending," wedding classical music to folk music, cruelty to tenderness, maudlin mannerism to abstract art, Darwinian determinism to surreal imagination, affectation to concision. He was the Henry Ford of animated film. His was a new kind of anthropomorphism, in that he "humanized" the flora and fauna that city dwellers no longer knew, fashioning a pastoral, innocent world where men and nature communicated on different levels. He always insisted that every detail be realistic. He acted as a filter between his assistants' talent and the public's taste, which he flattered and guided, by proposing animal types that embodied human types, had an erect posture, and eyes, looks, and clothing that defined them and made them come alive.

1. A portrait of Walt Disney in his early years.

2. Disney with his assistants in front of the studio during Mickey Mouse's golden years. Lined up in the front row, Mickey Mouse dolls.

3. Dumbo, the endearing, cheerful flying baby elephant.

4. The chimney-sweeps' dance on the rooftops of London, from Robert Stevenson's (1905–1986) *Mary Poppins*, with special effects by Ub Iwerks.

5. Ub Iwerks (1901–1971), considered the most brilliant of Disney's assistants and co-creator of Mickey Mouse. He worked as a freelancer from 1930

to 1940, then returned to Disney where he was in charge of special effects (also for Alfred Hitchcock's *The Birds*, 1963).

6. The dancing mushrooms, a delightful *Fantasia* invention.

7. *Snow White*'s seven dwarfs.

8. Snow White surrounded by small woodland animals, as famous as *Cinderella*'s small creatures and *Pinocchio*'s cricket.

9. Bambi, a shy fawn, looks at the world from behind its mother's legs.

ANNE FRANK
Seized by the Nazis in her Amsterdam hideout

Anne Frank was born in 1929 to a middle-class family in Frankfurt, the city of Goethe and the Rothschild dynasty. Frankfurt-am-Main had been the center of high German culture, where princes used to elect the Holy Roman Emperor. With the onset of "racial" persecution, the Franks fled to Amsterdam in Holland, and from 1942 to 1944 lived in hiding in a small, secret hideout, where they were fed and protected by acquaintances. The Netherlands had boasted an educated, well-to-do Jewish community since the sixteenth century. With their country occupied by the Nazis, the Dutch put up a strong resistance led from London by Queen Wilhelmina (1890–1948); many hid and aided Jews as much as they could, even risking their own lives. Sometimes, however, the protection failed, and informants got the upper hand. Like so many other Jews, the Franks were caught and deported to the Bergen-Belsen extermination camp. They all died with the exception of Otto, the head of the family and Anne's father, who later published the diary (somewhat expurgated) she had written while secluded in the Amsterdam garret.

1948 1949 1950 1941 1942 1943 **1944** 1945 1946 1947 1948 1949 1950 1941 1942 1943 **1944** 1945 1946 1947 1948 1949 1950 1941 1942 1943 **1944** 1945 1946 1947 1948

"This picture is how I would always want to look. But who knows, I might also go to Hollywood."
Anne Frank writing in her diary.

THE DIARY. In the secret Amsterdam hideout, Anne Frank kept a diary in Dutch with fair regularity, recording the minute events of her secluded life and her adolescent musings. Her terrible act of accusation consists precisely in the fact that she remained herself, a budding woman. Neither fear nor pain nor hardship corrupted her.

THE PUBLICATION. Published by Otto Frank in 1947, Anne's diary became immensely popular overnight. Among all the diaries written by Holocaust protagonists—butchers, heroes, and victims—that of an ordinary victim seemed exceptional. It aroused deep emotions and became the subject of plays, radio programs, and films. No one, however, noted that Anne had overcome her suffering through writing, and by so doing had affirmed the superiority of culture—which was treasured by twentieth-century Jewish people—over barbarity. Paraphrasing the infamous concentration camp motto, "Writing makes one free."

ANTI-SEMITISM. Attributing anti-Semitism only to German National Socialism, or looking for its roots in the history of the pagan ancient Roman Empire misses the point, for anti-Semitism has been pervasive in Christian civilization. In modern times, even some Enlightenment figures were anti-Semitic, Voltaire among them. Johann Gottlieb Fichte (1762–1814) wrote this about the Jewish people: "One could grant them civil rights only on condition that in one night their head be cut off and replaced by another." In the Soviet Union, when he was near death, Stalin was about to embark on an extensive "purge" of the Jews. Like many Bolshevik leaders, Trotsky was Jewish.

THE HOLOCAUST

The word *Holocaust* refers to the extermination of Jewish people at the hands of the Nazis—who were helped by innumerable other people—starting with the occupation of Poland in 1939. This was the most tragic anti-Semitic chapter in all of history. What set it apart from all other modern horrors was the fact that it was sanctioned by state laws, issued by the German Reich in 1933 and 1935, and by the kingdom of Italy in 1938. The butchery was accomplished through excessive labor, malnourishment, physical abuse, torture, medical and surgical procedures, weapons, and deadly gases, particularly in the concentration and extermination camps. Among the major camps were Bergen-Belsen, Buchenwald, Dachau, Flossenburg, Neuengamme, Ravensbrück, and Sachsenhausen in Germany; Mauthausen in Austria; Natzweiler in Alsace; Theresienstadt in today's Czech Republic; Auschwitz, Belzec, Chelmno, Majdanek, Stutthof, and Treblinka in Poland;

1948 1949 1950 1941 1942 1943 **1944** 1945 1946 1947 1948 1949 1950 1941 1942 1943 **1944** 1945 1946 1947 1948 1949 1950 194

Fossoli, Gries, and Trieste San Sabba in Italy. Starting in 1936, the camps came under the rule of the SS. In 1944, 35,000 SS and 10,000 regular army soldiers, aided by inmates (chosen for the most part from "asocial" elements such as common criminals and the mentally ill) made sure that the "final solution" would be enacted.

Every inmate was forced to wear an identifying badge on his or her chest: a red triangle marked the political prisoners; a pink one the homosexuals; a purple one the religious prisoners and conscientious objectors; a black one identified the asocial

elements; a green one the "common" prisoners; and a double yellow triangle (the "star of David") marked the Jews. Although most of the documents were destroyed by the Nazis, the total number of Holocaust victims was estimated at about ten million, including Gypsies, Polish, and Russians prisoners. Of these, six million or more were Jews, and about one million children.

1. Some pages from Anne's diary notebooks. Otto Frank supervised an edition that removed all criticism of her parents and any word that might spoil his daughter's image. It was a mistake because, as *The Book of Job* teaches, martyrs and saints are all the more exemplary for their imperfections.

2. A photo of young Anne Frank.

3. The house where the Frank family lived in hiding.

4. Millie Perkins in *The Diary of Anne Frank* (1959), directed by George Stevens (1904–1975), who accompanied the American troops and filmed the liberation of the Dachau concentration camp and the capture of Hitler's "eagle's nest" in Berchtesgaden.

5. 1938, Germany. The boycott of Jewish stores begins.

6. Poster celebrating the S.A.: Jews and priests beg the Brown Shirts for mercy.

7. 1941, Warsaw ghetto. A child charged with distributing "star of David" badges.

8. 1945, Belsen camp. Two young victims.

9. 1942, Warsaw ghetto. An emaciated child begging.

HO CHI MINH
Proclaimed the People's Republic of Vietnam

"He who enlightens" is the pseudonym of a man who lived an adventurous life. His true name is unknown. He was born in Central Vietnam between 1890 and 1892, the son of either a poor teacher or a lower court officer. Young Ho was registered with the Overseas Workers Organization in Paris in 1917. He entered history in 1919 when he appeared at the Versailles Peace Conference with a petition demanding freedom for Vietnam, at the time a French colony. At the 1920 French Socialist Party Congress held in Tours, he sided with the minority that founded the French Communist Party. A delegate to the Chinese Farmers' Congress, he remained in Canton where he worked as a translator at the Russian Consulate. He was jailed; upon his release, Ho Chi Minh expatriated to Siam (today's Thailand), where he organized terrorist attacks on the French in Indochina and a Communist uprising in North Vietnam. Expelled from Siam, after a jail term in Hong Kong he fled to Russia. By 1938 he was with Mao in Yenan. He was imprisoned by the Chinese Nationalists. Later, in Indochina, he organized guerrilla activities against the Japanese occupation and the local French colonial government that collaborated with the Japanese. At this time he founded the Viet-Minh League and guided the popular front struggle. In 1945 he proclaimed himself president of the Democratic Republic of Vietnam.

1942 1943 194 42 1943 1944 **1945** 1946 1947 1948 1949 1950 1941 1942 1943 1944 **1945** 1946 1947 1948 1949 1950 1941 1942

1946–1954. In 1946 Ho signed an agreement with Paris under which Vietnam was given autonomy. But it was only a piece of paper. In November 1946 the French bombed Haiphong: it was the beginning of the long Vietnam War. Ho Chi Minh had two valiant aides: Pham Van Dong and Vo Nguyen, nicknamed Giap (b. 1912). General Giap defeated the French Army, which led courageous French Prime Minister Pierre Mendès-France (1907–1982), a Socialist, to end the Indochina war by signing the Geneva treaty. South Vietnam and the United States later violated that treaty.

1956–1975. In 1954 Vietnam was partitioned. National general elections were going to be held. In 1956, a second Republic of Vietnam was formed, with Saigon as capital and a right-wing government assisted by the United States, which had refused to aid the French, only to replace them. In 1960, counting on assistance from North Vietnam, a National Liberation Front was set up in the South (the so-called Viet Cong), and war broke out between the two Vietnams. The United States took direct part in the war, gradually committing more and more men and resources. The United States opened peace negotiations in 1973, after being defeated by Giap, by the Vietnamese people, and by the American and international peace movement. In 1975, a peace treaty was signed and Vietnam was reunited.

OTHERS. Ho Chi Minh's national way to Socialism was unlike that of other leaders of emerging nations. For example, when, in 1974, Mengistu Haile Mariam put an end to Ethiopia's ancient empire with a military coup, he established a personal, repressive, dictatorship. Marshal Tito forced on Yugoslavia a very personal regime, and the hegemony of the Serbs, Croats, and Slovenes over other ethnic groups.

NATIONAL SOCIALISM

Ho Chi Minh was a cultivated cosmopolitan. During his long prison years in China, he wrote a Prison Diary *in classical Chinese verse. He spoke several languages. He refused to become an ideologue. An earnest man of the left, Ho Chi Minh attended the 1935 Comintern Congress and believed in the popular front policy. The Viet-Minh League (1942–1951) was one such front. When the farmers resisted the government's policy of forced land collectivization in 1955–1956, Ho left the prime minister's post and took on the job of Communist Party secretary. His Communism included both Marx and Lenin, but not Stalin. He had great respect for Mao but tried to keep him out of Vietnam. "Uncle Ho," as the people called him, despised Saigon's puppet generals, the prostitutes who entertained the American Marines and the pimps who procured them, and the large landowners and merchants who made their fortunes from the war.*

" *We must continue to fight until we achieve victory, even if it means twenty years of war or more.* **"**

Ho Chi Minh, July 1966

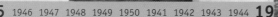

6

8

945 1946 1947 1948 1949 1950 1941 1942 1943 1944 **19**

1944 **1945**

7

Ho Chi Minh was not a brutal man. His vision was to achieve progress and industrialization within a patriarchal and agrarian society, without tearing it apart. He strongly believed in universal education, including for women. Ho Chi Minh despised Bao Dai, who in 1925 at the age of twelve was made Emperor of Vietnam and, having abdicated in 1945,

9

was placed on the throne again by the French in 1948 and finally deposed in 1955. Ho died in Hanoi in 1969. He forbade the cult of his person. He always fought for a united left, for peace, and for a respectful government-citizen relationship, and for a balance of tradition and modernization.

1. 1920, Tours. Young Ho at the congress that founded the French Communist Party.
2. Ho Chi Minh when he was president of North Vietnam.
3. 1966. President Ho Chi Minh, followed by General Giap, tours a military training camp.
4. 1954. Bao Dai, the wealthy Emperor of Vietnam, later president of Vietnam. After his deposition in 1955, he went to live on the French Riviera.
5. 1967, South Vietnam. A U.S. Marine camp in the forest.
6. 1947. Ho with Giap and other military and political chiefs during the war against France.
7. 1969. A painting of Ho Chi Minh by Renato Guttuso, an Italian Communist Party executive and a well-known representative of international Communist realism.
8. March 1968. Dead bodies of Vietcong soldiers. In the background, Marines on patrol outside the fortified area of Khe Sanh.
9. 1968, Paris. A closeup of Pierre Mendès-France, the French Prime Minister who put an end to the Vietnam War in 1954.

RITA HAYWORTH

Starred in *Gilda*

Margarita Carmen Cansino was born in the United States in 1918 to a Spanish Catholic family of dancers. She learned dancing at home. In 1935, at the dawn of her career (*Cruz Diablo*) she was already a noted starlet. In 1941 she was in *Blood and Sand*, a remake of a Valentino film directed by Rouben Mamoulian with handsome Tyrone Power and Linda Darnell (1923–1965). In 1944 she starred in *Cover Girl* with actor-dancer Gene Kelly. In *Gilda* she was paired with Glenn Ford, whose career she helped launch. In 1947 Orson Welles (1915–1985), her husband who was also a director, turned her into a blonde for *The Lady from Shanghai*. Later, for several years she no longer lived a public life, having become a princess through her marriage to Aly Khan, eldest son of billionaire Aga Khan, the leader of the Ismaelite Shiites. She triumphantly returned to the screen with the melancholy *Miss Sadie Thompson* (1953) by Curtis Bernhardt, in which she danced and sang two lovely songs. Her beauty, softened by time, had a yearning, longing quality. She was in *Pal Joey* (1957), *Separate Tables* (1958), *They Came to Cordura*, and *The Story on Page One* (1959). Her last movies were *The Money Trap* (1966) and *The Wrath of God* (1971). Rita Hayworth died in May 1987.

THE OTHERS. A great rival for the beauty prize was Ava Gardner (1922–1990), celebrated as "the most lovely animal in the world." Statuesque Arlene Dahl was a little less celebrated. Lauren Bacall (b. 1924), a consummate actress, was "The Eyes." Exotic Gene Tierney (1920–1991) was exciting yet ladylike. Enchanting Veronica Lake (1919–1973) was witty and vivacious. Hedy Lamarr (b. 1915) had a daring, although somewhat dated beauty. Maria Felix (also b. 1915), a magnificent brunette, was for twenty years the star of Mexican film.

MEN. The atomic bomb was not a maneater. When the multi-talented Orson Welles married her (1943–1947), she was Hollywood's most splendid star.

Like Marilyn Monroe, she sought culture, protection, a brilliant intelligence from her husband. They had a daughter. Hayworth felt misunderstood and they divorced; later they made a film together in which he killed her on the screen. In 1948 she married Aly Khan, a well-known high society man. They had a daughter. But the prince loved the whirlwind of society life, while Rita preferred to stay at home with the family. After their divorce, Rita returned to the screen. In the last years of her life she was always accompanied by attractive athletic girls, who were her bodyguards and nurses.

DECLINE. With Orson Welles, Hayworth learned to drink. After divorcing Aly Khan, she drank again. It was a solitary vice; Rita was never immoderate in public. In her last years she agreed to appear at gala dinners for a fee, especially in South America: she was still the atomic bomb, her beauty and hearty sensuality intact. Someone would sometimes note that she seemed strange, absent-minded, and shaky on her legs and thought it might be excessive drinking, but they were wrong: Rita developed Alzheimer's disease, which killed her.

THE ATOMIC BOMB

We don't know who first coined this nickname for Rita Hayworth, whether it was her producer's publicity office, or American soldiers in the closing years of the war, which ended with the dropping of the atomic bomb on Hiroshima and a second one on Nagasaki in August 1945. But the concept is clear: Rita was a flaming, explosive beauty, "the Great American Love Goddess." Neither haughty nor off-putting, Rita was reserved and, when she felt at ease, affable and cheerful. She was a woman of bewitching beauty: lustrous reddish-brown hair; luminous eyes; a lovely mouth with healthy teeth; long legs and well-shaped arms; strong, elegant hands; a full but not opulent bust; large but not squarish shoulders; perfect back and hips. All contributed to make of her a total beauty and when she danced—she was an excellent dancer—a sorcery of seduction.

Critics claimed she had a low forehead and shaved it. The critics, in occupied

5

6

Europe especially (where her movies could not be shown), also claimed that she was not a good actress. But, starting with Gilda, Rita Hayworth showed excellent acting skills. Her lovely open face and her sincere eyes, her strong Latin grace pervaded even her last films. She was likeable. Marilyn Monroe imitated her in many ways, not just in singing and dancing; smaller than Hayworth and lighter in color, she aimed to please and was liked by men and women alike. In the history of cinema, Hayworth is a reference point in the transition period from the domination of stars to an interest in directors.

7

8

1. 1950. Margarita Cansino, by now Rita Hayworth (Columbia's Harry Cohn changed her name), posing for the fashion photographer George Hoyningen-Huene.

2. Gene Kelly and Rita Hayworth in *Cover Girl*, directed by Charles Vidor, 1944. In 1941–1942 Rita made two films with Fred Astaire (1899–1987), Hollywood's greatest dancer. She also danced well in *Tales of Manhattan* (1942).

3. Orson Welles and a blond Hayworth in *The Lady from Shanghai*, 1947.

4. 1934. Young Rita as a flamenco dancer.

5. 1953. Hayworth in the role of Sadie Thompson

in *Miss Sadie Thompson*.

6. 1946. Hayworth in *Gilda's* famous dance where she whispered *Put the Blame on Mame*. The film is director Charles Vidor's (1900–1959) best. In a sadistic, abstract Buenos Aires gambling location, he introduced Hollywood to the theme of obsession and frenzy.

7. Tyrone Power and Rita Hayworth in *Blood and Sand*.

8. Rita's silhouette drawn on the B-24 bomber *Flamin' Mamie*.

"Now that she is dead I must try to forget her . . . What is important is to know how to get old well."
Orson Welles playing Michael O'Hara in *The Lady from Shanghai*

CHARLES DE GAULLE

Resigned to found Gaullism

Charles André Joseph Marie de Gaulle was born in 1890 to a Catholic family of the lesser nobility. He studied in Jesuit schools and later, like Bonaparte, at Saint-Cyr Military Academy, where he was to return in the 1920s as a professor of military history. During World War I he served in the regiment led by Henri Philippe Pétain (1856–1951). A general staff officer, in 1932 he was appointed Secretary of the National Defense Council. De Gaulle published innovative essays on the use of armored vehicles, which endeared him to Paul Reynaud (1878–1966) but not to the military chiefs, so that in 1936 he was forced to leave the council.

At the onset of World War II de Gaulle was in command of the Fifth Army's tank brigade. In June 1940 he was Assistant War Secretary in the Reynaud government, in charge of relations with England. He rejected the new Nazi-friendly Pétain government; from London he launched his first radio appeal calling on all Frenchmen to resist the Nazis. Head of the volunteer resistance army, he was made head of the French National Committee in London in June 1941; joint president of the French National Liberation Committee in Algiers in April 1943; and head of the French Republic's government in April 1944. On August 25, 1944 he entered Paris. In July 1945 he broke with the Communists, and in January left the provisional government. On April 15, 1947 he established the Rassemblement du Peuple Français (Rally of the French People), the embryo of Gaullism.

1

2

3

4

5

LORRAINE CROSS. In a France defeated and humiliated by a collaborationist government led by a World War I hero such as Marshal Pétain, de Gaulle proudly raised the Cross of Lorraine that had been Joan of Arc's banner and led the war of resistance against the Germans. At times supported by England and Russia, unpopular in the United States, he called to his side politicians, intellectuals, aristocrats, as long as they were men of integrity. In his radio speeches he spoke lofty, simple words, winning the hearts of all those who were proud of being French. His faith in a final victory was contagious. An honest man, he nourished himself with the past, was repelled by the obvious, and looked beyond the future.

TRAVELS. Between 1958 and 1969 de Gaulle traveled extensively abroad, vis-

GAULLISM

> *"Not one century has gone by without the world having been visited by the hideousness of war . . . unfortunately, men's history is that of their weapons."*
>
> Charles de Gaulle, "Recruitment Theory" in *Revue de l'infanterie* (*Infantry Review*), April 1, 1929.

A Gallic Catholic, pro-republic and anti-Communist, de Gaulle belonged to the democratic right; he was a peace-loving military man. He was in favor of a strong, effective government and national unity, and despised the mediocrity and corruption engendered by the parliamentary system. He wanted a strong head of state to lead the country and be responsible to the citizens who elected him. In 1958, as a result of the generals' putsch in Algiers, President Coty called him to public duty, and he was elected prime minister by parliament. De Gaulle then submitted a constitution for the Fifth Republic, which gave ample powers to the presidency. In January 1959 he was elected president. In 1961, the generals rose up again in Algiers and there was an attempt on de Gaulle's life. De Gaulle granted independence to Algeria. In 1962 there was another attempt on his life. De Gaulle was reelected president, this time in the general elections. In 1963 he vetoed the United Kingdom's entry in the European Common Market, because he considered it a U.S. satellite. In 1964 he recognized Communist China. He formed a strong bond with Adenauer's Germany. In 1965 he criticized U.S. intervention in the Dominican Republic, and later, U.S. intervention in Vietnam. De Gaulle initiated friendly gestures toward the Soviet Union and other Communist countries: he dreamed of one Europe, "from the Atlantic to the Urals." He was reelected in 1965, and took French troops out of NATO. He censured Israel for starting the 1967 war. He passed a law forcing corporations to share profits with their employees. During the May 1968 crisis, with the government deadlocked, de Gaulle took the situation in hand and called for new elections, where the left was defeated. On April 28, 1969 his referendum for new laws on the French *départements* and the senate failed. De Gaulle resigned. France had been reborn, and was now an atomic power.

7

6

1945 1946 **1947** 1948 1949 1950 1941 1942 1943 19 47 1948 1949 1950 1941 1942 1943 1944 194

8

9

iting the French Empire, South America, Canada, and Europe. His imposing, dignified figure, his unbiased views, his deep knowledge of history and geography, created everywhere a profound impression of the greatness, the courage, and the dignity of France. With him, Paris became once more the European cultural capital.

1. Paris. Charles de Gaulle in his study at the Elysée Palace. His speeches from this room made him popular with young people as well.
2. Charles de Gaulle in exile in London.
3. 1962, Germany. De Gaulle with Chancellor Konrad Adenauer.
4. Young de Gaulle when he was a student at the Saint-Cyr Academy.

5. Algiers, Algeria. A crowd listening to President de Gaulle's speech.
6. January 1943, Casablanca, Morocco. An Anglo-French-American conference. From the left: General Henri-Honoré Giraud (1879–1949), co-president until 1943 of the National Liberation Committee, President Franklin D. Roosevelt, General de Gaulle, and British Prime Minister Winston Churchill.

7. 1940, London. De Gaulle launches "the June 18th appeal" on the BBC.
8. President de Gaulle's funeral (1970).
9. Cover of a recent pocketbook edition of de Gaulle's *Le Fil de l'épée et autres écrits* (*The Edge of the Sword and Other Writings*). The book is still quite popular.

Published *Le modulor*

Charles-Édouard Jeanneret was born in the Swiss Jura Mountains at La Chaux-de-Fonds in 1887, and attended art school there. The horrors of the war, coupled with the spirited Babel of the period's avant-garde movements, inspired in him a love for order and for patient research that never left him. While he signed his paintings with his name, for his architectural work he chose for himself the pseudonym "Le Corbusier." In 1921 Le Corbusier opened an architect's office in Paris. In 1922 at the Fall Salon he exhibited his *Project for a City of 3 Million Inhabitants*. In 1924 he designed row houses for working class families. In 1925 he completed his *Neighborhood Plan* for the new Paris. In the 1920s and 1930s he designed large public buildings: for the League of Nations in Geneva, for Centrosoyuz and the Palace of Soviets in Moscow.

Le Corbusier was active in organizing international congresses on modern architecture. Although he increasingly took on more urban planning projects, they were built only rarely. The chapel of Notre-Dame-du-Haut (1950–1955) in Ronchamp, with its soft volumes and lovely lines, seemed to many a retreat from the modernity of the *Residential Complex* he had designed earlier for Marseille, and a retreat as well from the rough edges of the Modern Movement for which Le Corbusier was perhaps the leading spokesman.

945 1946 1947 **1948** 1949 1950 1941 1942 1943 1944 1945 1946 1947 **1948** 1949 1950 1941 19   1946 1947 **1948** 1949 1950 1941 1942 1943 1944 19

BRUTALIST ART. Those who visited the *Swiss Dormitory* (1930–1932) on the Paris University campus in the 1960s were shocked by its condition of neglect: it was run down, dull, and dusty. Le Corbusier's building materials have a short life; the sharpness of the lines is lost and tarnished by the crumbling materials. The *Residential Complex* gives the same impression; its essential and assertive language was called brutalist by the critics of the time. Indeed, true architectural "brutalism" was about to begin. In designing the Hunstanton School in Norfolk (1951–1954), Peter and Alyson Smithson left the structure and inner system of the building naked, and rejected any pretense at decoration.

A DISTORTED LESSON. In the second half of our century the concepts of architectural rationality and of the house as a living machine were now used by real estate developers and the building industry to erect millions of functional buildings that were nothing more than that. These buildings, all equal, were then multiplied without ornamentation or harmony of proportions, thus achieving economies of design, labor, and materials. According to the building industry and to developers, they were forms of modernity.

PAINTER. All his life Le Corbusier regretted that his reputation as a painter did not match his reputation as an architect and urban planner. But the opinion of the critics has not changed.

MODULOR

Modulor is the closing essay in Le Corbusier's Towards a New Architecture *(1923), a utopian meditation on architecture and city planning, which took its inspiration from the Purist manifesto* Après le cubisme *(After Cubism) written by Le Corbusier and the painter Amédée Ozenfant (1886–1966) in which they proposed a rational, orderly art free of emotion. A "modulor" is a system of harmonic measures proportional to the height, structure, and movements of a hypothetical man who is 6'1". These measures are then used as an architectural module for rooms, buildings, and cities. The building is supported by pillars, has an open plan, and uses primary materials such as concrete, iron, and glass, with low rectangular windows arranged*

8

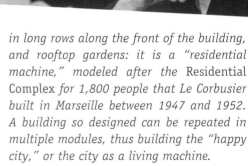

9

in long rows along the front of the building, and rooftop gardens: it is a "residential machine," modeled after the Residential Complex *for 1,800 people that Le Corbusier built in Marseille between 1947 and 1952. A building so designed can be repeated in multiple modules, thus building the "happy city," or the city as a living machine.*

In the 1930s Le Corbusier formulated restructuring plans for Rio de Janeiro, São Paulo, Algiers, Stockholm, even Paris. Le Corbusier believed that such harmony was feasible in an industrial city, where individual and crowd, man and technology, private and public are reconciled. In this Leonardoesque modulor we thus see the most fascinating urban utopia of the bourgeois twentieth century.

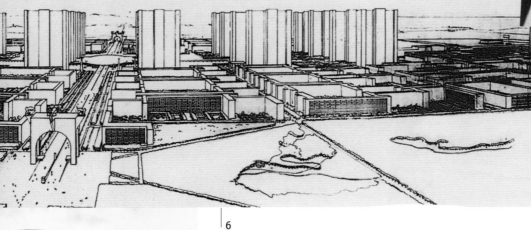

6

"The perception of order is the highest pleasure of the human spirit; its greatest satisfaction is in partaking or assisting in this order. **"**
A. Ozenfant and Le Corbusier in *After Cubism*, 1918.

7

KONRAD ADENAUER

First chancellor of the Federal Republic of Germany

Konrad Adenauer was born in January 1876 to a middle-class family in Cologne. He joined the Catholic Center Party as a young man and worked in city government. Adenauer was the city's burgomaster from 1917 to 1933. As such, he was responsible for endowing Cologne with an urban plan, a new port, a new university, a large stadium, and the idea of the Cologne Fair as well as its implementation. From 1920 to 1933 Adenauer was also president of Prussia's State Council. Hostile to Nazism, he was sent to jail twice. In 1945 the Allies reappointed him mayor of Cologne.

Adenauer was elected Chancellor of the Federal Republic of Germany (West Germany) in 1949. From 1949 to 1963, he was assisted by his capable minister of economic affairs Ludwig Erhard (1897–1977), who later became Vice Chancellor and succeeded Adenauer. Adenauer's main political goals were to restore Germany's sovereignty and to unite West Berlin. The 1954 Paris treaty ended the Allied military occupation of the city. In 1955, Germany became a member of NATO. Adenauer was reelected in a 1957 plebiscite. He resigned in 1963 and died in 1967.

BERLIN. West Berlin was a small area inside the German Democratic Republic (East Germany), which was part of the Soviet Empire. From June 24, 1948 to May 5, 1949 the access roads to West Berlin were blocked by Soviet soldiers. "The longest and most meaningful bridge of our century" to bring supplies to the city was organized by the U.S. military in Germany, who used an air bridge to deliver 2,323,738 tons of food, fuel, machinery, and other supplies. The Soviet blockade of Berlin, imposed in retaliation for the establishment of the Federal Republic of Germany, only had the effect of intensifying the bridge activity. On August 15, 1961, the German Democratic Republic built a high wall in Berlin, in an effort to reduce emigration from Communist Germany to Adenauer's Germany.

SAARLAND. Saarland is strategically important for its large number of factories and is rich in coal. It was given to Prussia by the Congress of Vienna in 1815, then returned to France by the Treaty of Versailles in 1919, then returned again to Germany by a 1935 plebiscite; it was occupied by the French in 1945. As of 1957, it became part of Germany.

ECLIPSE. Adenauer was successful in establishing sincere, friendly relations with France. He also believed that a united Europe had a future. And it was Adenauer—a man of the past, who came from an orderly, capitalist Germany—who gave back to his country the esteem and respect of the world. When John Foster Dulles died, President Eisenhower began a dialogue with Moscow; at that point, Adenauer became an embarrassment and was no longer taken into consideration.

RECONSTRUCTION

There was an economic boom in the Federal Republic of Germany between 1952 and 1959 that was supported by massive U.S. aid ($3.9 billion from 1948 to 1952), by an industrial structure that although damaged by the war had not been as severely damaged as the cities, and by cheap labor supplied by the three million Germans who immigrated from East Germany and another eight million who came from the territories east of the Oder-Neisse line. Such a speedy reconstruction was also favored by limited consumption and the adoption of American models for the building industry, for factories, and for the communication system. The free-market policy was pursued by Erhard as well, also against the pro-labor union faction of the Christian Party.

Adenauer was strongly pro-American and equally strongly opposed to Communism. Therefore, he was the favorite ally of U.S. State Secretary (1953–1959) John Foster Dulles (1888–1959). In August 1957 the Karlsruhe court ordered the Communist

7

Party (KDP) to disband; the party had received 610,000 votes at the 1953 elections. A neo-Nazi party was also disbanded; however, in 1953 Adenauer appointed as interior minister Hans Globke who under the Nazi regime had been an "expert on the Jewish question." An anti-militarist in the 1949 protocol, in reality Adenauer rebuilt the German armed forces and hoped they could be supplied with atomic weapons so as to effectively be of service to NATO. He wanted full sovereignty for Germany.

1948 **1949** 1950 1941 1942 1943 1944 1945 1946 1947 194   1946 1947 19

6

9

8

"We state our firm desire to keep the federal territory and to use all available means to prevent the reconstruction of any type of armed forces."

Protocol signed on November 22, 1949 by Adenauer and the High Allied Commissioners

1. March 1956, Ascona, Italy. Chancellor Adenauer during a brief vacation.

2. Partial view of Cologne in 1935.

3. May 1966, Tel Aviv. Adenauer pensive in the crypt of the Yad Vashem Institute, a memorial to the Jews killed in the Nazi extermination camps.

4. "No experiments": a pro-Adenauer 1957 election poster. The message and the intended audience are clear.

5. 1963, Berlin. Adenauer accepts from Willy Brandt the keys to Berlin

6. July 1962, Paris. Adenauer and de Gaulle at the Elysée Palace.

7. December 1965, Rohendorf. Adenauer reading his published diary. It is as disappointing as those of other great statesmen who were similarly reticent.

8. December 1957, Paris. Adenauer dining at the Bristol Hotel with daughter Lotte (at his right), and his secretary. He was in Paris for a NATO conference.

9. August 1961, Berlin. A French officer follows the construction of the Berlin Wall that was erected by East German soldiers.

DWIGHT EISENHOWER

Was supreme NATO commander

Dwight David Eisenhower was born to a poor Mennonite family in Texas in 1890. He studied at the U.S. Military Academy at West Point and began his military career in 1915. During World War I he was the instructor of an armored unit to be deployed on the French front. In 1929, then a major, he was called to Washington to work on an industrial mobilization plan in the event of war. In 1933 Chief of Staff Douglas A. MacArthur (1880–1964) made him his assistant. In 1941, after Japan bombed Pearl Harbor, Eisenhower was made assistant chief, then chief of the operations office and brigadier general. In 1942 he was made commander of the U.S. forces in Europe, then of the Allied forces in the Maghreb. Once the Nazi troops were defeated in Africa, he led the Allied landing in Sicily and the forces that brought Italy to surrender unconditionally. He was then sent to direct the Allied landing in Normandy and the war operations that brought the Nazi regime to an unconditional surrender on the Western front. Eisenhower was U.S. Army Chief of Staff from 1945 to 1947; in 1948 he accepted the post of president of Columbia University. From 1950 to 1952 he was the first Supreme Commander of NATO.

944 1945 194   1943 1944 1945 1946 1947 1948 1949 **1950** 1941 1942 1943

PRESIDENT. Eisenhower was the most popular man in America. In 1952 the Republicans asked him to run for the presidency; he accepted and was elected. The first Republican president in two decades, Eisenhower proclaimed the end of New Deal policies, signed an armistice with Korea, and intensified anti-Soviet policy. He also strengthened NATO and in 1954 created SEATO (an alliance of the U.S., U.K., France, Austria, New Zealand, Philippines, Pakistan, and Thailand).

He also financially supported Taiwan against Communist China.

FOR PEACE. Reelected in 1956, Eisenhower was unable to veto the social welfare programs passed by a Democratic Congress. He promoted the Camp David meeting with Khrushchev

(1959). However, the American U2 reconnaissance plane incident (the plane was shot down in Soviet air space) closed the door to the possibility of increased détente with the USSR. Eisenhower helped Latin America by providing those countries with two aid plans totaling one billion dollars. At

the close of his second term, in a final speech he warned the country against the dangers to peace of the "military-industrial complex" that had acquired so much power in determining U.S. domestic and international policy.

DULLES. John Foster Dulles (1888–1959) was Secretary of State from 1953 to 1959. He was sympathetic to the CIA (the intelligence agency set up in 1947) and its influence on the coun-

ATLANTISM

On April 4, 1949, the United States, Canada, Ireland, United Kingdom, France, Belgium, Denmark, Italy, Luxembourg, Norway, the Netherlands, and Portugal established the North Atlantic Treaty Organization (NATO). The treaty stated that "the parties agree that an armed attack against one of the member countries . . . will be considered an armed attack against all the member nations." In case of war the military forces of the twelve countries would join together "to reestablish and maintain security to the North Atlantic region." Later, Greece, Turkey, West Germany, and Spain also joined NATO, while in 1966 France removed its troops from the unified command because the post was always entrusted to a U.S. officer.

"*We are not saints. We know we make mistakes, but at least our heart is with the right cause.* "

President Eisenhower on an official visit to Chile, 1960

5

7

947 1948 1949 **1950** 1941 1942 1943 1944 1945 1946 1947 1948 1949 **1950** 1941 1942 1943 1944 1945 1946 1947   45 1946 1947

8

6

1. Young Eisenhower and his wife.
2. June 6, 1944. General Eisenhower with the paratroopers who are about to leave for Normandy.
3. Eisenhower and General Patton on the French front.
4. 1944. General Eisenhower during an inspection on the European front. Behind him is General Montgomery.
5. Eisenhower greeting the crowd during a trip to Ankara, Turkey.
6. President Eisenhower conversing with Pandit Nehru, the Indian Union Prime Minister and leader of the third world's non-aligned nations.
7. Richard Nixon, Vice President (1952–1960) during Eisenhower's presidency. Nixon was elected president in 1968 and continued the détente policy of Eisenhower's last term. Here he is speaking at Eisenhower's 1969 funeral. Nixon resigned in 1974 in the wake of the Watergate scandal.
8. April 1961, Camp David. President Kennedy receives Eisenhower's advice during the Cuban missile crisis. This photo by Paul Vathis won the Pulitzer Prize.

The first NATO commander was General Eisenhower. He was chosen for the formidable organizational skills he had shown during the war on the Western and Mediterranean fronts, and for his skills as a frequent mediator in those years, a rarity among so many prima donna *generals and politicians. However, the goal of the Atlantic Treaty was not the defense of that ocean; it was an anti-Communist alliance of democratic countries and* right-wing regimes that feared Soviet expansionism and accepted the leadership of the United States. In fact, Moscow retaliated by establishing the Warsaw Pact (May 14, 1955) which included the USSR, Poland, Bulgaria, Romania, Czechoslovakia, East Germany, and Albania. The latter withdrew in 1968. After the collapse of the Soviet Union, the Warsaw Pact disintegrated. On the other hand, the NATO membership has been augmented by the former Communist countries Poland, Hungary, and the Czech Republic, thus NATO's goal is no longer clear. Many are afraid it might become a mini-U.N. in support of United States policies.*

try's Cold War policy. Because of his passionate anti-Communism, he was not opposed to coups by extreme right-wing groups in Latin America and Asia, possibly even in Africa and Europe. Both the CIA (until 1975) and the FBI (which J. Edgar Hoover directed from 1924 to 1972), often played a covert, influential role in U.S. foreign policy.

The second half of the century began as Europe started to rebuild after clearing away the rubble of two world wars, painfully realizing it was changed forever. The Communist-Liberal alliance against the Nazi and Fascist regimes had unexpected effects: Germany and Italy, though heavily damaged by bombs and the loss of human lives, did not exit the scene, but began a strong comeback. Even Austria, which suffered Allied occupation until 1955, moved toward a quiet form of democracy. The United Kingdom was severely affected by the war: rationing of basic supplies continued for several years after the war and the loss of major power status was painful. For France, the loss of its colonies was a slow and agonizing process, given the fragmented state of parliament, the government's unsteady policy, and the country's deep ties to its colonial empire, where so many Frenchmen lived. Beyond the Pyrenees, Spain and Portugal were dormant. East of the Iron Curtain, a hushed Eastern

Europe dared to allow itself some pangs of free-

dom. Soviet Russia had used the war to affirm its

status as superpower. Now it strongly intervened

in Asia as never before, and was firmly resolved

to step into African and Latin American affairs.

Everyone was building or rebuilding, often

with care; for example, while the great

Aswan Dam was being built on the Nile, between

1955 and 1960, care was taken to save the

splendid Abu Simbel rock temples by "moving"

them upstream, thereby preventing them from sinking into the new lake. In the meantime, the

first Soviet rockets soared into the air. The advantage the Soviets held over the United States in

the race to the moon raised concern and fear in the West. Some events, however, provided a mod-

icum of relief in these tense times: three years after Stalin's death, at the 20th Soviet Communist

Party Congress, held in 1956, the Party Secretary accused Stalin of abominable crimes. And in

November 1960, young John F. Kennedy was elected president of the United States.

At the death of André Gide (1869–1951), 1947 Nobel Prize winner for literature, someone recalled that his novel *The Vatican Swindle* (1914) had told the story of a boy who killed a man for no reason. This "gratuitous act" was interpreted by some as symbolic of Europe's collective attempted suicides (1914–1918 and 1939–1945), and by others as an expression of total freedom, even to the point of murder.

This frenzy for self-expression (which generally involved a pressing search for joy) was especially strong in the 1950s.

1. Living Theater. 2. Julius and Ethel Rosenberg. 3. The aircraft carrier *Enterprise*. 4. Laika the dog aboard *Sputnik II*.

IN EUROPE, THE 1950S WAS THE DECADE OF THE CONSTRUCTION WORKER, AS THE CONTINENT'S HISTORICAL CITIES WERE REBUILT. WRECKAGE WAS CLEARED AND ANCIENT CHURCHES, PALACES, AND BRIDGES WERE REBUILT ALONG THEIR ORIGINAL LINES. NEW EDIFICES, STREETS, AND SQUARES WERE BUILT. SUBURBAN ORCHARDS WERE TURNED INTO NEW URBAN DEVELOPMENTS. HIGHWAYS AND NEW AIRPORTS WERE BORN.

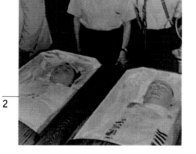

In these years new avant-garde movements emerged in the visual arts, music, literature, the theater (in 1947, Julian Beck and Judith Malina founded New York's Living Theater), film, and architecture. These were years of easy living: people wore jeans, listened to the juke box, rode motor bikes, read Alfred Kinsey's report on *Sexual Behavior in the Human Female*

(1953) and, starting in 1960, were able to use a contraceptive pill. The world was young again.

Winston Churchill, prophet of the Cold War, was returned to power for a short time in 1951 at the age of 77. In 1952, General Eisenhower was elected president of the United States, succeeding Truman. The following year, Stalin died. In May 1958 during the Algerian crisis, de Gaulle was recalled to power. Although men and women did not change much, reality around them did.

In the United States, the Committee on Un-American Activities, led by Senator Joseph McCarthy, brought down illustrious victims, usually leftist intellectuals. At Sing-Sing Prison, in 1953, Julius and Ethel Rosenberg were executed in the electric chair, in spite of clemency appeals by many, including Pope Pius XII, Albert Einstein, and the English philosopher Bertrand Russell. The Rosenbergs had been convicted of atomic espionage. J. Robert

Oppenheimer (1904–1967), the physicist who had directed the team that developed the atomic bomb, was dismissed in 1954.

In August of the same year, Soviet Premier Georgiy Malenkov announced that the USSR had perfected the hydrogen bomb. Fear of atomic war permeated this decade and fueled an arms race. Nuclear-powered

science: in general, the human sciences made considerable progress during this decade; for example, Jonas Salk produced the first polio vaccine in 1955.

The march toward freedom of former colonies in Africa and Asia was fast but painful, and strewn with victims. In 1951, Persia's Prime Minister Mohammad Mosaddeq (1881–1967) nationalized the petroleum industry and immobilized the shah; the latter however seized power again in 1953 in a military coup.

nists and 94,000 U.N. troops had been killed.

In July 1954 French Prime Minister Pierre Mendès-France, a Socialist, boldly ended the Indochina war and signed a peace treaty in the wake of the debacle at Dien Bien Phu. Indochina was soon made a party to treaties with the United States. The last super-power ambitions of France and the

On a different note, Tunisia and Morocco secured their independence, while in Algeria a bloody war raged between the colonial government, Algerian natives, and French settlers. In 1959, Fulgencio Batista's (1901–1973) dictatorship in Cuba was defeated by a guerrilla war, and Fidel Castro became Cuba's new master.

5. Jonas E. Salk.   6. Mohammad Mosaddeq.   7. Gillo Pontecorvo's film *The Battle of Algiers*.   8. On the way to European unity.   9. Alcide de Gasperi.

engines propelled submarines (for example, the *Nautilus*), and aircraft carriers (such as the *Enterprise*). When, in 1957, the Soviets successfully launched into orbit the *Sputnik I* and *Sputnik II* satellites (*Sputnik II* carried Laika, a female dog, on board), the West feared they might be spy satellites launched into orbit by intercontinental-range missiles.

There was also much positive news from non-military

Persia freed itself from British dominance.

In 1951 Japan signed a peace treaty in the wake of its World War II defeat. Japan was returned to full sovereignty in return for releasing its claims on Sakhalin, Manchuria, Taiwan, and Korea. During the Korean War, the removal of General MacArthur from command in turn removed the risk of a nuclear war in the eyes of many; an armistice was signed in 1953, after at least 1,340,000 Commu-

United Kingdom were put to rest jointly in 1956 by Washington and Moscow, when the two superpowers ordered the removal of French and British troops from the Suez Canal, after it was nationalized by Nasser (Egypt's leader, who in 1952 had forced King Farouk into exile). Even the Soviet Empire creaked: there were riots in East Berlin and in Poznan, Poland, and an uprising in Hungary.

Meanwhile, Europe was walking a painful, uncertain path toward unity. In 1951 the European Coal and Steel Community was formed, later EURATOM; in 1957, the Rome Treaty gave birth to a common market among Benelux (Belgium, the Netherlands, Luxemburg), France, West Germany, and Italy. Under the 1945–1953 leadership of Prime Minister Alcide de Gasperi (1881–1954), Italy began post-war reconstruction in a climate of democracy and under the shield of NATO and European unity.

MARIA CALLAS

Revived lyric opera

Maria Kalogeropoulos (1923–1977) was born in New York to a modest middle class family of Greek immigrants. Her socially ambitious mother doted on Maria's sister. After the parents separated, Maria, her sister, and her mother returned to Greece and took up residence in Athens. Both girls studied music. Maria studied the piano and found a good voice teacher, the Spanish soprano Elvira de Hidalgo (1892–1980). From 1938 to 1945 Maria sang at the Athens Opera. She was an awkward

young woman, with an imperfect voice. Yet she had an iron will and an astonishing, lifelong craving to learn. In 1947 she sang a stirring *La Gioconda* at the Arena in Verona, Italy. It was a second debut. Maria then met Maestro Tullio Serafin (1878–1968), perhaps the best vocal conductor of this century. In 1951 she sang *I vespri siciliani* at Milan's La Scala, and became a diva. After many triumphant years when Callas sang in theaters all over the world, her voice declined rapidly. She turned into a truly elegant lady who only gave concerts and recitals. Wounded by love, she went into hiding. She died suddenly in Paris. From her ashes was born a myth that the years have not tarnished.

1

2

3

6

MEN. "La Maria" wanted a man to love, and who loved her, at her side. During her climb to fame, this man was her husband, G. B. Meneghini, an older construction materials entrepreneur, whom she later divorced. Her intimate friends were two great tenors: handsome Franco Corelli and Giuseppe Di Stefano, both born in 1921. She also fell for the cultivated and polemical writer Pier Paolo Pasolini (1922–1975) who cast Callas in his 1969 film

Medea. Pasolini was very attractive to women but was a homosexual, and so this flirtation came to nothing. Her great love seems to have been shipping magnate Aristotle Onassis but he brought their relationship to a sudden end and married someone else.

OTHERS. Rivalry between the fans of Callas and Renata Tebaldi (b. 1922) made sopranos divas again. Magda Olivero and Antonietta Stella steered clear of the game. Others accepted the *prima donna* role in their private life. Birgit Nilsson, Joan Sutherland, Leyla Gencer, and Montserrat Caballé are unforgettable.

ALONE. In her letters, Callas returned again and again to her solitude, her inability to reconcile the woman and the artist in her character. Yet after her death, thousands of people claimed to have known the "divine" Callas or to have been her friend. "La Maria" became a *bel canto* myth. She was a myth of troubled femininity.

4

5

PRIMA DONNA

Maria Callas's voice was exceptional for its richness of coloring, for its mastery of phrasing, for its exceptional range from A below middle C to high F, for its agility and precision. Perhaps it was the imperfect timbre of her voice that gave her singing such a stirring, penetrating force. A light as well as dramatic soprano with contralto effects, her breathing and voice techniques recalled the bel canto of the nineteenth century. It was Callas who launched what came to be called the

"Renaissance of bel canto." She gave authoritative performances in operas that were not staged regularly, such as Medea by Cherubini and Il turco in Italia by Rossini. Her best repertoire included Rossini's The Barber of Seville and Armida, Bellini's Norma, I Puritani and La Sonnambula, Donizetti's Lucia di Lammermoor and Anna Bolena, Verdi's Aida, La Traviata, Il Trovatore, Macbeth and Don Carlos, Wagner's Tristan and Isolde, Die Walküre, and Parsifal; Puccini's Tosca and Turandot. That is not all, but it is breathtaking. She did not make many recordings.

The myth of the prima donna is largely based on statements from people who were close to her. Her stage presence and craft, they said, was equal to her vocal art. The raw, essential modernism of her acting highlighted the quality of her vocal execution and her musical precision. Her artistic intransigence caused turmoil behind the scenes and outbursts of enthusiasm in the theater. Once again, opera attracted large audiences and won new fans even outside Europe. As a society figure, Callas was a star equal to nineteenth-century divas or today's pop stars.

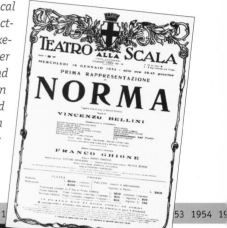

7

1955 1956 1957 1958 1959 1960 **1951** 1952 1953 1954 1955 1956 1957 1958 1959 1960 **1951** 1952 1953 1954 1955 1956 1957 1 53 1954 19

9

8

10

1. Maria Callas in a scene from Puccini's *Turandot* at La Fenice Theater, Venice, January 1948.
2. A costume of Maria Callas made in the atelier of La Scala for *Anna Bolena*. Her old costumes are religiously housed in the wardrobes of La Scala. They are displayed sometimes during exhibitions dedicated to the soprano.
3. Ulisse Sartini, *Maria Callas*.
4. The facade of La Scala Theater, Milan (Giuseppe Piermarini, 1775–1978).
5. An aerial view of the Arena, Verona, Italy (1st century A.D., 1913 opera season).
6. 1969. A drawing by Pier Paolo Pasolini portraying Callas in *Medea*.

7. 1957. New York, Waldorf Astoria Hotel. Callas in a vaguely Egyptian costume at a masked ball. The jewels are authentic and belonged to the Harry Winston Collection.
8. The hands of Maria Callas playing the piano. She used her hands on stage like a consummate actress.
9. Poster for a *Norma* premiere at La Scala on January 12, 1952. Two other great singers sang with Callas: Ebe Stignani as Adalgisa and Nicola Rossi Lemeni as Oroveso.
10. 1960, Paris. Maria Callas dining with Aristotle Onassis.

"Callas is sweet and has no claws. But she does her duty, works hard and is never satisfied with her work. This is why they say I am aloof, but it is not true."
Maria Callas to Italian writer Dacia Maraini

EVITA PERÓN

Left history and became a myth

María Eva Duarte was born to a modest family near Buenos Aires, Argentina in 1919. She became a well-known radio actress. In 1943 she met General Juan Domingo Perón (1895–1974) who had participated in a recent coup, and began an affair with him. Perón rose steadily, becoming vice president of Argentina and minister of labor and of war. In 1945 he married Evita. She became his most trusted political advisor. Together, they led the fight for unionization of the newly urbanized laborers (*los descamisados*, or "the shirtless ones") and seduced the new entrepreneurial class who vied with the old landed and financial aristocracy for power. Arrested on charges of being a Nazi sympathizer on October 9, 1945, Perón was released after a week-long general workers strike spurred on by Evita. At the 1946 presidential elections their party, the Single Revolutionary Party, won an absolute majority.

Perón was handily reelected in 1951. Evita became *de facto* minister of labor, health, and education. She was a strong ally of the Church against Communism, and the acting vice president of the regime and the country. She died of a tumor in the summer of 1952.

A POSTER. Evita supported her husband without overshadowing him. A 1951 electoral poster showed a well-dressed gentleman looking at x-ray plates bearing this message: "Higher salaries—stadiums—social laws—access to education—hospitals—vacation centers . . ." On top: "Look at his X-rays," and below: "Is there someone who owes nothing to Perón?"

MOTHER. Evita did not have a comfortable childhood, and she was childless. Her dedication to motherhood and children's issues was genuine and brought results. She created and supervised a total literacy program; she guaranteed free childbirth care, free nurseries and kindergartens in the cities, and free compulsory education. The children and the elderly received completely free medical care.

UBIQUITOUS. Evita established the Eva Perón Foundation and endowed it with vast state funds. Today, the foundation is everywhere in Argentina. It distributes food and clothing to the poor (still today, food staples are very inexpensive in Argentina). The *pampa* which was established as a province and was called Evita, attempted to undermine the power of the great ranchers. The foundation even assists the *gauchos*.

JUSTICIALISMO

1. July 1950. The presidential couple leave the Casa Rosada to attend a performance at the famed Teatro Colón.
2. November 1996, Buenos Aires. On a wall in the working-class district of Boca, electoral posters still carry in the foreground the image of Evita.
3. Vatican City. Evita Perón among the dignitaries of the papal court. Pius XII received her with the highest honors reserved for Catholic queens.
4. Santiago del Estero, a small, nondescript town. An evening outdoors organized by the Peronist Party. Dancing, beer, and *asado* (barbecued meat) to make people merry.
5. Eva Duarte as the young wife of General Perón.
6. August 6, 1952, Buenos Aires. A vast mass of people attends the funeral of Evita Perón on Avenida de Mayo.

7. March 1973, Argentina. Presidential elections won by Hector Campora, in preparation for Perón's comeback. The winning image is still that of Evita.
8. Evita Perón surrounded by miners during union bargaining negotiations. Argentina is rich in mineral resources and hydrocarbons.

The Peronist policy of justicialismo *(making justice), a nationalist doctrine, was opposed to U.S. "dollar diplomacy" and was anti-parliamentarian, inter-class, and Catholic. Socially, the doctrine was corporate and tended to be rabble-rousing. Unlike Fascism, however, it enacted strong laws benefiting the working classes. The unions became a supporting tool of the dictatorship, strengthening it in difficult times and even holding in check the army. At the same time, Peronism developed protective measures for domestic industry, which were effective in a country such as Argentina that is rich in raw materials. The weak points of the Peronist doctrine were the fact that it ruled by dictatorship and was unconstitutional, restricting democracy and political debate; ultimately, the discretionary powers of the administration favored corruption at all levels and in all the nerve centers*

7

8

69 1960 1951 **1952** 1953 1954 1955 1956 1957 1958 1959 1960 1951 **1952** 1953 · · · 1958 1959 19

6

of government. Other weak points were a tendency to excessive government spending, and appointing the army to supervise the agreement between capital and labor.

Strong anti-Peronist pressure was applied by powerful international financial groups and by the United States in particular. Even before Evita's disease was known to be fatal, the army forbade her candidacy for vice president, because her radical justicialismo had such a strong hold on the unions and the professional middle classes.

"With the deepest grief the people mourn Evita, a martyr of labor, who has achieved immortality. "
Death announcement on the first page of *Democracia* newspaper, 1952.

NIKITA KHRUSHCHEV
Secretary of the Soviet Union's Communist Party

Khrushchev was born in 1894 in Kalinovka (Ukraine) to a family of small property owners. As a boy he was a blacksmith's apprentice, then a mechanic and a miner. In 1918 he joined the party. A strict Stalinist, in 1935 he was appointed first secretary to the Moscow party organization. He was a merciless executor of the great Stalinist purges, first in the Caucasus and in 1937 in Ukraine, and first secretary of the Russian Republic's party term after term until 1949; in 1939 he was called to the Politburo. In October 1941 he led an active resistance unit in Ukraine. In 1949 he was appointed agriculture minister. An expert in party structure, he was considered one of Stalin's successors. In September 1953 he replaced Georgiy Malenkov as first secretary of the Soviet Party. Having eliminated Lavrenti Beria, who was interior minister and chief of the secret police, in 1955 he appointed Marshal Nikolai Bulganin premier, replacing Malenkov. In 1957–1958 he removed his strongest rivals from office. No Soviet Party leader enjoyed so much power after Stalin's death. He was removed in 1964, and died a pensioner in 1971.

1

7 1958 1959 1960 1951 1952 **1953** 1954 1955 1956

2

1951 1952 **1953** 1954 1955 1956 1957 1958

4

3

THE ECONOMY. The successes Stalin claimed in 1948 were secured by exploiting the labor force and the economy of the Soviet satellite countries. With the fifth five-year plan (1951–1955), the USSR became the world's second industrial power, but only for heavy industry. The peasant masses were hungry and disgruntled. Khrushchev ordered that vast tracts of virgin land be used for agriculture and initiated the sixth five-year plan: by 1957 it was already a failure. The Presidium gave a vote of no-confidence to Khrushchev, but the Central Committee reinstated him. In 1958, after a bloodless purge of Malenkov, Molotov, Kaganovich, and Zhukov, Khrushchev's dictatorship began.

IN THE WORLD. In 1955 the USSR decided to withdraw its troops from Austria, provided it became neutral. Eisenhower and Khrushchev met in Geneva: nothing of substance was concluded, but at least the meeting was cordial. In 1956, Egypt made overtures to the USSR and in November the two superpowers blocked the French, British, and Israeli troops in the Suez Crisis. In 1957, relations took a turn for the better between China and the USSR, based on declarations of mutual respect. In 1958 Khrushchev stated: "We would like to again make a toast with our war allies. We are seeking peaceful solutions." In 1959 Vice President Nixon stated in Warsaw: "What is important is to be able to find ways of mutual cooperation for peaceful purposes, while respecting our diversity." On September 12, the Soviets sent a rocket to the moon. Later, Khrushchev met with Eisenhower at Camp David; once back in Moscow, he praised the friendship uniting the two countries.

On May 1, 1960 he announced that a U-2 reconnaissance plane had been shot down in the Soviet skies and the American pilot captured. As a result, the Paris summit failed.

THE FALL. In 1960 Fidel Castro joined the Socialist camp, whereupon Khrushchev sent Soviet missiles to Cuba to be used for Cuba's defense. They were removed after a confronta-

REVISIONISM

On June 3, 1955, in Belgrade, the Soviet leaders affirmed the policy of non-intervention in domestic affairs; this resolved the dispute that had been brewing between the USSR and Yugoslavia since the 1948 "schism." The policy recognized the right of nations to pursue different roads to Socialism. The public report read by Khrushchev to the 20th Party Congress (held February 14–25, 1956) announced a return to Leninism; the secret speech, however, denounced the cult of Stalin's personality and for the first time denounced Stalin's crimes and acts that violated Socialist laws. According to Khrushchev, excesses should be corrected, but not the structure of Soviet power.

This process of "destalinization" opened the way for a mass strike for better living conditions in the Polish industrial city of Poznan. Khrushchev flew to Warsaw and placed in power Wladyslaw Gomulka, who had been interned in a Stalinist prison. In turn, Gomulka freed the Primate of Poland Wyszynski, who had been languishing in prison for three years, and opened a dialogue with the Catholic Church. But the illusions of destalinization fell with the events in Hungary; there, the revolution brought Imre Nagy to power, but when Nagy announced his decision to withdraw Hungary from the Warsaw Pact, Soviet and other Warsaw Pact troops moved into Hungary. The revolution was crushed on November 7, 1956.

5

51 1952 **1953** 1954 1955 1956 1957 1958 1959 1960 195   1960 1951 19

6

8

7

"It was Stalin who engineered the concept of 'enemy of the people' . . . mass arrests and deportations . . . executions without due process . . . all of this created a situation of mistrust, fear and even despair."

Khrushchev, Secret Report to the 20th Congress of the Soviet Communist Party, 1956

9

tion with President Kennedy and after the United States agreed to abstain from armed intervention in Cuba. In 1962 Soviet-Chinese relations soured; Romania claimed the right to an independent policy; and the economy took a turn for the worse. Khrushchev's cautious reforms had failed.

1. 1958. Leonid Brezhnev in Moscow. In 1960 Khrushchev appointed him president of the Presidium of the Supreme Soviet.
2. August 1957, East Berlin. Khrushchev greets the crowd on an official visit.
3. September 20, 1960, New York. Nikita Khrushchev embraces Fidel Castro.
4. June 1961, Vienna. Khrushchev in private con-

versation with President John F. Kennedy.
5. May 10, 1960, Moscow. Khrushchev mockingly waves photographs of U.S. Captain Francis Powers, whose U-2 reconnaissance plane was shot down over Soviet territory.
6. August 30, 1964, Czechoslovakia. Khrushchev speaks to the crowd. Next to him is Alexander Dubcek, then secretary of Czechoslovakia's

Communist Party.
7. June 1963, Moscow. Khrushchev and "his" cosmonauts in Red Square.
8. November 1943, Kiev. Then Soviet proconsul in Ukraine, Khrushchev speaks to the people amid the bombing rubble.
9. 1964, Alexandria, Egypt. A guest of Nasser, Khrushchev greets the crowd.

ERNEST HEMINGWAY

Won the Nobel Prize for literature

One of the best loved twentieth-century writers, Hemingway was born in Illinois in 1899. Toward the end of World War I he was in Italy as a volunteer soldier and reporter. In 1921 he published his first short story, *Up in Michigan*. A romantic, libertarian spirit, and a clever architect of his own fame, Hemingway made it a point of being in all the places where an important event was taking place. He was in Paris in the years of the "lost generation" (as Gertrude Stein called it), although Paris was also a city where art, music, and literature stars were made. Hemingway was in Spain during the Civil War and followed revolutions here and there in the world, though he also enjoyed gambling and womanizing in Havana, Cuba, then a playpen for wealthy Americans. He enjoyed macho pastimes, as long as they were wild and bloody: bullfights, big-game hunting, deep-sea fishing in Mexico, Spain, Kenya, the Rockies, and the Caribbean, and memorable evenings spent drinking on the French Riviera, in Venice, London, Pamplona, New York. Hemingway was always there. In the meantime, he met all the important people and tirelessly wrote journalistic reports, short stories, and novels. He died in Idaho in 1961 of a self-inflicted gunshot wound.

51 1952 1953 **1954** 1955 1956 1957 1958 1959 1960 1951 1952

WORKS. In addition to the ones already mentioned, these are Hemingway's other major novels: *The Sun also Rises* (1926); *A Farewell to Arms* (1928), *Death in the Afternoon* (1932), *The Green Hills of Africa* (1935), *To Have and Have Not* (1937), *For Whom the Bell Tolls* (1940), *Across the River and Into the Trees* (1950).

HE WAS LOVED. In the 1930s and later, Hemingway's prose stirred several generations of writers. Hollywood turned several of his works into films: *A Farewell to Arms* (1932), *For Whom the Bell Tolls* (1943), *To Have and Have Not* (1944), *Gulf of Mexico* (1950), *The Snows of Kilimanjaro* (1952). Great actors such as Gary Cooper, Gregory Peck, Errol Flynn, Spencer Tracy, Ingrid Bergman, Susan Hayward, and Ava Gardner interpreted Hemingway's characters.

THE OTHERS. Hemingway has been more widely read in the world than other, just as important, American artists such as William Faulkner (1897–1962) or Ezra Pound (1885–1972), one of this century's leading American poets. He has also been more loved and more widely read than other twentieth-century greats such as Luigi Pirandello (1867–1936), Marcel Proust (1871–1922), James Joyce (1882–1941), or Franz Kafka (1883–1924).

A JEWEL. Even the most hostile of critics was able to find a jewel in Hemingway's literary production. In his works, violence, struggles to the death, and youthful purity express tragedy and are drawn with an economy of expression and a perfection of form that are the antithesis of mannerism.

HEMINGWAY THE REPORTER

In articles as well as fiction, Hemingway wrote about current events, nature, the city, and human beings. He looked for characters in the lower middle classes; his heroes are humble men and women engaged in the struggle for survival and freedom. Often the leading characters are shown as they engage in extreme, violent actions under dangerous conditions. For the most part, they are plain-speaking and not educated. Hemingway is credited by literature critics with inventing the "realistic dialogue," with the gift of always finding the right word and the skill in creating with minimal staging a great degree of tension and atmosphere. His works read as if they were journalistic reports of current events; only at the end does the reader realize that what he has read, whether a short story or a novel, was a small masterpiece. For all of these qualities, and for his nomadic life and penchant for strong emotions, Hemingway is considered by many the master of our century's journalistic prose, especially important given the centrality of the media today.

But with time and habit, even an impeccable style can sometimes misfire. When he wrote The Old Man and the Sea (1952), Hemingway believed he was creating a second Moby Dick, though in an unforgiving page, literary critic Dwight Macdonald killed the novel noting that the pervasive "self-advertising" of the novel "is a singular contrast to the concise, bare style that gave fame to young Hemingway."

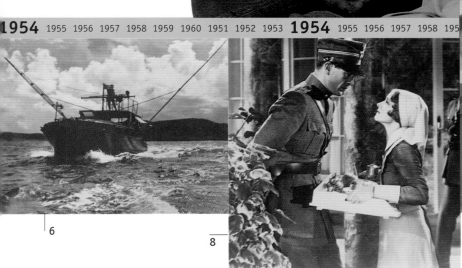

7

1954 1955 1956 1957 1958 1959 1960 1951 1952 1953 **1954** 1955 1956 1957 1958 195 ... 952 1953 19

6

8

9

"*He wanted to build a pedestal to his own psychological monument, using not only literature, but also, and especially, the choice of specific actions.*"
Italian author Alberto Moravia

1. December 1939, Sun Valley, Idaho. Hemingway at work on *For Whom the Bell Tolls*.
2. Thacher, Ava Gardner and Gregory Peck in Hemingway's *The Snows of Kilimanjaro* (1952), directed by Henry King.
3. A page from *For Whom the Bell Tolls*. Hemingway copiously and patiently edited his work to achieve the style he wanted.
4. 1944. Hemingway at the right of General Charles T. Lanham, inspecting the Siegfried Line.
5. An aging Hemingway on an adventure trip.

6. *Pilar*, Hemingway's boat fitted for deep-sea fishing.
7. Ingrid Bergman and Gary Cooper in *For Whom the Bell Tolls* (1943), directed by Sam Wood.
8. Cooper and Helen Hayes in Hemingway's *A Farewell to Arms* (1932), directed by Frank Borzage. The author was unhappy about the films made from his books, maybe because they revealed the inner rhetoric of their plots.
9. 1961, Cuba. Ernest Hemingway and Fidel Castro.

JAWAHARLAL NEHRU

Led India to non-aligned nation status

The father of modern India was born in 1889 in Allahabad, on the Ganges River, to a high caste family. Nehru studied at Harrow and Cambridge in England from 1905 to 1910. In 1918, having joined the Congress Party, he took part in Gandhi's civil disobedience campaign, which cost him a jail term from 1921 to 1923. Released, he was appointed Congress secretary, and was to be its president for many years and the leader of its left wing. A man of both Eastern and Western culture, tolerant and pragmatic, he did not share Gandhi's ethical and mystical philosophy. He was more interested in the farmers' and workers' movements, and in 1930 led the unifica-

tion of the Indian trade unions. After spending another thirteen months in jail in 1940–1941, he led the party's delegation in the negotiations with the English authorities. This time he was sent into internal exile from August 1942 to June 1945. In 1946 he formed an interim Indian government, leading the negotiations with Viceroy Mountbatten for the transfer of power, and proclaimed the independence of the Indian Union, becoming Prime Minister from August 15, 1947 a position he held until his unexpected death in New Delhi in May 1964.

1

3

6

9 1960 1951 1952 1953 1954 **1955** 1956 1957 1958 1959 1960 1951 1952 1953 1954 **1955** 1956 1957 1958 1959 1960 1951 1952 1953 1954 **1955** 1956 1957 1958 1959

2

THE INDIAN UNION comprises 1,268,883 square miles, a billion inhabitants by the year 2000, 25 states, 7 territories, 2 official languages, 9 additional languages spoken by several million Indians, 7 main religions, average January temperatures (as recorded at the 11 main meteorological stations) ranging from 50° to 80°F, annual precipitation ranging from 26 to 245 inches. India is a vast country of extraordinary complexity. Only under English rule did its territory constitute a single empire. The Indian prime minister enjoys great powers rooted more in Nehru's tradition than in India's Constitution.

STRIFE. Religious strife divided India into three states and border conflicts raged along the Himalayas, unleashing wars that posed a threat to the world, though the West seemed to pay little

attention to them. In 1962 China crossed the Indian border, initiating a war that it won. Nehru was devastated. In 1965, India declared war on Pakistan over the Kashmir border, and again in 1971 in support of Bangladesh's secession from Pakistan, winning both. Today both India and Pakistan are nuclear powers.

4

THE NEHRU FAMILY. Indira Gandhi (1917–1984), who was Nehru's daughter, was head of the Indian Congress Party in 1959 and prime minister from 1966 to 1977, wielding absolute power in the last two years. After losing a bid for reelection and returning to private life, she was again prime minister from 1980 to

1984, when she was killed. Her post was filled by her son Rajiv Gandhi, who ruled until 1991, when he was killed by a religious fanatic, the same fate suffered by his mother. Although the Congress Party has collapsed since then, the Nehrus' charisma has not.

5

NON-ALIGNMENT

A "westernized Oriental gentleman," Nehru governed an immense country of villages, great misery and untold riches, developing industry, a network of waterways and railroads, primitive and insufficient roadways, with fast-multiplying middle-class urban elites, an extraordinary cultural tradition, respectable universities, good hospitals (where they existed). Like any high-caste Indian, he both feared the United Kingdom and felt anger toward it, yet he respected its greatness, and wanted India to be part of the Commonwealth. He was aware that India belonged to a third world, which differed from the first two: the United States and Soviet spheres of influence. In 1955, at the Bandung (Java) conference, he was the great diplomat who cemented the "non-aligned" front which, in addition to India, included Sukarno's Indonesia, Nasser's Egypt, and Tito's Yugoslavia.

Despite their purported neutrality, however, they were not truly neutral with respect to the United States and the USSR, since they claimed to be Socialist countries that adopted a national way that differed from the Soviet (or Chinese) way. These countries felt a modicum of sympathy for the Soviet Union from which they asked (and received) economic aid while, clearly, the United States tried to "become allied with the more conservative third-world nations" which in 1955 included Iraq, Turkey, Pakistan, Iran, the Philippines, and Thailand. In the wake of the Cuban revolution, even some Latin American countries moved closer to the Afro-Asian non-aligned movement. While it lasted, this front played a dignified, autonomous role between the two world blocs.

8

195... 52 1953 1954 **1955** 195... ...9 1960 1951 1952 195...

9

"*Independence. India: the miracle of a nation. The state born from Gandhi's utopia, but even more, from Nehru's intuition.*"

Amartya Sen

1. August 14, 1947. Nehru proclaiming India's independence. Next to him is the Viceroy Lord Mountbatten of Burma; on the throne's steps, the viceroy's wife.
2. Indira Gandhi (on the right), next to her father, Shri Jawaharlal Nehru.
3. The Pandit ("Sage") Nehru. Unlike Gandhi, and though he was the more cultivated and cosmopolitan of the two, Nehru was an impassioned nationalist.
4. President Eisenhower visiting the president and vice president of the Indian Union.

5. 1947, India. Nehru between Lord Mountbatten and his wife. According to rumors, Nehru was in love with her, and the feeling was reciprocal.
6. Women at a well in an Indian village.
7. A street in Benares (Uttar Pradesh), a major holy city.
8. Laborers at work in the lagoon port city of Cochin (Kerala), at one time the site of the Dutch East India Company.
9. Equipment being moved by man-powered boats in Cochin, Southwest India. Modern roadways are still almost non-existent.

NASSER
Nationalized the Suez Canal

Gamal Abdel Nasser was born in 1918 to a lower middle class family. He attended the Cairo Royal Military Academy. A career officer, in 1948–1949 he fought in the war against Israel, at which time he was promoted to colonel. Like many of his military colleagues he then entered politics and gravitated toward the fundamentalist movement, censuring the immoral secularism and the excesses of King Farouk's court (1920–1965). On July 23, 1952 he was among the first "Free Officers" who deposed the king and forced him into exile, replacing him with Major General Muhammad Najib (1901–1984), a rather opaque figure with many ties to the past. On November 13, 1954, Nasser finally removed Najib from his post and assumed absolute power as the Rais, the revolution's leader. In 1956, a referendum was held that approved the new Constitution which, in turn, assigned ample powers to the president. Nasser was thus elected president, a position he held until his death. During a crisis later that same year, he succeeded in nationalizing the Suez Canal after English and French troops had occupied Port Said and the Sinai Peninsula. Both the United States and the USSR supported Egypt's position, forcing the invading troops to leave. Nasser died of a heart attack on September 28, 1970. Nineteen heads of state attended his funeral. Forty-six people died in the throng that attended his funeral, held at the Nasser Mosque in Kubbeh, Cairo.

SUEZ. The only canal joining the Mediterranean to the Indian Ocean, revenue from its traffic still yields large profits for the country that controls it. The canal also divides Africa and Asia, and is a symbol of the international weight of a country that is the most influential Islamic nation in the Old World. When the Suez Crisis broke out in 1956, Nasser exclaimed: "World War III has begun." Even Hitler had dreamed of seizing the canal so as to strangle England. Although World War III did not break out, the solution imposed by the United States and the USSR marked the end of the colonial power of both France and the United Kingdom.

130 HOURS. On May 5, 1967 Nasser closed the Gulf of Aqaba to Israeli ships. On June 1, Israel appointed General Moshe Dayan (1915–1981) defense minister. In the early hours of June 5, Dayan unleashed the war. In 130 hours, he snatched strategic territories from Jordan and Syria and the whole Sinai area from Egypt. Arab pride was humiliated.

SADAT. Anwar el-Sadat (1918–1981) was to be the second Rais, Nasser's natural heir. He had been in the shadow as Nasser carried out his coup in 1952, later became one of his closest assistants and a trusted political advisor. More pro-West than Nasser, he guided Egypt in the 1973 Yom Kippur War, the only war against Israel that Islam did not lose, then to the Camp David (1978) and Washington (1979) agreements with Israel that returned Sinai to Egypt and spawned the fundamentalist plot that was to kill him.

NASSERISM

1. 1952. Cairo. The chiefs of the republican revolution: Major General Najib, the apparent leader at the time, raising his hat. Colonel Nasser is at his right.

2. President Nasser.

3. 1970, Cairo. Politicians attending Nasser's funeral, gathered around his portrait. From left: King Hussein of Jordan, Tunisian Prime Minister Bahi Ladgham, French Prime Minister Jacques Chaban-Delmas, the Negus of Ethiopia, and Archbishop Makarios III, President of Cyprus.

4. A view of Lake Nasser from the temples of File Island.

5. In a Port Suez cafe, a Nasser portrait hit by a bullet during the 1967 war.

6. Aswan. A Nasser mural and a poster of Sadat. Celebrations for the opening of the dam.

7. Anti-Nasser demonstration in Israel.

8. Suez Canal Zone. Egyptian war vehicles and equipment captured by the Israelis during the 1956 war.

9. October 1, 1970. President Nasser's funeral in Cairo.

Nasser's revolution, which made Islam the state religion in 1956, attempted to break the then existing power system, which was based on an alliance between the old Mameluke aristocracy, the landed bourgeoisie, the banking industry, and businesses in the hands of a Levantine elite. Nasser wanted to bring the military, the government bureaucracy, teachers, and influential journalists into the mix. He championed the disadvantaged peasants and the urban masses. He was a proponent of the United Arab Republic (which was briefly a reality) consisting of Egypt and other Mediterranean or Middle Eastern Muslim countries. He aimed to truly decolonize his people. He requested Soviet support for this endeav-

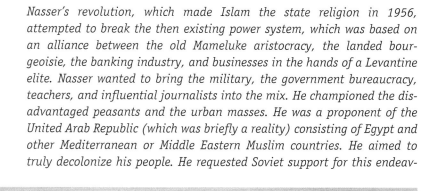

7

6

8

9

or, and although he expelled Soviet "technicians" he was able to secure Soviet financing for large projects.

Nasser succeeded in keeping a middle course between both blocs by pursuing a policy of non-alignment along with other important statesmen such as Nehru and Marshal Tito (Josip Broz, 1892–1980); the latter in 1948 had successfully uncoupled Yugoslavia from the Soviet Empire. On the Israeli issue as well, Nasser's position was complex; therefore his Israeli policy was sometimes contradictory. When he died at the age of 52, the world paid him the tribute owed to one of the leading statesmen of his time.

"Colonial rule . . . hurts those who rule and those who are ruled."
Joint declaration of Nasser, Nehru, and Tito, July 16, 1956

ELVIS PRESLEY

Rock 'n' roll's world star

Elvis Aaron Presley was born in Tupelo, Mississippi in January 1935 to very young parents (his father was a 19-year-old trucker, his mother a clerk). He grew up in poverty. An obedient child, he enjoyed listening to country music and the blues on the radio and tried to imitate the singers. For his thirteenth birthday, as there was no money for a bicycle, his parents gave him a guitar. In 1948 the family moved to Memphis, Tennessee, where Elvis attended high school, graduating in 1953. He was not a problem teenager, except for his penchant for flashy clothes that made him stand out. Elvis sang in school productions; self-taught, he slowly honed his style. While working as a trucker, one day he parked his rig near the Memphis Recording Service and paid $4 to make his first record. The inde-

pendent producer Sam Phillips listened to the record, and in the spring of 1954 gave him a contract. His first concert, held in Memphis, was a resounding success. In November 1955 Presley's contract was assigned to RCA for $40,000. The following January he recorded another single with *Heartbreak Hotel* and *I Was the One*, which sold one million copies. His six appearances on the Dorsey Brothers CBS television show made him a national star.

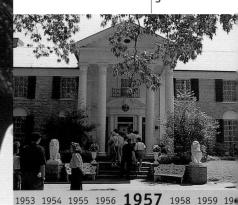

3

certs a year Elvis would meet girls whom he invited to his never-ending parties. The men at the parties were Presley's assistants, the so-called "Memphis mafia."

GRACELAND. Gold costumes, a solid gold Cadillac, and the Graceland mansion on Memphis' Elvis Presley Boulevard. This is the stage on which the boy who had no friends lived when he was not on tour, and where he rehearsed, strumming the guitar while sitting on his bed. He went on tours only in the United States, with the exception of Germany, where he served while he was in the military from 1958 to 1960. The night of August 16, 1977 he played tennis for five hours on his private Graceland courts. At three in the afternoon the following day, Elvis died.

2

1

LADY LUCK. Thirty-three films between 1956 and 1973 (plus *This Is Elvis*, 1981), 62 LP albums between April 1956 and July 1977, 29 extended plays from March 1956 to April 1967, over one hundred singles from July 1954 to June 1977. By 1961 he had already sold 86 million records. By the end of 1966 he had been the recipient of 66 gold records. For many years in a row, he earned twenty million dollars a year.

ACTOR. For several years, instead of giving concerts, Elvis starred in films from which his records were extracted. Almost without exception, they were "B" films on themes that favored the audience's identification of the character with the actor. Elvis was a poor actor and a mediocre dancer. His stage presence improved greatly when he started singing while shaking the

mike, brandishing his guitar, and moving his body to the rhythm of his music. Before him, only black singers used to do that, but not on TV. Afterward, many copied him.

WOMEN. In May 1967 Presley married Priscilla Beaulieu. The following February Lisa Marie was born. In 1973 the couple divorced. In hundreds of con-

ROCK 'N' ROLL

Elvis Presley's voice had a range of two and a third octaves. "No artist had a greater influence on popular music than Presley," stated music scholar Henry Pleasants. Presley had a large repertory. His fair rendition of the old Neapolitan classic O' Sole Mio, sung in English, sold millions of copies. Wild songs with a throbbing rhythm alternated with country ballads. What were his sources, who were his teachers? According to many, the answer was Dean Martin, plus the country and bluegrass rhythms he had unconsciously absorbed, together with gospel music, even echoes of Italian opera. He interpreted all his songs in a uniformly clean style, as if only the background noise distinguished studio pieces from live recordings. His interpretations were always so well-balanced that all his different influences were fused in one unique style. The expressiveness of his body language was spectacular: maybe only the great Edith Piaf (1915–1963) reached this intensity. Presley's body movements, along with his voice, made him an explosive rock star. From his first professional concerts, his public performances let loose in his female fans a violent, bewildering sexuality. "My first public performance . . . I was singing one of my songs and everybody was screaming and rocking . . . My manager said it was because I was shaking my legs . . . I sang an encore at the end of the show, and the more I shook my legs, the wilder the audience went." "Elvis the Pelvis" sent the audience wild: after him, a raging audience became the mark of the rock concert.

1. Presley in a frame from *Love Me Tender* (1956), directed by Robert D. Webb, the first of his 33 films.
2. Elvis in *Aloha from Hawaii*, which was seen by 1.5 billion people in 40 countries.
3. 1992. The beginning of the "Elvis Weekend" for tourists visiting Memphis, Tennessee.
4. Presley in a classic concert pose. His outfit is also a classic: shirt open on top of the jacket's collar, white socks, sideburns, medium-long slicked-back hair, and forelock.
5. The original poster for *Girl Happy* (1965), directed by Boris Sagal.
6. August 14–16, 1997, Memphis. On the anniversary of Presley's death, visitors to Graceland wear his likeness on T-shirts, caps, handbags, kerchiefs, even on the skin.
7. October 1957. Presley sings *Hound Dog* at the Los Angeles Pacific Auditorium. He is wearing a gold lame jacket.
8. August 14–16, 1997, Memphis.

7

8

4

5

6

> **"*Presley had no right to behave like a sexual maniac in a show that was broadcast to the whole country.*"**
>
> Actor-showman Jackie Gleason, after the *Dorsey Brothers Show*

PELÉ

Won the soccer World Cup

Edson Arantes do Nascimento was born in a ramshackle house in Três Coraçoes in the state of Minas Gerais (Brazil) in October 1940, the son of "Dondinho," a local soccer celebrity. The family was poor, and Pelé's ambition, even when playing soccer, was to have a real job, for example, as a hospital orderly. His dream finally came true after ten years or so. Edson, nicknamed Dico as a child, moved with his parents and brothers to Baurù, in the state of São Paulo, when he was four years old. As a kid he shined shoes at the railroad station. Much later, Pelé wrote: "Poverty is a misfortune that depresses the mind, tires the soul and poisons life." When he was eight his parents enrolled him in school, which he attended for six years. At that time his nickname became Pelé. He played on the September Seven, a children's soccer team that played barefooted. In the meantime, he worked in a shoe factory. At the age of twelve, playing on the Amériquinha team, he won the Baurù children's league competition. Playing in the Bac junior team, Pelé met the great coach Valdemar de Brito, a former national team champion. Brito recruited him for the Santos team in 1956. Thus began his brilliant career: three World Cups for Brazil's national soccer team (1958, 1962, 1970), 1280 goals, and phenomenal success, composure, and intelligence.

1

2

3

4

5

955 1956 1957 **1958** 195   1955 1956 1957 **1958** 1959 19

A WORLD SPORT. In 1901 the National Soccer Teams Federation already existed; that year, the final game for England's cup was followed by 110,000 fans; by 1905, there were almost 10,000 teams. But soccer was popular elsewhere as well. In 1889 the Dutch and Danish federations were established; in 1893 federations were established in Argentina, in 1894 in France, in 1895 in Switzerland, in 1898 in Italy, in 1900 in Uruguay, in 1902 in the Kingdom of Bohemia (now the Czech Republic), in 1904 in Germany and Austria, in 1912 in Russia, in 1914 in Brazil.

NEW COUNTRIES. Beginning with the 1960s, social changes such as increased work mobility, waves of immigration, and television, made soccer popular in many other countries. Teams such as Korea (1966), Morocco (1970), Zaire (1974), Algeria (1982), Cameroon (1990), and Jamaica (1998) distinguished themselves in international competitions. The only countries where soccer has not made many inroads are the United States, where all efforts at making it popular have failed so far, and Japan.

MAGIC 10. According to the "system" number 10 is assigned to the inside left forward, a center forward position. With Pelé, number 10 often became the magical element in the game, neither pure center fielder, nor pure forward, but a player who invented for others or even played the most dangerous balls for the opponent. Later, 10 was the number worn by Gianni Rivera, by the exceptional Diego Maradona, Arthur Zico, Michel Platini and Ronaldo. Replacing Pelé on the Brazil team, Johan Crujiff chose number 14 instead of number 10, refusing to be a second-rate number 10.

THE SOCCER PLAYER

Pelé was probably the greatest player in the history of soccer. He worked mostly with his right leg, but also easily with the left, and was capable of powerful head shots; he was acrobatic, kicked an accurate offside shot, was quick at the goal post, and was a sublime dribbler. He was extremely fast and a great finisher. He was a complete soccer player. As he became older, he played more and more a forward position, even changing the position of number 10. Married with children, he had no vices: he was the perfect professional player, a lofty example of athlete and man. In 1975 he left the Brazilian national team to join the New York Cosmos. One of his reasons was his desire to promote soccer in the United States. A careful manager of his talent and wealth, he advertised for consumer name brands without overdoing it. He did not play the mercurial star and

6

8

9

7

did not lose his head. Pelé used his color to give as much international fame as possible to a sport that was born in haughty, class-conscious England. His playing, like that of other Brazilian champions such as Garrincha, Vavà, and Didì, lacks meanness, is very elegant, full of imagination and joy that makes it fun to play. After retiring from active sports, his star status continued and he became a myth, respected as few others in this sport. Another very respected champion was Sir Stanley Matthews, who played for the first time in the English national team and left professional soccer in 1960 at the age of 50.

958 1959 1960 1951 1952 1953 1954 1955 1956 1957 1957 **1958**

1. 1971, Santos. Pelé in his office as general manager of Campina Grande Bank.

2. Pelé in a classical pose. He is not very tall, has no spectacular physique, is not overly handsome. His fame rests purely on his excellence on the field.

3. February 1966, Munich. Pelé and Rosemary Cholbi, his wife, during their honeymoon in Bavaria, Germany.

4. May 1963, Amsterdam. Pelé's legs under the care of a massage therapist.

5. Pelé, no longer in his youthful prime, playing with the Corinthians.

6. May 1977, Cannes. Pelé playing during an interview about the film *Pelé,* for which he wrote the soundtrack.

7. Pelé and Diego Maradona, two South American soccer stars. As a person, the Argentine Maradona is very different from Pelé. Maradona loves the night life and blustering gestures.

8. Mexico City. Pelé waiting to pounce during a game.

9. July 1966. A rare image of Pelé tending goal.

MARILYN MONROE

Starred in *Some Like It Hot*

Norma Jean Baker Mortenson was born in Los Angeles in 1926. The illegitimate child of an alcoholic mother, she grew up between orphanages and foster homes. At age eighteen she was already a photography model. In 1946 she divorced James Dougherty after a marriage that lasted only a few weeks. A starlet, she was given a break in 1950 with two tiny parts in John Huston's *The Asphalt Jungle* and Joseph Mankiewicz' *All About Eve*. In 1953 she triumphed in Henry Hathaway's *Niagara*, *Gentlemen Prefer Blondes*, directed by Howard Hawks, and *How to Marry a Millionaire*, directed by Jean Negulesco. By then, she was already famous outside of the United States. Billy Wilder directed her in two memorable comedies, *The Seven Year Itch* (1955) and *Some Like It Hot* (1959). In between, she also starred in Joshua Logan's *Bus Stop* (1956) and *The Prince and the Showgirl* (1957), directed by the great Laurence Olivier (1907–1989) who also starred in it. In 1960 she was in *Let's Make Love*, directed by George Cukor and in 1961, again directed by John Huston (1906–1987) in *The Misfits*. On August 5, 1962, while filming *Something's Got to Give*, directed by Cukor, Marilyn Monroe died in Brentwood in her sleep from an overdose of pills.

1

2

3

4

MEN. Marilyn's second husband was Joe DiMaggio (1914–1999), the New York Yankee legend. A good, concrete man, he could not understand his wife's insecurity. Her third husband was playwright Arthur Miller (b. 1915), who instead of helping her to become cultivated and mature, destabilized her. Marilyn was persuaded she was not the great actress that she ought to be. She studied at the Lee Strasberg Actors' Studio, but luckily did not adopt their excessive acting style. Rumor had it that she had a relationship with Yves Montand while filming *Let's Make Love*, directed by Cukor (1960).

AN AMBIGUOUS DEATH. Was it suicide? Tragedy? Homicide? Marilyn's death has never been solved. Her use of barbiturates was well known, and it was rumored that she drank too much and that she had been involved with both John and Robert Kennedy. Taking into consideration her fragile state of mind and the Kennedys' lifestyle, that rumor does not appear improbable.

Rumor also has it that the night before her death she sought help from a very powerful man who, instead of helping, silenced her.

EVERGREEN. Marilyn's films are often rerun on TV, and tapes of her films still sell briskly. In *All About Eve*, next to Anne Baxter and Bette Davis (1908–1989)—possibly Hollywood's greatest actress—she was able to stand on her own, although her part was tiny. Her wisecracks in light comedies and the words of some of her songs, such as "Diamonds Are a Girl's Best Friend," are unforgettable, as is "noodles," the word she used to describe piano music in the style of Rachmaninoff.

MEANWHILE, Mattel launched the Barbie doll, a combination of Marilyn and Sandra Dee: it was to become an icon for millions of little girls and their mothers. The great French actor Gérard Philipe (b. 1922) and the great jazz singer Billie Holiday (b. 1915) died. On the royal scene, Belgian King Albert II married Paola Ruffo of Calabria; Farah Diba married Mohammed Reza Pahlavi (1919–1980) who was Shah of Iran from 1941 to 1979.

SEXY

"What does Marilyn wear in bed?" "A drop of Chanel No. 5." This witty remark captured Marilyn Monroe's most lasting image. In the Hollywood movie industry, it marked the shift from the fatal vamp to the sexy star. After Monroe, the expression "sex symbol" would be used also for male stars with sex appeal, especially for actors who, like Marilyn, evoked tenderness, such as Montgomery Clift (1920–1966), James Dean (1931–1955), even today's Leonardo DiCaprio, actors that still have the child in them and thus manage to project fragility. In looking at Marilyn's silhouette, observing her medium height and child-blond hair, a

1. Monroe as a very young pin-up girl.
2. Poster for *The Asphalt Jungle* (1950), directed by John Huston, starring Sterling Hayden and Louis Calhern. Monroe had a small part next to these two excellent actors.
3. Poster for *Niagara* (1953), directed by Henry Hathaway (1898–1985). While Jean Peters was the lead female star, Monroe did not go unnoticed.
4. Laurence Olivier next to Monroe in *The Prince and the Showgirl* (1957), directed by Olivier.
5. Monroe in a frame from *The Seven Year Itch* (1955), directed by Billy Wilder.

6. Anne Baxter, Bette Davis, Marilyn Monroe, and George Sanders in *All About Eve* (1950), directed by Joseph L. Mankiewicz.
7. A shop-window full of Marilyn Monroe's portraits.
8. Monroe with Tony Curtis and Jack Lemmon, who dressed as women, in *Some Like It Hot* (1959), directed by Billy Wilder.
9. May 1953. Monroe and Jane Russell on the cover of *Life*. They starred in *Gentlemen Prefer Blondes*, directed by Howard Hawks.

1960 1951 2 1953 195

1957 1958 **1959**

student of Konrad Lorenz would say that she had typical "cub shapes" that inspired tenderness.

Marilyn also provoked male desire with her "curves" though maybe not as much as Mae West (1892–1980) who starred in the scandalous Sex (1926) and was an exceptional vamp-clown whom Monroe took as model, along with Rita Hayworth. Like Rita, Marilyn was instantly likable, even to women (unlike her French rival Brigitte Bardot [b. 1934]). Like Mae West, Marilyn Monroe was intelligent and had an unfailing acting instinct that she honed through hard work. Her film quips were open and knowing; her look, kindhearted and funny, yet sharp. Unlike Mae West, Marilyn was not an iconoclast.

*"Wake up, Marilyn.
Time to take the plane to New York."*
Marilyn Monroe's wake-up message to herself,
recorded shortly before falling asleep forever.

JEAN-PAUL SARTRE

Published *Critique of Dialectical Reason*

Jean-Paul Sartre (1905–1980) was born in Paris to a middle-class family. He studied at the École Normale Supérieure and received a grant to study in Berlin (1933–1934). Sartre fought in World War II and was taken prisoner by the Germans. Like the Enlightenment thinkers, he expressed his ideas in essays, novels, plays, and newspaper articles. Together with his life companion, writer Simone de Beauvoir (1908–1986), Merleau-Ponty and others, he founded the important review *Les Temps Modernes* in 1945. Later, he also supported *Libération,* the newspaper of the restless left; in 1980, he entrusted his ethical testament to the *Nouvel Observateur*. From the late 1940s to about 1968, Sartre was

MA168
DEBUT
D'UNE LUTTE
PROLONGEE

1

the soul of cultural and artistic society in Saint-Germain-des-Prés, the Paris quarter he made famous. Sartre was a convinced "fellow traveler" of Communism, although in his late years he turned against Soviet Russia and supported Mao and, in his last years, he distanced himself from Marxism and proposed an ethic based on brotherhood and solidarity.

5

2

3

4

WRITINGS. Sartre received the Nobel Prize for literature in 1964, which he declined on political grounds. His novel *Nausea* (1938) has been widely translated, as was *The Wall* (1939), a collection of short stories and, later, *The Roads to Freedom* cycle (1945–1949). His plays include *The Flies* (1943), *No Exit* (1944), and *Dirty Hands* (1948). Sartre's most important philosophical works are *Being and Nothingness* (1943), *Situations*, a collection of published essays, and *Critique de la Raison*

Dialectique (*Critique of Dialectical Reason* (1963) of which only the introduction was translated in English as *Search for a Method*). In innumerable manifestoes, articles, and essays Sartre discoursed at length on many disparate subjects of current social, philosophical, ethical, and political relevance.

FRIENDS. Sartre's friends were his École Normale classmates such as the philosopher and sociologist Raymond Aron (1905–1983) who was close to

de Gaulle and the guru of French Liberalism.

EXISTENTIALISTS. Tens of thousands of young people in post-war Europe called themselves "existentialists." Young men and women wore the same black T-shirts and jeans, smoked *Gitanes*, listened to the records of Georges Brassens (1921–1981) and Juliette

Gréco (b. 1926), and read the verses of Jacques Prévert (1900–1977). They adored Saint-Germain, the Café de Flore, films with Jean Gabin (1904–1976) and Michèle Morgan (b. 1920), and everything Parisian. Except, they had never been to Paris.

OFFSPRING. The philosopher sided with the new generation against the

ANGST

> *"Victor: 'Why do we sing under the bombs?'*
> *Sartre: 'In singing you find all your freedom again . . .*
> *and in that moment freedom overcomes death . . .'"*
> From "Militant Sacrifice," January 1973, in *On a raison de se revolter*
> (*The Right to Rebel*)

"The essence of being," that is, of human existence, "lies in his becoming." This is how Martin Heidegger in Being and Time *(1927)* unwillingly ushered in twentieth-century existentialism. The radical finite nature of man is defined as "lucid anxiety" by the existentialists, particularly by Sartre, who wrote (in Being and Nothingness) that the problems of the human condition constitute an ongoing, relentless tension between the "for itself" (consciousness) and the "in itself" (that of which consciousness is conscious). The fundamental task of man is to try to reconcile these aspects, but this is impossible and so man is "condemned to be free." Freedom and a feeling of responsibility, both absolute, generate anguish. With his Search for a Method, *Sartre reformulated his existentialism in the direction of social analysis to complement Marxism, the "unsurpassable horizon of our times."*

6

9

1958 1959 **1960** 1951 1952 1953 1954 1955 1956 1957 1958 1959 **1960** 1951 1952 1953 1954 1955 1956 1957 1958 1959 **1960**

10

7

8

What everyone understands in the thinking of Sartre is that life is anguish, a sense of nausea for the bourgeois who hide behind "bad faith," and that this feeling can give birth to the struggle for freedom. On March 15, 1974 Sartre stated that the "the revolution will happen when the majority find themselves so aware of their situation of being oppressed by the minority that they will fully understand their own strength." For today's young leftist generation, angst is out, but revolution is still in.

Algerian and Vietnam wars, in favor of peace, against the Communist Party, in favor of Maoism, and took increasingly extreme left positions, in protest marches and at the Sorbonne University. "I was with the young people . . . but deep down" he confessed in 1974, "I did not understand them." By then, Sartre was isolated in his ongoing activism on behalf of leftist issues. The left, the center, the right, culture, power, they all venerated him as a great figure but no longer listened to the man.

1. Anonymous, May 1968. *The Beginning of a Long Struggle*, poster.
2. Sartre and Simone de Beauvoir, arrested for distributing "La voix du peuple," which had been banned.
3. 1946, Paris. Sartre in a well-known portrait by Henri Cartier-Bresson, the great photographer who wrote about the poetry of "the decisive moment."
4. April 19, 1980, Paris. The 30,000-strong crowd

attending Sartre's funeral in Mortparnasse Cemetery.
5. Simone de Beauvoir, Jacques Laurent Bost, Jean Cau, the "offensive" writer Jean Genet (1910–1986) and Sartre in a Paris café.
6. Sartre and de Beauvoir at a café table during a trip abroad.
7. 1978. Italian state TV broadcasts *Le mani sporche* (*Dirty Hands*) with Marcello Mastroianni and Giuliana De Sio, directed by Elio Petri.

8. 1968, Paris. Student demonstration. In the foreground are visible the portraits of the "saints" of that young leftist generation.
9. May 1, 1968. Sartre at Sorbonne University. The philosopher later noted that the students had booed him because the organizers of the demonstration had treated him like a star, which had annoyed the students.
10. Sartre is interviewed in the middle of a crowd.

1961 – 1970

RUDOLF NUREYEV

JOHN XXIII

JOHN F. KENNEDY

CASSIUS CLAY

HELENA RUBINSTEIN

THE BEATLES

CHE GUEVARA

ARISTOTLE ONASSIS

NEIL ARMSTRONG

ANDY WARHOL

In the West, the number of high school and college students continued to grow; unemployment was low and the percentage of workers engaged in agriculture continued to drop; the factory work week became shorter. In many countries, and not just those ruled by Socialists or Communists, the government owned industries; thanks to pensions, health insurance, and free or inexpensive education, many countries provided social security to their citizens. Transportation and communication infrastructures took a giant leap forward. People took longer vacations, and spent them away from home. More and more people became homeowners and enjoyed a comfortable lifestyle, with spacious bathrooms, mass-produced furniture, stereos, televisions, and all sorts of household appliances. These items "freed" housewives, but only to a point, since domestic salaries increased and many

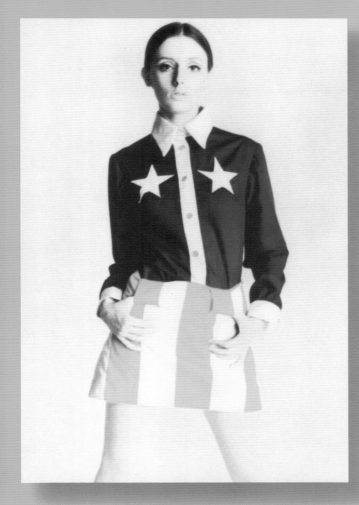

families could no longer afford full-time help.

Twiggy, a famous model of the 1960s,

Women demanded various kinds of freedom:

represented a new type of woman: fem-

freedom from the dictates of the man of the

inine even without "curves."

house, from being limited to modest jobs, from inequality in housing, salaries, access to the professions, from double standards of morality and traditional codes of conduct.

For the first time in history, a skinny woman with small breasts—personified by the model Twiggy—became a model for millions of women; an indication that thinness was now a choice, not the result of abject poverty, and that maternity was no longer a woman's only vocation. Many saw an explosion of joy and youth in 1968. Peace and justice seemed within the grasp of many. There was a preoccupation with redefining roles, since it seemed at the time that the work of a few could suffice for all.

In 1961, for the first time, a man—the Soviet Yuri Gagarin—flew around the Earth in an artificial satellite. In these years, there was almost full employment in the West, although many new machines replaced blue-collar workers—such as batching and packaging machines and die tools that manufactured machines.

This decade ushered in the second generation of computers, although they were still enormous in size. In 1961, German Communist authorities built a wall that split Berlin into two cities, in an effort to prevent their

beginning with energy consumption. Colossal gas and oil pipelines were built, boring through mountains and desolate wastelands. Oil was also transported by supertankers. In 1967, one such tanker, the *Torrey Canyon*, sank and spilled its oil, causing an environmental disaster

1. IBM 7070.   2. Oil pipeline in the desert.   3. Young Biafrans.   4. Suharto.   5. Poster from May 1968.

on the English coast.

THE PASSWORD OF THE DECADE WAS CONSUMERISM: IT BECAME FASHIONABLE. IN THE WEST, MILLIONS OF BLUE-COLLAR WORKERS MOVED INTO THE MIDDLE CLASS, CHANGING ITS BEHAVIOR AND MENTALITY. THE ACHIEVEMENT OF PROSPERITY ALSO MEANT CHANGED SPENDING HABITS, WITH FEWER SAVINGS IN ORDER TO FLAUNT A NEW SOCIAL STATUS. STATUS SYMBOLS WERE ONE HALLMARK OF THE DECADE.

countrymen from escaping to the west. In 1964 Martin Luther King Jr., the Baptist minister who led the fight for the equal rights of African-Americans, received the Nobel Peace Prize. Four years later he was murdered, but the struggle continued and is still bearing fruit.

In the developed countries consumption grew at a fast pace,

In 1966, floods in the art-rich cities of Florence and Venice touched all culture and art lovers. Young Europeans rushed to salvage works of art. People began worrying about the health of the environment. One medication, Thalidomide, was found to cause genetic defects in children, so even medicines became a cause for fear. Advances in surgery made miraculous feats possible: in 1967, Christiaan Barnard, a South African surgeon, transplanted a young woman's heart into the chest of an old man, who survived 18 days. The era of organ transplants had begun. World population growth caused anxiety; but Pope Paul VI, in his encyclical *Humanae Vitae* reaffirmed Pius XII's total ban on contraceptives. The "good pope" John XXIII died in 1963. In the same year, President Kennedy was murdered; he had recognized the justice of the U.S. black civil

Brutal power struggles agitated the newly independent states: in the Congo (renamed Zaire, now the Republic of the Congo), there was a bloody secession war in Katanga province (1960–1963) during which Prime Minister Patrice Lumumba (1925–1961) was murdered and U.N. Secretary-General Dag Hammarskjöld died in an airplane crash. In Nigeria, Biafra's attempted secession war (1967–1970) resulted in millions of deaths. And these were only the most tragic events.

In the East,

the cultural revolution, which was not understood in the West, since many claimed it had no victims, and seemed more a sign of renewal, of wanting to give space to the younger generation.

The decade began with "beat" kids in jeans and leather jackets and an undercurrent of anarchy and violence. This sentiment was admirably interpreted by Anthony Burgess in his novel *A Clockwork Orange* (1961). Mary Quant and Courrèges' miniskirts became popular, along

was *One Hundred Years of Solitude* (1967) by Gabriel Garcia Marquez; the cult film, *2001: A Space Odyssey* (1968) by Stanley Kubrick. The 1969 Woodstock Festival marked the times.

But not everything was flowers and love. In 1967 a brutal right-wing dictatorship seized power in Greece; in 1968 the Warsaw Pact crushed Prague's spring of freedom. The Vietnam War, begun in

5

la lutte continue

8

9

6. Flower children. 7. Buttons from the 1960s. 8. Poster advertising *A Clockwork Orange*. 9. Defoliated forest in South Vietnam. 10. Concorde jet.

rights movement and had resolved the Cuban Missile Crisis. The following year, Nikita Khrushchev was deposed. The world mourned the loss of three great leaders. In Africa, decolonization advanced full speed: between 1960 and 1966, 32 independent states were born. In 1962 de Gaulle ended the long Algerian war by granting independence to that colony and ordering the arrest of the leaders of OAS, the French soldiers' and settlers' terrorist organization. Several years later, director Gillo Pontecorvo shot an epic movie on the subject, *The Battle of Algiers*.

6

India fought China over their Himalayan border and Pakistan over the province of Kashmir. In 1966 in Indonesia a coup took place in which President Sukarno (1901–1970), a moderate leftist, was deposed by General Suharto—an unscrupulous profiteer. In 1966 in China Mao launched

7

FLOWER POWER

HIPPY POWER

MAKE LOVE NOT WAR

BLACK IS BEAUTIFUL

STUDENT POWER

with Paco Rabanne's plastic wear and Yves Saint-Laurent's and Pierre Cardin's svelte, chic couture.

The decade moved full speed toward the 1968 youth revolution: France's May days, communes, clogs, gypsy clothes, long hair, and pot.

The novel of the decade

10

1960, continued even though the younger generation called for an end to the bombings and the use of napalm incendiary bombs and forest defoliants such as Agent Orange.

In 1969 the French-English supersonic jet, the *Concorde*, perhaps the most beautiful commercial passenger plane ever, was introduced.

RUDOLF NUREYEV

Asked for political asylum in France

Rudolf Nureyev was born in 1938 near Irkutsk in Siberia. He studied folk dance, and was seventeen when he began attending the Kirov Ballet dance school, the faithful keeper of the imperial theater tradition. Three years later he was already a star, causing a sensation with his performances in *La Bayadère, Sleeping Beauty,* and *Giselle.* He had an athletic chest; powerful, not too long legs, as befits a dancer; and a highly expressive face, hands, and back. He developed an exceptional technique, a very personal rendition of the *ballon* and *élévation* movements, and a strong, noble, virtuoso style. During the striking success of his 1961 Paris tour he asked for political asylum, both for career reasons and because he was impatient with the passé style of Soviet ballet. He joined the Grand Ballet du Marquis de Cuevas; later, he was a permanent guest star with London's Royal Ballet where he danced with the splendid Margot Fonteyn (1919–1991), unquestionably the queen of English ballet. He also danced with other groups and with the best dancers of the time, among them Carla Fracci (b. 1936), the *prima donna* of Italian ballet. He was among the best representatives of a movement for cautious reform of classical-romantic choreography. Nureyev died of complications from AIDS in 1993.

1965 1966 1967 1968 1969 1970 **1961** 1962 1963 1962

2

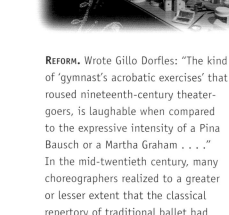

1

3

REFORM. Wrote Gillo Dorfles: "The kind of 'gymnast's acrobatic exercises' that roused nineteenth-century theater-goers, is laughable when compared to the expressive intensity of a Pina Bausch or a Martha Graham . . . ." In the mid-twentieth century, many choreographers realized to a greater or lesser extent that the classical repertory of traditional ballet had to be rejuvenated. Some suggested interesting new choreographies; among them, Nureyev with his performances of *La Bayadère* (1963), *Swan Lake* (1964), and *The Nutcracker*

(1967). Out of his experience with Martha Graham came the original ballet *Lucifer* (1975).

OTHER MEDIA. Nureyev's *Giselle* (1961) was shown on television and met with an extraordinary success. He was less lucky in film: neither *I Am a Dancer* (1971) nor *Valentino* (1977), directed by Ken Russell was successful.

IN THE MEANTIME, the French author Louis-Ferdinand Céline (b. 1894) died; he had been both a philanthropist and a Nazi sympathizer, and one of the

more innovative writers of our century. Architect-trained André Courrèges (a former designer for the house of Balenciaga and creator of some of the loveliest evening gowns of the time) opened his Paris couture house. American Eero Saarinen (b. 1910), a leading architect of the time, died. Dag Hammarskjöld (b. 1905), U.N. Secretary-

General, died in a plane crash in the Congo; he was posthumously awarded the Nobel Peace Prize. French film director Alain Resnais, working from a screenplay by French author Alain Robbe-Grillet, filmed *Last Year at Marienbad*, which became a cult movie for the originality of its cinematographic language.

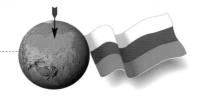

BALLET STAR

1. Nureyev during makeup.

2. Nureyev and Carla Fracci in rehearsal.

3. 1973, London. Nureyev in *The Prodigal Son*. The elegance and technical precision of his acrobatic performances were unparalleled.

4. Nureyev at the Zurich Opera House in *Manfred*, which he choreographed.

5. 1965, London. Nureyev in *Prince Igor*.

6. June 1974, Paris. Nureyev performing at the Palais des Sports.

7. 1974, Paris. Rudolf Nureyev and modern dancer Carolyn Carlson in *Tristan*.

8. March 1963, London. Nureyev and Fonteyn in *Marguerite and Armand* by Frederick Ashton, at the Royal Opera House.

9. A touching photo of Nureyev, in his last painful years.

Becoming a ballet star, the leading dancer, is the dream of every boy or girl who is willing to face the harsh discipline and the long, daily regimen of ballet school, training and exercise, which dancers must keep up until they retire. Starting in the nineteenth century, a ballet star was also a social celebrity, was paid an astronomical salary, and received fabulous gifts. In the romantic nineteenth century, however, the object of all this attention was a woman. There were few exceptions, among them, the Italian dancer Enrico Cecchetti (1850–1928), who founded the Russian school and from 1910 to 1918 was with the Ballets Russes.

In our century, traditional ballet continued to have women stars of exceptional artistic stature (Anna Pavlova, Olga Preobrajenska, Ida Rubinstein, Galina Ulanova, to name a few). Women were especially sensitive to the need for a radical reformation of the classical-romantic ballet. They were also the major interpreters of free, modern dance, from the mythical Isadora Duncan (1878–1927) to the great Martha Graham (1900–1991) and the cultivated Katherine Dunham (b. 1914), all American artists, and the gifted German dancer Pina Bausch. Many of these artists were also choreographers.

61 1962 1963 1964 1965 1966   69 1970 **1961** 1962 1963 1964 1965   962 1963 196

> *"His art and his magnetic personality generated such high levels of enthusiasm that a true cult grew around his person."*
> Renée Mandl

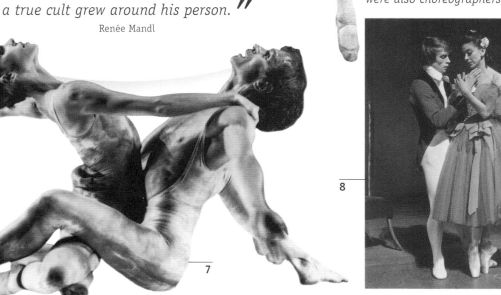

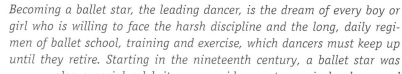

The male ballet stars of our century were classical dancers, and some were also great choreographers: among the unforgettable are Vaslav Nijinsky (1890–1950), Mikhail Fokine (1880–1942), Léonide Massine (1876–1979), Serge Lifar (1905–1986), all Russians. Last among these—possibly also thanks to modern media—Nureyev was the only ballet star to reach the masses and touch their hearts with the splendor of his youth, the overwhelming force of his talent, and the reserved sadness of his agonizing twilight.

161

JOHN XXIII

Opened Vatican Council II

Angelo Giuseppe Roncalli was born to a family of farmers in the village of Sotto il Monte, Bergamo, Italy, in 1881. He studied in the local seminary and in the Seminary of Rome, and was ordained a Roman Catholic priest in 1904. During World War I he was a sergeant in the Health Corps, then chaplain. Appointed secretary to the bishop of Bergamo, in 1921 Pope Benedict XV called him to Rome and asked him to direct the Congregation for the Propagation of the Faith for Italy. He was then named archbishop in 1925, apostolic delegate and visitor to Bulgaria, apostolic delegate and director in Turkey and Greece in 1935, apostolic nuncio in Paris in 1944, and cardinal patriarch of Venice in 1953.

On October 28, 1958, when Pius XII died, Roncalli was chosen to succeed him, and took the name of John XXIII. Three months later, perhaps basing himself on studies that Pius XII had commissioned and then set aside, he announced that he was calling an ecumenical council, the 21st such council held by the Catholic Church in its 2,000-year history. The council opened in St. Peter's Basilica in Rome on October 11, 1962. Pope John died of stomach cancer on June 3, 1963.

1967 1968 1969 1970 1961 **1962** 1963 1964 1965 1966 1967 1968 1969 1970 1961 **1962**   1964 1965 1966 1967 1968 1969 1970 1961

TRADITION. Pope John did away with the papal court that was composed of lay people and cut the ancient bond the papacy had with the Roman nobility. He did not bestow aristocratic titles on his family, as was his prerogative. He did, however, retain the use of the papal tiara, the gestatorial chair, the ceremonial fans, and the Swiss Guards. He loved the ancient splendor and pomp, gold and incense; for he knew that to simple people they spoke of God and of heaven, of grace and forgiveness. He was a Roman pope who had experienced the richness of the Byzantine rites.

WORK. Even when sick, the elderly pope worked gladly and serenely. He was a scrupulous organizer of the council, and supervised all its documents, personally guiding the Central Committee. He was not intimidated by the 2,500 bishops he gathered in St. Peter's: he held in check those who wanted too much change, and encouraged those who mistrusted change. He attended the general sessions, and allowed 42 non-Catholic observers to attend, some of them women. When someone predicted that the pope would not see the council to its conclusion, he replied that God's providence is immortal.

HUMANITY. Breaking with a centuries-old tradition, the pope enjoyed inviting guests to dine with him: simple, refined repasts, a few cigars, lively conversation, and pointed questions. The pope defended himself from a retinue that was accustomed to scheming. He encouraged the observation, judgments, and opinions of outsiders. He began to reorganize the departments of the Vatican and reformed the papal universities. In 1963 he was awarded the Balzan peace prize. To please him, the USSR freed the Ukrainian archbishop Slipyi. John XXIII died leaving the council divided.

"We ought to bring back value and splendor to the human and Christian qualities of thought and of life."
John XXIII, November 14, 1960

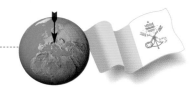

THE ECUMENICAL COUNCIL

John XXIII had lived away from Rome and knew the uneasiness the Church felt in other lands, and the defects of the Roman Curia. He was especially aware of the open wound created in the Church in 1870 by the suspension of Vatican Council I following the proclamation of the dogma of papal infallibility that had been the subject of controversy at the council. In the spring of 1959 he reaffirmed the ban on Catholic political parties forging alliances with Communist parties; all the while, however, he showed respect for the opinions of Communists and for Eastern European countries. With firm faith in divine providence, he called the council in the belief it would strengthen the Church's organization, modernize its liturgy and customs, express in a manner appropriate to our times the unchangeable principles of faith and morality, open a brotherly dialogue with the various Christian Churches, and assuage the perplexity and distress felt by so many faithful.

The pope was a conservative who loved life and had faith in man; this is why Catholics as well as non-Catholics called him simply "the good pope." In 1961 his epistle, Mater et Magistra, while stating nothing truly novel about the Church's social doctrine, did express a deep solidarity with the poor and disadvantaged.

Without upsetting the Vatican hierarchy closest to Pius XII, the pope appointed innovative cardinals and other prelates to highly responsible positions, and created an Office for the Union of all Christians.

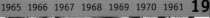

1. 1953, Elysée Palace, Paris. President Vincent Auriol of France places the cardinal's biretta on Monsignor Angelo Roncalli, the papal nuncio to France.
2. 1962, Vatican. The pope chairs one of the council's sessions in St. Peter's.
3. An official photograph of John XXIII wearing the pope's traditional tiara.

4. October 11, 1962, Vatican. The pope on the gestatorial chair, surrounded by cardinals and the Vatican court, on his way to St. Peter's Basilica to open Vatican Council II.
5. 1961, Vatican. The pope during an audience granted to Queen Elizabeth II, head of the Anglican Church.
6. 1953, Venice. Solemn entrance of the newly

elected patriarch cardinal Roncalli.
7. 1965, Imbersago, Como, Italy. A commemorative statue of John XXIII at the sanctuary of Our Lady of the Woods.
8. 1958, Vatican. A moment of the solemn assembly called in St. Peter's by the new pope.
9. On a vendor's stall in Venice, a photograph of John XXIII together with other souvenirs of the city.

JOHN F. KENNEDY

Assassinated in Dallas, Texas

John Fitzgerald Kennedy (1917–1963) was born in Massachusetts to a family of Irish ancestry that had recently made a fortune and that had political ambitions. A graduate of Harvard in 1940, in 1941 he commanded a torpedo boat in the Pacific that was later sunk. A back injury he received during the war gave him trouble for the rest of his life. With his elder brother killed in the war, John became the heir to his father's ambitions. He was elected Congressman in 1946 and Senator in 1952. In 1956, he wrote *Profiles in Courage*, which won him the Pulitzer Prize. He married Jacqueline Bouvier, an attractive young woman from a leading New England family, who had received a European-style education. With Eisenhower coming to the end of his presidential mandate, John received from his family's party, the Democrats, the presidential nomination. He won the election against Vice President Nixon, the Republican candidate, by a very narrow popular vote margin of 118,574 votes. He was President of the United States from January 1961 to November 22, 1963, when he was assassinated during a pre-election campaign tour in Texas. In less than three years, however, he had succeeded in fashioning a new image for the United States and upholding the ideals of optimism and social justice.

2

1

THE PRESIDENT'S TEAM: Dean Rusk, former President of the Rockefeller Foundation, was Secretary of State; Robert S. McNamara, former President of Ford Motor Company, was Secretary of Defense; Arthur Goldberg was Secretary of Labor; Adlai Stevenson was Ambassador to the United Nations; his brother Robert Kennedy (1925–1968) was Attorney General.

A THORN IN THE SIDE was Castro's Cuba, which did not tolerate U.S. interference. The April 1961 Bay of Pigs landing—led by nostalgic supporters of former dictator Batista who had escaped to Florida and were armed by the CIA—failed.

USSR. The USSR supplied Cuba with experts and nuclear bases. This led to the 1962 Missile Crisis. Kennedy blockaded Cuban ports, forcing Khrushchev to withdraw the missiles and dismantle the launching ramps. In August 1961, Khrushchev had shown a firmer hand in building the Berlin Wall. In August 1963 in Moscow, Khrushchev and Kennedy signed the nuclear test ban treaty.

THE KENNEDYS. Womanizers it was rumored, they were fond of Hollywood: patriarch Joseph was involved with Gloria Swanson (1899–1983) while his sons, it was said, were involved with Marilyn Monroe; one daughter married actor Peter Lawford. The Kennedys were social climbers: Joseph was Ambassador to Great Britain, three of his sons served in the Senate and one of them, JFK, married Jacqueline Bouvier,

3

HOPE

The New Frontier was the path to which Kennedy pointed the American people. With the American West conquered, the social reforms of Franklin D. Roosevelt in place, Nazism and Fascism overthrown, and the United States securely established as the leader of the Western world, the youngest president in the history of the country outlined the democratic objectives that he intended to achieve. The Alliance for Progress (August 1961) announced an aid plan for Latin America of $20 billion over ten years, while the Peace Corps aimed to send young volunteer experts to developing countries.

Kennedy was able to increase the minimum wage, to launch government aid for schools, and to ensure free health care for the elderly. He also initiated a far-reach-

❝Let us together explore the stars, conquer the deserts, uproot disease, explore the depths of the oceans and encourage the arts and commerce. ❞
John F. Kennedy, in his inaugural speech.

1. The confident style John F. Kennedy used when speaking to audiences.
2. Paris, June 1961. Presidents Kennedy and de Gaulle pay homage to the war dead in France.
3. November 1960. The Kennedy family photographed at home in Hyannis Port, Massachusetts. Front left: father Joseph and mother Rose. Behind JFK is Robert, who was murdered during his 1968 presidential campaign. Front right: JFK's wife, Jacqueline, seated next to her brother-in-law Ted.
4. 1960. John F. Kennedy with his wife and daughter Caroline.
5. R. and K. Bowen replaced the Stars and Stripes of the Marines victorious in the Pacific—a famous 1945 photo—with a rose to create a pacifist poster in 1969 in the "New Frontier" style.
6. Three frames from the film made by Abraham Zapruder during the assassination of Kennedy. The murder investigation's official determination was that there had been a "lone gunman."

7

5

6

CHICAGO DAILY NEWS

PRESIDENT IS KILLED

Texas Sniper Escapes; Johnson Sworn In

Story Begins on Next Page

965 1966 1967 1968 1969 1970 1961 1962 **1963** 1964 1965 1966 1967 1968 1969   1966 1967 1968 1969 1970 1961 1962 **1963** 1964 1

ing program of racial equality and used his presidential authority to intervene in the internal affairs of racist states. 1960–1961 was a period of recession, but Kennedy's policies ensured for the 1960s an average GNP growth of 4.3 percent at constant prices, although more than 5 percent of the labor force was unemployed. In his last year in office, Kennedy initiated a tax reduction plan totaling $11 million to spur investments.

His every action was echoed throughout the world. Millions of men and women believed in his positive guidance toward a new frontier of justice and peace among men and peoples. This was the spirit of the sixties.

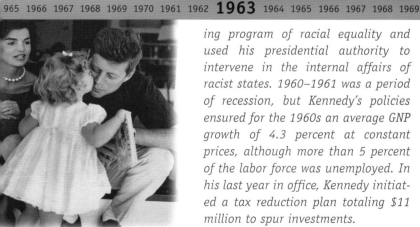

8

7. A photo of the assassination on the front page of a newspaper.
8. Martin Luther King, Jr. (1929–1968), apostle of anti-racism, speaking to the crowds during the August 28, 1963 March on Washington. Kennedy even used the army to support the struggle against racism and wrested control of the National Guard from the governors of two states. The objective was to allow young black students to attend college. Winner of the Nobel Peace Prize, King was assassinated in Memphis in 1968.

whose sister was a former "Most Serene Highness." They were widely considered America's "Royal Family."

WANTED. In a poster that appeared in Texas on the eve of his fatal trip, underneath the photo of the president

were these words: "This man is wanted for treason against the United States . . . for having subjected the sovereignty of the USA to a United Nations controlled by Communists . . . for having aided and abetted race riots inspired by Communists . . . . "

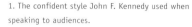

CASSIUS CLAY

World heavyweight champion

Named after his slave grandfather, Cassius Clay was born in 1942 in Louisville, Kentucky. He had an unremarkable childhood and adolescence. He was born for boxing: according to his trainer, he would change style, innovate in the ring week after week. At the age of 18, already 6 feet tall, he had won a string of amateur fights and was middle-heavyweight champion at the Rome Olympics. His motto was already: "I am the strongest, the greatest, the handsomest!" In 1964, at the age of 22, he fought Sonny Liston, a true slugger, and won the world heavyweight championship. The 1965 return match held in Miami lasted one round

(2'12") and Clay again prevailed. By then, he had converted to Islam and changed his name to Muhammad Ali. Between 1965 and 1967 he won against the challengers Floyd Patterson, George Chuvalo, Henry Cooper, Brian London, Ernie Terrell, and Zora Foley. Each time he would predict the round in which he would knock out his opponent, and then conduct the match accordingly. He had the great ability to shape his boxing to take advantage of his adversaries' weaknesses, while at the same time provoking them with jeers and taunts. No wonder many people hated him. In April 1967 the U.S. government conscripted him.

COMEBACK. After 43 months of inactivity in jail, the Supreme Court reinstated Muhammad Ali. In 1970 he won two matches; in 1971 Joe Frazier grounded him, winning on points. The title holder then accepted a rematch that took place in 1974 in Kinshasa (in what was then Zaire), a land from which so many Africans had departed on slave ships bound for America. It was christened "the fight of the century." Ali fought George Foreman, who was eight years younger. Ali's strategy was to be on

close guard and to let Foreman tire himself out in the first five rounds; he then began to counterattack, and K.O.'d Foreman in the eighth round. This victory was followed by four more brilliant years.

DANCE. The 1964 Liston-Clay fight was shown live on large screens in movie houses. Clay "floated like a butterfly and stung like a bee." This was the beginning of the champion's career that made him a millionaire. Even more important, it was the movie

camera that made it possible for the world to appreciate Clay's incredible dance around his adversary, splendid legwork unsurpassed among heavyweight fighters. Like a bullfighter, Clay would tire his adversary out until he exploded in random violence. His hits were hard and on target, and so fast that only in slow motion replay was it possible to understand how he had won.

STRATEGY. Clay's "strategy of demoralization" consisted of statements, gestures, predictions, and insults that

created a psychological weakness in his opponent, giving him a sense of inferiority. Clay was not an offensive, crude boaster: he was intelligent and well-read, a thinker who fought first of all with his mind.

AFRICAN-AMERICANISM

Three ideas always inspired Muhammad Ali: men are free; God marks a path for every one where truth will shine; Muhammad's path led him to bring boxing back to Africa, the land of some of the world's greatest boxers. Having refused to serve in the Vietnam War, in 1967 he stated, in a nutshell, that as a black man, he did not want to kill yellow men to please the white man. Whereupon the U.S. government revoked his title and his boxing license, sentencing him to a jail term and fining him $6 million. The government had been suspicious of him since he became friendly with Malcolm X (1925–1965), a charismatic black leader, and prominent member of the Nation of Islam, which preached the ethical inferiority of white men.

Clay was different from the other great black boxing heroes: he was not deferential like Floyd Patterson, nor a snob like Sugar Ray Robinson, nor a scoundrel like Sonny Liston or Mike Tyson. Much like the mythical Marcel Cerdan (1916–1949), he exhibited an intense love for humanity and the ideals of justice for the disadvantaged and the oppressed. In the 1930s African-Americans started to assert themselves in the world of music and dance; in the 1950s, they became accepted in Hollywood; in the 1960s they aspired to the respect

"He lorded over the entire history of boxing, as if fate had willed for . . . him to meet boxing as his own destiny, and for him to become boxing."
Alexis Philolenko, *Storia della boxe (History of Boxing)*

7

8

due to human beings, and to respect for the culture, the talents, the dignity of their people. Clay censured those blacks who slavishly imitated whites and tried to be part of their world. He gave hope to poor black kids, and empowered them.

`70 1961 1962 1963 **1964** 1965 1966 1967 1968 1969 1970 1961 1962 1963 **1964** 1965 1966 1967 1969 1970 1961 1962 1963 **1964** 1965 1966 1967 1968 1969 1970`

9

6

1. Muhammad Ali's children: from left, Hana, Samilla, Rasheda, Laka, Maymay, Muhammad.
2. Ali on an airplane. He loved to be photographed while reading the Koran or religious or political books.
3. An expressive close-up of Ali.
4. December 8, 1971, New York City. Ali beats Oscar Bonavena.

5. February 16, 1978, Las Vegas. Ali is beaten by Leon Spinks in the heavyweight championship match.
6. 1965. Malcolm X speaks to a crowd. He was murdered later that same year.
7. February 25, 1964, Miami Beach. Clay challenges and beats Liston, world heavyweight champion, in the seventh round.

8. February 7, 1967, Houston. Muhammad Ali-Ernie Terrell match. Ali won, thus keeping his title.
9. February 25, 1964, Miami Beach. Clay-Liston match. Quick as lighting, Clay dodges Sonny Liston, a formidable bruiser. The winning champion is only 22 years old, and before him stretches an unparalleled career.

HELENA RUBINSTEIN

Died rich and famous in Paris

Helena Rubinstein, known today simply as HR, was born around 1872 in Krakow, the ancient capital of Poland, the oldest of eight girls, to an international merchant and art collector. She grew up in a lively, wealthy home. An avid reader, after completing high school she wanted to study medicine but was turned off by the sight of blood and the smell of disinfectants. She learned how to manage a large household from her mother; from her father, she absorbed the experience and the sense of the business world. Her strong family and the affection of family and friends gave her a sense of self and made her an optimist. After a love affair ended, she left to visit cousins in Australia. As the Australian climate was harsh on women's skin, Rubinstein started importing the cream she had used at home, with modest success. Back in Europe, not content with the prospect of being a housewife, she studied with dermatologists, nutritionists, endocrinologists, and surgeons. Again in Australia, she set up company branches, and her business grew. Rubinstein would exhaustively test the products she invented. She had a great sense of organization. All this contributed to her wealth and success.

1

2

3

CARING FOR THE BODY. When all is said and done, Rubinstein started a business, like countless others; yet she accomplished much more than that, for she helped create one of the great myths of our century: the care of the body and the pursuit of a physical sense of well-being. Helena was among the first to understand the importance of a proper diet, of physical exercise, of a way of life focused on preventing the deterioration of the body. For her, beauty was the result of care, will power, and perseverance: self-discipline assisted and promoted by cosmetic products. She did not see this activity as an end in itself, but as the right way of existing in a world where we have a duty to promote beauty in all its forms. As the ancient Greeks used to say, beauty *is* goodness.

ART. Rubinstein was an avid collector of art objects, paintings, and sculptures, and befriended artists, writers, and poets. However, even this hobby was secondary to her business and she did not allow her personal image to take the place of her products' image.

EAU DE FRANCE. Here is Rubinstein's recipe against age wrinkles: 32 grains of incense powder (*Olibanum*), 32 of benzoin powder, 32 of Arabic gum powder, 48 of sweet almond powder, 16 of cloves, 16 of nutmeg, 8 ounces of scentless alcohol. An English grain is equal to 0.0648 grams.

OTHER BRANDS became well-known in this period. For example, Max Factor became the makeup of Hollywood's silent-movie stars. Later, Elizabeth Arden was to open many beauty salons in the more important cities, and Guerlain, an old French family of perfume makers, was to become well-known for its excellent perfumes.

BEAUTÉ AND BEAUTY

Helena Rubinstein made several trips to Europe from Australia; finally, she established herself in London, with her company's headquarters in the home of the Marquis of Salisbury, then English Prime Minister—which she transformed and decorated. London's high society did not look favorably on outsiders, but the city was a cradle of luxury in a fabulously rich empire. Rubinstein worked hard at her business and lived grandly. She married a well-known literary figure and they had two sons. She was happy in her roles of wife and mother, but also needed to be active in her beauty business. She was able to please the most demanding ladies and served royal and aristocratic families. During World War I, queens and empresses would employ special couriers to supply them with Rubinstein products. Helena herself used to say: "Wars come and go, but beauty must last forever."

Although Lon-

5

4

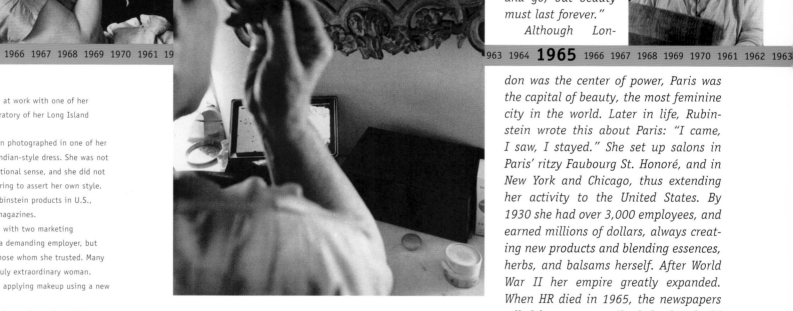

6

1. Helena Rubinstein at work with one of her chemists in the laboratory of her Long Island factory.
2. Madame Rubinstein photographed in one of her homes, wearing an Indian-style dress. She was not a beauty in the traditional sense, and she did not dress trendily, preferring to assert her own style.
3. Ads for Helena Rubinstein products in U.S., British, and French magazines.
4. Helena Rubinstein with two marketing executives. She was a demanding employer, but was generous with those whom she trusted. Many remember her as a truly extraordinary woman.
5. Helena Rubinstein applying makeup using a new type of brush.
6. Rubinstein relaxes by reading a financial newspaper. An excellent, meticulous businesswoman, she had great self-reliance.

don was the center of power, Paris was the capital of beauty, the most feminine city in the world. Later in life, Rubinstein wrote this about Paris: "I came, I saw, I stayed." She set up salons in Paris' ritzy Faubourg St. Honoré, and in New York and Chicago, thus extending her activity to the United States. By 1930 she had over 3,000 employees, and earned millions of dollars, always creating new products and blending essences, herbs, and balsams herself. After World War II her empire greatly expanded. When HR died in 1965, the newspapers called her a queen. She helped to build the myth of beauty and well-being, which was to become even more important in later years.

"Being surrounded by lovely objects . . . is important for the health of the soul . . . as important as being able to attract because of our physical aspect. "
Helena Rubinstein, *The Art of Feminine Beauty*

THE BEATLES

At the height of their career

At the end of 1957, John Lennon (1940–1980) and Paul McCartney (b. 1942) were already playing guitar and singing together at the Cavern Club, a Liverpool, England, club. In 1958 Paul brought another guitar player, his friend George Harrison (b. 1943) into the band, and they played in many clubs, including several in Hamburg, Germany. They took the name of the Beatles, an homage to the beat. In 1962 they hired a clever manager, Brian Epstein, and in the same year they were joined by drummer Ringo Starr (b. 1940). Their first recorded single was *Love Me Do;* the second, *Please Please Me,* which in the following year was the title of their first nationally successful album. In 1963 *With the Beatles* was the best-selling album in England.

In 1964 the Beatles first toured the United States and achieved worldwide acclaim. They also starred in their first film, *A Hard Day's Night*. In the same year, statues of the Beatles were added to Madame Tussaud's Wax Museum in London. In 1965 they starred in their second film, *Help!*, and Queen Elizabeth II named them members of the Order of the British Empire. In a 1966 interview, John Lennon claimed that the Beatles were more popular than Jesus Christ, which angered many people. Their records were burned in the United States and there were riots during their last international tour. After that, each of the Beatles started to perform independently.

A GOLDEN SUNSET. In 1967 the Beatles recorded their sensational album *Sgt. Pepper's Lonely Hearts Club Band*. They also sang live, over satellite TV, to an audience of 400 million, *All You Need is Love*. They were attracted to the Maharishi Mahesh Yogi, an Indian guru, and followed his transcendental meditation course. When Brian Epstein died, Apple Records, the Beatles empire, was born. They filmed *Yellow Submarine*, a cartoon movie. In 1970 Paul McCartney left the group, and

they each embarked on solo careers, but their solo successes were not as great as their earlier success as a group.

JOHN LENNON. A composer, singer, guitarist, and keyboard player, John was perhaps the most intellectually gifted of the four. In 1969 he married Yoko Ono, an ambitious Japanese musician and artist, one of the reasons, it was rumored, for the Beatles' breakup. John formed a band with her, The Plastic Ono Band. John also published

poetry. He was killed in 1980 by a mentally deranged man in New York City, in front of the building where the couple lived.

SWINGING LONDON. Young men dressed in Edwardian attire, girls in Mary

POP MUSIC

1. The Beatles and friends with their mystical guru in India.

2. The Beatles in the splendid years of their youth and success. They had the courage to dare new forms. They had luck and talent.

3. 1994. Thirty years after the Beatles performed in Hollywood.

4. A giant poster of the Beatles during their Tokyo tour.

5. The Beatles in Elizabethan-inspired costumes. The spirit of *The Merry Wives of Windsor* was alive in some of their costumes and tomfoolery.

6. No longer mischievous, the Beatles' pose reflects their waning youth.

7. Fans weeping at John Lennon's tragic, unexpected death.

8. *Sgt. Pepper's Lonely Hearts Club Band,* a light-hearted album cover of the Beatles in the heyday of the flower power age.

9. 10. Covers of two other famous albums: *Please Please Me* and *Yellow Submarine*.

Popular music, pop for short, is not folk music—the latter is based on a country or ethnic group's culture or tradition—nor is it country music, which is the popular music of non-urbanized areas. Rock in all its varieties is, however, a pop music genre. The term "pop" came into use in the 1960s, but is not synonymous with light music. Pop is generally performed in English because 1960s London was the capital of young fashion, and because since the 1930s American English has been the language of jazz, of Bing Crosby, Frank Sinatra ("The Voice"), and Fred Astaire (1899–1987), the unsurpassed dancer and singer. On the other hand, light music usually has a national flavor and belongs to all ages, while pop is the music of young Americans or those who want to imitate them. And it was the Beatles' music that ignited a fire in the pop music world that spread from Liverpool to the American coasts, even to Japan. The group was the perfect embodiment of the synthesis that is pop: band music, with the band members in flexible roles as composers and performers, and great attention to rhythm and to sound amplification. The Beatles were also unique for their rich melody (rare in pop music), and their especially endearing, youthful grace.

1 196... 1965 **1966** 1967 1968 1969 1970 1961 1962 1963 1964 1965 **1966** 1967 1968 1969 1970 1961 1962 1963 1964

5

6

7

8

9

10

Quant miniskirts, night made into day in crowded city streets, young people drinking beer and singing while strumming their guitars and smoking pot like the American beat writers of the fifties, young people flocking to London from all over Europe. And they did not forget to bring home the latest Beatles album.

"None of us ever thought about things like the future . . . some nights were good, some were bad, in our tours . . . our only fun was . . . getting together at night to smoke grass or things like that."
Ringo Starr

CHE GUEVARA

Murdered in Bolivia

Ernesto Guevara de la Serna was born in 1928 to a middle-class family in Rosario, Argentina, and attended medical school. Argentina was then a wealthy South American country whose resources came mainly from farming and cattle. The attraction of the Mexican peasants' revolution was still very strong, and Guevara left Peronist Argentina and emigrated to Mexico, Ecuador, and Costa Rica. He befriended Guatemala's Democratic president, Jacobo Arbenz Guzmán, and became his assistant. The coup engineered by the CIA in Guatemala forced him to flee. He made friends with the Cuban exiles who had fled Fulgencio Batista's dictatorship (1952–1959). Landing in Cuba with Fidel and Raúl Castro, he fought in the guerrilla war (1957–1959) that attacked the dictator from the Sierra Maestra in the southeastern part of the island. He first killed a man in the Arroyo del Infierno attack. Castro called him to the revolutionary executive committee. In 1959, they liberated Havana. For several years, Che was Cuba's minister of industry. But Che did not like occupying a position of power. On October 3, 1965, Castro announced that Che had relinquished his Cuban citizenship. After that, wherever there was a breeding ground of rebellion, Che was there. On October 9, 1967, the Bolivian dictatorship suddenly announced that a revolutionary had been killed in the Waucakakwazu jungle: it was Che.

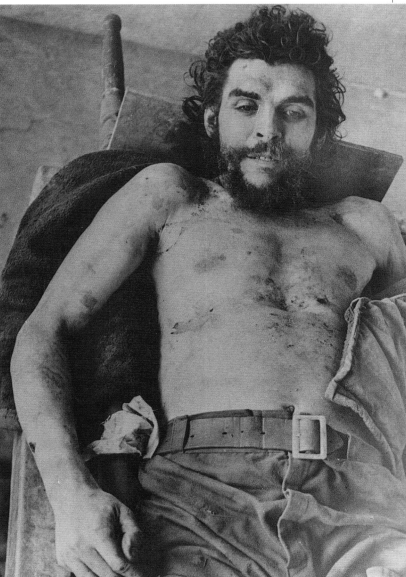

964 1965 1966 **1967** 1968 1969 1970 1961 1962 1963 1964 1965 1966 **1967** 1968 1969 19

SHAKING THE WORLD. In 1964 Che was given the welcome of a statesman and hero in Socialist countries that were sensitive to his message of freedom. He visited China, Africa, and Algeria. He dreamed of gathering forces to light one hundred, one thousand fires of revolt.

CHE'S WRITINGS. Che wrote letters, historical essays, and theoretical works that he published where he thought they might make an impact. In 1966, in Paris it was *La guerre de guérilla* (*Guerrilla Warfare*) and *Le socialisme et l'homme à Cuba* (*Man and Socialism in Cuba*). In 1968, his *Reminiscences of the Cuban Revolutionary War* was published in London. In Turin, Italy, in 1974 a collection of *Scritti, discorsi e diari di guerriglia* (*Guerrilla Writings, Speeches, Diaries*) was published.

THE EVE OF A MOVEMENT. Che was 39

" . . . I swear I will not stop until the capitalist octopus is destroyed . . . I want to perfect myself to become a true revolutionary. "
Young Che writing to Aunt Beatriz

GUERRILLA FIGHTER

Latin America's modern history began with the struggle for independence from Spain. In 1898, the United States won the Spanish-American War and seized the Philippines and Cuba from Spain, turning them into de facto U.S. colonies. In 1903, President Theodore Roosevelt (1901–1908) organized a mini-revolution and seized land from Colombia, which was then excavated to create the Panama Canal. In 1910–1928 a whole series of revolutionary movements shook Mexico, as landless peasants claimed a share of the land. Great leaders such as Pancho Villa (1878–1923) and Emiliano Zapata (1879–1919) led the guerrilla war against the golpista presidents.

The expansion of the United Fruit Company brought a new type of colonialism to Latin America, forcing single-crop farming on local communities, with disastrous results for the natives. Young Guevara wrote that the United Fruit Company was like an octopus, with an appalling amount of power. For him, the only possible form of protest against capitalism was guerrilla warfare. A handsome, well-educated radical ideologue who suffered from asthma, Guevara

was always courageous and never sought power for himself. He became the very image of the guerrilla chieftain ready to gamble his life for the rights of the wretched and the oppressed against the implacable power of capitalism. His equivocal death, perhaps the result of a betrayal, made Che into a saint, a hero for all people, young and old, who yearn for freedom and justice, a model for guerrilla fighters all over the world.

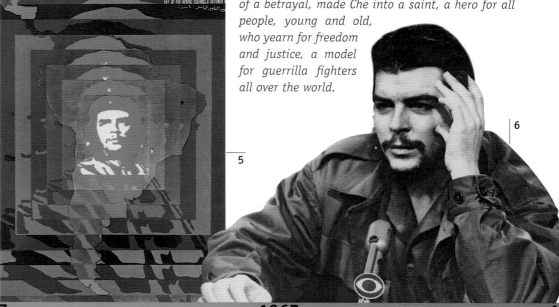

5

6

1967 1968 1969 1970 1961 1962 1963 1964 1965 1966 **1967** 1968 1969 1970 1961 1962 1963 1964 1965 1966 **1967** 1968 1969 1970 1961 1962 1963 1964 1965 1966 19

7

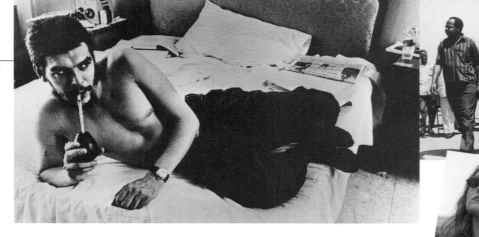

4

when he died surrounded by the misery of peasants stupefied by poverty and fear of the military, like a revolutionary St. Francis of Assisi. The following year was 1968. From Berkeley to the Sorbonne, his image on buttons, T-shirts, and posters, Che became the martyr saint of rebel youth. Even today posters of Che can be found in student dorm rooms along with those of the other martyrs of

eternal youth, James Dean and Elvis Presley.

MEANWHILE, the networks broadcast shows such as *Bonanza* (NBC, 1962–1973), *Star Trek* (NBC, first series 1966–1969), *The FBI* (ABC, 1965–1974). In June the Six Day War was fought in the Middle East and Israel captured the Sinai territory from Egypt and seized land in Syria and Jordan.

8

1. Mexico. Guevara with Universo Sanchez before joining the guerrilla warfare against Batista in Cuba.

2. On the left is Che; at his left is Fidel Castro. An impromptu meeting of the chiefs of staff during the guerrilla war in Cuba's Sierra Madre.

3. October 10, 1967, Vallegrande, Bolivia. A close-up of Che Guevara dead.

4. Che Guevara relaxes sipping *maté*, a mildly stimulating infusion made with *Ilex paraguariensis* leaves, traditionally used in South America.

5. A portrait of Che transformed into a graphic icon of our times. Even today some magazines for young people periodically give away Guevara posters.

6. Cuba. Che speaks on the radio.

7. 1966. Che Guevara is welcomed by the authorities upon arriving in the Congo.

8. Young people marching. It could be any city in the West. The poster of Che is a common symbol of all the different leftist groups.

ARISTOTLE ONASSIS

Married President Kennedy's widow

Aristotle Onassis was born in 1905 to a merchant family in Smyrna, a port city in Anatolia containing Greek, Jewish, Armenian, and Turkish districts. In 1918 the city counted 300,000 inhabitants, one third of them Greeks who had strong feelings of national identity, which intensified as Turkish nationalism fermented. In 1914, Italy was promised Anatolia in exchange for entering the world war. However, at the conclusion of the war the powers meeting in Paris in 1918 authorized Greece to occupy the region. Atatürk then led a Turkish insurrection that routed the Greeks and seized the area. The city's Greek quarter was set on fire and sacked, the Greeks killed. Among those lucky enough to survive the attack was Onassis, who emigrated to the United States.

By the 1950s he was a shipowner who became wealthy transporting petroleum. He married Athina Livanos, who came from an important shipowning family. Onassis even built an airline and owned vast real estate properties, including hotels. He was *the* Greek tycoon, dividing his time between New York, London, Paris, and Monte Carlo. His last marriage was to Jacqueline Bouvier Kennedy, widow of President Kennedy.

62 1963 1964 1965 1966 1967 **1968** 1969 1970 1961

"*Greece has one of the largest merchant fleets in the world which was developed . . . thanks particularly to the unscrupulous initiatives of shipowners such as Niarchos and Onassis . . .***"**
Silvio Paolucci, *L'Europa (Europe)*.

THE PHANARIOTS. In the seventeenth century a new class began to rise in the Ottoman Empire. They were either Greek or of Greek customs and they took their name from their city quarter (Fanar, which means lighthouse) in Istanbul on the Golden Horn. They were active in trafficking and shipping, and had ongoing relations with the large Mediterranean ports, from Venice to Alexandria. The Phanariots usually knew several languages and were useful to the Turkish court. They were governors of the Balkan principalities. They were to be the soul of the Greek Renaissance. They were an example to all Greek merchants and patriots, from Anatolia and the Nile River delta to the Black Sea ports and the Arab sheikdoms.

THE THEATRICS OF POWER. *Forbes* regularly publishes a reliable list of the wealthiest people in the world. Some of these modern-day Croesuses are known figures, but some are unknown to the masses. The known billionaires often appear in the press that covers their leisure time activities and their love stories, but the press rarely discusses their "real" business, and then only when the game is over.

THE SILENCE OF POWER. Very powerful

THE JET SET

Onassis bought an entire island, Skorpios, in the fashion of the great shipowners. The other major Greek shipowning families, such as Niarchos and Livanos, are related to Onassis by marriage. A Ulysses in his leisure time, he wandered the Mediterranean on a yacht where the powerful of the Earth were his guests, especially the powerful of yesteryear. He was close to Maria Callas, the opera star, but went on to marry Jackie Bouvier, an icon of the Kennedy cult. Like other Greek tycoons, he was followed by the paparazzi and by dark rumors. Onassis lost his son Alexander in a tragic accident. His image grew; he was a Greek-Yankee autocrat of our time.

5 | 9 |

1966 1967 **1968** 1969 1970 1961 1962 1963 **1968** 1969 | 1964 1965 196

7 | 8 | 6 |

men and women often prefer to be silent. While they also travel on jets, they use spaces exclusively reserved for them in the airports. They visit famous places before they become famous. They rarely travel: they make others travel. They write little: they make others write. They use discreet methods of communication. If we were to meet them face to face, they would probably go unnoticed.

At his death in 1975, Onassis left all his estate to his daughter. Later, Onassis's daughter married an unknown Russian, had a child, and died young. The tabloids that make their money from gossiping about the jet set—what used to be called high society—usually make no distinction between those who really belong to the jet set and those who join it for a short time or who are merely hangers-on. Often, even the names of the most powerful individuals and families are unknown. Stories about the flashy Onassis were fodder for the tabloids.

NEIL ARMSTRONG

The first man to walk on the moon

Neil A. Armstrong was born in Ohio in 1930. An engineering graduate (like the Soviet Yuri Gagarin), he married and had two children. During the Korean War he served as a Navy pilot. In 1962 he went to work for NASA as a civilian, and in 1966 was made a member of the *Gemini 8* crew. The second man on the team was Air Force Colonel Edwin Aldrin, from New Jersey, also

1

3

born in 1930, an MIT graduate in space mechanics. Michael Collins, the *Apollo 11* pilot, born in the same year, a former West Point cadet, had already flown as a member of the *Gemini 10* crew. The *Apollo 11* mission lifted off from Florida's Kennedy Space Center on July 16. The spaceship approached the moon and started orbiting around it. While Collins remained on board, Aldrin and Armstrong left the ship on the LEM (Lunar Excursion Module), and on the night of July 20 Armstrong went down the ladder and left his boot mark on the moon's dusty soil. Later, it was Aldrin's turn. They collected 50 pounds of rock samples and took many photographs. All the images were transmitted to Earth, and the moon landing was seen all over the world on television. On July 24, the *Apollo 11* landed on schedule in the Pacific Ocean with the astronauts safely on board.

63 1964 1965 1966 1967 1968 **1969** 1970 1961 1962 1963 1964   66 1967 1968 **1969** 1970 1961 1962 1963 1964 1965

2

THE FIRST STEPS. On October 4, 1957 Soviet technology shocked the world when it sent into orbit the first artificial satellite, *Sputnik I,* which weighed 184 lbs. and completed a full revolution around the Earth in 95 minutes. On November 3, 1957, the Soviet Union sent into orbit *Sputnik II,* which weighed more than 1,100 lbs. and carried a dog on board, Laika, that survived six days—as long as there was oxygen in the capsule. It demonstrated that a mammal can survive even in the absence of gravity.

TOWARD THE MOON. On September 13, 1959 a Soviet missile crashed on the moon's surface; it carried instruments that during the flight had picked up and transmitted scientific data to Earth. The Soviet government then announced that no country should try to colonize the moon. The following month, in October, a Soviet probe, the

Luna III, captured on film the hidden face of the moon, transmitting the images to Earth.

THE FIRST COSMONAUT. On April 12, 1961 a small spaceship called the *Vostok I* was sent into orbit manned by Soviet

Major Yuri Gagarin (1934–1968). It circled the Earth in an elliptical orbit, at an altitude of between 108 and 209 miles. The whole world was deeply touched by this feat.

SHADOWS OF WAR. Von Braun estimated that Soviet technology was about five years ahead of United States technology. The powerful long-range Soviet missiles had an especially deep impact on public opinion. People thought that the artificial satellites circling the Earth were espionage instruments. The NATO countries were not especially pleased about the extraordinary scientific advances evidenced by Soviet space exploration.

4

176

LANDING ON THE MOON

We don't know when human beings first noticed that the moon appears sickle-shaped in the sky, grows larger night by night, becomes a perfect disk, then wanes until it's a sickle-shaped sliver and the cycle begins again. Nor do we know when man started measuring time based on the lunar months or realized that the lunar cycle corresponds to other cycles in the natural world.

In various times and cultures, the full moon has been interpreted in various ways. According to the fourteenth-century Italian poet Dante, one could see in it the face of Cain. From the Greek poet Lucian of Samosata (second century A.D.), to Ludovico Ariosto (1474–1533), to Cyrano de Bergerac (1619–1955), just to mention a few, writers and poets imagined travels by sea,

1969 1970 1961 1962 1963 1964 1965 1966 1967 1968 **1969** 1970 1965 1966 19

empires, and follies on the moon. A decisive step toward a physical approach was taken by Galileo Galilei (1564–1642) in 1610. The telescope he invented (or perfected), permitted the eye to see enlarged images of the lunar crust and he rationally described seas and mountains. The Italian poet Giacomo Leopardi (1798–1837) sang of the moon as a "wandering and lonely, unapproachable land." When Armstrong landed on the moon in 1969, that was no longer the case.

1. Armstrong, Collins, and Aldrin in a photograph distributed by NASA, like the other photos on these pages. Von Braun was director of NASA at the time.
2. July 20, 1969, the moon. Footprint of a human step.
3. July 20, 1969, the moon. Armstrong salutes the United States flag he pitched on the moon's surface.
4. April 12, 1961. Yuri Gagarin, the first cosmo-

naut, in the *Vostok I* space capsule that was put into orbit.
5. July 16, 1969. lift-off.
6. July 24, 1969. Aircraft carrier *U.S.S. Hornet*, Pacific Ocean. President Nixon follows the retrieval of the *Apollo 11* capsule.
7. July 1969. The Earth as seen from *Apollo 11* at a distance of 100,000 miles.
8. July 1969, Houston. Aldrin and Armstrong in the NASA space center's cafeteria.

"That's one small step for [a] man, one giant leap for mankind."
Neil Armstrong, July 20, 1969

Filmed *Trash*, an underground cult movie

Andrew Warhola (1930–1987) was born in Pittsburgh. After studying at the Carnegie Institute of Technology, he worked as an advertising artist and tried his hand at painting in the early 1950s. In 1952 he held his first show in New York, with drawings for author Truman Capote (1924–1984), the arbiter of society life. He achieved amazing international success starting in 1964. His work was shown in New York at the gallery of Leo Castelli—the art dealer who "invented" mass art (the term "pop art" was coined by English critic Lawrence Alloway) and at Sonnabend in Paris. In 1966–1967 his works were shown in contemporary art museums in Philadelphia, Amsterdam, Stockholm, Chicago, Paris, and London.

Warhol was probably the best-known pop artist; he traveled extensively, watching the world in silence through his camera lens. Warhol also made films. He was rich and influential. His home and studio ("the Factory") were the undisputed sanctuary of underground culture. He died of complications from AIDS. Hundreds of gifts to himself from his trips around the world were found in his home, the packages unopened.

Andy Warhol

1962 1963 19   **1970** 1961 1962 1963 1964 1965 1966 1967 1968 1969 **1970** 1961 1962 19

> *"Perhaps future generations will think of Andy . . . as the saintly prostitute of the history of art who . . . passively accepted the attentions of the public . . . which buys an artist rather than his art."*
>
> Barbara Rose

FRIENDS. After his death, Warhol's friends appeared from every corner. The Factory had been open to young people. Some became friends and assisted Warhol in his work. Unstable, often united by drug use and involved in love-hate relationships, Paul Morrissey, Brigit Polk, Joe Dallesandro, Billy Linich, Gerard Malanga, Jed Johnson were all linked with his work in some way.

OTHERS. Other U.S. pop artists were not so trendy in life. Roy Lichtenstein (b. 1923), who started as an abstract expressionist painter, is known for his huge images of cartoon characters and masterpieces of the past. Robert Rauschenberg (b. 1925) started as a New Dada artist and won the grand prize for painting at the Venice Biennial in 1964. Sculptor Claes Oldenburg (b. 1929) is known for his soft sculptures and gigantic food sculptures. Tom Wesselman (b. 1931) made his

UNDERGROUND

1. Self-portrait, 1967. Acrylic, screen-printing on canvas.

2. 1967. The famous banana painted by Warhol for the cover of the *The Velvet Underground & Nico* record album, which Warhol himself produced.

3. A panel of *Elvis I and II,* 1964. Aluminum and screen-printing on canvas.

4. Joe Dallesandro and Jane Forth in a frame from *Trash,* the film Paul Morissey and Warhol directed in 1970.

5. *200 Campbell's Soup Cans* and, front, *Campbell's Soup Can with Can Opener.* The dimensions are impressive: both works are about 6' high. Acrylic on canvas.

6. *Marilyn Dyptich,* 1962. Two panels. Acrylic, screen-printing on canvas.

7. Top: *Muhammad Ali* (Cassius Clay), 1977, and *Grace Jones,* 1986. Bottom: *Roy Lichtenstein,* 1976, and *Mao,* 1973. Acrylic, screen-printing on canvas.

8. *Vote McGovern,* 1972. Detail, print on paper. The face is that of President Nixon, who in 1972 was re-elected over Democratic candidate George McGovern.

Pop art was the 1960s movement that shook the foundations of the international art world. The twentieth century had already seen famous U.S. artists such as Man Ray (1890–1976) and Jackson Pollock (1912–1956). Pop art was an American movement; its leading artists were all American. Pop art was a figurative art that took daily life and banal situations as its subjects and often used graphic art techniques from advertising. Everyone looking at it thought they could understand it. Of all the pop artists, Warhol probably enjoyed the longest popularity and had the greatest influence on the mass media's techniques and styles. His techniques were impersonal, cold, industrial, and included photo-collage, photo silk printing, and multiple reproductions.

As subjects, Warhol chose the icons of Hollywood such as Marilyn Monroe, Marlon Brando, Liz Taylor; of music—Elvis Presley, Grace Jones; of politics—Nixon, Mao; of fast food—Campbell's soup, "the 20th century Mona Lisa"; the horror of daily life—Race Riot, Electric Chair; road accidents, or "poetic trivia" such as flowers. Each subject was interpreted, reduced, colored, and multiplied in a glacial, automatic, decorative report that was glaring, refined. In films, this

966 1967 1968 1969 **1970** 1961 1962 1963 1964 1965 1966 1967 1968 1969 **1970** 1961 1962 1963 1964 1965 1966 1967 19   64 1965 19

objectifying was applied to taboo themes such as drugs, nudity, alternative sexual lifestyles, urban waste, underground deviance. People, things, places, trips, acts, animate and inanimate objects, sleep, silence, all met without emotion, in a dim light. Warhol's films also made him an idol.

name with a striking series of "great" American nudes.

SUCCESS. Pop art and the activism of Warhol, who was also a publisher, had a strong influence in the West; it also

marked a split between U.S. and European artists. Americans no longer believed in the primacy of the Old World, while Europeans strove to regain it. It was not a question of politics, for all the new art trends still considered

themselves to be "left-wing." America's art and culture at the time was striving to impose itself on the world.

MEANWHILE. Two winners of the Nobel Prize for literature died in 1970: the

English mathematician, philosopher, and pacifist Lord Bertrand Russell (b. 1872) and the French novelist François Mauriac (b. 1885). The Osaka World's Fair, which opened in 1970, highlighted the power and wealth of Japan.

1971

MARLON BRANDO

THE RIACE BRONZES

KONRAD LORENZ

WILLY BRANDT

JUAN CARLOS I

THE TERRA-COTTA ARMY

BOKASSA

GOLDA MEIR

RUHOLLAH KHOMEINI

RONALD REAGAN

In the West color television became a common household appliance. Many could now afford a vacation home, or could pay for vacations abroad. Clothing, cars, house furnishings, toys, appliances . . . everything had to have a famous logo. The volume of consumer goods skyrocketed. In 1972 *The Limits to Growth,* a study prepared by MIT and commissioned by the Club of Rome, was published; it painted a disturbing picture of the Earth's environment, with catastrophic mid-term projections. Because both the study's sponsor and the university had close ties to the corporations and groups that were the prime movers of industrial development and the growth of consumerism, the study had a powerful impact on public opinion. In December 1973 the oil-producing countries, organized in the OPEC cartel, approved a substantial increase in the price of crude oil, reminding the world that fossil fuel is not an inexhaustible resource.

I n 1976 a chemical plant spewed a deadly cloud of dioxin in Seveso, in northern Italy, with adverse effects on the local population and the coun-

Much devastation was caused by the 1978 oil spill from the *Amoco Cadiz* tanker, which sank along the coast of Brittany in northern France, spilling 220,000 tons of crude petroleum into the ocean. The marine and coastal environments were devastated by several such disasters, with immediate effects on plant and animal life.

tryside. In 1979 a nuclear disaster occurred at the Three Mile Island nuclear power plant in Pennsylvania. Wealth and high consumption seemed to threaten the Earth; in the long run, even the very life of the planet. In 1872 Yellowstone National Park, the first national park, was born out of a romantic awareness of the environment. A century later, the first environmental groups were born. In the 1970s environmentalism became a mass movement that saw the birth of associations to safeguard the environment and the natural, historical, and artistic heritage of countries. Animal-rights and anti-nuclear associations were also born. The "Greens" became an important political force first in Germany and then throughout Western Europe.

The 1971 Pakistan elections heightened that country's tensions and the gap between the western region and Bengal, the smaller region east of India. The conflict between Prime Minister Zulfikar Ali Kahn Bhutto (1929–1979) and the leader of East Pakistan, Mujibur Rahman, was intensified by President Yahya Khan, who called in the army. An emigration of biblical proportions saw people moving from East Bengal to the Indian Bengal region. India then attacked Pakistan and eventually eastern Pakistan became an independent state, taking the name of Bangladesh. Bhutto was deposed in 1977 and hanged by his successor, Zia

ul-Haq. Elsewhere, while a guarded détente was developing between NATO and Warsaw Pact countries and between the United States and China, in 1971 half a million people marched on Washington to protest the Vietnam War. Many in the United States could not accept the loss of American soldiers, the killing of Vietnamese civilians, or the war's inhumane methods. In 1975 Saigon fell; the United States had stopped bombing North Vietnam in 1973. The *Washington Post* published a

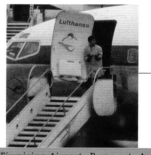

story on a break-in at the Watergate Democratic campaign offices during the 1972 election campaign. Undone by his own lies in connection with the scandal, Nixon resigned on August 8, 1974.

Several high-level politicians were suspected of accepting bribes to favor the purchase of Lockheed aircraft; in Holland, Prince Bernhard, married to the Queen, was among the accused.

An undeclared war raged in the Middle East. Palestinians were without a homeland, pushed from one territory to another, occasionally massacred by Muslim fundamentalists; some embraced terrorism. Lebanon was a raging fire. In 1979 President Carter succeeded in bringing together Egypt and Israel for peace talks at Camp David. In 1973, Chile's military staged a coup, murdering Socialist President Salvador Allende, who had nationalized the copper mines, and a long, brutal dicta-

1. Against the Vietnam War. 2. Prince Bernhard. 3. A Palestinian terrorist at Fiumicino Airport, Rome. 4. Andreas Baade

THIS WAS THE DECADE OF THE SHEIKS. ALTHOUGH DEMOGRAPHICALLY TINY AND POLITICALLY UNIMPORTANT, THE MIDDLE EAST OIL-PRODUCING POTENTATES ARE FINANCIAL GIANTS WHO ALSO INVEST HEAVILY ABROAD. ON PAPER, IN 1975, EVERY UNITED ARAB EMIRATES CITIZEN HAD AN AVERAGE PER CAPITA INCOME DOUBLE THAT OF A U.S. CITIZEN. UNDERDEVELOPMENT NO LONGER WAS SYNONYMOUS WITH POVERTY.

torship followed; in 1976 in Argentina, an even more brutal military dictatorship seized power. However, the 1974 coup in Portugal was bloodless (it was dubbed "the carnation revolution"): it brought democracy to the country and independence to the Portuguese colonies of Mozambique and Angola. East Timor, on the other hand, was invaded by Indonesia and plummeted into a civil war. In 1974, there was a

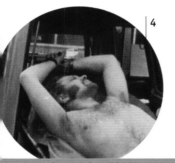

4

military *putsch* in Ethiopia: Haile Selassie, the 225th King of Kings, was deposed and replaced by a bloody left-wing dictatorship.

While Islamic terrorists hijacked airplanes, Western European terrorists caused different kinds of calamities. In Ireland, the Catholic-Protestant "troubles" intensified. In Italy, the death in

1972 of a wealthy publisher marked the beginning of a wave of terrorism. In 1978 the Red Brigade, a left-wing terrorist group, kidnapped and killed Aldo Moro, President of the Christian Democratic Party; in 1980 a terrorist bomb killed over 80 people at the Bologna railroad station.

In Munich in 1972, Palestinian terrorists murdered Israeli athletes during the Olympic Games.

6

The activity of the German Baader-Meinhof left-wing terrorist group between 1971 and 1977 ended with an unlikely collective suicide in jail.

Horror was both public and private. In California, in 1969, Charles Manson and three followers of his "Satanic sect" entered the mansion of film director Roman Polanski and killed his pregnant wife, Sharon Tate. In 1973, in Italy, the *camorra* kidnapped J. Paul Getty III and cut his ear off to secure a ransom of

one million dollars; in 1975, near Rome, writer and film director Pier Paolo Pasolini was murdered. Pasolini had just finished *Salò*, a film depicting the Marquis de Sade's *The 120 Days of Sodom* atrocities, set in the short-lived 1945 Fascist Republic of Salò.

In 1978, in a Guyana jungle, 913 followers of the People's Temple, a California sect, committed mass suicide.

7

8

Some of this century's greats died in this decade: among them, the American poet Ezra Pound (1885–1972) and the German philosopher Martin Heidegger (1889–1976).

In 1976 in France, René Goscinny died (b. 1927). He created the Celtic heroes Astérix and

Obélix, illustrated by Uderzo. His cartoons depicted the ancient Romans as cowardly dolts, making you wonder how they could ever have conquered an empire that stretched from Portugal to Mesopotamia.

In 1976 the American economist Milton Friedman received the Nobel Prize in economics. Friedman, a radical free-market proponent, was an advisor to Chile's dictator Pinochet and greatly influenced right-wing English and

errare Romanum est, hi! hi

9

10

American politicians. In 1977, in Paris, the Pompidou Centre, a new type of museum and cultural center, opened its doors. It was built on the grounds of Les Halles, which had been demolished in 1971.

In 1980 Italy's Umberto Eco published *The Name of the Rose*, which became an international bestseller.

5. State funeral for Aldo Moro.   6. J. Paul Getty III.   7. Mass suicide of People's Temple followers.   8. Ezra Pound.   9. Obélix by Goscinny.   10. The Pompidou Centre.

MARLON BRANDO

A star in transition

Buddy Brando was born in 1924 in Omaha, Nebraska, to a small businessman and a frustrated amateur actress who became an alcoholic. A difficult high school student, he was sent to a Minnesota military academy that expelled him in 1943, just before graduation. He then moved to New York where he enrolled in Erwin Piscator's school and joined his acting company. The great director said this of Brando: "He possesses an interior rhythm that never fails." He met Elia Kazan, who in 1947 was to found the Actors' Studio, directed by Lee Strasberg and Stella Adler. In 1947 he starred in his most memorable stage triumph as Stanley Kowalski in *A Streetcar Named Desire*, under Kazan's direction. The play was made into a movie in 1951, in which he starred with Vivien Leigh (1913–1967). Having left the stage in 1950, Brando starred in *The Men,* a motion picture masterpiece, *Julius Caesar* (1953) (where he played Antony), and Kazan's *On the Waterfront* (1954). But other

performances were not as fortunate: overly made up, he starred in *Viva Zapata!* (1952), and in the ludicrous *Desirée* (1954) where he played Napoleon. In 1954 he also starred in *The Wild One*, where he played a "bad guy," glorifying what came to be known as the Brando type.

1

2

3

4

"No actor in the history of film was able to use his body with such a sharp sense of the expressive force it projected. "
René Jordan

FLOPS. A series of failed films in the 1950s: *Guys and Dolls* (1955), with Frank Sinatra and Jean Simmons; *Teahouse of the August Moon* (1956); *Sayonara* (1957), the most composed of his youthful work; *The Young Lions* (1958) with Montgomery Clift and Maximilian Schell; *One-Eyed Jacks* (1961), which he also directed; *The Fugitive Kind* (1959) with Anna Magnani; *Mutiny on the Bounty* (1962) in the role of Christian that had been Clark Gable's.

OUT OF LUCK. It was difficult for a director to create a masterpiece with Brando in the leading role. However, in the 1960s Brando made a number of films in which he gave exceptional performances by remaining true to himself while muting the aggressiveness of his more youthful roles. In *The*

Ugly American (1963) he played a born loser; in *Bedtime Story* (1964) (in which he co-starred with David Niven), he distorted some of his past performances; in *Reflections in a Golden Eye* (1967), directed by John Huston, co-starring with Liz Taylor, he played a demented homosexual offi-

cer. None of these films were box office successes when they were first released.

MATURITY. While his private life became increasingly troubled, Marlon Brando became increasingly active in the fight against racism and war. Francis Ford Coppola's *The Godfather* (1972), made

CHILDISH MACHO

Not too tall, compact and athletic, with a very handsome face he spoiled when he broke his nose in fist fights with stage hands, Brando as a young man was extremely shy, full of sex appeal, and endowed with the gift of communicating his emotions and physical states viscerally, with his body. But he was so arrogant and uncommunicative that he created problems for directors. During his years as a leading actor he refused to coordinate his acting with that of the other actors, so as to create a unified, collective whole, the achievement of great films. The only film in which he grandly enunciated his speeches instead of blurting out his usual "mumbled thoughts,"

was Julius Caesar, where he played the role of Antony. In Brando's art, the "Stanislavski method" as interpreted by the Actors' Studio—acting through the body, with incongruous poses, elusive gestures, and small tics—in reality a hammy style—became the embodiment of the self-conscious anguish and unease of the young misfit who can afford to noisily rebel, because he has a "return ticket."

This Brando, brooding, at once macho and childish, was a worldwide success: with critics, the box office, and imitators. James Dean (1931–1955) modeled himself after him, and was even more uncommunicative. Paul Newman, Al Pacino, Robert De Niro, all imitate Brando, like most all the Actors' Studio students, with the exception of the more polished among them, such as Karl Malden and Dustin Hoffman. Montgomery Clift (1920–1966) was the first model, even for Brando. But it is the Brando of The Wild One who was imitated by young people all over the world, who dressed and posed like him.

76 1977 1978 1979 1980 **1971** 1972 1

1972 1973 19

|5

|6 |7 |8 |9

him enormously successful again; the success continued with the assertive Last Tango in Paris (1973). From this time on he specialized in cameo roles where his obesity, his baldness, his face misshapen by his unhappy old age formed the physical base for performances of a superb, self-destructive mannerism.

1. 1954, Hollywood. Marlon Brando and Grace Kelly receive the Oscar for best leading actors.
2. 1954. Brando in *On the Waterfront*, directed by Elia Kazan, in which he played the role of Terry Malloy, which won him an Oscar and the Cannes Film Festival prize for best actor.
3. 1950, New York. Brando is already a famous stage actor.
4. 1941, New York. Orson Welles, James Light and, on the right, Erwin Piscator.
5. 1953. Brando plays Antony as he pronounces the famous oration before the dictator's lifeless body in *Julius Caesar*, directed by Joseph L. Mankiewicz

(1909–1993), a subtle Berlin-born filmmaker.
6. 1952. Brando in *Viva Zapata!*, one of the more touching political films directed by Elia Kazan.
7. 1972. Brando in Francis Ford Coppola's *The Godfather*. Brando refused the Oscar for this role, in protest against the U.S. treatment of Native Americans.
8. 1954. Brando stars in *The Wild One*, directed by Lazlo Benedek (1907–1992), a Hungarian-born filmmaker.
9. 1951. Brando and Vivien Leigh, wonderful interpreters of the Tennessee Williams play *A Streetcar Named Desire*, directed by Kazan.

THE RIACE BRONZES
Reemerging, they gave life to one of the century's myths

On August 16, 1972 diver Stefano Mariottini, while submerged in Calabria's Ionian Sea about 600 feet from the coast of Riace, near the ancient Aeolian colony of Kaulonia found two larger-than-life, nude, male bronze statues. While they were immediately catalogued as Greek, from the 5th century B.C., the experts disagreed on the subjects represented—whether men, heroes, or gods—and about their creators. The experts decided to call Bronze A the statue with long flowing hair (78"), and Bronze B the other statue (77½"). In 1998 the art historian Paolo Moreno made a convincing case for identifying the statues as representing Tydeus, by Ageladas, and Amphiarus, by Alcamenes. The statues had been cast around 450 B.C., part of the Seven of Thebes group that

was meant to decorate Argos's *agora*. While the statues were intact, their helmets, shields, and spears, which were presumably all in silver, were missing. The statues were immediately restored, then exhibited in 1980–1981 in the Archeological Museum in Florence and at the Quirinale Palace (the official residence of the President of Italy) in Rome. In less than 200 days, 700,000 visitors saw the statues.

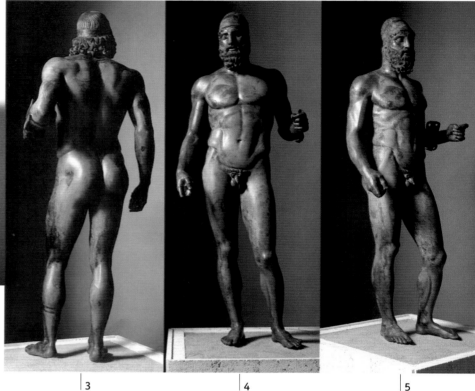

1
2
3
4
5

"Ageladas's powerful statue taught this to his students: to Myron, the secret of breath contained within the bronze; to Phidias, the sense of life; to Polykleitos, a virtual energy."

Paolo Moreno, *L'arte dei Greci* (*The Art of the Greeks*)

THE NUDE. The extraordinary appeal of statues such as the Riace Bronzes rekindled an interest in the male athletic physique. The image of the female body adapted to this trend, and women body-builders and martial arts experts started to proliferate. The androgynous type also met with suc-

cess: found in either young men or young women, it is nimble rather than athletic, ambiguous like an adolescent figure.

PERFORMANCE. The body was exhibited, sometimes defaced; sadomasochism became more widespread and a routine

THE BODY AS MYTH

Museum visitors who saw the Riace Bronzes in Florence and Rome and, later, in their permanent home, the Archeological Museum in Reggio Calabria, were touched by their beauty. Conscious of their cultural as well as monetary value, people were spellbound by the television programs broadcasting their images abroad and by the scientific debate that continued for years. This was also a period in which it became fashionable to devote hours to the gym, to aerobic dance and exercise, to martial arts and body-building; in other words, to the care of the body. Clothing, always important, now had to display a famous name or logo. It became trendy to decorate the head, the limbs, the chest with jewels, piercing, chains, head-dresses, tattoos, scars, wild colors. At the center of attention was the naked body because it communicated eroticism, and because it projected a self-satisfied narcissism; this fashion also included masochistic and defacing tendencies.

This trend was launched by Anglo-American culture, in the United States in particular, and gave life to corresponding fetishes and idols: Jane Fonda (b. 1937), an Anglo-Saxon type (see her 1968 film Barbarella*), the Afro-muscular type of Grace Jones, a singer and actress who came to promi-*

nence in a James Bond movie, and the Afro-anorexic type of Donyale Luna, a model who acted in Carmelo Bene and Federico Fellini movies. The male idol dominated, with figures such as Mickey Hargitay, Sylvester Stallone (b. 1946), and Arnold Schwarzenegger (b. 1947), who began their careers as muscle-builders.

part of the performance of avant-garde artists. Post-modern artists appropriated the classical nude models, both male and female. Even high fashion created evening gowns around the "seminude" theme. After transvestitism, male striptease became a trend: finally, men also have become objects.

DOMINANCE. In Mozia, Italy, another Greek statue from the fifth century B.C. was discovered, a larger-than-life marble statue of a young man dressed in a thin, draped robe. This statue also enjoyed some popularity in the 1970s but, unlike the Riace Bronzes, did not become an idol.

1. 1972. Donyale Luna in Carmelo Bene's (b. 1937) *Salome*. The model's anorexic physique perfectly suited the character she played.
2. The head of Riace's Bronze A. According to Moreno, it is *Tydeus*, by Ageladas.
3. Back view of Riace's Bronze A.
4. Front view of Riace's Bronze B. According to Moreno, the statue is *Amphiarus* by Alcamenes.
5. Three-quarter frontal view of Riace's Bronze B.
6. 1985. Sylvester Stallone in *Rambo: First Blood Part II*, directed by G. P. Cosmatos. With *Rocky* and *Rambo* the actor who acts with his muscles became accepted. *Rocky* received three Oscars.
7. Front view of Riace's Bronze A.
8. 1998. Exhibition of male and female body-builders.
9. 1982. The Austrian Arnold Schwarzenegger, protagonist of *Conan the Barbarian*, directed by John Milius. In 1975 he left his body-building career; he has been doing movies since 1970; in 1980 he played the role of Mickey Hargitay on TV.

972 1973 1974 1975 1976 1977 1978 1979 1980 1971 **1972** 1973

1980 1971 **1972** 1973 1974 1975 1976 1977 1978

KONRAD LORENZ

Nobel Prize winner in physiology/medicine

Konrad Zacharias Lorenz was born in Vienna in 1903. In childhood he developed the ability to stay immobile for hours, thus accustoming the animals he was studying to lose all interest in him and behave "normally." He was a long-time observer of jackdaws (*Corvus monedula*), a bird that lives in groups, and the subject of his first published research. Lorenz was an excellent student, studying biology at New York's Columbia University and receiving a medical degree and a Ph.D. in zoology in Vienna, in 1928 and 1933, respectively. In 1937 he qualified as professor of comparative anatomy and published a study in which he contrasted the various animal behavior theories based on instinct to those based on the study of hereditary mechanisms. He began teaching comparative psychology in 1940. In 1943 he proposed extending the field of ethology to the human species as a type of "domesticated species." In 1951 he was called to the Max Planck Institute of Munich, where in 1961 he was appointed head of the Behavioral Physiology Department. In 1973 he was the Nobel Prize recipient for medicine and physiology, which he shared with Nikolaas Tinbergen and Karl von Frisch. In 1973 he was appointed to head the Animal Sociology Department at the Behavioral Research Institute of the Austrian Academy of Sciences. Konrad Lorenz died in 1989.

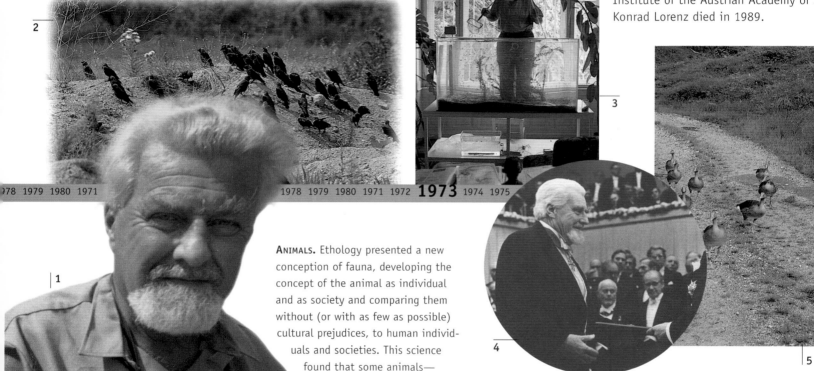

ANIMALS. Ethology presented a new conception of fauna, developing the concept of the animal as individual and as society and comparing them without (or with as few as possible) cultural prejudices, to human individuals and societies. This science found that some animals— primates among them—are capable of invention and can communicate their inventions to their peers; also, that many animals share a complex world of affections, even outside of sexuality and parental relations. Ethology has studied reciprocal altruism among animals, and has recorded recurrent homosexual behavior in various species.

ECO-ETHOLOGY. Research studies on inter-species relations, and the relationship between animal species and the environment and its resources (eco-ethology) are important. These studies can help compare animal and human species behavior vis-à-vis the environment.

THE DUTCH SCHOOL. Tinbergen and the Dutch school have assessed the survival value of various types of behavior using rigorous field experimentation; they have also studied animal communication in its social context, as a means to increase the degree of fitness of various species.

WAR AND RITUAL. Ethology has determined that while some animals developed lethal morphological structures, such as talons and tusks, they also developed inhibitions that ritualize their use. For example, the buck fighting its peer for the harem butts its horns with those of the adversary but without impaling it, even when it could do so. The defeated wolf lies

188

ETHOLOGY

1. 1967. Konrad Lorenz in an expressive close-up.

2. A group of jackdaws. Ethology has studied their sociality.

3. Lorenz in front of his aquarium. Observation of a tiny fish, the stickleback (*Gasterosteus*) yielded some of the most important early ethological discoveries.

4. December 10, 1973, Stockholm. Lorenz receives from King Karl Gustaf XVI the Nobel Prize for physiology and medicine.

5. Lorenz walking with "his" ducks.

6. Ethological justice. A man and his dog both naked in San Gregorio, California.

7. A common seagull.

8. 1969. Lorenz swims while observing "his" geese, which follow him.

9. A gorilla and its cub. Ethology helps develop in cultivated men and women a certain degree of openness to considering animals—mammals at least—as persons belonging to other species.

A science founded in the 1930s, ethology studies animal behavior, especially the time span from birth to reproduction. The science analyzes both instinctual and learned behavior—in both the individual animal and the group—for survival, mating, offspring raising, and defense of the territory; the relationship between stimuli and behavior in individuals at different stages of growth, parents and offspring, members of the same family and group, and various forms of competition and territorial behavior. The science compares and contrasts these and relates them to the behavior of comparable species, both in their natural state and in laboratory conditions.

7

8

0 1971 1972

6

9

"By observing myself, I can safely say that the shared laughter can not only avert aggression, but also create a perceptible sense of social solidarity.**"**

Konrad Lorenz, *On Aggression*

Lorenz is credited with important discoveries in both ethology and comparative psychology: among these, the distinction between innate and learned behavior, the interaction between these two types of behavior in imprinting—the post-natal period when the animal is receptive to external stimuli and processes reactions that will determine its future behavior. In fact, individual behavior is an expression of an individual's genetic heritage integrated with what the individual receives culturally through its peers and with its own experiences. An important part of Lorenz's work was applied to the study of animal aggressiveness as compared to human aggressiveness.

down and offers its neck to the winner who pulls back, satisfied with the offering act. For a very long time, war among men was also for the most part a ritualized event. However, noted

G. Celli, "the concept of total war which Hitler perfected coincided with the complete de-ritualization of the phenomenon; the atomic war being the perfect example."

WILLY BRANDT

Forced to resign

Herbert Frahm was born in 1913 in Lübeck to a blue-collar family of Social Democrats. He entered politics at a very young age. In 1931 he left the German Social Democratic Party (SPD) for the more radical SAP. He changed his name to Willy Brandt when Hitler came to power in 1933. The party sent him to Oslo. For 12 years, enjoying Norwegian citizenship, Brandt moved between Sweden, Norway, and Spain (including a few missions to Berlin), where he fought with the left-wing factions and worked as a reporter, all the while acquiring an international outlook. Back in Berlin in 1945 as press attaché for the Norwegian Military Mission, Brandt regained his German citizenship and rejoined the SPD. He was convinced that his party had to be protected from Communist aggressiveness, that the United States was doing a good job providing freedom to his country, and that the NATO alliance was useful to Germany. At the Bad Godesberg Congress the SPD distanced itself from Marxism-Leninism and so Brandt's rise began. Burgomaster of West Berlin in 1957, federal chairman of the SPD in 1964, he was also a personal friend to Kennedy during the most delicate phase of Washington's relations with Bonn. He was foreign minister and vice chancellor during the great 1966 coalition and, starting in 1969, Chancellor of the Liberal-Democratic Socialist coalition. He was forced to resign in 1974 when one of his inner circle, Gunther Guillaume, was accused of spying for East Germany.

OUTSIDE GERMANY, many suspected that behind the Guillaume affair there was a secret power struggle within the SPD. A recipient of the Nobel Peace Prize in 1971, even after resigning, Brandt remained party chairman and was the leader of the Socialist International. As such, he continued his Ostpolitik, to bring democracy to the countries of the Mediterranean and those ruled by the Communist Party.

At his death on October 8, 1992, Brandt was one of the most loved and respected men in the world.

THE LEFT. Brandt's tenure as chancellor coincided with a period of intensified European radicalism. Also, terrorist fringe groups appeared in many countries. In June 1972 the German Federal Police arrested some members of the radical left Baader-Meinhof group, headed by Andreas Baader and his wife, Ulrike Meinhof, including Baader himself and Holger Meins, Jan Carl Raspe, and Gudrun Ensslin. Their activity spawned a series of political crimes but also unconstitutionally repressive laws. In 1976–1977 many of them "committed suicide" while in jail.

LONG-TERM EFFECTS. By accepting the outcome of World War II, Germany in fact put it into question. By defusing explosive East-West relations, Ostpolitik weakened all those who based their fortune on the USSR-USA conflict—secret services, dictators, speculators. It encouraged a democratization of the Communist Party in free countries, and spotlighted the reactionary element in those groups that were hiding behind the alibi of the "red menace."

OSTPOLITIK

Brandt was mayor of Berlin in August 1961 when the Communists built the infamous wall to prevent East Germans from escaping to freedom. On that occasion, and at other times of increased East-West tension, Brandt's response was lucid and composed, convinced as he was that "there are two states of the German nation." Having been Foreign Minister during the tenure of Christian Democratic Chancellor Kurt Kiesinger, Brandt in turn, once Chancellor, appointed the Liberal Walter Scheel to the same post. Brandt, the first Social Democratic Chancellor since the war, was the first Western statesman to meet on equal terms with the Premier of the German Democratic Republic (East Germany) (in 1970). On August 11 of the same year he was in Moscow for three days to sign the treaty in which the USSR and the FRG (Federal Republic of Germany) renounced the use of force in their reciprocal relations. On December 7, 1970, West Germany and Poland signed, in War-

saw, a treaty normalizing their diplomatic relations, thus recognizing the German-Polish border. At the same time, Brandt publicly atoned for the evil inflicted upon the Jews. In October 1972, in Beijing, Walter Scheel declared the reestablishment of diplomatic relations with Mao's China. In November, in Bonn, the two Germanies signed the "Basic Treaty" regulating their relations. At that time, Brandt's own acts and words and his government's actions made a deep impression internationally, for it became clear that the majority of Germans had accepted the consequences of losing the war and that good will could move the Iron Curtain. Many liked Brandt's Germany, proud and courageous.

8

7

74 1975 1976 1977 1978 1979 1980 1971

75 1976 1977 1978 1979 1980 1971 1972 1973 **1974**

6

9

"He understood that one had to accept the existence of the German Democratic Republic and the Oder-Neisse border and therefore, the irreversibility of the outcome of World War II."
Massimo L. Salvadori, Italian historian.

1. Brandt in his mature years.
2. May 1, 1959, West Berlin. Brandt the Burgomaster celebrates Labor Day.
3. June 8, 1973, Jerusalem. Willy Brandt with Israeli Prime Minister Golda Meir and Israeli President Ephraim Katzair.
4. 1958, New York. West Berlin's Burgomaster speaking at the U.N. By then, Brandt was already a

well-known political personality, highly respected for his strong ideals and sincerity.
5. Willy Brandt with Leonid Brezhnev, in an attempt to establish better relations with the USSR.
6. December 1976, Madrid. First PSOE (Spanish Socialist Workers' Party) Congress. Italian Socialist

Pietro Nenni is on the left, Spanish Socialist Felipe Gonzales and Willy Brandt are on the right.
7. December 7, 1970, Warsaw, in the former Jewish ghetto. Chancellor Brandt kneeling to honor the more than half a million victims of Nazism killed in 1943 in that part of the city alone.

8. 1967, Bucharest. Brandt on an official visit to Romania. To the right, the independent Communist dictator Nicolae Ceausescu (b. 1918, executed with his wife Elena in December 1989).
9. 1958, Berlin. Brandt in the rubble of the city being rebuilt.

JUAN CARLOS I

King of Spain

Juan Carlos de Borbón was born in Rome, Italy in 1938 to the exiled son of the former king of Spain. His childhood and adolescent years were haunted by the conflict between his father and Spanish dictator Francisco Franco. His father, the Count of Barcelona, was a conservative democrat who had harshly criticized Franco's regime.

Having no male children and only one greedy son-in-law, Franco decided to fashion for himself an heir. Thus he removed Juan Carlos from his parents, brought him to Spain, and subjected him to a strict education in military academies and with private tutors, learning languages, sports, dancing, geography, history, Spanish and international law, and so on. Juan Carlos was given a small military court at his private residence of Zarzuela, which he was never to leave.

In 1955 Franco declared Juan Carlos his successor. In 1961, Juan Carlos became engaged to Princess Sophia of Greece (daughter of right-leaning European royalty) who renounced her Greek Orthodox faith to marry him. Married in Athens in 1962, they have four children. In 1971, Franco called him to rule at his side, as a kind of co-regent. In 1974, hospitalized, Franco entrusted him provisionally with executive powers, which Juan Carlos took up on October 30, 1975. On November 22, 1975, two days after Franco's death, he ascended the throne.

DRAMAS. The crown of Spain entered a period of crisis when Isabella II took the throne in 1833 and her uncle Don Carlos, her son and her nephew contested it, waging a war against her. Isabella II abdicated in favor of her son, Alfonso XII, who was in exile and succeeded in returning to Madrid only in 1875. He died in 1885 at the age of 28 and left a posthumous heir, Alfonso XIII, under the regency of the mother, Maria Cristina of Austria. The king married Eugenia of Battenberg, daughter of Princess Beatrix of England. During his reign, Spain lost the Antilles and the Philippines to the United States in the Spanish-American War.

ALFONSO XIII. Handsome, gallant, and adventurous, the king was crushed between the socialist, anarchist, and republican camps, whose policies he opposed, and the military and reactionaries. From 1923 to 1930 he supported Primo de Rivera's dictatorship and when democracy was reestablished, the Republican government sent him into exile. The king died in Rome in 1941. His first two sons were born hemophiliacs; the fourth died in a car accident. His third son, who became pretender to the throne upon the father's death, was Don Juan, Count of Barcelona.

THE BOURBONS. Member of a premier royal dynasty, Juan Carlos is very much a Bourbon. He is the son of Maria de las Mercedes de Borbon y Orleans of Borbone-Sicily. His great-grandmother Maria Cristina was great-granddaughter of a Spanish *Infanta*. His great-great-grandparents were Isabella II and Francis of Assisi Ferdinand M., who were Bourbons on both their parents' sides.

THE PEOPLE'S KING

His destiny was to be the king of all the people, so as to stabilize the country and allow the children of the anti-Franco martyrs to live in peace with the children of the victims of Communist violence. Thus Juan Carlos refused to have his own party. In 1976 he entrusted the government to Adolfo Suarez, former secretary of Franco's Falange Party (the only legal party at the time). In so doing, he ensured the repatriation of the surviving leaders of the Spanish Republic and the Communists, and led the country to adopt a new Constitution and hold democratic elections in 1977, in which Suarez won a majority.

On February 23, 1981, Lieutenant Colonel Tejero del Molina seized the Cortes and several military chiefs requested the king to transfer government powers to the armed forces. Juan Carlos, in a speech broadcast on national television, pledged to defend at all costs the constitutional monarchy. Thus the coup failed. The king allowed the Falange and left-wing radicals to slowly exhaust themselves,

taking moderate action against Basque terrorism, favoring some degree of autonomy for certain regions and respecting electoral results that alternated between democratic-socialist and center-right parties. In 1992 in Barcelona, on the 500th anniversary of the discovery of the Americas, he inaugurated the 25th modern Olympics. Spain was again a great power, respected and influential. Modernization, which moved at a swift pace from 1960 to 1973, with an annual growth rate of 6–7 percent, continued, although not uniformly. The Kingdom of Spain is now an important member of the European Union in every respect.

1973 1974 **1975** 1976 1977 1978 1979   1971 1972 197

9

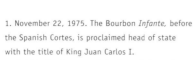

8

"After 1975, it was Juan Carlos' authority and prestige that ensured that the moderately progressive forces would prevail.**"**

Giampiero Bordino, *Il mondo dal 1970 ad oggi*
(*The World from 1970 to Now*).

1. November 22, 1975. The Bourbon *Infante*, before the Spanish Cortes, is proclaimed head of state with the title of King Juan Carlos I.
2. Madrid. The European Union Summit in a solemn reception given by the king and queen of Spain.
3. Juan Carlos I at an official ceremony. He wears the insignia of the Grand Master of the Order of the Golden Fleece.
4. July 1959, Portofino. Don Juan Carlos leaving a

yacht. Behind him is Don Alfonso. Franco at one time or another had fanned hopes that the throne would be given to the Count of Barcelona, to Juan Carlos, to his cousins, to the princes of the Carlista branch, and to the Borbone-Parmas.
5. 1973 or 1974, Spain. *El Caudillo* Francisco Franco accompanied by the designated heir, Don Juan Carlos de Borbón.
6. June 1977, Madrid. A family photo of the

Spanish royal family. Next to the king are his parents, the Count and Countess of Barcelona.
7. Barcelona. The king and queen inaugurate the Contemporary Art Museum.
8. Madrid. Juan Carlos and his queen with Pope John Paul II on an official visit to Spain.
9. November 1975, Madrid. Juan Carlos leaves the Cortes Palace after being proclaimed king of Spain.

THE TERRA-COTTA ARMY
The past resurrected

In 1974, less than a mile from the walls of Shih huang-ti's mausoleum near Xian, Shensi province, a large subterranean chamber was discovered full of terra-cotta statues of soldiers dating to the emperor's time. Subsequently, other chambers were unearthed and excavation is still in process in the area. It's as if a whole military unit in battle formation had been buried in each of these chambers: men armed with swords, axes, crossbows, bows, quivers, halberds, javelins, bronze lances. Some wore elaborate armor. There were several wooden war chariots and horses. In the pits and along the hallways, the army of terra-cotta was

1

3

ranked in battle order: the rows and the outside columns each faced front. The statues of the soldiers are 6' to 8' high, those of the horses are 5' high and 6½' long. All of this must have required a vast number of master artists and workers, baking ovens, huge supplies of clay and wood. News and photographs of the terra-cotta army found their way into the media, but it was not until a couple of years later that the public started realizing the magnitude of the discovery. The discovery of over 500 horses, 130 chariots, 10,000 soldiers including infantrymen, archers, knights and coachmen (and these were just the statues that were found in the first three chambers) had an impact that shook twentieth-century culture and society.

2

4

SHIH HUANG-TI. His name was Chao Cheng and he was king of Ch'in, one of the warring states. Between 230 and 221 B.C. he conquered the other kingdoms and founded the Chinese Empire, thereafter taking on a new name. For the first time, the territories and peoples of most of China were united. Shih huang-ti introduced in his empire uniform units of measurement and weight, one common currency, one written language, which was the same in all the provinces. By so doing he rendered his empire uniform, thus centralizing power.

CH'ANG-AN. In a territory approximately 4 by 3 miles, archeologists excavated Ch'ang-an, capital of the Ch'in dynasty who were the first emperors of China (221–206 B.C.). Dwellings made of beaten earth were identified. The main body of a monumental building rises on a vast base complete with flights of steps, doors, and symmetrical interior spaces. Walls and stairs are constructed of hollow bricks and embellished with circles, rhombuses, phoenixes, and dragons, while the walls are covered with frescoes. The eaves are decorated with cloud

designs, typical of the Ch'in period.

BEAUTY. Ancient Western sculpture has accustomed us to the uniqueness of a work of art, copied over the centuries in an infinite number of reproductions with different media. Faced with a whole army of terra-cotta, our sensitivity reels; however, the realism, the measured gestures and countenances, the impeccable workmanship, the dignified bearing of the statues hint at another idea of classicism, no less noble than that of Western art.

5

ARCHEOLOGY IN AID OF HISTORY

The scientific methods of archeology were developed in the second half of our century; they have since become an irreplaceable, sure-fire tool of historical research, along with paleo-anthropology, paleo-botany, and auxiliary sciences. The finds excavated from the Xian pits have an exceptional value that gives life and a richer meaning to an exceptional monument, the only one visible by the artificial satellites orbiting the Earth: the Great Wall of China. Parts of the wall were built by various Chinese states for defense purposes; however, after unifying China, Shi huang-ti connected the northern segments and made it into a wall over 3,000 miles long whose eastern extremity extends to the Liaoning Peninsula. The grandiose walls erected by the Roman emperors cannot even remotely be compared to this structure. The

6

8

1977 1978 1979 1980 1971 1972 1973 1974 1975 **1976** 1977 1978 1979 1980 1971 1972 19   1975 **1976**

same emperor caused the Ling Channel to be dug, which, together with natural waterways, still connects the Yangtze River navigation system to that of the Pearl River. These public works attest to a treatment of the territory that was typical of very strong states.

   Thanks to the statues discovered in the Xian pits, we also know what type of armed forces ensured that the Ch'in king would succeed in subjugating other warring states and keeping his empire in check. Chariots, horses, weapons, men, defenses, battle line-ups of the various units, everything is reflected in the position of the statues, lined up in an order that has resisted time and constitutes a unique find for military archeology.

7

9

❝The statues and their formations are a dazzling testimony to the rigid soldierly discipline that allowed Shih huang-ti to unify the empire. ❞
Chinese History Museum of Beijing

1. The museum edifice built above the underground chamber where the army of terra-cotta statues are located.

2. The interior of the museum. The vastness of the whole and the order of the ranks can be clearly perceived.

3. Another view of the interior, from another angle. The impression is of looking at a real battle formation.

4. Four horses lying on the ground, as if knocked down in an accident.

5. A coachman on the ground, clasping the reins.

6. A closed, covered coach with horses and driver.

7. Horses and soldiers. Because of the distance, the horses seem taller than the men.

8. A detail of the battle line-up. Note that the faces, headdresses, weapons, and attire are not uniform; they vary.

9. Another detail of the formation. If we compare the statues' height to that of the average Chinese, even today, we have a sense of their grandeur.

BOKASSA

He crowned himself emperor of the Central African Republic

Jean Bédel Bokassa was born in a Bérengo village in 1921, then part of French Equatorial Africa. Bokassa enrolled in the French colonial army, the only way for a non-aristocrat to secure a future. In 1960 the country proclaimed its independence and took the name of the Central African Republic. In 1969, the country had an area of 240,300 square miles and a population of about 2,304,800, about 70 percent of them illiterate farmers. The region of Bakouma is rich in uranium; the country also extracts gold and diamonds, though mostly of inferior grade. There are no railroads, and only a few hundred miles of paved roads. The rest of the

roads are not always accessible by car. The Congo-Ouubangi waterway is navigable, however. On New Year's Eve in 1966, Colonel Bokassa completed his *coup*, naming himself Marshal and bedecking himself with decorations and honors. Napoleon was his guiding spirit. He proclaimed himself president for life. His policies consisted of constant changes of direction and wild purges that sowed terror in the country. In March 1975 French President Valéry Giscard d'Estaing (1974–1981) was his guest. D'Estaing expressed his friendship and reportedly received a box of good diamonds in return for promising his help.

19

1

2

3

4

5

MENGISTU. Haile Selassie I, King of Kings, was deposed in 1974 after conquering Eritrea, which gave his country an outlet to the Red Sea. His place was taken by Mengistu Haile Mariam, head of state and of government, chairman of the Provisional Military Administrative Council (Derg) and since 1984 general secretary of the Workers' Party (Web), which had the task of achieving a Marxist-Leninist "Ethiopian Socialism." After the 1977–1978 war with Somalia for control of Ogaden; the wars of secession by Eritrea, Tigray, and other provinces; clashes with the Coptic Church; drought, famine, and deportations; another popular front

conquered Addis Ababa and in 1991 forced the dictator to flee the country.

AMIN DADA. Uganda, an independent African state since 1962, with a population of 9,549,000 in 1969 and a territory of 93,070 square miles, was a confederation of small and large monarchies. Prime Minister Milton Obote crushed them and in 1966 became president of a unified republic. Major Idi Amin Dada seized power in a January 25, 1971 coup. He immediately issued a number of decrees that suspended individual freedoms, constitutional rights, and political activity, even granting full civil jurisdiction to the

military courts in 1973. He purged the army, replacing it with ethnic groups that supported him. Amin was responsible for thousands of political and even unmotivated killings; the refrigerators in his presidential palace were said to contain human corpses. Amin clashed with his neighbors, and Tanzania began assisting his internal opposition, causing the dictator to flee on April 11, 1979 to Libya first, then to Saudi Arabia.

NO VICTORS. There are no winners in

African Bonapartism. Instead of military victories, there are tribal slaughters. Powerful, modern weapons have distorted the meaning and sense of ethnic conflicts.

AFRICAN BONAPARTISM

Bokassa's dream came true on December 4, 1977. In front of TV cameras, the press, and the diplomatic corps, President-for-Life Bokassa crowned himself Emperor Bokassa I. The ceremony, the customs, the words and gestures imitated Napoleon I's coronation. Times and interests changed; in 1979, with French assistance, he was deposed and fled abroad. Former President Dacko was recalled into power, soon replaced in yet another coup. The emperor unexpectedly returned home in October 1986. He was arrested, tried, and sentenced to death, a sentence later commuted to life imprisonment. Thus Bokassa exited the stage of history.

Bokassa is a picturesque example of a common figure on the African continent. We must note that it was European imperialism that distorted traditional African political structures, since originally states consisted of tribes ruling over the land on which they lived, who often subjected and enslaved other ethnic groups. Nomadism was still alive with frequent, even cruel, mass migra-

"Before the end of the decade some positive events took place in Sub-Saharan Africa: . . . the defeat in the same year of bloody dictatorships . . . in Uganda . . . Equatorial Guinea . . . and the Central African [Republic]."

G. Bordino, *Il mondo dal 1970 a oggi*
(*The World from 1970 to Now*).

6

8

1975 1976 **1977** 1978 1979 1980 1971 1972 1973 1 72 1973 1974

9

tions. It was Europeans who created colonies with neat boundaries, tracing the course of rivers and using ruler and pen. Those colonies sometimes enclosed whole ethnic groups and tribes, and sometimes just parts of them. At the time of decolonization, the only class to possess modern skills and techniques was the military. Thus military juntas or leaders wrested power from the tribal kings—often with the intent of improving their people's living conditions—and still compete for it with coups d'état. This is what happened in Angola, Benin, Burkina Faso, Burundi, the former French Congo, Equatorial Guinea, Nigeria, and so on.

1. An image of Bokassa dominating the crowds. During his dictatorship he acquired about a thousand medals and decorations, a collection worthy of Goering.

2. Bangui. Bokassa on the throne, in dress uniform.

3. Valéry Giscard d'Estaing, President of the French Republic (1974–1981) and leader of the Liberal-Conservative Party.

4. December 4, 1977, Bangui. Bokassa allows himself to be photographed and filmed by TV, wearing his scepter, crown, and imperial mantle.

5. Bangui. At the coronation, the foreign guests are in the foreground; in the background is the

cream of Central African society.

6. Mengistu Haile Mariam, who defeated the empire of the lions and was dictator of Ethiopia for many years.

7. October 2, 1975, New York. Idi Amin Dada, President of Uganda, speaking at the United Nations. Of all African military dictators, he was considered the most uncouth and ferocious.

8. December 4, 1977, Bangui. Bokassa I sitting on the throne in all his glory, in the shadow of the huge imperial eagle.

9. A poster dedicated to a general during the terrible Biafran secession war from Nigeria (1967–1970).

GOLDA MEIR

Died far from the political scene

Golda Mabovitch was born in Kiev in 1898 and migrated with her family to the United States in 1906. In 1917 Arthur J. Balfour (1848–1930), then British foreign secretary, published a statement in which he pledged to give the Jewish people a "homeland" in Palestine. Golda emigrated to Palestine in 1921, working in the Merhavya kibbutz and in a factory collective. She joined the Jewish General Federation of Labor and became its secretary and executive. In 1946–1948 she headed the political department of the Jewish Agency, which was the embryo from which the state of Israel was declared in 1948 by David Ben-Gurion (1886–1973), then leader of the Mapai (Labor) Party. In 1948–1949 Golda Meir was appointed minister to Moscow; in 1949–1956 she was labor minister; in 1949–1952 she was also social security minister; in 1956–1966 foreign minister; in 1968, Mapai's general secretary. She succeeded Levi Eshkol to the prime ministership in 1969, to which she was reelected in 1973. She governed until the Yom Kippur War, which found her unprepared. She lived her last years as a private citizen until her death in 1978.

2

1

1 1972 1973 ... 72 1973 1974 1975 1976 1977 **1978** 1979 1980 1971 1972 1973 1974 1975 1976 1977 **1978** 1979 1980 1971

3

YIDDISCH FOLKS SCHULE
MILWAUKEE WIS. JULY 16-16

5

MINISTER. As foreign minister Golda (she called herself Meir starting in 1956) skillfully exploited Soviet expansionism in the Middle East (which was to succeed in Aden (Sudan), and in Libya with al-Gaddafi's revolution), making of Israel the most trusted U.S. ally in the region.

SIX DAYS. In 1967 hawkish Ben-Gurion was defense minister. On June 5, Moshe Dayan (1915–1981), then an army staff officer and later defense minister, unleashed an attack that in six days destroyed the Egyptian air force, conquered the Sinai Peninsula and Syria's Golan Heights, the Arab section of Jerusalem and the remainder of Palestine, thus forcing another

200,000 Palestinians to join the already 1.3 million Palestinian refugees. On November 22, 1967 the U.N. approved Resolution 242, which demanded that Israel withdraw from the occupied territories. Israel so far has not complied.

PRIME MINISTER. Meir inherited a difficult situation when she succeeded Eshkol upon his death. Israel bombed the Egyptian cities along the Suez Canal and did not return the land they had won, thus resisting Washington's

pressure. As a result, Palestinian terrorism escalated, culminating in the infamous attack on Israeli athletes at the Munich Olympic Games. Israel escalated by retaliating in Jordan, Lebanon, and Syria and by sending settlers to the occupied territories. The peace was broken when Egypt, then Syria, attacked on October 6, 1973 and the oil-rich Arab nations suspended the supply of oil to Western countries. The outcome on the battlefield was still undecided, when Israel's enemies declared victory and

Henry Kissinger, then U.S. Secretary of State, forced Israel to accept a treaty that improved the situation of its enemies. Israel suffered heavy losses, had to increase spending, applied new taxes, and suffered a high rate of inflation. On April 4, 1974 Golda Meir resigned.

WOMEN AND POWER

Notwithstanding women's emancipation, the twentieth century has not seen many women achieve political power. In Western Europe several queens continued to rule, among them the iron-willed Wilhelmina of The Netherlands (1880–1962), mother of Queen Juliana and grandmother of today's Queen Beatrix. The women who became presidents or prime ministers have been few and far between. The same situation applies to women who control important companies: for family reasons, they entrust power to the husband or son, in any case, to a man. In the third world, the first part of the century saw powerful women rulers: in China, the widowed Empress Tsou-Hsi ascended the throne in 1861; in Ethiopia, it was Empress Taitu.

In Asia, where women are generally subordinate to men, women reached several powerful positions in the second part of the century. There were women prime ministers in India, Pakistan, and Sri Lanka. In China, Taiwan, and the Philippines the wives of dictators such as Mao Dzedong, Chiang Kai-shek, and Ferdinand Marcos acquired power as their husbands' waned. At the death of Perón in Argentina, his last wife, who—unlike Evita—had been vice president, briefly assumed power. Maybe the twenty-first century will see more women in leading positions.

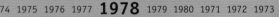

74 1975 1976 1977 **1978** 1979 1980 1971 1972 1973

1. 1921, Palestine. Golda Myerson at work in Merhavya's kibbutz fields. A kibbutz is a farm collective modeled after the Soviet *kolkhoz*, which were set up especially during the first Soviet five-year plan (1928–1932). It has an egalitarian structure based on democratic principles and reflects the Zionist socialist soul.
2. An expressive portrait of Golda Meir in her robust older years.
3. July 1916, Wisconsin. A group portrait, with the young Golda among her classmates at the Milwaukee Yiddisch Folks Schule.
4. 1970, Sinai Desert. Prime Minister Meir visiting Israeli troops.

5. November 1, 1973, Washington, D.C. Golda Meir conversing with President Nixon.
6. Elderly Ben-Gurion in the study of the kibbutz where he lived.
7. 1970, Sinai. Israeli troops in Sharm el-Sheikh pay their respects to Prime Minister Meir.
8. June 30, 1978. U.S. Vice President Walter Mondale on a private visit to Mrs. Meir.
9. 1970, Bucharest. Prime Minister Meir, on an official visit to Romania, speaks in a synagogue.

"*Golda Meir's goodwill tour in the United States was memorable. Even personalities from outside politics or Zionism . . . made contributions to help Israel.*"
F. Cohen, *Israel: Forty Years of History*

Founded the Islamic Republic of Iran

Ruhollah Musawi Khomeini was born in 1900 in Qom in what was then Persia and is now called Iran. After his secondary schooling, he studied with the eminent Shiite law scholar and theologian Bayeri in Qom, and specialized in law and morality at the Koranic College. In 1925 Reza Kahn, a Cossack general, declared himself shah, establishing the Pahlavi dynasty. His aim was to modernize Persia. In 1960, at the death of Ayatollah Berugerdi, Khomeini was chosen to lead the opposition to the new shah, Mohammed Reza Pahlavi, who was accused of corruption, secularism, and subservience to U. S. interests. In 1962 he was appointed head of the *ayatollahs*. Khomeini was arrested in 1963 and

sent into exile the following year, first to Turkey and then to the Iraqi holy city of An-Najaf. There his opposition became increasingly hardline and he turned for inspiration to mysticism and a kind of social and ethical radicalism. Gradually, this position found a large following in his country. Meanwhile, in Persia massive demonstrations were taking place, as the shah and his court gradually lost prestige and had to depend on the aristocracy and the capital's upper middle class. Having been expelled even from Iraq, Khomeini took refuge near Paris.

4

973 1974 1975

1977 1978 **1979** 1980 1971 1972 1973

1

2

3

5

SHIITE AND SUNNI. Shiite Muslims are those who follow the *shi'a* (faction) of Ali, cousin of Mohammed and husband of the prophet's only daughter Fatimah, who was passed over for the succession in favor of the first caliphs, whom the Shiites consider usurpers. Several Shiite sects exist today, some with strong mystical and esoteric currents. The Sunni are orthodox Muslims; they constitute the majority and follow the *sunna*, or "beaten path," that is, the acts of the Prophet

and of the early Islamic community.

ISLAM. It is the major religion in Arabia, in the Fertile Crescent, in Egypt, Sudan, in the Maghreb from Libya to Morocco, in Iran, Azerbaijan, Tajikistan, Turkey, Uzbekistan, Turkmenistan, Kyrgyzstan, Pakistan, Bangladesh, Malaysia, Indonesia, and vast regions of Sub-Saharan Africa. There are large Muslim minorities in the Volga Valley,

in Siberia and Kazakhstan, India, Sri Lanka, Burma, the Philippines, Lebanon, and the Balkans. By now, there are also Muslim communities in Western and Central Europe. Worldwide, Muslim believers total about 900 million, and the year 2000 for them corresponds to the year 1420–1421.

IRAN. Iran is rich with a strong, ancient national culture, which was not subjugated by the Arabs and had a deep influence on Islam. The ancient Persian Empire was threatened and depleted of provinces by Russia and the United Kingdom; after World War II, following Israel and Saudi Arabia, it became a United States outpost in the region. Khomeini's revolution has brought the country closer to the Palestinian movement for a homeland and to Muammar al-Ghaddafi, the "Guide of the Libyan Revolution."

ISLAMIC FUNDAMENTALISM

In January 1979, having been deserted even by his Western allies, the shah and his family fled the country. On February 1st Khomeini returned and was given the welcome accorded to a holy man and a hero. After a referendum on April 1st, he proclaimed the Islamic Republic of Iran. It was a political, moral, and social revolution. Khomeini ruled Iran until his death in 1989; in those years, the clergy took control of all the nation's power centers. The campaign launched by Khomeini in 1979 against the United States led to a raid on the U.S. embassy in Teheran and the seizure of several dozen hostages who were freed two years later. In 1980 Iraq attacked Iran over border issues. This led to an extremely bloody war that lasted some ten years, and served to toughen the Shiites' fundamentalism as they fought the Sunni state of Iraq.

Whether Sunni or Shiite, Islamic fundamentalist groups were rampant. They murdered President Sadat of Egypt, threatened the king of Morocco, and even Palestinian President Arafat; they armed the Sudanese Muslims against their Christian and animist countrymen and took violent action against intellectuals and Westernized women in Algeria. Shiite fundamentalism is even hatching in a secular state such as Turkey, and is conquering Afghanistan in a blood bath. The goal of Islamic fundamentalism is to restore to society the guidance of the religious class (the ulamas), marginalize women, return to a system of patriarchal despotism, separate the sexes, foster Islamic science, and wage a holy war against the infidels.

9

1975 1976 1

8

7

"His inflexible and relentless commitment to bring down the dictatorship and stop capitalism inevitably made of him the symbol of the movement."
G. Vercellin, *Iran e Afganistan* (Iran and Afghanistan)

1. Qom. A view of Fatimah's mosque in this holy Shiite city.
2. Teheran. A giant portrait of Ayatollah Khomeini dominates the crowds.
3. Teheran. In the foreground, a portrait of Khomeini. In the background, a group of inmates in Evin Prison.
4. February 1979, Teheran. Khomeini and Yasser Arafat in private conversation.
5. June 7, 1989. An immense crowd gathers around the urn carrying Khomeini's ashes.

6. 1980, Teheran. Elected President Bani-Sadr ritually kisses Ayatollah Khomeini's hand.
7. June 7, 1989. An ocean of people attend Khomeini's funeral.
8. Trained in military camps, *chador*-clad Iranian women get ready to defend Khomeini's revolution, which marginalizes them.
9. Teheran. Ahmad, Khomeini's son, en route to the American Embassy to ask the Muslim students who seized a group of Americans, to release women and blacks.

RONALD REAGAN
President of the United States

Ronald W. Reagan was born in 1911 to a lower middle-class family in Illinois. An average student, he was a sports broadcaster on the radio, then found his way to Hollywood where he became the king of "B" movies, making more than 50 films for Warner Brothers and marrying Jane Wyman, an actress. In the meantime, he had progressive ideas and was an actors' union representative, moving up the ranks to become president of the Screen Actors Guild. Fired from Warner Brothers, he married an obscure starlet, Nancy Davis, and lived modestly until 1954 when he was recruited for a TV program where he made his name as a supporter of lower middle-class values that were provincial, more reactionary than conservative. He made his name politically giving speeches during the 1964 presidential elections, and in 1966 was elected governor of California on the Republican ticket. In the 1970s, having shifted to more moderate positions, Reagan became the leader of a vast grassroots conservative movement that led him to the presidential nomination in 1980 and to two presidential terms. At the end of his second term, in 1988, he retired to private life.

3

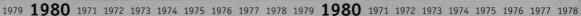

1979 **1980** | 1979 **1980** 1971 1972 1973 1974 1975 1976 1977 1978 1979 **1980** 1971 1972 1973 1974 1975 1976 1977 1978

1

2

FOR PRESIDENT

VALUES. During his tenure as governor of California, Reagan reduced taxes and shrank the state's budget, claiming that helping the poor only made them lazy. Reagan took positions against homosexuals, drug addicts, abortion. He favored mandatory Christian prayer in school. He appointed conservative judges to the Supreme Court, forming a majority of conservative judges. Thanks also to Vice President Bush (former head of the CIA), he maintained close links with high-level financial circles and with mass-market conservative publishers that strengthened his image as a winner.

THE GREAT COMMUNICATOR. In his acting days, later as representative of the actors' union, and finally as California governor, Reagan learned how to use the media. He had an uncanny ability to appeal to strong, deeply felt popular sentiments. A mediocre actor, he was formidable in his role as president: short, clear sentences, simple, unambiguous words, the winning gestures of a strong, benevolent grandfather. Still troubled by their loss to a third-world country such as Vietnam, and beset by a drug epidemic, aggressive displays of homosexuality, and the spread of AIDS, Americans needed to be reassured about America's power, and Reagan did just that.

STAR WARS. Reagan's anti-Soviet policy culminated in a space arms program intended to protect the United States from aggression by the "Evil Empire." The cost of the Star Wars program was stratospheric, to which was added the cost of a dynamic policy to retaliate

REAGANOMICS

"*In the United States, how many people were homeless during Reagan's presidency? In 1980 we had 125,000. In January 1984, 216,000. In August 1988, 402,000.*"

From C. Jencks, "The Homeless," in *The New York Review of Books*, April 21, 1994.

The dollar is the currency of the international economy, not tied to parity systems with other currencies. The budget can reach serious deficit levels but foreign countries will not stop buying dollars or using them. However, Reagan decided to achieve government savings by following Margaret Thatcher's example. He thus proceeded to shrink the federal government structure and entitlements that had been put in place by the New Deal, with drastic cuts to welfare and the lifting of EPA environmental controls. On the other hand, he reduced individual and corporate income taxes to spur investment. The strategy worked for business but not for the disadvantaged classes, and further increased the ecological imbalance. Reagan was reelected in 1984. The same policies did not work as well during his second term. Consumer expenditures rose, instead of investments; the poverty gap widened and an interventionist and aggressive foreign policy further burdened the budget. In addition to this, financial and political scandals, the growing autonomy and hostility of

6

7

1971 1972 **1980** **1980**

8

9

Congress, and a certain decline in Reagan's health had a negative effect on the last period of his mandate. His decisions were increasingly conditioned by his staff. At the time he left office however, Reagan's popularity was undiminished.

wherever the Soviets might strike or intervene wherever there was a possibility of unseating them. Moscow lacked the economic resources to accept the challenge and lost. In 1986 Gorbachev inaugurated a policy of détente, and Reagan followed suit. He will thus be remembered in history as the winner of the 40-year-old Cold War and the destroyer of the USSR.

1. Moscow. Ronald Reagan during a speech at Moscow University, under a bust of Lenin.
2. Phoenix, Arizona. A soup kitchen distributing free meals.
3. October 1983, Grenada. The action of U.S. troops put an end to the pro-Castro government of this Caribbean island republic.

4. New Hampshire. Reagan presidential election poster.
5. 1966. Reagan has just been elected governor of California.
6. 1980, Washington. Reagan's inauguration; with him is outgoing Democratic President Jimmy Carter.

7. Reagan and his horse in the western *The Last Outpost* (1951).
8. Beirut. U.S. troops at the airport during the international action (1982–1984) to end the war in Lebanon, after Israel's 1978 invasion.
9. 1984. Reagan and Vice President George Bush celebrate their reelection.

1981

1991

JOHN PAUL II

JR EWING

THE PERSONAL COMPUTER

NIKI LAUDA

MIKHAIL GORBACHEV

ANDREY SAKHAROV

MARGARET THATCHER

ENZO FERRARI

AKIHITO

LEONARD BERNSTEIN

A t the end of the 1960s two films—*Easy Rider* (directed by Dennis Hopper, 1969) and *Zabriskie Point* (directed by Michelangelo Antonioni, 1970)—prefigured the end of the hippie world and the transition to a more competitive society. The war in Vietnam (1965–1974) destroyed the illusions of many young people, and marijuana found a new competitor in lysergic acid: LSD. Drugs and hallucinogenic substances became affordable for more people and an easy way to escape from reality. In the real world, the rise in petroleum prices dictated by countries belonging to OPEC (the cartel of petroleum producing countries) caused a long recession in the industrialized nations. The new decade saw the expansion across the continents and into more manufacturing centers and markets, of multinational companies set up by the economically advanced countries in order to diversify investments and business sectors.

S ociety became increasingly competitive and escape from reality became more widespread, first with heroin and later with cocaine. These drugs supported a criminal economy whose huge profits were laundered into the legal economies of many countries to the extent of modifying them, with the help of organized crime as well as military potentates and politicians. AIDS grew to epidemic proportions, initially

November 1989. A soldier of the dying German Democratic Republic gazes through a crack in the Berlin Wall, a symbol of the collapsing Iron Curtain.

spread by drug addicts and male homosexuals. The Soviet bloc tottered and fell, weakened by the

war in Afghanistan (1979–1989) and the revolutions of 1989. The Cold War was at an end. Signs of

affluence spread: personal computers, ready-to-wear fashion, overseas travel, and private invest-

ment in the stock market. Wall Street was ruled by yuppies, highly successful young urban profes-

sionals who came to symbolize the 1980s. Less obvious was a huge increase in the number of

homeless. The third world split: on the one hand, in the Far East there was significant economic

growth while, on the other, in Africa, many countries were on the verge of collapse.

1981

1990

The eighties. According to some, the century, and maybe history, died here. State planning as a form of government was on the decline, the social safety net of the developed countries was in danger, while other countries had never enjoyed it. Epochal conflicts became more muted: Communism was in its last, agonizing throes, and the United States was the absolute superpower.

The watchword of the decade was laissez-faire politics. Very little government, plenty of mar-

sa was elected president of Solidarnosc, a group of independent unions. In 1983 he was awarded the Nobel Peace Prize. In 1990, he became president of the Republic of Poland, then was slowly pushed aside. Managing a post-Communist country was not an easy task.

Cinema, the art of the century, entered a box-office crisis; to counter it, the studios started to produce blockbusters with mind-

1. Lech Walesa.   2. Yves Montand and Simone Signoret.   3. Giancarlo Giannini and Hanna Schygulla in *Lili Marleen*.

THE SOVIET BLOC WAS IN SERIOUS CRISIS. HALF A CENTURY OF COLD WAR WAS ABOUT TO END. THE UNITED STATES WAS ON THE WAY TO BECOMING THE ONLY SUPERPOWER. AN ENORMOUS CONCENTRATION OF WEALTH WAS USED TO ACQUIRE COMPANIES AND FACILITATE GIGANTIC MERGERS. LARGE MULTINATIONAL CORPORATIONS ACHIEVED THE ABILITY TO EVADE NATIONAL CONTROLS.

ket freedom, and may the strongest win. And on the sidelines of the first world, the old liberal ideals of national independence, personal freedom, freedom of thought, expression, religion and work, swelled up like a tide.

Lech Walesa, born in 1943, the son of Polish farmers, an electrician in the Gdańsk shipyards, a traditional Catholic and nationalist, was the champion of this movement, and received the blessing of the pope, a fellow Pole. An active union representative, often arrested, in September 1980 Wale-

numbing special effects. But the art film was still alive and well: Rainer Werner Fassbinder (1946–1982), a German playwright and film director and a crude, inspired teller of contemporary tales, made films quickly and with little investment. In 1981 his *Lili Marleen* was also a commercial suc-

206

cess. Old stars died, such as the great French actress Simone Signoret (1921–1985), here in a photo from 1960 with her husband, Yves Montand (1921–1991).

It was by now clear that the United States and the Soviet Union would never go to war. The role of Tito, who died in 1980, had shrunk in his last years. These were also the years of Anwar el-

religious fanatics. Libya with its eccentric Muslim dictator was left outside the mainstream.

Yasser Arafat (b. 1929), trained as an engineer, also risked his political career. President of the Palestine Liberation Organization since 1969, antagonized by the extremist wing of his organization, not trusted by many Muslim countries, leader of a dispersed people, in 1988 he persuaded the PLO to approve a program calling for the coexistence of the state of Israel and of a free Palestinian state in the contested territory, following a November

stories" by which he meant the vast ideological visions that since the Enlightenment had conditioned Western civilization. The phenomenon of postmodernity marked literature, the arts, architecture, even history and the people's mindset. On the other hand, the economic and monetary sciences were never so influential, and filled a space

that had once been the province of philosophy, especially moral philosophy and ethics.

In 1986 the explosion of a reactor in Chernobyl's nuclear power plant, in Ukraine, unleashed radioactivity that affected tens of thousands of people, a dramatic lesson in the dangers of nuclear power. In 1989, the Chinese government suppressed vast student protests in favor of democracy that were being held in Beijing's Tiananmen Square. At the 1984 Los Angeles Olympics, the myth of Carl Lewis, winner of the 100, 200, 4 x 100 meters, and long-jump, was born.

In November 1982, Leonid Brezhnev

4. Indira Gandhi.   5. Yasser Arafat.   6. Attempt on Reagan's life.   7. Berlin, Brandenburg Gate, 1990.   8. Carl Lewis.   9. Leonid Brezhnev lying in state.

Sadat (1918–1981): elected president of Egypt in 1970, recipient of the Nobel Peace Prize in 1978 (shared with Israel's Menachem Begin), he was assassinated by the Muslim Brotherhood. Indira Gandhi (1917–1984) also died; she had been Prime Minister of India from 1966 to 1977, then from 1980 to her death. Like Sadat, Gandhi was murdered by

1947 U.N. resolution that was never implemented.

In 1979 a French philosopher, Jean-François Lyotard (b. 1924), published *La condition postmoderne* (*The Postmodern Condition*). The adjective "postmodern," first used in Spain in the 1930s, was used by Lyotard to refer to the disappearance of the "great

The March 30, 1981 attempt on Reagan's life was the seventh attempt on the life of an American president. The Falklands War (April–June 1982) fought by Great Britain and Argentina was a colonial war of mid-size powers. On October 3–4, 1990, Berliners celebrated the second unification of Germany in front of the Brandenburg Gate.

(1906–1982) died. He had ruled the Soviet Union since 1964. He played superpower politics and at the same time pursued a cautious policy of détente with the United States. Unfortunately, Russia aged with him, the victim of inefficiency, corruption, and ideals that were by then only empty slogans.

JOHN PAUL II
Survived an attempt on his life in St. Peter's Square

Karol Wojtyla was born in 1920 in Wadowice to a humble Polish family. In his youth he was a factory worker and a poet. Having felt the religious vocation, he became a priest in 1946, and a protégé of Cardinal Wyszynski. Appointed auxiliary bishop in 1958, in 1964 he became Archbishop of Kraków and in 1967 was made cardinal. Extremely dynamic, of pure Roman Catholic faith, greatly devoted to the Virgin Mary, he kept up intense contacts with his colleagues, which became easier as East-West relations began to thaw. In the meantime, the papacy of the mystical John Paul I (Albino Luciani, 1912–1978) lasted a mere 43 days, just the time he needed to abolish the use of the papal "we" and the solemn coronation ceremony. Pope John Paul I however, did not remedy the uneasiness which Paul VI's papacy had brought. He was fearful of the changes wrought by Vatican Council II, torn between a cult of the traditional Curia and a

love for modernity. The second 1978 conclave put Karol Wojtyla on the throne, the first non-Italian pope since 1523. Unknown to Italy and the Catholic masses, direct and good-natured, Wojtyla energetically set to work and gained enormous popularity. On May 13, 1981, he was seriously wounded in an attempt on his life in St. Peter's Square in Rome.

2

1

3

89 1990 **1981** 1982 1983 1984 1985 1986 1987 1988 1989 1990 198

7

CARDINALS IN THE EAST. Hungary's Cardinal Jozsef Mindszenty (1892–1975), sentenced to life in prison by the Communist regime, was freed in the 1956 revolution and allowed to take refuge abroad. He became a symbolic figure of the martyred Church in Iron Curtain countries. In Poland, the Church had represented the nation's identity since at least the eighteenth century when the Polish kingdom was partitioned among Austria, Prussia, and Russia. The Catholic faith has acted since then as a cohesive element. The bishops, however, did not particularly stand out as protectors of the Jewish community slaughtered by the Nazis. Stefan Wyszynski (1901–1981), Poland's primate was influential both at home and in Rome.

PETRUS. The pope's activity is prodigious. He published a new canon

law code (1983 and 1990). He reformed the Roman Curia, making it more international. He brought to completion the process by which the Vatican's state secretary is now prime minister. He appointed more than one hundred cardinals. He voiced his opinions in many important documents, on ethical issues (he has a degree in moral philosophy from Rome), on theology (he received a degree in theology in Poland), and contemporary issues such as kidnappings for ransom, war, and capital punishment.

DOCTRINE. The pope has strongly reaffirmed Pius XII's teaching on contraception, abortion, divorce, church celibacy, and the ban on women in

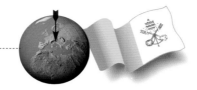

THE WANDERING APOSTLE

Mehmet Ali Agça, a young radical right-wing activist from Turkey, was sentenced by the Italian courts to life imprisonment; the motives for his actions have never been understood. What is certain is that the presence of a pope who lived from age 25 to 58 in a country of the Soviet Empire gave voice to the anti-Communism of Catholics in Poland, Slovakia, Lithuania, Croatia, and Hungary. The pope is a master in the use of the mass media, and the world's TV channels pay special and generous atten-

84 1985 1986 1987 1988 1989 1990 **1981** 1982 1983 1984 1985 1986 1987 1988 1989 1990 **1981** 1982 1983 1984 1985 1986 1982 1983 1984

He has defended human rights, and declared his strong opposition to euthanasia and to genetic engineering. Finally, he has taken responsibility for sins the Church committed centuries ago.

tion to him, not the least because he is an unusual figure. The world watches when he chairs bishops' synods, proclaims saints and blesseds (chosen particularly from among the clergy and religious orders) or announces holy years. The world follows him when he presides at spectacular ceremonies, gives weekly homilies to the pilgrims gathered under his window, or visits the churches of Rome—his diocese. An extraordinary multimedia liturgy takes place during his visits in Italy and abroad, accompanied by the sale of books, photos, and commemorative objects and the presence of enthusiastic welcoming crowds. John Paul II has toured over one hundred countries in the Old and the New Worlds. In Bologna, Italy, he attended a rock concert. The image of this pope, now old, somewhat stooping, with a shaking arm caused by Parkinson's disease, yet fearless, has become a symbol of our time.

1. January 1998, Cuba. Fidel Castro and John Paul II.
2. May 13, 1981, Vatican City. Attempt on the pope's life.
3. Poland. The pope speaks to General Wojciech Jaruzelski, Poland's Premier (1981–1989) who ruled the country up to the demise of Communism.
4. Cardinal Joseph Ratzinger.
5. Nicaragua. The pope speaking under a giant portrait of Augusto Sandino (1893–1934), a hero of the war that brought an end to the country's military occupation by the United States (1912–1933) and who inspired the front that banished dictator Somoza in 1979.
6. Mexico. Throngs of people surround the pope.
7. Cardinal Jozsef Mindszenty, Hungary's primate. In 1998 Pope John Paul II beatified archbishop Stepinac, a pro-Nazi Croat who was sentenced and thrown into prison by Tito's courts.
8. Cardinal Stefan Wyszynski, Poland's primate.
9. New York. A store window during John Paul II's visit.

the clergy. He has condemned homosexuality, and in recent years has been critical of the guiding principles of capitalism. He has often appointed bishops who are not well-liked in their own dioceses. He has condemned the theology of liberation and those Catholic theologians who are lax in their obedience to Rome.

"*Karol Wojtyla, archbishop of Kraków . . . elected pope in October 1978 . . . in that role too he will . . . make a decisive contribution that will change the destiny of the Polish regime (and of the communist world in Europe).*"
G. Bordino, *Il mondo dal 1970 a oggi*
(*The World from 1970 to Now*)

JR EWING
His TV show conquered France

I n 1982 John Ross Ewing, aka JR, patriarch of the *Dallas* clan, conquered market No. 59: cultivated, savvy France. *Dallas* was an American TV serial created by David Jacobs and produced by Leonard Katzman, which was broadcast on CBS from April 2, 1978 to May 3, 1991. It was named after the Texas city where Ewing Oil, the company owned by Jock Ewing and family, was located. During its 356 episodes, it reached up to 85 million viewers in the United States alone. It is popular in most countries of the world, and it became one of the ten most watched TV programs of all time. The plot? It begins

like a sort of *Romeo and Juliet* set in the world of oil tycoons and continues through deaths, killings, hatred, betrayals, deceptions, drunkenness, vile calculations, loves, revenge, social climbing, sinful relationships, departures, returns, and all the traditional, sensational scenes of the classic romance novel, with a special predilection for spousal betrayals.

8 1989 1990 1981 **1982** 1983 1984 1985 1986 1987   1981 **1982** 1983 1984 1985 1986 1987 1988 19

OTHER SHOWS. The American entertainment industry has flooded the world with successful TV films, serials, and soap operas. At an even more elementary level, Brazil has produced very successful *telenovelas* (which are usually broadcast daily in the afternoon, like the soap operas).

Among the best-known U.S. productions: *The Bold and the Beautiful*, a soap opera narrating the saga of the Forrester designers (CBS, since March 3, 1987); *Dynasty*, a serial narrating the saga of the Carrington Oil family, with a woman as the "lead villain" (interpreted by Joan Collins);

Falcon Crest, a serial saga narrating the life of the Giobertis, a California winery-owning family, who quarrel over a vast property, with an older "lead villainess" interpreted by Jane Wyman (former wife of President Reagan).

THE POWERFUL. It is impressive that millions of TV viewers interpreted the modest farmhouse, the dreary living rooms, the middle-management-type offices, and the Ewings' flashy, provincial clothes as the luxury and chic of the rich and famous.

SERIAL

The serial is a particular type of fiction written for television, divided into episodes and segments structured around commercial breaks. Using a simple cinema-theater-TV language, complete with its own conventions, it narrates the events in the life of a character or a family. Unlike other TV films, which often portray the life of a social nucleus different from the family and end a story with each episode, the serial goes on by interweaving the lives of its characters in many chapters (episodes), just like the popular nineteenth-century serialized novels that were published in installments. Like them, the successful serial yields plenty of lore on mass mentality and taste, especially when it becomes successful in many countries and is followed passionately by the "global village" masses.

The gist of the *Dallas* plot is biblical: the "lead villain," who is the protagonist and replaces the "juvenile lead" which has become obsolete—is JR (actor Larry Hagman) who undermines his father Jock Ewing's (actor Jim Davis) power, following the plot of "Absalom against David," and persecutes his younger brother Bobby (Patrick Duffy), following the plot of "Cain against Abel." The Southfork Ranch is the royal palace where the intrigues take place (including semi-incestuous relations patterned after "Tamar and

1. The Ewings in the horse corral, a must for every large ranch.
2. Larry Hagman—JR—on a promotional tour in Russia.
3. JR, a Texan, keeps his 10-gallon hat on even while taking a dip.
4. The city of Dallas, Texas in the background of the serial's title.
5. JR with his younger brother Bobby.
6. Mother Ewing with her "jewels."
7. JR with relatives, friends, and enemies in gala dress.

8. Jock Ewing, the empire's founder, with son Bobby and daughter-in-law Pamela (actress Victoria Principal).
9. Southfork, the Ewings' ranch. Clearly, not a match for the mansion of press tycoon William Randolph Hearst (1863–1951), or those of oil men John D. Rockefeller (1839–1937), J. Paul Getty (1892–1976) or Muda Hassan al Bolkiah, since 1967 Sultan of Brunei and reputed to be the wealthiest man in the world, even wealthier than Elizabeth II.

7 | 8

982 1983 1984 1985 1986 1987 1988 1989 1990 1981 **1982** 1983 1984 1985 1986 1987 1988 1989 1990 1981 **1982** 1983 1984 1985 1986 1987 1988 1989 1990 1981 19

6

Amnon"), while the glass headquarters of the Ewing Oil Company in Dallas is the temple where the cult of the All-Powerful-Dollar is celebrated. In addition to Adam, Cain, and Abel we also have "mother Ewing," an Eve type and, like Eve, not completely innocent. There is also a role for the "whore of Babylon," which is filled by different women characters and, ending with Shakespeare, there is an Iago behind every corner.

WICKEDNESS. The star of *Dallas* is JR, the meanest, most hypocritical, spiteful, petty, greedy, and insensitive, of the Ewings. He is only moderately handsome and a bit of a swine. So, is wickedness in action what attracts the masses in this last quarter century?

"The characters in Dallas are all more or less subjected to the same events: struggle for wealth and power, life, death, defeat, victory, adultery, love, hate, envy, illusion and disappointment."
Umberto Eco

9

"Man of the Year"

The personal computer (PC) is a stand-alone computer that does not need to share processing or resources with other computers and is built for use by one person at a time. Born in 1980, the idea had already been around for centuries. If the calculator's ancestor was the adding machine invented in 1642 by the French mathematician and philosopher Blaise Pascal, we can say that the true inventors of the modern PC are the mathematician and inventor Charles Babbage (1792–1871) and his colleague, the mathematician Augusta Ada Byron (1815–1852), who developed the working principles of the modern digital computer. The first personal computer, built by IBM Corporation, signaled that a dream held by many computer industry people of the seventies—such as Steven Jobs (Apple's co-founder) and Bill Gates—had come true: to put a computer in every American home. Since the 1980s, the PC has radically changed the way millions of people work and live, by making very powerful machines available to anyone at a relatively low cost. Just to give an example, the advent of desktop publishing created six million jobs in five years (1982–1987) in the United States alone. In recent years, the Internet has allowed people to combine the PC's power with unlimited database resources.

2

3

7 1988 1989 1990 1981 1982 **1983** 1984 1985

1981 1982 **1983** 1984 1985 1986 1987 198

4

1

IBM was born in 1914 as the International Business Machines Corporation and in 1924 merged with Computing Tabulating Recording (founded in 1911). The idea upon which IBM was to build its fortune at the end of the 1950s was that of a "family of computers" where the same software could be used on any machine operating with the same type of processor. In 1981 IBM introduced its personal computer. It has quickly become the standard used today by over 100 million people.

INTERNET. The Internet is an open connection system linking computer networks that allows the computers and their programs to directly exchange information. At the beginning of 1995, over 50,000 networks and five million computers were linked over the Internet, increasing at the approximate rate of 9 percent per month. According to projections, by 2001, 100 million Americans and over 60 million Europeans will be linked through the Internet.

BILL GATES. William H. Gates III founded Microsoft Corporation with Paul Allen in 1975. He was among the first to envision the future of home computing. He entered millions of households through the sale of his DOS (disk operating system), and later with Windows. Thanks to Bill Gates' long-term vision, Microsoft is the world's leading software house.

5

COMPUTER SCIENCE

Computer science is the discipline covering the design, programming, and use of computers. Undoubtedly the father of computer science was the English mathematician Alan Turing. During World War II, Turing, a professor at Cambridge, and other scholars decoded enemy communications using practical applications of mathematical theories. Later, extraordinary technological advances—such as the miniaturization of electronic components—gave a tremendous impetus to computer science.

It is difficult to measure the use and application of the computer worldwide, as the most significant and reliable data are from the United States, while figures relating to other countries are less reliable. There are approximately 60 million PC users in the United States and 30 mil-lion in Europe. In the 1990s computer science became a part of our working life as well as our way of communicating and our leisure time. In the United States, a recently published dictionary contained 9,700 computer-related words. In today's spoken language, at least thirty to fifty everyday words or jargon expressions are computer-related and did not exist before the computer age. This is true of the five most widely spoken languages in the world.

1982 **1983** 1984 1985 1986 1987 1988 1989 1990 1981 19

1. Rome. A room in the Flore Internet Café. Even before the birth of the Internet, computers were used for games among friends, and not just by the younger generation.
2. 1984. A promotional image of the computer generated by the Rainbow digital PC.
3. November 1989, Tokyo. Inside the stock exchange. The computerization of work and of stock exchange services is a leading factor in the progressive globalization of the securities market.
4. 1989, Yokohama. Fuchinobe High School students during a computer lesson.
5. Principality of Monaco, April 1992. Bill Gates at an international Microsoft meeting.
6. Potomac, Maryland. Elementary school children in front of the computer.
7. Cologne, Germany. The image of a fashion catalogue published on a CD-ROM.
8. February 1997. An ad page for one of the most popular browsers, Microsoft's Internet Explorer.
9. 1993, Paris. A powerful Macintosh Powerbook equipped with internal modem.

"With the reduction in the price of computers, it will be more economical to center everything in the home. Some families will again become the units of production, as was the case before the industrial revolution."
Storia del computer (History of the Computer), 1984

NIKI LAUDA

Formula One world champion again after seven years

Niki Lauda was born in Austria in 1949, to a family of industrialists. He had no aptitude for school, his passion and dream being car racing. His family was opposed and tried placing all kinds of obstacles in his way. But young Lauda, with a cool, calculating nature, was seriously determined and won. He began his career as a driver in the lesser categories; he ran for BRM and at the end of 1973 joined Ferrari, the house that had won its last championship in 1964 with John Surtee. Luca Cordero di Montezemolo, a young aristocrat close to the Agnelli family (which owned an important stake in Ferrari) was the team's manager in 1973–1975. In 1974 Lauda won two Formula One Grand Prix, and in 1975 he went on to become world champion. In 1976 he was the favorite for

Germany's Grand Prix. On August 1, during the race, he went off course, hit a rock, and bounced back on the track; his car was hit by two other cars and went up in flames. Extracted from the flames, Lauda was hospitalized with severe burns to the head, multiple fractures, and serious lesions to the bronchi and lungs. He looked death in the face. That night he received the last rites.

2

1

3

4

BUSINESS. Formula One is an international business involving large automobile manufacturers and other related industries, including the tire manufacturers and the fuel and electronic component industries. It also involves multinational consumer goods companies such as cigarette and soft drink makers that pay high prices to sponsor the stables and profit from the champions' publicity. Lauda, a businessman, was personally involved in his contracts.

RISK. Lauda was one of the few race car drivers who tried—in vain—to organize fellow drivers to deal with their "masters"—the car manufacturers, the teams, the sports federations, the sponsors, the track bosses. The high compensation drivers receive certainly does not repay them for the enormous

risks they run. Tennis, for example, also a billion-dollar sport, entails no risks. Lauda is a very rational man, and not many people agreed with him.

IS THERE LIFE AFTER RACING? In addition to racing, Lauda is in the airplane business: he owns a small, though not

insignificant, airplane fleet. He continued in his family's business tradition, and was not just a racing champion. He was not the first driver to come back after a serious accident, but his accident was especially devastating. Nuvolari and Fangio, perhaps even Ayrton Senna (who died in a track

A CHAMPION'S COMEBACK

"I am coming back because I want to be world champion for the third time."

Niki Lauda, 1982

On September 10, after the August 1, 1976 accident and after undergoing extensive treatment and surgery, Lauda was back on the racing track for Italy's Grand Prix and came in fourth. Racing was still very painful: the helmet hurt his skin; he had eye and lung problems. He did not win in 1976; he did so in 1977. In October of that year he left Ferrari to join Brabham; in 1979 he announced his retirement from racing. After that, not much changed in Lauda's behavior. He was still an exceptional test driver and technician. He raced with a clean, modern style that seemed automatic in its precise focus aimed at performance and success, free of excess or bravado.

6

9

1982 1983 **1984** 1985 1986 1987 1988 1989 1990 1981 ... 1988 1989 1990 1981 1

Nor did his words and behavior outside the track change. Asked about his secret as a champion, he coldly replied: "I always ask myself what I must do in order to come in first." And when he did win, it meant he had given himself the right answers.

Niki Lauda shielded his private life by simply avoiding the public eye. He said very little about his relationship with colleagues and the houses for which he raced, responding with minimal courtesy to those who succeeded in questioning him. In 1982 Lauda announced he would race again. He was 33 years old, and this was his second comeback. Now racing for Marlboro-McLaren, in October 1984 he won the world championship for the third time. On August 17, 1985 he permanently retired.

7

8

accident), were maybe more pleasant or greater champions, although it is foolish to compare drivers of different times in a sport that changes radically every few years. However, no one was more serious or less picturesque than Lauda. He exemplified the modern sports champion.

1. April 1976. Lauda relaxes in his Salzburg home.
2. Niki Lauda. The cap partially hides the scars of the 1976 accident.
3. Niki Lauda on the winners' platform with Alain Prost, another champion.
4. March 1977. Lauda raises the trophy for most courageous sportsman of the year.
5. August 1, 1976, Nürburgring. Drivers Merzario, Edwards, Ertl, and Lunger place Lauda's body at the track's edge after extracting him from the car on fire.
6. August 1, 1976. Lauda's Ferrari bursting into flames; next to it, the last car to hit the Ferrari, a Surtees T16 driven by the American Brett Lunger.
7. Luca Cordero di Montezemolo, who later became

Ferrari's organizer, with Niki Lauda in the Ferrari stand.
8. 1979. Niki Lauda piloting an airplane, part of his fleet, Lauda Air.
9. 1977. The T2 Ferrari Niki Lauda used in his second world championship. All visible space is filled with sponsor names.

MIKHAIL GORBACHEV
Last Secretary of the Soviet Union's Communist Party

Mikhail Sergeyevich Gorbachev was born in 1931 to a family of farmers in Privolnoye, a village in the Stavropol region. In 1955 he graduated from Moscow law school and was sent back to Stavropol where he began his political career. In 1971 he was a member of the party's Central Committee in Moscow; in 1978 he was a member of the Secretariat and in charge of agriculture; in 1980, a regular member of the Politburo. When Yuri Andropov (1914–1984) succeeded Brezhnev in 1982, Gorbachev began his climb to the top of the hierarchy, which continued as Konstantin Chernenko (1911–1985) became general secretary in February 1984. Gorbachev was appointed Party Chairman with the support of Andrei Gromyko (1909–1989), the great diplomat.

Gorbachev inaugurated the "new course" at the 27th Party Congress. In 1989, after Gromyko's death, Gorbachev became President of the Soviet Union. In a 1988 speech at the U.N. he had proclaimed the transition from an era of confrontation to an era of international cooperation. He withdrew the Red Army from Afghanistan. He signed agreements with both Reagan and Bush to reduce nuclear armaments. He approached China and discontinued the politics of power the USSR had pursued in Africa. He supported reformers in the Warsaw Pact countries, favoring their 1989 revolutions, and recognized the inevitable reunification of Germany. He signed accords with EEC countries, wished for a "common European house" and in 1990, with the Paris Charter for a New Europe, he put an end to the Cold War era. In 1990, he was awarded the Nobel Peace Prize.

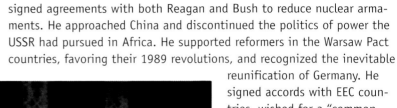

DIALECTIC. Starting in 1989 the number of Gorbachev followers dropped, while that of radical reformers swelled; the latter won the local elections in the various republics of the Soviet Union, and pushed for the abolition of the state economy and the single-party system. The embarrassing withdrawal from Afghanistan after a ten-year war (1979–1989) increased discontent in the Red Army. The nationalist problem had been exacerbated by Stalin's policy of mass deportations and of "Russification" of those republics of non-Russian ethnic stock. With Gorbachev's abolition of state atheism, the Moscow Patriarch returned to his pre-revolutionary power and Islam reasserted itself in the Asian republics.

OTHER POWERS. The disintegration of the USSR was followed by increased agitation by the Red Army and the all-powerful "military-industrial complex," the conservative Communists who remained in the state and party organizations, the fragments of the KGB (the formidable secret service that gained power during the Brezhnev dictatorship [1964–1982]), and the academic departments closest to the sciences, to technology, and the extraction industries.

COUP D'ÉTAT. Although Gorbachev stayed a central course, he proved incapable of governing; nevertheless, in 1990 he was reelected President for another five-year term. On August 18, 1991 he was detained together with his wife and daughter in Foros (Crimea). But the coup failed thanks to Boris Yeltsin, the President of the Russian Republic, and Gorbachev was freed to return to Moscow. On December 21, the presidents of eleven Soviet republics announced to Gorbachev that the USSR no longer existed. On Christmas Day, the Soviet flag was lowered from the Kremlin tower and in its place the flag of the Russian Republic was unfurled. The former president, now a private citizen, has remained in Russia, protected by his Western friends.

GLASNOST AND PERESTROIKA

"In the Russia of fifty years ago, what Gorbachev said would have sent him to the firing squad. Five years ago, it would have sent him to a jail for dissidents."

Stephen Cohen

In February–March 1986, at the Soviet Union's Communist Party Congress, Gorbachev presented his "new course," to be marked by glasnost (openness) and a democratization in the relations between government and citizens. Glasnost was to be achieved through perestroika, the "restructuring," through far-reaching reforms, of government structures, especially those that concerned the economy. In international relations, Gorbachev advanced the idea that a new mindset was needed to deal with national security problems in light of the reality of nuclear weapons. Gorbachev created a deep, lasting impression when he rehabilitated Stalin's enemies (among them, Bukharin), abolished the gulags and political exile, took the first steps for freedom of the press and of

1983 1984 **1985** 1986 1987 1988 1989 1990 1981 1982 1983 1984 **1985** 1 ... 81 ... 1982 1983 198

association, and for a "pluralistic single-party system," and enacted laws to establish an opposition, relatively democratic elections, freedom

of speech at political congresses, and the birth of a mixed economy. In the summer of 1988 a reform plan began the restructuring of the party.

All of these reforms went hand in hand with the peaceful dismantling of the Soviet Empire in Europe, and were received with joy and admiration in the West. In the Soviet Union however, the economic situation was disastrous, living conditions became dire and the party's eclipse left a power void, just as local nationalist groups became increasingly unruly. Special forces deployed in Georgia in 1989 created a slaughter. Subsequently, the Baltic Sea republics revolted along with Armenia and Azerbaijan; the Donbas miners went on strike, and party membership plummeted. Clearly, the Soviet Union was disintegrating. Perestroika turned out to be unfeasible, as it conflicted with the personal interests of the powerful bureaucratic class. Without glasnost, power and money passed from the party to high-level party bureaucrats.

1. February 1989, Afghanistan. The impotent Red Army leaves Kabul.

2. July 1989, Paris. Gorbachev during a press conference at the Elysée Palace.

3. Moscow. Party Secretary Gorbachev and his wife, Foreign Minister Eduard Shevardnadze (later President of Georgia), Soviet President Gromyko, Council President Nikolay Ryzhkov together with Erich Honecker, East Germany's dictator.

4. November 30, 1988, Moscow. Gorbachev speaks to the Supreme Soviet.

5. May 1988, Moscow. Presidents Gorbachev and Reagan meet at the Kremlin.

6. 1986, Ukraine. The Chernobyl nuclear power plant, which exploded on April 26.

7. 1989, German Democratic Republic. In Berlin, protesters demand strong reforms.

8. February 1983. Yuri Andropov, Party Secretary who succeeded Brezhnev.

9. August 1991, Moscow. After the coup, Yeltsin takes charge of the situation and faces the insurgents' tanks.

ANDREY SAKHAROV

Suffered internal exile

Andrey Sakharov was born in 1921 in Moscow. His father, Dimitri, was a physics professor and a well-known popular author. Andrey earned a physics degree at the University of Moscow in 1942 and until 1945 worked in the war industry; later, he was involved in research and until 1948, in quantum physics. In 1947 he received a doctorate in physical and mathematical sciences. He studied thermonuclear reactions—the processes of fusion within the nuclei of light elements such as deuterium, hydrogen, and tritium. He worked with the Igor Tamm group on the principles of making a hydrogen

bomb. Also important in Sakharov's work was his research on the properties of plasma. In 1953 he was made a regular member of the Soviet Academy of Sciences. In the wake of the Communist Party's 20th Congress, Sakharov denounced the danger of nuclear tests. Later, in 1964 he strongly attacked the unsound biological theories of Trofim Lysenko, which Stalin had supported. In 1968 his dissent manifesto, *Progress, Coexistence and Intellectual Freedom* was published in the USSR and in New York.

4

1

2

PLASMA. It is practically the fourth state of matter; it is composed of ionized but macroscopically neutral gases, the number of positive and negative charges in each volume being equal. Plasma is important in astrophysical research because it can engender thermonuclear fusion—the process caused by the high-temperature, high-pressure conditions found inside stars. Sakharov noted that as a result of its high level of conductivity, plasma freezes internally the force lines of its magnetic field. Therefore, an external magnetic field cannot penetrate plasma; this allows for the creation of large volumes of plasma contained by magnetic fields. From these systems the explosive buildup of magnetic force results. Research on controlled thermonuclear fusion is extremely important because, unlike fission, it does not produce radioactive waste.

SAKHAROV was not the leading Soviet physicist of his time. As a recipient of the Nobel Peace Prize in 1975, however, he became an international figure. That, together with his strong will and probably the fear that he might be used abroad for his research work on nuclear fusion, saved him from exile (unlike the reactionary author Alexander Solzhenitsyn). The powerful international community of physicists kept the Sakharov case alive. After seven years of internal exile, Gorbachev granted him leave to return to Moscow. Sakharov then entered politics: he favored a *perestroika* that could lead to a dissolu-

3

tion of the USSR Communist Party. Elected to Parliament, he died in Moscow in 1989.

SAMIZDAT. It is the publishing and dissemination of independent publications in a country, such as the USSR,

where publishing is a state-controlled industry. The first such publication was the *Synthaxis* review (1959). The phenomenon grew along with the first dissident groups. In 1967, after the arrest of Anatoly Ginzburg and others, the great *samizdat* era began, with

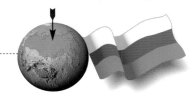

DISSENT: CULTURE AND FREEDOM

At first it was primarily the poets who criticized Bolshevism and fell victims to the secret police. Yet in the 1950s, unlike Western scientists who generally became apolitical, supported by vast research funding (especially in the United States), Soviet scientists became politically active.

When Sakharov first expressed his dissent he was already a renowned physicist. In his 1968 book he claimed that only the cooperation of the two superpowers and a reconciliation of the two opposing ideological and social structures, applied systematically, could save the world from catastrophe. As a result, he was immediately removed from his scientific work. In 1970 he founded a human rights committee. In 1973 he attacked the concentration of power and the class self-

ishness of Soviet bureaucracy. In 1976 he was among the founders of a group to monitor the implementation of the Helsinki treaty (1973 and 1975) on European safety and cooperation. Increasingly pro-West, he went so far as to state that the Soviet regime was the world's center of totalitarianism. On January 22, 1980 the Soviet Presidium took away his privileges and exiled him to Gorky (now Nizhny Novgorod).

4 1985 **1986** 1987 1988 1989 1990 1981 1982 1983 1984 1985 **1986** 1987 1988

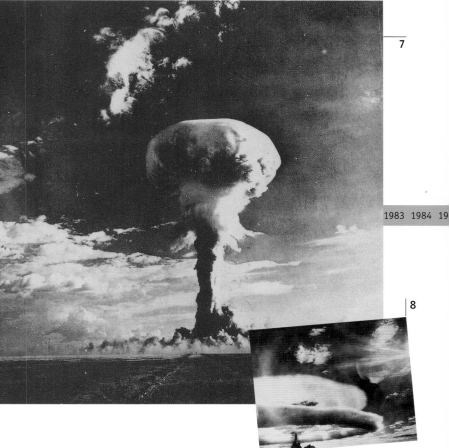

1983 1984 19

6

1. Moscow. A view of the imposing university structure built during the Stalin era.
2. A portrait of Andrey Sakharov during his years as a dissident.
3. The gray minibus carries Sakharov's remains, followed by a small funeral crowd.
4. Sakharov with his wife Yelena Bonner, who was allowed to leave the Soviet Union for medical treatment, even during her husband's internal exile.
5. Moscow, May 1, 1967. A missile unit marches in Moscow's Red Square on Soviet Labor Day.
6. March 1955. A portrait of Soviet Marshal Giorgyi Zhukov (1896–1974), Stalin's closest military ally during the "patriotic war," and the true author of the Soviet Eastern front victory over Hitler. He was Defense Minister from 1955 to 1957 and a great supporter of nuclear weapons.
7. August 12, 1953, Soviet Union. A hydrogen bomb explosion.
8. Soviet Union. A "superbomb" explosion.

publications by the Medvedevs and A. Marchenko, the widow of Osip Mandelstam (1891–1938), a poet who died while in internal exile. The government sent the dissidents to labor camps or special mental institutions or expelled them from the country.

"It is not a coincidence that the leading national and international spokesman of Soviet dissent was a scientist . . . who had been among the first to create the Soviet hydrogen bomb at the end of the nineteen-forties."
Eric J. Hobsbawm, *Ages of Extremes—The Short Twentieth Century 1914–1991*

MARGARET THATCHER

Three times the United Kingdom's Prime Minister

Margaret Hilda Roberts was born in 1925 to a well-to-do family of shopkeepers. She received a degree in chemistry from Oxford in 1951, and in 1953 was admitted to the Bar. In 1959 she was elected to the House of Commons as a Conservative. From 1961 to 1964 she held modest appointments in the Macmillan government; later, she was a "minister" of various departments for the Conservative "shadow government" when the party was out of power. With the Conservative Party regaining power in 1970, Thatcher was made Minister of Education and Science. At the Conservative convention of 1975, she was chosen to lead the party, and in May 1979 led the party to victory, thus becoming Prime Minister. She was reelected to the office in the 1983 and 1987 elections.

After ten years she clashed with members of her own administration who favored the U.K.'s entry into the European monetary system and with her Chancellor of the Exchequer, whom she replaced with John Major. The Labor Party's victory in the European Parliament elections, and opposition by many Conservatives and the public at large to a new municipal tax on individuals (the infamous "poll tax") forced Thatcher to resign on November 22, 1990. John Major took her place.

THE IRON LADY. Mrs. Thatcher fought the labor unions. She signed new laws outlawing the calling of solidarity strikes and forbidding labor leaders to call strikes without first consulting with the rank-and-file. In 1985, after a year of continuous strikes, she prevailed upon the powerful miners' unions, the backbone of British labor, to end their walkout.

PEOPLE'S CAPITALISM. Thatcher's policies brought about a 3 percent annual rise in the GNP starting in 1981, which lasted several years. Between 1979 and 1987 the number of people owning stock tripled. Thatcher supported selling municipally owned real estate to tenants: as a result, home ownership rose from 52 to 66 percent. In 1986, inflation fell to 3.4 percent.

EUROPE. The dream of a united Europe received only lip service from those countries that were not under Roman influence during antiquity, that did not belong to the Holy Roman Empire in the Middle Ages, and that did not suffer protracted foreign invasions in modern times. Mrs. Thatcher was the faithful spokesperson for an Anglo-centric vision of the world.

CULTURE. As Minister of Education, she ended the program that provided free milk to elementary school children. She had no interest in supporting culture; as a result, in the 1980s Paris became once more the leading European capital of tourism.

THATCHERISM

1. 1980, London. Prime Minister Thatcher receives Elizabeth, the Queen Mother, widow of George VI, at No. 10 Downing Street.

2. February 1986, Canterbury. Mrs. Thatcher and President Mitterand of France sign the treaty to build a tunnel below the English Channel, thus physically linking the two countries.

3. Margaret Thatcher during her first years in power.

4. October 13, 1984, Brighton. The Grand Hotel after the IRA attack on the Conservative Party convention.

5. Mrs. Thatcher with President Ronald Reagan; their economic policies often coincided.

6. Confrontation between strikers and strike-breakers during a strike against the Thatcher government.

7. South Atlantic Ocean. The British Navy in the Falkland Islands.

8. November 22, 1990, London. On the day of Thatcher's resignation, poll tax protesters in front of No. 10 Downing Street.

9. 1989, Liverpool. The industrial crisis after ten years of Thatcher government.

Mrs. Thatcher was the first neo-laissez-faire politician to gain power in the U.K. She aimed to drastically lower social welfare and taxes, privatize state-controlled companies, industries, and services, and pass laws limiting the decision-making powers of labor leaders. Having come to power after a series of strikes—the first woman Prime Minister ever of a country that had been ruled by six or seven queens—she cut the government budget, privatized state-owned companies, raised indirect taxes, did away with currency controls, raised the cost of money, and lowered the highest tax bracket from 83 to 60 percent, thus favoring the wealthy capitalists. The inflation rate was cut from 17 to 11 percent in 1981; however, in 1980 the unemployment rate rose to 6.1 percent and, in 1986, to 11.8 percent, while production continued to lag. In 1982 she quickly reversed Argentina's invasion of the Falkland Islands, and won the war.

This victory revealed the new electoral base on which Thatcher's popularity rested: people of modest means and station—who looked wistfully back to the empire and shared her xenophobia and her anti-European sentiments—and the middle and upper-middle class who approved her anti-labor policies, her policies favoring the development of an advanced tertiary economy, and a proud sort of nationalism. The Crown supported the Prime Minister, as it must constitutionally, albeit coolly. Thatcher ushered in the values of an aggressive, technological bourgeoisie that was much influenced by the United States but had little or no style.

"*She has Marilyn's mouth and Caligula's eyes.*"
François Mitterand

ENZO FERRARI

His unforgettable "red cars" survive him

Enzo Ferrari was born in Modena, Italy in 1898, the son of Alfredo Ferrari, whose mechanical shop supplied the state railways. An average student, he was an enthusiastic athlete, enjoyed *operettas*, and was a fan of the first automobile races. In 1914 he was already reporting for a sports newspaper, writing about soccer. After his father and his older brother died in 1916, Enzo Ferrari taught in the firemen's mechanical school in his hometown. He served in the war from 1917 to 1918. After his discharge he worked in Turin for an automobile wrecking company. He entered the world of car racing working first as a test driver, then as a race car driver for CMN of Milan. At the Targa Florio 1919 race he came in ninth. From 1919 to 1924 he was a valuable driver, mostly for the Alfa Romeo company.

In 1929 he founded Scuderia Ferrari, a racing team, with capital from Alfa Romeo and Pirelli Tires. He was one of his company's drivers until 1931 together with the champion Tazio Nuvolari (1892–1953) and the Varzis, Giuseppe Campari, Luigi Fagioli, Luis Chiron, and Guy Moll. After liquidating the company, Ferrari went on to manage Alfa Races from which he resigned in 1939 to buy a plot of land in Maranello, Modena where he established his new company, Auto Avio Costruzioni Ferrari. In 1940 his first car, the fast 815 Ferrari, was built; the first driver was Alberto Ascari (1918–1955). The *Cavallino* was born.

2

5

82 1983 1984   198.

1

EVERYONE'S RED CAR. When Ferrari died in 1988, many of his beloved relatives and friends had preceded him: his oldest son Dino, his wife, and some of his beloved drivers. Even the company was no longer his; though, to tell the truth, neither does it belong to Fiat: as a myth, it belongs to everyone. For the past forty years, the Dinos, the Testarossas, and all the other racing and road cars: the open two-seaters, the coupes, the GT's, have been the dream of half of the world's young men who look at them spellbound on newspaper pages or in films where they are driven by today's thriller heroes. Red toy models for children and reproductions for adults are bestsellers.

SPONSORS. From the first day he built his racing team with investments from Alfa Romeo and Pirelli, Ferrari had an uncanny ability to find investment capital. In Europe he was considered the inventor of sports sponsoring. Shell, Bosch, Whitworth, Champion, Siata, Memini, all automotive industry companies, were some of his pre-World War II sponsors. After the war, the sponsors multiplied. In the end,

"On August 14th, in Maranello, the world's most famous Italian died."
From a newspaper of the times.

THE RED CARS

1. Enzo Ferrari with engineer Lampredi.

2. Enzo Ferrari as a young race car driver.

3. The Ferrari 125 raced by Alberto Ascari, who won the 1949 European Grand Prix.

4. The Ferrari 500 F2 with which Alberto Ascari won the Formula One Grand Prix in 1952 and 1953.

5. The Lancia D50-modified Ferrari, used by Fangio to win the 1956 world prize.

6. The Alfa Romeo P3 raced by the Ferrari team in 1932.

7. The Ferrari driven by José Froilan Gonzalez when he won his first Formula One Grand Prix on July 14, 1951 in Silverstone. It is a 375, designed by the engineer Lampredi.

8. The Ferrari 156 used by Phil Hill to win the 1961 world prize. Designed by Paolo D'Alessio.

9. June 4, 1988. A photo of Pope John Paul II visiting the Ferrari works. He is greeting the faithful in a Ferrari Mondial 8. (From *Autosprint*).

The Ferrari logo, a rampant black colt (Cavallino) on a yellow background, appeared for the first time in 1932 on Ferrari Racing Team cars, a present from Countess Baracca, mother of World War I Italian ace Francesco Baracca (1888–1918), who sported the emblem on his fighter plane. The "red cars" were born before the Ferrari Company. The dazzling Alfa Romeo P3 used by the Ferrari Team was built in 1932. In 1949 Ascari won the European Grand Prix in Monza with a Ferrari 125. In 1951, Gonzalez's 375 was the first Ferrari to win a Formula One Grand Prix at Silverstone (the race was inaugurated in 1950). In 1952 and 1953 Ascari was Formula One world champion in a Ferrari 500 F2. In 1956, it was Juan Manuel Fangio who drove a Ferrari that was originally a Lancia D50. The fourth Ferrari world title was won by Mike Hawthorn in 1958:

1986 1987 **1988** 1989

83 1984 1985

Ferrari was acquired by Fiat.

MEANWHILE, Salman Rushdie's publication of *The Satanic Verses* incurred Ayatollah Khomeini's wrath; he sentenced the author to death, authorizing anyone to execute him. President Mitterand invited 75 Nobel Prize winners to Paris, to a meeting having as theme the danger and promises at the threshold of the twenty-first century. In Burundi, the Tutsi aristocracy, of Nilo-Hamitic origin, exterminated the Hutu majority.

he drove a Ferrari 246. In 1961, the world title went to Phil Hill, who drove a Ferrari 156. In 1964, it went to John Surtees, who drove a monocoque body Ferrari 158. Between 1953 and 1972, out of 20 world races, Ferrari won 13. In 1975, Ferrari again won the Formula One world title with Niki Lauda. In 1979 Jody Scheckter won with a Ferrari 312T4. This was the last Formula One won by Ferrari cars. Its founder, the mythical builder of racing cars, Enzo Ferrari, who received an honorary engineering degree, died in 1988. His gritty determination, his rare talent of putting together a team and stimulating them to create a winning car, his ability to turn a brand into a myth, live on.

AKIHITO
Japan's 125th emperor

Akihito was born in 1933, the son of Hirohito and Nagako, daughter of Prince Kuno. Like all the emperors of his race, Akihito has no personal history, rather, he is a descendant of *Jimmu Tenno*, last emperor of the age of the gods and first emperor of the age of men, whose reign began around 660 B.C. and who was reputed to have lived over 130 years, a normal time span for Akihito's ancestors. Jimmu was great-grandson to Ninigi, who was granted sovereignty over Japan because he was grandson to Amaterasu, the Sun-goddess. All of Japan's emperors descend from Amaterasu, in a single, direct line. Not all of them ruled; often their tasks were taken over by regents or by the *shogun* (military governors). At the time Akihito was born, this was neither myth nor lore, but sacred history enshrined in the Constitution, whose article 3 (later abolished in 1945), stated that the emperor "has a heavenly, divine and sacred nature." At an appropriate age, when he became crown prince, Akihito married a "commoner," Michiko Shoda who gave birth to their son and heir, Naruhito. In 1989 after a long illness, Emperor Hirohito died; with him, the Showa era came to an end. He was succeeded by Akihito, who ushered in the Heisei era (in which peace was to be achieved). In 1993, Akihito's son, Naruhito, married a young non-aristocratic career diplomat, Masako Owada.

83 1984 1985 1986   8 **1989** 1990 1981 1982 1983 1984 1985 1986 1987 1988 **1989** 1990 1981 1982 1983

> ❞*In 1994, Japan was the largest net creditor nation in the world, for 690 billion dollars, while in perfect juxtaposition the U.S. have become the largest net debtor nation in the world, to the tune of 700 billion dollars.*❞
>
> Geminello Alvi, *Il secolo americano* (*The American Century*)

THE HIROHITO ISSUE. In a metropolitan area of twelve million people, the old emperor (born in 1901, regent since 1921, and emperor since 1926), lived isolated, in a palace surrounded by trees and an imposing wall. The Imperial Office administered huge assets, dealt with politicians and the press, and protected the isolation of the dynasty. But Hirohito was a problem: he was responsible for the authoritarian, military, and capitalistic regime that had led the country to war and defeat.

CORRUPTION. Thirty years after the atom bomb was dropped, Japan was reborn as a major industrial and financial power. Gerontocracy, a strict hierarchical system, the subservience

NO MORE *MIKADOS*

1. Tokyo. A picture of the isolated imperial residence.
2. 1990, Tokyo. Akihito in the religious coronation costume prescribed by the Shinto ritual.
3. 1993, Tokyo. Crown Prince Naruhito with his fiancée, both in Western clothes.
4. Tokyo. The wedding of Crown Prince Akihito to Michiko.
5. November 12, 1990, Tokyo. A demonstration against the imperial family.

6. November 12, 1990, Tokyo. One step in Akihito's crowning ceremony, conducted by the Imperial Agency according to tradition.
7. 1964, Tokyo. Emperor Hirohito at the stadium for the opening of the Olympic Games.
8. 1994, the Vatican. Emperor Akihito and his wife during a visit to Pope John Paul II.
9. February 24, 1989, Tokyo. The Shinto funeral for Emperor Hirohito.

The emperor Mutsuhito and his reign, called the Meiji era (1868–1912), coincided with the abolition of the shogunate and the feudal system, the transfer of the capital to Tokyo, the birth of the Constitution, government ministries, the parliament, the imperial army, heavy and light industry, the rebirth of imperialism after centuries of isolation, and of Shintoism, the ritualistic religion that up to that time had been dominant only in the imperial palaces. In 1894 Mutsuhito signed, with Britain, the first joint agreement between an Eastern and a Western country. Yoshihito (Taisho era) and Hirohito succeeded Mutsuhito; Hirohito brought Japan to the height of power in the East and

7

6

8

1988 **1989** 1990 1981 1982 1983 1984 1985 1986

then to Hiroshima's catastrophe. But not even General MacArthur, U.S. proconsul in the East, considered abolishing the monarchy or deposing the mikado. This ancient imperial title fell to disuse and a new Constitution was adopted that secularized the Tenno.

In today's Japan, government power rests with a strong prime minister, his party, and a two-chamber parliament; the Tenno's power has been reduced to mere symbolism. The emperor lived isolated in his palace, extremely wealthy and silent. Hirohito's death and Akihito's coronation took two years, in accordance with a sacred ritual that was highly criticized and was the cause of demonstrations. Japan is again a great power, a wealthy country seeking genuine democracy. Today, however, Akihito and his son are seeking a new role for the crown at a time when Japan is once more in the throes of an economic crisis.

of women to men, the employees' obedience to the company, still prevail in Japan. Working hours are long and hard, and tradition still rules. Urbanization has erased the village communities and the extended family. Competition is fierce even in elementary school. The party that for decades monopolized power was found to be corrupt: Prime Minister Tanaka was

involved in the Lockheed scandal, and in 1987 Prime Minister Takeshita was involved in the Recruit Cosmos scandal.

NATIONALISM. A famous historian wrote: "Together with the Germans, the Japanese shared the ability of combining barbaric behavior with a sophisticated aesthetic sensitivity."

9

LEONARD BERNSTEIN

Popularized classical music

Leonard Bernstein was born in 1918 in Lawrence, Massachusetts, to a family of Russian Jews. After studying music at Harvard, in 1940–1941 he studied conducting with Fritz Reiner and Serge Koussevitsky, and was the latter's assistant in Boston in 1942. His vast, deep musical erudition allowed him to become a composer, and he wrote music throughout his life. He performed in many U.S. and European cities as a pianist and conductor. In 1956 he became permanent conductor of the New York Philharmonic Orchestra; as such, he led the orchestra on a long European tour in 1959, performing even in the Soviet Union. In 1968 he left the New York Philharmonic and became guest conductor of the most prestigious symphony orchestras in the world, even going on tour with them. He had an intense recording and television career, creating musical programs that were popular in the United States and abroad. In 1979 he received the UNESCO award for music. His international popularity kept growing, fueled by his musical versatility, the warmth and the simplicity of his style and demeanor, and by his interest in all types of music for young people. He died in New York, his adopted city, in October 1990.

1

3

6

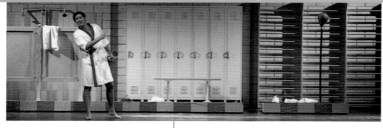

2

`4 1985 1986 1987 1988 1989 1990 1981 1982 1983 1984 1985 1986 1987 1988 1989 1990 1981 1982 1983 1984 1985 1986 1987 1988 1989 1990 1981 1982 1983 1984`

4

5

COMPOSER. Among the many chamber music works, symphonies, operas, and ballets that Bernstein created, the following stand out: *Jeremiah Symphony* (1944), *Dybbuk Variations* and *Divertimento for Orchestra* (1980); among the ballets, *Fancy Free* (1944) and *Facsimile* (1946); and *Trouble in Tahiti* (1952), *Dybbuk* (1974), and *Mass* (1972), operas for singers, musicians, and dancers.

FILM AND THEATER. In 1944 Bernstein wrote the musical score to a famous musical, *On the Town* which, thanks to Stanley Donen and Gene Kelly's talent, was made into a successful film in 1949. Also for Broadway he wrote *West Side Story* (1957), which was made into a film in 1961 and has become a genre classic for its outstanding set design and choreography. Other musicals by Bernstein include *Wonderful Town* and *Candide*.

FOR BRANDO. It is a little-known fact that the score for *On the Waterfront*, Budd Schulberg's film directed in 1954 by Elia Kazan, was composed by Bernstein. The film clearly took its inspiration from the great Soviet cinema and from the U.S. social exposé films of the 1930s. While Marlon Brando and Karl Malden gave superb performances, the dialogue and the noise are often banal. Bernstein's music, almost emphatic, provides an extraordinary counterpoint to the black and white images.

MAESTRO. Bernstein loved to be surrounded by young musicians, singers, and students who assisted at his performances and stayed up with him until the late hours of the night. Some of them followed in his footsteps. For example, Seiji Ozawa (b. 1935), Japanese-born, considered among today's best talents, especially for twentieth century music, was Bernstein's assistant.

226

MUSICAL PLEASURE

1. 1968, New York. Bernstein as Chaplin's piano accompanist.

2. A stage photo for *Trouble in Tahiti*, staged at La Scala in the 1983–1984 season.

3. A dance scene from *West Side Story*, directed by Wise and choreographed by Robbins.

4. 1980. Bernstein at the piano. Next to him are Seiji Ozawa and the composer Aaron Copland (1900–1990).

5. 1968. Bernstein conversing with Louis Armstrong.

6. Bernstein during a rehearsal. Bernstein was not given to emphatic gesturing, but had a very expressive style of conducting, highly nuanced and joyful.

7. Mid-1960s. The highly prestigious New York Philharmonic Orchestra under the baton of Leonard Bernstein.

8. A poster for *West Side Story* (1961), a film directed by Robert Wise and choreographed by Jerome Robbins, starring Natalie Wood, George Chakiris, and Richard Beymer.

9. June 1982, Venice. Bernstein paying homage to the grave of Igor Stravinsky; a touching picture by Silvia Lelli.

A dedicated musician and tireless worker, Bernstein enjoyed life, and music was his greatest pleasure. A magic moment in his career was when Milan's La Scala Theater called him to direct Italian opera, the first foreigner to receive such an honor. In the 1950s his interpretations of Cherubini's Medea *and Bellini's* La Sonnambula—*both with Maria Callas as soprano—became the stuff of legend for opera lovers the world over, similar to Verdi's* Falstaff *staged by Luchino Visconti in Vienna in 1966 or Herbert von Karajan's (1908–1989) interpretations of Puccini operas or the world premiere of* Wozzeck *by Alban Berg (1885–1935), conducted by Erich Kleiber (1890–1956) in 1925. Bernstein was an unsurpassed interpreter of Mahler's symphonies, Mahler being, like Bernstein, an eclectic composer, sensitive like him to the sheer physical pleasure of sound and the expressiveness of rhythm.*

The heritage of Bernstein the composer included elements of traditional Jewish music, religious Christian music, American song and jazz—piano jazz in particular—in addition to the cultural heritage of "high-brow" European music. Bernstein moved among these elements in an open, respectful manner, as documented in his 1959 book, The Joy of Music. *On the podium he developed a mimicry, a set of gestures and*

1986 1987 1988 1989 **1990** 1981 1982 1983 1984 1985 1986 1987

9

7

dance movements that remained impressed in the memory of those who saw him as exceptional evidence of the joy that art can bring.

❝*An irrepressible personality full of musical enthusiasm is that of Leonard Bernstein . . .*❞

Giovanni Tintori, *Direttori d'orchestra sul podio della Scala* (Conductors on the Podium of La Scala).

8

Eric Hobsbawm, a contemporary British historian, has written that "the destruction of the past or, rather, the destruction of the social mechanisms that linked the experience of our contemporaries with those of preceding generations, is one of the singular and stranger phenomena of the closing years of this century." Certainly, the most endangered of these mechanisms is the family. The extended family of the early 1900s, transmitting ideas, values, and modes of behavior that were then enriched and reinforced in school and in the work environment, has become the nuclear family. In the 1970s, an alternative family model involved communal living. Other alternative family models today involve single men and women living together or alone and complex "blended" families. When Diana Spencer died, four generations of the House

of Windsor and representatives of the Anglican

Church took part in a ceremony honoring the memo-

ry of a woman who had left the family. Here was "a

singular and strange phenomenon," proof of the con-

fusion that marked the times, the people, the places

and the culture of this decade.

In 1993 the European Community became the European Union. The original members, Benelux (Belgium, the Netherlands, Luxemburg), France, Germany, and Italy were joined by Denmark, Ireland, the United Kingdom, Greece, Spain, and Portugal and, after 1995, by Austria, Finland, and Sweden. In 1999, many of these countries already shared a common currency—the *euro*. Yet the European Union does not have a parliament to legislate democratically, nor a government that would answer to parliament, nor a true leader, nor a political platform. Is this a Union?

In 1996, the U.N. General Assembly approved (with 158 yea votes and 5 countries abstaining) a ban on nuclear experiments. However, France, India, and Pakistan (1998) continued to conduct nuclear experiments, and despite a number of nuclear arms reduction treaties, several smaller countries developed their own nuclear capabilities. In 1991, the Warsaw Pact military structure dissolved,

yet NATO continued to expand.

In 1991, the United States and its allies attacked Iraq upon the latter's invasion of Kuwait. In addition to this Gulf War, there was a war in Yugoslavia. The disintegration of that country resulted in the independence of Croatia, Slovenia, Macedonia, and Serbia. Then Serbia and Croatia began a prolonged war to divide up Bosnia, which—being mostly Muslim—wanted to be independent, but was instead torn to pieces.

Murders and all kinds of violence marked this decade. Rajiv Gandhi, the Indian Prime Minister, was killed in 1991 by religious fanatics (as his mother Indira, another Prime Minister, had been in 1984). In 1991, the USSR and the Russian Empire that the Romanovs had built over the span of four centuries, was dissolved. In 1993, Czechoslovakia split into two republics. In Italy, a separatist movement sought autonomy and independence for the northern region of the country. The utopia of a United States of the World that had engaged political writers in the period between the two world wars was clearly dead. What is more, religious, ethnic, and racial conflicts continued to intensify.

In 1994, a new outburst of ethnic hatred in Rwanda resulted in one million dead and two million refugees, and still the conflict between the Tutsis and the Hutus did not seem to be concluded. In

1. The Persian Gulf War.   2. War in Bosnia.   3. Rajiv Gandhi.   4. One million dead in Rwanda.

1990s. THE UNITED STATES AND A VARIETY OF ECONOMIC INSTITUTIONS ENJOY PLANETARY HEGEMONY. AT THE SAME TIME, THE EARTH IS IN THE THROES OF AN ECOLOGICAL IMBALANCE.

1989, 200,000 people marched on Washington in support of the homeless (3 million in the United States). In Brazil in 1992, the second U.N. conference on the environment was held, but no concrete steps were taken to stop the dissipation of resources. In Lille, France in 1996, the G-7 Summit (of the seven leading industrialized nations) took place. The leading topic was unemployment, which

downsizing of Rooseveltian welfare policies, it was clear that the era of the social safety net had come to an end. The following year, the FAO world conference on nutrition denounced the frightening gap in living conditions between countries and between

Colorful cults flourished. Some cults embraced terrorism, such as the Japanese Aum Shin Rikkyo sect that in 1995 poisoned the air in Tokyo's subways. Others were self-destructive, such as the Order of the Solar Temple sect that in 1994 caused 53 suicides on two continents. The relationship of adults to children was often brutally exploitive. Labor practices involving children were a mainstay of several thriving Asian nations; and the murder of street children became disturbingly widespread in Brazil.

Bill Gates made billions of dollars with his computer programs, and was tried by the U.S. government for monopolistic practices.

The Cassini space probe project envisioned the exploration of Saturn, and the landing of a probe on Titan, one of Saturn's moons. We will already be in the twenty-first century when that happens.

5. Fernando Collor de Mello.　6. Aum Shin Rikkyo's sect in Japan.　7. War in real time on CNN.　8. Bill Gates.　9. The Cassini space probe.

in many developed countries hovered at about 10 percent. The political winds did not favor the needy classes: starting in 1992, many countries voted for right-wing, albeit mostly democratic, governments. When President Bill Clinton, in 1996, accepted a radical

social classes in the same country, to no avail.

In the meantime, in 1992, in Italy, a series of trials laid bare the corruption linking political leaders to both state-owned and private corporations. In Brazil, President Fernando Collor de Mello was forced to resign on charges of corruption. Today multinational corporations, banks, international agencies, and financial groups control the global economy.

On another note, the communications industry kept breaking new frontiers. Thanks to satellites, CNN showed the 1991 war against Iraq's dictator Saddam Hussein in real time. The Internet created a global village, and portable cellular telephones were mass produced for consumers.

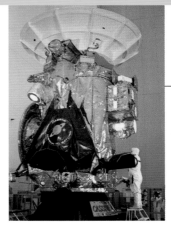

Signed a billion dollar contract with Sony

Michael Joseph Jackson was born August 29, 1958 to a poor black family in Gary, Indiana, the seventh of nine children. A precocious musical talent, at the age of five he was one of "The Jackson Five" with his brothers; they performed wherever they could. After school he was busy rehearsing and had no time for playing with children outside of his family. Soon, Michael was the star of the band and was launched by Motown Records. At the end of the 1960s, he left Motown and after a role in the film *The Wiz* he was already his own savvy manager. Jackson's singles topped the record charts. In 1979 his LP *Off the Wall* was a success; in 1982, *Thriller* sold 40 million copies.

No longer part of his brothers' band, as a solo performer Michael shone. His films, his commercials, and his videos became cult objects for millions of young people all over the world. After 10 years of press silence, in 1993 Jackson granted a live interview from his Neverland Valley, California ranch (about 27,000 acres including a zoo and an amusement park) that was watched by a TV audience of over 60 million. He was hounded by disturbing rumors, and his 1994 wedding to Lisa Marie, Elvis Presley's only child, was a world event.

1995   **1991** 1992 1993 1994 1995 1996 1997 1998 1999 2000 **19**

ADVERTISING. In 1984 the Jackson Five, and especially Michael, advertised for Pepsi Cola, under a contract that was "between ten and fifteen million dollars." During the filming of the commercial, "two burners fell on Michael and his head caught fire." The insurance settlement was a million dollars, which the performer used to found the Michael Jackson Burn Center.

BEING AND OTHERNESS. Michael Jackson's

1980s transformation is the achievement, on a large scale, of a longing felt by many teenagers. Tattoos, nose rings, lip rings, nipple rings, earrings abounded, together with sculpted hairdos, tinted and re-tinted hair, slit and torn clothing, strange, affected voices, eyes hidden behind dark glasses, shocking thinness or obesity, shock-

ing face colors: anything to make the body into a work of art.

CHILD PRODIGIES. It is rare for a child to continue to be appreciated as an artist after puberty. Shirley Temple (b. 1928) was the only great child diva of the screen: she enjoyed great popularity between the ages of four and eleven. In 1949 she left the cinema for a career in politics. Liz Taylor (b. 1932), who first appeared

INVENTING HIS IDENTITY

Who is Michael Jackson? A child prodigy; a singer and dancer. He is admired by older women: the singer Diana Ross at the beginning of his career, Liza Minnelli and Elizabeth Taylor later on. Jackson is active in charity work with Taylor and Madonna. He is rumored to have been involved with the actress Brooke Shields. He has a troubled relationship with his father, but loves his mother. Puberty was a disaster for him: he refused to look at himself in mirrors. He has developed a rare skin condition that turns his skin white. Looking at pictures of Michael the young man, we see a different face than he had as a child. "I am not ashamed of being black, not at all," he has stated. His overall look is that of Puck or Peter Pan. Dancing in flashy, sequined costumes, he is all quick move-

"He has a great voice, a daring sense of freshness and energy. He is also a fabulous dancer."

Paul McCartney

7

8

98 1999 2000 **1991** 1992 1993 1994 1995 1996 1997 1998 1999 2000 **1991** 199   96 1997 1998

6

1. The Jackson Five. Michael, the youngest, is in the foreground.
2. August 14, 1997, Copenhagen. Michael Jackson in concert.
3. In front of his helicopter, in Disneyland, flanked by Minnie and Mickey Mouse.
4. August 7, 1994, Budapest. Michael and Lisa Marie Jackson distribute gifts to hospital children.
5. May 26, 1994, La Vega, Dominican Republic. The last page of the marriage certificate of Michael Joseph Jackson and Lisa Marie Presley. The groom's signature is very visible.
6. 1993, California. The amusement park in Jackson's Neverland Valley ranch.
7. Michael Jackson in a cautiously affectionate pose.
8. 1983, Los Angeles. Michael Jackson (second from left) in the video for the album *Thriller*, directed by the great John Landis. The longest (14 minutes) and costliest (half a million dollars) video ever produced up until that time.
9. Michael Jackson (left) in a *Michael Jackson Moonwalker* frame, directed by C. Chivers and J. Kramer.

on the screen at the age of nine, continued to star until the 1990s and won two Oscars as an adult. Mickey Rooney, an outstanding actor born in 1920, had a continuous acting career from the time he was seven until well into his sixties. Between 1939 and 1941 he also starred in three unforgettable films with Judy Garland (1922–1969), who was a great star and singer from the age of thirteen until her untimely death.

ment and tiny, perfect steps. Legendary and unapproachable, strange stories circulate about Michael Jackson. "For me, the innocence of children is an endless creative source" he says. However, he has been accused of molesting children.

9

BILL CLINTON
Elected 42nd president of the United States

William Jefferson Clinton, called Bill, was born William Jefferson Blythe III, in 1946 in Hope, Arkansas. A big, exuberant boy, Clinton went to Georgetown University and to Yale law school where he met Hillary Rodham, whom he later married. She became a successful lawyer. He entered local politics and was elected governor of Arkansas (population about 2,400,000), at a young age. In June 1992 he won the Democratic Party nomination for president. In November, he beat President George Bush, who had triumphed in the 1988 election and whose Persian Gulf War had redeemed the humiliation suffered in Vietnam. In 1996, Clinton was elected to a second term. Because of pressure from Congress, his domestic programs could not be as ambitious as he (and especially his wife) would have liked. In any

case, he promoted, or at least supported, a protracted phase of economic expansion, which created jobs and wealth. The agreement he signed with Boris Yeltsin and the modest aid granted to Russia allowed the United States to engage in politics as a world power. In 1993, in Washington, Israel Foreign Minister Shimon Peres and PLO Chairman Arafat signed an agreement, with the United States as guarantor, providing for the mutual recognition of both entities and for a limited-autonomy state for the Palestinians. This in all likelihood, was the pinnacle of worldwide popularity for Clinton.

3

999 2000 1991 000 1991 **1992** 1993 1994 1995 1996 1997 1998 1999

1

2

4

YOUTHFUL INDISCRETIONS. In the United States, political candidates are subjected by the mass media to true morality trials, often founded on simple rumors. Charges were leveled against Clinton when he was a presidential candidate that he pulled strings to avoid being drafted for the Vietnam War, and that he used drugs. His defense was that he did

take part in anti-war demonstrations and did smoke marijuana, but without inhaling.

MONEY. In the course of their careers, the Clintons, who perhaps never believed they would ever become so prominent, managed to become relatively wealthy. In at least one case their financial dealings were exces-

sively casual. The scandal involving the Whitewater Development Corporation hounded them, and caused some of their friends to be indicted, tried, and sentenced.

SEX. While President of the United States, Clinton was accused by several women of sexual indiscretions. He was also accused of abuse of power, since

it is difficult to refuse the most powerful man on Earth. Mrs. Clinton reacted with stoicism and displayed spousal solidarity. In 1998–1999 the Republicans impeached Clinton on charges of perjury and obstruction of justice but failed in their attempt to remove him from office.

LORDING IT OVER THE PLANET

Bill Clinton came to power when the decline of the Soviet Union was already a fait accompli and mighty Russia was collapsing along with its society, its economy, and its Red Army. Although elected twice with a mere plurality, hounded by a prosecutor investigating a whole series of charges, and opposed by a Republican-controlled Congress, Clinton is by far the most powerful "prince" of the Earth since the time of the great Chinese and Roman emperors. The fatal growth crisis suffered by a now unified Germany, and Japan's 1997 economic-financial crisis contrast with the indisputable hegemonic role of the United States, while the European Union traverses a delicate transition phase toward a common currency.

The way in which Clinton exercises this hegemony however, does not reflect an ideology that, developing the principles of FDR's New Deal, could open to all the prospect of a better standard of living, more social justice, and improved relations among states and nations. With the end of U.S.-USSR antagonism, the United States is unopposed and can firmly express its point of view on international issues, even threaten to impose it by force, relying on NATO's support and on the U.N.'s timid response. In practice, the United States is extending to the world the policies it applied to Latin America one hundred years ago, in particular the policies of Theodore Roosevelt. A Yankee way of treating the world, made more palatable by the youthful looks of Clinton, Vice President Gore, and their wives.

"The only way for Americans to meet the challenges of the 21st century is to have the best educated and best trained work force in the world."
Bill Clinton, 1992

1. January 1993, Washington. Buttons on sale for President Clinton's inauguration parties.

2. July 1992. William Jefferson Clinton, the Democratic Party candidate.

3. June 6, 1994, Utah Beach, Normandy. Presidents Clinton and Mitterand photographed on site, on the fiftieth anniversary of the landing that turned the war on the Western front.

4. September 1997. Freshman Chelsea Clinton at Stanford University with Mom and Dad. The Clintons' style is that of middle-class America.

5. 1996. A pop festival in the United States. Nostalgia for the 1960s.

6. January 20, 1993, Washington. Capitol festivities for Clinton and Al Gore's inauguration, after the Reagan-Bush era.

7. January 22, 1993. Clinton submits to Congress his health insurance plan, which will be rejected by the majority, partially as a result of strong lobbying by health insurance companies.

8. 1993. The new president plays the saxophone.

9. 1996. Clinton celebrates his 50th birthday with his wife and daughter.

YITZHAK RABIN

He walked the path of peace with the Palestinians

In 1922, the Jewish people had yet to establish a "homeland" in their Biblical fatherland; and Palestine, which had been wrested from the Turkish Empire, was in English hands. In that year, Yitzhak Rabin was born in Jerusalem to a family of Russian emmigrants. In 1940, he graduated from the Agricultural Institute and the following year enlisted in the Palmach, the elite Haganah corps—a Jewish paramilitary underground group. He took part in military and terrorist actions in Syria and Lebanon against the French, and in 1946 in Palestine against the English, which landed him in jail for six months. When Ben-Gurion proclaimed the state of Israel, Rabin was a brigade commander; after the war, in 1949, he took part in the negotiations with Egypt. In 1960 he was appointed to the Joint Chiefs of Staff, which he headed (1963–1968) when he directed the war operations in June 1967. From 1968 to 1973 he was ambassador to Washington, an essential role in view of the aid Israel was receiving from its great ally. In 1973, he was elected as a Labor Party MP to the Knesset, and appointed minister of labor. When Golda Meir resigned in 1974, he took her place. In 1977 a financial scandal forced Rabin to resign and leave politics. He was to return in 1984 as minister of defense in the national unity governments (1984–1990), and led the brutal repression of the Palestine revolt (the 1987 *Intifada*) in the occupied territories. In the 1992 elections he was the Labor Party candidate.

97 1998 1999 2000 1991 1992 **1993** 1994 1995 1996 1997

1999 2000 1991 1992 **1993** 1994 1995 1996 19

1

2

3

4

GENERALS FOR PEACE. In the twentieth century, exceptional military men were able to cut through seemingly intractable solutions and make peace. For example, de Gaulle put an end to the Algerian War; the Lisbon generals ensured Portugal's safe passage from dictatorship to democracy and liquidated the empire; Sadat made peace between Egypt and Israel, and paid for it with his life: in his case, he was killed by Islamic fundamentalists.

TERRORISM. Early in his career, Rabin was a terrorist working for the independence of the Jewish people, in a land where the Palestinians were living peacefully before the Jews staked their claim, citing their biblical roots in the area.

THE BOOK AND THE LAW. The Jewish Bible, the Muslim Koran, and the Christian Bible are the sacred texts of the three "religions of the book." In Christian countries the law and the state are more or less clearly separate from the Book. In Islamic countries however, the law and the state are either inspired by, or dependent upon (in fundamentalist countries) the Book. In Israel, after a long secular period that took its inspiration from Socialist experiments such as the kibbutz, biblical fundamentalism and right-wing parties came to dominate the country, setting policy and attempting to mold society according to religious dictates.

THE PEACEMAKER

Rabin won the election in June 1992 and formed a coalition government with the capable Shimon Peres as foreign minister. In December, the Intifada *movement intensified. Rabin ordered 413 Palestinian rebels deported to Lebanon, which refused to admit them. The rebels then set up a makeshift camp in a no man's land. International public opinion grew increasingly favorable to the Palestinian cause. Ultra-secret negotiations—with Norway acting as broker—finally led to Washington, where in September 1993 a Statement of Principles was signed, which effectively provided for the mutual recognition of Israel and the PLO, for a transition phase toward Arab autonomy in the occupied territories, and possibly, the establishment of a Palestinian state. The hard-core wings of the Palestinian liberation movement (the Hamas and the Shiite Hezbollahs), Iran, Syria, and Iraq (which had just lost the Gulf War), opposed the agreement. Ironically, the fundamentalism of the Israeli right and of the intransigent religious groups was just as dangerous, if not more dangerous, than Arab fundamentalism.*

"*He was more Israeli than all of us.* **"**
A commentator on Israeli military radio
the day after the assassination.

1991 1992 **1993** 1994 1995 1996 1997 1998 1999 2000 1991 1992 **1993** 1994

9

6

7

1. Yitzhak Rabin as a young soldier among his comrades.
2. 1989, Israel. A thoughtful Rabin.
3. December 1992. Hamas Palestinian rebels deported to a no-man's land between Israel and Lebanon.
4. 1967, Suez Canal. Israeli Chief of Staff Rabin inspects the damage inflicted on Egyptian forces during the Six Day War.
5. August 30, 1993, Israel. A cabinet meeting where the impending peace accord is discussed.

6. November 5, 1995, Tel Aviv. Rabin and Peres, just prior to the assassination.
7. 1995, Israel. An image of Rabin's funeral.
8. Rabin and Hosni Mubarak, President of Egypt, who survived a Muslim Brotherhood attack in 1995.
9. September 13, 1993, Washington. The Statement of Principles on the transition phases for autonomy and a future Palestinian state has just been signed. Arafat and President Bill Clinton with the Israeli leaders. In October 1998 Clinton forced Benjamin Netanyahu and Arafat to more gestures of good will.

When, in 1994, Rabin, Yasser Arafat, and Peres received the Nobel Peace Prize, Israeli rightists attacked Palestinians in Hebron, and Hamas unleashed a series of terrorist acts against Israelis. In 1995 Prime Minister Rabin was murdered in public by a fundamentalist Israeli student, part of a plot that Israeli justice has yet to bring to light. The even more peace-oriented Shimon Peres took Rabin's place; however, in 1996 he stepped down in favor of Netanyahu's right wing, which put a brake on the implementation of the 1993 agreement and encouraged new Israeli settlements in Palestinian territory. Those not blinded by religious fundamentalism take note that France has over one thousand mosques, that 8 million Muslims live in Western Europe, and 4 million in North America.

NELSON MANDELA
President of the Republic of South Africa

Nelson Rolihlahla Mandela, of the powerful Xhosa ethnic group, was born in Transkei in 1918. After obtaining a law degree, in 1944 he was among the founders of the African National Congress' Youth League whose purpose was non-violent struggle. In 1948 the Boers, who were then in power, passed strict racial laws forbidding sexual relations with whites; they also passed apartheid laws, banned the movement of blacks, and created puppet ghetto states. Police brutality increased. Mandela protested against territorial segregation, and was arrested in 1952 for organizing a series of strikes. He made news again in 1955 during a

protest against the establishment of seven black reservations. Arrested in 1956, he was tried in 1958. With the ANC suppressed, it was replaced by the Pan-Africanist Congress. In 1961 Mandela went underground. With the failure of a strike for the proclamation of a Republic, the blacks were left at the mercy of the Boers. At that point Mandela founded the party's armed wing.

Captured in 1962, he was sentenced to five years of forced labor, then to life imprisonment. He became the symbol of the struggle against apartheid. A mammoth concert was staged in London for his 70th birthday. While in jail, he began negotiations with President Botha, then with his successor, Frederick W. de Klerk. Released in 1990, this undisputed leader of the reborn ANC—which he shifted to moderate positions—received the Nobel Peace Prize and in 1993, after the new Constitution was signed into law by de Klerk, ran as a presidential candidate. In 1994 he was elected President of the Republic of South Africa in the country's first free elections with universal suffrage.

000 1991 1992 1993 **1994** 1995 1996 1997 1998 1999 2000 1991 1992 1993 **1994** 1995 1996 1997 1998 1999 2000 1991 1992 1993 **1994** 1995 1996 1997 1998 1999 20

ZULU. In the 1994 elections Inkatha's Zulus received only 43 seats, against the 252 seats won by Mandela's ANC. The Inkatha was organized by the racist government in opposition to the ANC. The Zulu people (Bantus from Natal) are descended from the glorious kingdom of the bellicose King Chaka (1787–1827) who fought an epic war against the English, who finally subdued him in 1827.

SLAUGHTER. March 1960, Sharpeville, a

black suburb of Johannesburg: the police killed 69 protesters and wounded 180. June 1976, Soweto, a black ghetto: 100 dead, over 1,000 wounded. Two examples of the ferocious repression of mass rebellion. A shocking number of political murders was committed by the police and by white right-wing extremists, who even killed democratic whites. Even internationally known figures such as Frank Chikane or Cape Town's Anglican archbishop, Desmond Tutu (1984 Nobel

Peace Prize), were subjected to repressive measures.

MAU MAU. Kenya, a Zanzibar sultanate, later British protectorate (1895) and colony, suffered a bloody revolt (1952–1956) by the Mau Mau, a

Kikuyu (Bantu) secret society, in which Jomo Kenyatta (1893–1978), the main leader of Kenya's black independence movement, was also involved. Coming to power in 1963, he was the Republic's president until his death.

238

RACIAL INTEGRATION

"We arm ourselves to kill the black masses."
South Africa's defense minister talking to officers, December 1959

Racial integration is the goal citizens and democratic states want to achieve once they realize the makeup of the world's population. It is a difficult goal to achieve in those states originally established as colonies. In Africa, European powers often carved out colonies whose territories did not correspond to the aboriginal African states, at the same time disbanding ancient kingdoms. The goal of integration is not only to integrate different "races" but also different groups within the same "race."

In South Africa, at present, the white population (12.7 percent) includes Boers of Dutch origin along with English, German, and French Calvinist stock; about 2.5 percent of the population is Indian, with a few Chinese; the "colored"—mostly the offspring of white men and Hottentot women—are 8.5 percent; the Bantus are 76.3 percent and include eight major tribes, 35 percent of whom are Zulu. There are 11 official languages and 5 main religions, which include numerous Christian denominations (77 percent), animistic cults (10.5 percent), and mixed cults. To the old class division of shepherds and farmers were added the miners and factory workers; and while nomadic life still exists, urbanization is spreading. Social problems compound racial problems, while integration, here as elsewhere, imperils the survival of ethnic cultures. These are momentous issues for the future, and similar problems exist in Asia and Latin America.

TREASON TRIAL
The Accused
DECEMBER 1956

1. September 1966, Transvaal. The police attack textile workers on strike.
2. Nelson Mandela in his early years, wearing the Xhosa attire.
3. A frame from *Zulu* (1964), directed by Cy Endfield, a film dealing with the nineteenth-century Anglo-Zulu war in Natal.
4. 1996, London. The President and the Queen. In 1994 South Africa returned to the Commonwealth.
5. West Driefontein. Miners at work. The country is rich in gold (uranium-enriched), silver, platinum, iron, manganese, diamonds, and coal.
6. 1960, Sharpeville. Some of the 180 people wounded and 69 killed by police that opened fire on 5,000 protesters.
7. South Africa. President Mandela speaks to the martyr-town of Soweto.
8. December 1956. Mandela among the 144 arrested and tried for treason.
9. 1950s, Kenya. A black prison camp. Before

January 1956, more than 10,000 Kikuyu were accused of belonging to the Mau Mau and were hanged (the gallows is visible in the right back corner of the picture). The Kikuyu's war, led by Jomo Kenyatta, was the first war of liberation black Africa won against colonialism.

MADONNA

In search of a new style

Madonna Louise Veronica Ciccone was born in Rochester, Michigan, near Detroit, in 1958. Her mother died when she was 7. As a young girl she intermittently studied modern dance and music and made ends meet by doing odd jobs. In 1980 she starred in her first movie, *A Certain Sacrifice*, a soft-porn film. In 1983 her first album and video, *Madonna*, enjoyed fair success: her look was that of a trashy Latin singer. With her second album, *Like a Virgin* (1984)—strongly backed by MTV promotion—she broke through and became a star. In 1985 she co-starred in the film *Desperately Seeking Susan*, a box-office success. In those years she sold 75,000 records a day. In 1985 Madonna earned a million dollars a week during her six-week Virgin Tour. Her success as a

woman artist was unprecedented. *Penthouse* and *Playboy* published revealing early photos. She married the actor Sean Penn, known as a "bad boy." Their film, *Shanghai Surprise*, flopped. In 1986 she sold 17 million copies of her album *True Blue*, then starred in *Who's That Girl?*, another film flop. On the other hand, her 1987 *Girlie Show*, which toured 18 countries on three continents, attracted an audience of two million. A first-rate international star, Madonna is currently deeply committed to the fight against AIDS.

1992 1993 1994 **19** 1994 **1995** 1996 1997 1998 1999 2000 1991 1992 1993 1994 **1995** 1996 1997 1998 1999 2000 1991 199

ACTRESS. In 1988 Madonna starred in the play *Speed the Plow*. In 1989 her fourth album, *Like a Prayer*, was released, a mature work that became an instant classic. Later, she divorced Sean Penn and starred in a Pepsi ad campaign. Because her video of *Like a Prayer* was deemed blasphemous, the campaign was suspended. In 1990 she had great success in Warren Beatty's *Dick Tracy*, a film chock-full of stars.

SEX. After years of growing success, the double album *The Immaculate Collection*, launched together with a video, was still successful. Madonna went on the *Blond Ambition Tour* and in 1991 her tour documentary, *In Bed with Madonna*, enjoyed fair success. In 1992 her book, *Sex* ($50 per copy) instantly sold 750,000 copies; later, double that. In 1996 she decided to have a child,

little Lourdes Maria. The father was a young male fitness trainer whom she did not marry.

EVITA. In 1996 Madonna played the title character in the film *Evita*, a provocation for the Argentinean people, both followers and enemies of Perón and Peronism. Although the film was not a box-office success,

quite a few critics called it a great performance. Madonna said this in comparing herself to Eva Perón: "We are very different. The only thing we share is that we both came from nowhere and made ourselves with our own efforts . . . . It was more difficult, and at the same time easier, for her: to reach her position, she got married. I did not."

BREAKING THE RULES

1. Madonna on her *Blond Ambition Tour*.
2. Madonna in a soft-porn film, reflected in a mirror.
3. New York. Madonna performing in the *Live Aid* charity concert.
4. Madonna in the film *Evita*. She is less known for interpreting Marie, an acrobat, in Woody Allen's *Shadows and Fog* (1992).
5. Madonna with Carlos Léon, father of little Lourdes Maria.
6. Madonna in a clearly erotic scene, petting in the street.

7. 1985. Rosanna Arquette and Madonna in *Desperately Seeking Susan*, directed by Susan Seidelman.
8. Madonna with her daughter, Lourdes Maria.
9. Cover of the 1984 album *Like a Virgin* (Sire label). At that time, Madonna stated: "Sex is dirty only if you don't wash."

In Madonna we have a woman who adopted the techniques of the unscrupulous male star. Madonna trampled on male pride, exhibiting her body and her over-the-top (whether real or pretended) sexuality. With the same lack of scruples she travels the pop world, from disco music to easy-listening songs, as a composer and performer of other artists' work. She also trespasses on religion: from a Catholic background, well-versed in Marian imagery, she uses popular female religious stereotypes to attack them. She went so far as to dedicate a record to the Pope.

Madonna does everything in the star-fabricating fashion of American pop culture, with total earnestness, accepting the system, with faithfulness to questionable details and

7

6

1996 1997 1998 1999 1991 1992 1993 1994 **1995**

9

8

with postures interpreted ironically. The extreme pop vulgarity of the images, gestures, and contexts either created or chosen by Madonna in her technologically impeccable and powerful tours, is meant as a tool to reach as wide an audience as possible. Her close, professional relationship with her father, her long-standing loyalty to her violent yet fragile husband, her decision to procreate, all point to a very strong, coherent personality. Rather than embodying an androgynous lesbianism, Madonna is an accomplished, virile woman. This is what constitutes the iconoclastic novelty of her public persona.

"*Madonna pushes to extremes the absurd, offensive aspects of life. A most exasperated femaleness.***"**
Morrissey, of The Smiths band

DIANA SPENCER

She divorced the Prince of Wales

Diana was born in 1961, one of Earl Spencer's children. She received a normal education. Her parents were later divorced. As a young woman, she moved to London and found a job. The man she was to marry was born in 1948 to Elizabeth II and Prince Philip: he is Charles of Windsor, heir to the throne, who was involved with a married woman. The court played matchmaker to provide a more suitable partner for Charles, and the marriage took place in 1981 in St. Paul's Cathedral, before the eyes of a TV audience of 750 million people. The press persisted in calling the princess "Lady Di," and the Prince of Wales continued his affairs. The bride, trained in the tasks she was expected to fulfill, gave two princes to the dynasty: William and Harry. At court, Diana felt she had no space to breathe, no love, nor, she said, satisfaction. She became the darling of the press. She quarreled with her husband, was kept at a distance by her mother-in-law, attempted suicide five times, and took on lovers. In 1996 the Prince of Wales divorced her in the wake of his brother Andrew, the Duke of York's, divorce. Diana continued to be in the public eye: she took up charity work, and publicized efforts against the use of mines in war. She took a lover, Dodi al Fayed, an extremely wealthy Egyptian. They died together on September 1, 1997, in a car accident in Paris, while attempting to escape the paparazzi.

1

000 1991 1992 1993 1994 1995 **1996** 1997 1998 1999 2000 1991 1992 1993

2

3

4

5

OUT IN THE OPEN. Elizabeth II, who became queen at the age of 26 and married for love, put up with her husband's escapades and blunders, and was unrelenting in doing her duty. Her sister Margaret was different: unable to marry the love of her life, she entered into an unsuitable marriage and acquired unseemly habits. The queen's daughter, Anne, divorced and began a new life on more solid footing. One of the queen's sons, Andrew the Duke of York, married a beautiful, irrepressible redhead, but the marriage didn't last. The queen's daughter-in-law Diana was a concern: she would grant TV interviews, air her private life in public, and rouse the kingdom's people against the Crown.

THE SPENCER FAMILY should not be confused with the Spencer-Churchills; they became earls only in the eighteenth century. The second earl acquired fame for the lovely library he collected; the fifth for having sold it and for his political activity. In modern times, the Spencers became known for their cavalier habits.

THE CROWN. Elizabeth II's wealth is enormous, her role hard to fathom in a monarchy where the sovereign has no power. Until Diana's divorce, the monarchy was kept strong by the subjects' love for the Queen Mother, widow of George VI, by a liturgy strengthened over many centuries, and by the traditional quality of English society. But the people's stormy love affair with the royal family's lovely "victim" endangered the continuity of the institution of the monarchy. Elizabeth found a remedy in attending her

242

QUEEN OF HEARTS

The Princess of Wales didn't follow the traditions of the Court of Saint James. Her grandmother-in-law, the Queen Mother, had interpreted tradition with a garish style, her mother-in-law Elizabeth II had adopted the "working woman" style, and Aunt Margaret had adopted a crumpled style. Diana set a style of her own. She was famous for her lightning-fast crushes and obstinacy, and was determined to assert herself against everyone. Accustomed to an ordinary life, lacking pretense, healthy and robust, this girl was enchanted at the prospect of becoming part of the world's first family. Unfortunately, she had no idea that in that world importance is gained only by strictly following protocol, working hard, and always maintaining an appearance of goodness, superiority, and cheerfulness. Betrayed by her husband, she allowed herself

1. The Prince and Princess of Wales on their wedding day.
2. The Princess of Wales visiting a home for handicapped children.
3. July 29, 1996, London. Diana leaving the Chelsea Harbour Club gym.
4. Switzerland. Diana, Princes of Wales and Sarah, Duchess of York on the ski slopes.
5. A picture of Diana in a very sporty outfit.
6. August 1997. Diana Spencer and Dodi al Fayed during their Mediterranean cruise.

7. November 3, 1982. Queen Elizabeth II, together with the Princess of Wales on the way to the opening of Parliament.
8. September 5, 1997, London. Flowers left outside the gates of Diana's residence: mute witness to the deep sorrow of the people.
9. September 6, 1997, Westminster Abbey. Diana's casket being borne toward the altar.

9 2000 1991 1992 1993 1994 1995 **19**
1998 1999 2000 1991 1992 1993 1994 1995 **199**

unbecoming escapades; she enjoyed exercise, massage, and pop music. She carried on her charity work. But, above all, she flaunted her dissatisfaction, what she claimed were her romantic rights and her needs, and in the meantime she had fun. Millions identified with her. And so a lovely, not very serious, and very unlucky princess became the queen of hearts.

|7

|8

|9

daughter-in-law's funeral, mourning her loss, and paying her taxes.

HER DEATH. Books, pictures, and articles narrated Diana Spencer's life and illustrated her charitable works. In August 1997 the tabloids published photos of her at Portofino on the Italian Riviera,

with Dodi al Fayed. Similar pictures taken in the same resort 60 years earlier, showed Edward VIII with the lover for whom he gave up the throne, and while Edward VIII was to have an endless sunset, Diana was to die a horrible, heartbreaking death, which aroused deep pity.

"She touched the lives of so many and brought joy and well-being to Great Britain and the world."
Tony Blair, U.K. Prime Minister

MOTHER TERESA
She died among her beloved poor

Agnes Gonxha Bojaxhiu was born August 27, 1910 near Skopje, in what is now the Republic of Macedonia, to a family of ethnic-Albanian Catholic farmers. In 1928 she entered the Order of the Sisters of Saint Mary of Loreto. A sharp young woman full of good will, the Order sent her to Dublin to complete her studies, then to Darjeeling in Western Bengal. She was to remain in India, assisting abandoned and malnourished children, the homeless, the people dying in the streets. In 1948 the Holy See granted her permission to leave the Order and, with the authorization of the Archbishop of Calcutta, she established the Order of the Missionaries of Charity whose mission was to increase Christian charity through good works and examples, an Order at once active and contemplative. Some twenty years later, the Missionaries of Charity were to grow to 1800 sisters in 67 countries. In 1977, Paul VI awarded to Mother Teresa of Calcutta the Pope John XXIII peace prize. Two years later, she received the Balzan Brotherhood prize and the Nobel Peace Prize. In 1995, the missionaries were a benevolent, vivid presence also among the destitute of the urban wastelands of the West, with 559 houses in 115 countries. On September 13, 1997, Mother Teresa was buried in her beloved Calcutta amidst the honors of a state funeral.

MISSIONARIES. The nineteenth century was the great period of Christian missions to Asia and Africa, continents that had been conquered and subjugated by the leading European powers. To the local populations, the missionaries held up the West as a model of civilization, culture, and science. The Christians' lack of appreciation for local methods, customs, and systems was often unconscious, but always offensive.

HOSTILITY. In 1922 Shanghai the Anti-Christian Federation was established by college students who were incensed because "with some notable exceptions, the missionaries held no esteem for Chinese culture." Once in power, Mao Dzedong persecuted the Chinese Church that was subject to Rome. Gandhi also took an anti-Christian position, for he found it absurd that God would damn for eternity all those who thought differently from Christians.

NEW MISSIONS. Starting with the end of World War II, a new missionary spirit was born, next to the traditional one, and it was not limited to the Missionaries of Charity who were formed in the womb of Hindu culture. The Combonians, an order of Italian Catholic priests, are a remarkable example of missionary work founded on brotherly assistance to indigent populations, whom they defend from Western exploitation and the new local dictatorships. For this, they are often misunderstood and sometimes persecuted. Like Mother Teresa, they leave conversion to divine providence.

994 1995 1996

997 1998 1999 2000 1991 1992 1993 199

1

2

3

4

5

244

SAINTHOOD

Mother Teresa was a tough woman, a formidable spokeswoman for her mission, self-assured and extremely active even after undergoing heart bypass surgery. Simple, free of all pretense, she was rooted in a culture that had been massacred by history. Lacking any rancor or hostility, she founded her Order on a radically egalitarian vision that took its cue from a conception of poverty inspired by The Book of Job. *The Order's habit is a white Indian sari trimmed with the Madonna's blue color. The main house of the Order in Kalighat, near Calcutta, is a decent building, according to local standards. The preaching of the Gospel is left to God's will, as is passing moral judgment on the dying, the indigent, the children left to their own devices.*

The Missionaries of Charity are caregivers, nurses, washerwomen, servants to the most wretched of the wretched. Superior to no one, they are everyone's equal. Self-confident, Mother Teresa sat with the world's

" *This woman has left a mark on history.* **"**
John Paul II

7

97 1998 1999 2000 1991 1992 1993 1994 1995 1996 **1997** 1998 1

1996 **1997**

6

8

9

leaders and accepted money without passing judgment on the donors and their motives. Mother Teresa had total faith in God, and so avoided all polemics with the world and even with her Church. Her heroic charity was a service to God through God's creatures, but it happened as if outside of history. This is why, seen in the midst of the confusion and complexity of our times, Mother Teresa appears so great.

1. Mother Teresa and her Missionaries of Charity on the bus that picks up the most destitute and the dying lying in the streets of Calcutta.
2. Mother Teresa during one of her meetings with Pope John Paul II.
3. Mother Teresa next to one of the poor people housed by her Order.
4. Mother Teresa with a young child. In poor countries, malnutrition often affects nursing infants through their mothers.
5. The Missionaries of Charity praying Eastern-style.
6. Mother Teresa with the 1979 Nobel Peace Prize certificate.
7. The look of a young girl forced into prostitution, from the film *Salaam Bombay!*

8. An infirmary in one of Mother Teresa's houses.
9. September 13, 1997, Calcutta. Funeral honors for Mother Teresa at the Church of St. Thomas, who was apostle to India. Greater Calcutta has about 12 million inhabitants; Bombay, 13 million.

HELMUT KOHL

German Chancellor for sixteen years

Helmut Kohl was born in 1930 to a very modest Catholic family in Ludwigshafen-am-Rhein, in the Palatinate. In college he studied law, history, and political science. After working for a local chemical company, he entered politics and joined the Christian Democratic Union (CDU). He distinguished himself in the party's youth organization and moved up to become a regional party executive. From 1959 to 1976 he was a Deputy in the Rheiland-Pfalz Diet, near the border with Belgium and Luxemburg. He was Land Council President from 1969 to 1976, and in 1973 was appointed CDU political secretary, thus moving into national politics. A great consolidator, he became Bundestag Deputy in 1976 and head of his parliamentary group. When the Social-Liberal coalition split, he was the CDU candidate for the post of Chancellor. In 1982, with the fall of Helmut Schmidt, who had been in power since 1974, the CDU returned to power and Kohl became Chancellor, assisted by the capable Foreign Minister Hans-Dietrich Genscher. Kohl supported a double NATO policy (either successful negotiations with USSR for European disarmament, or Euromissile bases, which were installed in 1983). He continued a policy of cooperation with France and of support and friendship with the German Democratic Republic.

STYLE. The nineties were the years in which Kohl's direct, somewhat rough style asserted itself. His faith in Germany equaled the faith Bismarck had in Prussia. As soon as the Allies, winners of World War II, waived the last restrictions (September 1990) and Germany regained its unlimited sovereignty, Kohl went ahead full speed with national unification. He took care to soothe the USSR with massive aid and a limit on Germany's armed forces, confirmed with Poland the painful 1945 Oder-Neisse border, bet on Europe's monetary unification that was to signal the end of the German mark's power, financed the modernization of the former East Germany by burdening the budget, encouraged the extension of NATO—a pet project of the United States, and inaugurated joint French-German armed forces.

BERLIN. Politics needs symbols. There were so many factors opposed to moving the capital from Bonn back to Berlin: the opposition of Western Catholic Länder and of Bonn, the cost of the transfer, the Kaiser-Hitler image Berlin still projected, Berlin's location—too far to the east, the proximity to the border with Poland (where at least 200,000 Germans still live). All this notwithstanding, Kohl decided to move the capital back to Berlin.

DECLINE. The 1998 victory of the Social

THE FOURTH REICH

Until 1994, elections kept returning the CDU-Liberal coalition to power. The Chancellor was steadfast in his Atlantic Alliance policy and supported a Europe-centered development. He did not follow Anglo-American social welfare policy, but adopted other methods to reduce the public debt and encourage industrial production. He favored the immigration of ethnic Germans born in Iron Curtain countries, including the USSR. When Hungary removed the barbed wire along its border with Austria on September 11, 1989, 15,000 East Germans entered West Germany in three days.

In November the Berlin Wall fell, and Kohl immediately exploited the situation. With the support of the European Community Committee, he took advantage of strong French and English anti-Communist feeling—both countries being at a loss for a decent reason to oppose him; of Gorbachev, who had opposed reunification but now made an about-face, seeing its inevitability; of U.S. embarrassment, since it lacked a moral reason to stop him. Then Kohl proceeded to merge the Democratic and

the Federal Republics of Germany without any transitional phase. On October 3, 1990, he proclaimed the new Republic of Germany. In two months he organized the entire territory, and on December 2 the election campaign began. Germany now had one parliament, one government headed by Helmut Kohl, an area of 137,800 square miles (smaller than the Second Reich), and a population of over 80 million Germans, the most populous European country after Russia. The Fourth Reich was born.

6 1997 1998 1999 2000 1991 1992 1993 1994 1   1995 1996 199

7

8

9

"There are no more enemies in Europe."
François Mitterand, November 1990

1. October 22, 1982, Germany. The first meeting between Chancellor Kohl and President Mitterand, both supporters of the European Union.
2. Chancellor Kohl's broad smiling face, an icon of optimism.
3. Dresden, the Athens of the North, former capital of the Saxon electorate, almost destroyed by Allied bombing in 1945, welcomes Kohl after unification.
4. 1990. Kohl signs autographs in unified Berlin.
5. 1989, Berlin. The wall is still a half reality, under the grandiose Brandenburg Gate, a symbol of the Hohenzollern Empire.

6. November 8, 1992, Berlin. Kohl among 300,000 people marching against the dangers of Neo-Nazism.
7. Clinton and Yeltsin. With Gorbachev and Bush, they are the foreign statesmen most responsible for the peaceful integration of the two Germanies.
8. October 3, 1990. Berlin celebrates the country's unification in front of Parliament. It is Kohl's best speech.
9. March 19, 1990, East Berlin. An electoral poster.

Democratic Party meant the end of Kohl's career, at least for the time being. But to the careful observer, this domineering, not yet 70-year-old politician with limited diplomatic abilities, seems a leader-in-waiting. Maybe for the European Union, should it become a political entity some day.

BORIS YELTSIN

Lives out his somber sunset

Boris Nikolayevich Yeltsin was born in 1931 in a village near Sverdlovsk (now Yekaterinburg), in the Asian Ural Mountains. A building engineering graduate, he joined the party in 1961, and in 1976 was secretary of the Sverdlovsk district. In May 1985 Gorbachev appointed him to the Central Committee as minister for construction, and in December to the post of first secretary of Moscow's party. In this post he led a front-line battle against corruption and in support of a reform-oriented bureaucracy. In March 1986 he was a candidate for the Politburo. He accused Gorbachev's *perestroika* of being too cautious and multiplied his contacts with the masses. He was removed from the Moscow secretariat on charges of demagoguery in 1987, and in 1988 he was removed from the

Politburo. He came back in March 1989, triumphantly elected to the new People's Congress. On May 29, 1990, he was elected president of the Russian Federation. Increasingly critical of Gorbachev's group, and increasingly favoring a market economy, he resigned from the party to head a radical group. In August 1991 he courageously led the resistance to a reactionary Communist coup, and achieved his putsch, which signaled the death of the Soviet Union. He remained as president of Russia, which occupies 72 percent of the territory of the former Soviet Union and is the sixth most populous country in the world.

ETHNICITY. With the fall of the Soviet Communist Party and the state economy, the first nationalistic passions erupted. Today, 29 million non-Russians live in the Russian Federation: they are Turkish Tatars, Mongols, North Caucasians, Finns, Germans. A slightly lower number of Russians live in other former Soviet Republics. Where they are a visible minority, often these ethnic groups suffer discrimination.

SALARIES. The government is unable to meet its payroll on time. The armed forces lack clothing, spare parts, and sufficient food staples. Soldiers returning home from outposts across the dismantled Soviet Empire lack shelter and income. The ruble devaluation has greatly reduced the buying power of salaries and pensions. The health, culture, and transportation systems are in shambles. The sale of

medium and small companies and the privatization of large industries spawned enormous corruption. Great wealth contrasts with widespread misery.

CZAR BORIS. Godunov (1598–1605), the usurper who eased the way to the throne for the Romanovs, was Czar Boris. The press now calls Boris Yeltsin a czar, since he has turned out

to be not a statesman, but a clone of the Soviet system, incapable of long-term political plans and solicitous only in fending off rivals. Suffering from heart disease, Yeltsin jealously guards his power, mindless of past and future disasters. Will he also be immortalized by a Pushkin or a Mussorgsky?

RUSSIA IN CRISIS

Ushered into power by the people's enthusiasm following his repression of the 1991 Communist coup, Yeltsin was to continue in power even after parliament forced him to resign from the post of prime minister. With a 1993 referendum he had the new Constitution (modeled on the U.S. charter) approved and, imitating Gorbachev, ruled by executive decree. In 1993 he even had the parliament attacked with cannon fire—something not even Czar Nicholas II had dared to do. He grew increasingly suspicious of possible rivals, and increasingly incapable of managing political, economic, social, and ethnic conflicts, in Russia as well as in the twenty-odd republics of the Russian Federation, and among the Federation and the

> *"An old party boss who combined the necessary talents for getting ahead in old politics (toughness and cleverness) with the skills required by new politics (rabble-rousing, joviality and skill in exploiting mass communications) . . ."*
>
> Eric J. Hobsbawm, *Ages of Extremes—The Short Twentieth Century 1914–1991*

19

97 1998 **1999** 2000 1991 1992 1993 1994 1995 1996

8

9

7

6

independent republics spawned by the demise of the USSR. He persevered in his policy of transition from a state-planned to a market-based economy but, like his predecessor, was unable to ensure an effective transition. He coined new currency again and again; as a result, inflation skyrocketed; from 1991 to 1994 domestic net production decreased 50 percent.

In the midst of sprouting reformist, authoritarian-nationalist, moderate, and Communist-nostalgic parties, Yeltsin was unable to create a new political game. In 1993 foreign debt had already reached $80 billion, made up for the most part of debts incurred by the now defunct USSR, which Russia had assumed, along with the USSR's seat on the U.N. Security Council.

1. January 1992, Moscow. Yeltsin photographed in the Kremlin.

2. June 12, 1996, Moscow. Yeltsin fans at a rock concert in Red Square celebrating the fifth anniversary of his election to the presidency.

3. May 3,1996, Yarplov. President Yeltsin visits a military base.

4. August 1991, Moscow. Yeltsin and Gorbachev at the first session of the Russian Parliament after the failed coup.

5. February 7, 1992, Paris. With Mitterand.

6. March 1991, Moscow. In front of the Kremlin,

200,000 people demonstrate against the government's policies. Yeltsin became the leader of the radical democrats.

7. 1993. President Yeltsin in the holy city of Vladimir. The new Russia returned to the clergy the powers that the House of Romanov had restricted, and that the Soviets had abolished.

8. December 1992, Moscow. Yeltsin with Chancellor Kohl, who generously supported his presidency.

9. 1991. Yeltsin after quashing the reactionary coup d'état against Gorbachev's reforms.

JUBILEE AND OLYMPICS
A cycle comes to a close

Jubilees. The Jubilee marks a special year in the calendar, a year that breaks with the rules, renews them, and rejuvenates the world. Egypt's long-reigning pharaohs used to celebrate Jubilees, though not regularly, to begin their reign anew, repeating their entry into the abode of the gods and renewing the strength received in the crowning ritual. The ancient Hebrews also celebrated a special year, the seventh—or sabbatical—and every fifty years a special Jubilee. In that year the land was left fallow, Hebrew slaves were freed and debtors were excused from repaying their debts. Thus the land was made fertile again and wealth was redistributed to the benefit of the indigent. There is also a Catholic Jubilee, possibly the most famous of all, when the pope grants plenary indulgences— the remission of penalty for sins committed—to those who undertake pilgrimages, usually to Rome, visit certain churches, receive the sacraments, and so forth. The Jubilee is called the Holy Year.

Pope Boniface VIII declared the first Jubilee on February 22, 1300, for that same year; for the occasion 200,000 pilgrims journeyed to Rome, a huge number in those times. Giotto and Dante were among the pilgrims. A second Jubilee was celebrated 50 years later. Politics permitting, starting with Sixtus IV (1471–1484), the Holy Year fell every twenty five years, but in the nineteenth century there was only one, in 1825. To the Jubilee, for different reasons, are added extraordinary jubilees. All the pilgrims' prayers serve to entreat special graces for the good of the Church and for the pope's intentions. The Holy Year 2000 promises to be memorable.

Olympics. The Olympic Games were part of a religious festival in honor of Zeus, the Greek god of rain, who was worshipped on the dry plain of Olympia, in the temple of Elis. The games were celebrated every four years, probably even earlier than 776 B.C., the first recorded date. It was a holiday for all Greeks on the continent, the islands, and the colonies. During the Olympics, which took place in mid-summer, all wars among Hellenes were suspended. At first they lasted one day, then five.

The competition involved foot races, wrestling, the pentathlon (long jump, foot race, discus throw, javelin throw, and wrestling), boxing, chariot racing, horse racing, the pancration (wrestling and boxing), and the hoplite race (running wearing full hoplite armor). Only men participated in the games. Even princes took part. Like the other athletes, their reward was simply a laurel wreath and glory. Great poets such as Pindar sang the praises of the Olympic heroes and sculptors immortalized them in statues. Acting on the suggestion of Saint Ambrose, in 393 A.D. Emperor Theodosius forbade the games and later ordered the burning and destruction of the stadium.

At the Sorbonne in 1892, Baron Pierre de Coubertin proposed to create the modern Olympic Games, "to preserve for athletic endeavors the noble and chivalrous character they had in the past." Greece was again an independent country, and slowly sports became a popular pastime there. The first modern games were held in Athens in 1896. In the year 2000, the billion dollar Olympics will not return to Athens. They will celebrate not the beauty of the athletes, but their records.

CYCLES

Since ancient times, man has sought to discover and measure the cycles of the world, of living beings and inanimate things. The cosmic year is the time the sun, the moon and the major planets require to return to the same position from which they started their cycle. Heraclitus (sixth to fifth century B.C.) spoke of a great year, the period the universe takes to return from the original fire to the fire in which the cycle ends and begins. Empedocles (fifth century B.C.) thought in terms of a cycle first ruled by love, then by hatred. The idea of a millennium-long cycle made up of exactly one thousand years surfaced in Europe at the end of the sixteenth century, although it was attributed to early medieval men and women who lived as the one

"*Sports must be conceived as a generator of art and an occasion for art. It generates beauty because it creates the athlete, a living sculpture.***"**

Pierre de Coubertin, *Leçons de pédagogie sportive*
(*Lessons in Sports Education*), 1921

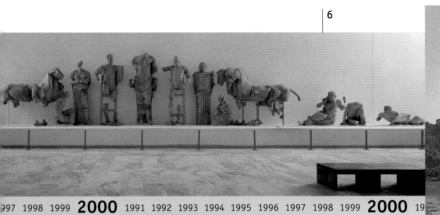

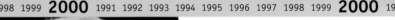

997 1998 1999 **2000** 1991 1992 1993 1994 1995 1996 1997 1998 1999 **2000** 19   1996 1997 19

1. Postcard commemorating the 1950 Jubilee, with the image of Pius XII, the reigning pope, and a list of the previous Holy Years.

2. Pharaoh Rameses II the Great (1279–1213 B.C.) flanked by the gods Amon and Mut.

3. Statue of the athlete Agias, winner of the pancration race, 335 B.C.

4. The most important churches of Rome in a 1575 etching. Those marked with a small cross granted Jubilee indulgences.

5. Israel. Ancient olive grindstones in Tirat Yehudah.

6. Surviving statues from the eastern pediment of the temple to Zeus in Olympia, destroyed by Christians. They are datable to 470–456 B.C. and represent the chariot race with Pelops and Enomaos.

7. Pierre de Coubertin (1863–1937), who conceived the idea of the modern Olympic Games.

8. U.S. athletes at the 1896 Olympics. Garret, third from the left, won the discus-throwing competition.

9. Olympia. The stadium where the games took place, without tiers.

thousandth year of the Christian era was approaching and who saw it as the impending end of the world. Millenarianism is an ancient Hebrew belief—still prevailing among some sects—according to which at the time of the advent of the Messiah the just will receive a golden millennium before the final judgment. Even the idea of a century—one hundred years—is recent, having been set forth by Lutheran theologians in Magdeburg as they compiled, starting in 1559, a church history divided into centuries. Previously, the term "century" meant, as it did in Latin, "epoch, or age": it could last longer or less than one hundred years. For example, Leo X's century only lasted eight years, from 1513 to 1521, when he died suddenly. Our century, which according to some has only lasted from 1914 to 1991, is therefore a "short century" like so many others.

1901 2000

Which personalities were known in every corner of the globe in the twentieth century? We can't know for sure because the information available is insufficient. We could try reading the newspapers of the time . . . but how many people were reading newspapers in 1910, and where? Copies of radio broadcasts—so influential for so long in manufacturing love and hate—are extremely rare. International research on the most popular personalities at the onset of the age of television would be priceless. A worldwide telephone survey, on the other hand, would not be statistically valid, because it is unlikely that the man or woman who has a telephone in Nigeria represents the average Nigerian citizen. Yet the country, with 88,500,000 people (and a per capita annual gross national product of just $260) has more inhabitants than Italy, Sweden, and Bulgaria combined. Thus our choice of the magnificent one hundred is somewhat arbitrary, although we took into consideration their fame abroad and what they embodied for the

masses. Thus they rightfully deserve to be called myths, or icons.

Icons are not individuals, but figures for lay worship, produced by history, by the media, and by the collective imagination. They include people who may have been insignificant in the sense that they achieved nothing memorable, yet the world saw in them values they shared. Almost none of this century's myths are creators of "high" culture. Authors, painters, sculptors, composers, scientists, historians, philosophers, sociologists, and economists, were all practically unknown to the masses. One thing is clear: the myth's legitimacy comes from the masses. Also excluded are some major actors and entertainers, exceptional athletes who were worshipped by particular nations (but not by others) or by elites of taste but not by the mass of humanity. In every epoch a hero is the mirror of the society that worships him. In our century, the role and prestige of the elites gradually shrank until at the end of the century mass society looked at itself and loved what it saw as its most popular values, in the models that most faithfully reproduced them, like Truman Burbank, the young insurance agent of the film, *The Truman Show*. These are the new icons, the new myths.

A 1930s radio. Notoriety was achieved through hit songs, jazz, opera, news reports, sports commentaries, serial dramas, and press statements.

A 1935 Philips TV set. With TV, anonymous people acquired a face, a personality, and gestures. They became famous, and people started referring to them by name or even by nickname, as if they were friends.

After the book

After reading this book, we would like to suggest some avenues for further reading. *Icons of the Century* is also a history of the modern mass mentality, of the irresistible impact of American culture in globalizing language, in addition to the economy. It is the history of ideas replaced with images on a mass scale; generally speaking, of rationality replaced with emotion. Finally, of replacing images with icons. In sum, a history of commoditization and reification not of the poor—who have always been treated as commodities—but of leaders in all fields.

Personality, myth, and icon

Through the years, the quality of the personalities changed. It is debatable whether the most famous of jazz artists was also the best, but there is general agreement that he was a great artist with a unique personality. By the 1970s, pop music entertainers had become media figures, the only difference between them being their degree of international success. Movie idols became assembly line products, molded with similar methods and procedures. The cost of promoting a "human product," a record or a film, kept increasing, compared to the cost of the product itself. And the qualities sought in an actor or an entertainer (like the style in an author) were no longer clarity, strength, or intensity, but the ability to absorb, to be malleable. Only in this way could the star be dressed and made up into a dazzling totem set on a merry-go-round of kaleidoscopic images and sounds.

Louis Armstrong and Michael Jackson have nothing in common, for the jazz icon belonged to the radio age, of friends engaged in conversation, of music enjoyed in clubs, by lovers, or in solitude, of music measured against one's own sensitivity or

A 1948, U.S.-made 1100 Wurlitzer juke box. With a coin or a token one could choose from 24 selections. The flashy, futuristic body enhanced the pleasure of listening to music.

memory, even when surrounded by the din of the juke box. For the masses, a performance by Michael Jackson is a decibel orgy, a visual storm, where the consumer enjoys the icon while rapt with narcissistic longing or a thrilling loss of self.

As the century passed, the quality of political icons also changed. Now, as in the time of the Roman consuls, the winners represented the interests of the power groups who elected them. The complex, cultivated, gifted personalities of the most popular U.S. presidents of the first half of the century were unique, and very different from those of later presidents. In his radio fireside chats, Franklin Roosevelt communicated plans, analyses, proposals. Ronald Reagan, on the other hand, was a great communicator, but more than ideas, he communicated irrational, chauvinistic reassurances. This personality crisis was not limited to the United States. In Russia, Stalin was a dictator but also an extraordinary, idealistic statesman; Brezhnev, by contrast, an opaque oligarch gradually led his country to the brink of collapse. Today, Yeltsin seems to be little more than a reckless adventurer. And,

Four-color separations of offset composition. Developed in the second half of the century, this process ensured the international success of the illustrated book and the popularity of color reproductions.

Three U.S. Nobel Prize winners born outside the country. From top: Georg von Bekesy (medicine, 1961), born in Hungary; André Cournand (medicine, 1956), born in France; and Emilio Segré (physics, 1959), born in Italy.

among fascist leaders, General Perón stands in marked contrast to Jorge Videla.

New meanings, new global languages

Many things have changed since the 1960s, and the changes keep coming at an increasingly faster pace. Of course, there was a crisis in traditional values. Dignity, decorum, and integrity fell on hard times, while the meaning of other values shifted. Now, elegance no longer means a refined style with a touch of novelty or exuberance. Even perfume is no longer the same, since a person is now expected to change it to suit his or her moods or the occasion. Style gave way to the look. Traditional role models disappeared: the good kid, the nice girl, the honest breadwinner, the true lady, the doctor who makes house calls, the obedient housewife, the faithful maid, all vanished along with the bourgeoisie that had produced them.

This crisis also spread to language. American English became the *lingua franca* of tourism, finance, industry, commerce,

and diplomacy, as well as science because U.S. academies and scientific institutes are richer, publish more, and pay higher salaries than others. The first true international language was that of American university professors. The same language now dominates movies—in many countries Hollywood movies aren't even dubbed—and in pop music the languages of music and images have blended. Often, the lower classes of the great European nations did not inherit a good education, and they now increasingly live outside the cultural and social context in which they were born. The roots of the elite classes of those same nations have weakened, having fallen prey to the winning models (read: what sells most). Young people who want to be "in" now buy American goods and imitate

Jasper Johns, *Three Flags*, 1958. For this abstract expressionist painter, the American flag, an icon worn by use, is an easy tool in a refined, expressive game of colors and elementary shapes to scale.

Americans. Fads spread like lightning, especially extreme urban looks: jeans, rock music, flower children, camping, pot, zen, yoga, piercing, and videos. And the list goes on. Young people still do the same old things, except that they now do them in the same way, "globally," which most find foreign and, therefore, alienating.

The globalization of elite values has played a major role in this change. American pop art conquered the global markets and made even the sophisticated artistic product more similar to mass consumer artistic products such as those associated with advertising. The world's production of books now increasingly resembles American best-seller lists, a result of adopting publishing industry systems and methods that seek out similar best-sellers. Many literary talents and scholars no longer find publishers. As in the Middle Ages, "high," or research, culture slowly withdraws into self-consumption

L. Ron Hubbard (1911–1986), who in 1959 founded the multinational "church" of Scientology, today a wealthy and powerful organization.

Georg Soros, a billionaire financial advisor and investor, here receiving an honorary degree from the University of Bologna.

when it has no value for the globalized economic system. A philosopher can publish only if he is a professor, for in this case, he will be read by colleagues and students. But the students who do not become his colleagues will no longer read him. The period in which Bergson's books sold like hot cakes is over. What sells today are the gurus.

The sales pitch: gurus and icons

We can credibly state that the guru is the representative figure, the collective icon of our century. A witch doctor for sale, equipped with undefined, uncontrollable knowledge, he dispatches responses and messages that find a growing market. Eclectic, postmodern, trans-religion, and trans-discipline, he specializes in whatever comes his way: politicians, executives, film stars, the generally unhappy. Often he works alone, meaning that he acts as investor, manager, star, telepreacher. His selling techniques have progressed from the merchandising of goods to presentation, motivation, contextualization, manufacturing, and planning. He plays a crucial role in all of these and employs various sciences and technologies that have become subordinate to the guru's activity. Because profit must follow production just as thunder follows lightning, only what sells is produced; thus, only what already has been sold (that is, its copy) is made. Because it must have as wide a market as possible, it must displease neither whites nor blacks, Turks nor Japanese; its target audience must be homogeneous.

The resulting product must be free of cultural idiosyncrasies that, while making it suitable for some, render it foreign or unpleasant to others. Hence, many items that are valuable in and of themselves are never produced. What is shocking is that the motors of today's cars are directly derived from the Model T Ford, for this is the product that sells. How long would it take for a new, better motor to become "global"? One marketing adage tells us that we should go slow with real innovation.

A similar process applies to human beings. They must be able to adapt to everyone and everything, everywhere. They must have no personal look, character, taste, or aspiration. Anything different requires a bit of time to get used to, and we can no longer afford to spend time getting used to things in today's economy. We blame a truly novel artist for not making himself or herself understood. So that, on average, those who "emerge" as candidates for iconhood look increasingly alike: not too macho, not too feminine, not too young, old, ugly, attractive, refined, peculiar, or individualistic. If they aspire to embody a "typical" category, then they must represent it in its markedly average values: the macho must be somewhat macho, but not too macho; the intellectual must be a pseudo-intellectual but not too cerebral; the politician must be a wheeler-dealer, not genuinely committed. The truly "extreme" aspect of everything frightens us and does not create an audience, because it must be understood.

What must be understood does not sell

Everything that has already been sold and consumed can be understood; better yet, it does not need to be understood. The same happens for the individual who becomes a piece of merchandise. When not just his

work is on sale but his metamorphosis into a myth, an icon as well. Tom Mix ("a living catechism" according to Jean-Louis Rieupeyrout), Roy Rogers, and the Barbie doll take their place in the consciousness of their worshippers in a space free of second thoughts or criticism. It is not the "historical placement" that turns a person into an icon, for we know that many Christian saints are still revered even though the Church has proved that they never lived. Icons may be burned, hidden in the attic and forgotten, yet their worshippers will not turn their backs on them. In 1998, President Clinton, in front of a grand jury and the TV cameras, drank a famous soda straight from the can, just like all those who watched him.

To be a myth

A special type of transference occurs between the masses and an icon. Each icon becomes the image not of a man or a woman, but of his or her heroic virtues. In the icon the banality of each one of her worshippers is transformed into universal, supreme value.

Icons are beautiful, good, bright, all-powerful, superlative in an indefinable manner. The adoration the icon receives from its fans in a concert, a game, or a media event is clearly a type of worship, also expressed in shamanistic-type trances. The fan becomes the icon, while projecting himself into it. In that instant the icon is the double of each one of its fans, it is an individual and it is the masses. For the person "possessed" by the fans, it is a state of suffering, as we can tell by the flight so many stars took from their iconic status, starting with Greta Garbo.

Once an icon disappears, the worshipper will accept, receive, and venerate another icon. This is a sequence that sometimes ends with maturity—a psychological condition that young people are reaching later and later in life. Sometimes, this sequence is picked up again when dissatisfied adults seek to become numb with new icons, worshipping them in a less noisy, possibly, but no less intense fashion.

In the meantime, it has become commonplace

to replace religion not with the search for rational values, but for "alternative" small faiths: alternative medicines, sects, diets, magical practices.

In the year 2000, the recurring comets of the Olympics and the Jubilee make their appearance, surviving remnants of absolute faiths, myths inherited from our past and translated into satellite-ready languages. Pilgrims and fans, on the road and on the Internet, share the world's roadways. The event need not happen, as long as it appears. In the meantime, other things happen, historical events that we can no longer perceive or grasp in their rhythm or sense. Vast transformations are taking place, as large as humankind that experiences them, and as the powers that determine them.

Something new and positive is being born, but we are not aware of it. It will have its myths and icons, but we know not what their substance will be.

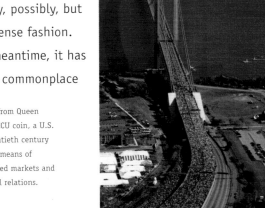

Bibliography

Bibliographical Note

The books listed here include only essays, articles, monographs, books, and major works that were quoted or used in writing this book.

7000 anni di Cina a Venezia (*7000 China Years in Venice*). Catalogue of the exhibition at the Palazzo Ducale of Venice, organized by the Museum of Chinese History of Beijing. Cinisello Balsamo: Silvana Editoriale, 1983.

Almanach de Gotha (*Gotha Almanac*), 1893. Gotha: Justus Perthes, 1893.

Alvi, G. *Il secolo americano* (*The American Century*). Milan: Adelphi, 1996.

Annuario 1995 (*1995 Yearbook*). Milan: Rizzoli Corsera, 1996. For Israeli radio quote about Mr. Rabin.

Annuario 1997 (*1997 Yearbook*). Milan: Rizzoli Corsera, 1998. For Amartya Sen's quote about Mr. Nehru and John Paul II's quote about Mother Teresa.

Aprà, Adriano "Il divismo cinematografico negli U.S.A." ("U.S. Cinema Stars"), in *Bollettino per biblioteche*. Pavia, 1981.

Architettura del XX secolo (*20th Century Architecture*). Milan: Electa, 1993.

Bartezzaghi, Stefano. "Nostalgia, l'equivoco italiano" ("Nostalgia, the Italian Misunderstanding") in *La Stampa*, March 17, 1997.

Barthes, Roland. *Miti d'oggi* (*Today's Myths*). Milan: Lerici, 1962.

Bausani, A. "La Persia dalla conquista islamica ad oggi" ("Persia from the Islamic Conquest to Today") in *L'Impero bizantino e l'Islamismo*, in *Nuova Storia Universale dei Popoli e delle Civiltà* (*The Byzantine Empire and Islam, in New Universal History of Peoples and Civilizations*), vol. 6, t. 1. Reprint. Turin: Utet, 1997, pp. 371-508.

Benedetti, M.T. *Dentro l'immagine. L'impressionismo* (*Inside the Image. Impressionism*). Milan: Mondadori, 1993.

Beonio-Brocchieri P. *Storia del Giappone* (*History of Japan*). With postscript by A. Tollini. Milan: Mondadori, 1996.

Boccafogli, R. *Ferrari . . . un sogno nato nella neve* (*Ferrari . . . A Dream Born in the Snow*). Milan: SEP Editrice, 1997.

Bordino, Giampiero and Martignetti, Giuliano. *Il mondo dal 1970 a oggi* (*The World—1970 to Now*). Supplement to *Nuova Storia Universale dei Popoli e delle Civiltà* (*New Universal History of Peoples and Civilizations*), vol. XXI. Turin: Utet, 1997.

Broad, L. *Winston Churchill*. 2nd ed. London-New York: Hutchinson & Co., Ltd. 1946.

Buja, C. *Elvis Presley*. Milan: Targa Italiana, 1988.

Calasso, Roberto. "Il guanto di Gilda" ("Gilda's Glove") in *Panorama*, October 25, 1977.

Calendario Atlante De Agostini 1998 (*De Agostini 1998 Atlas Calendar*). Novara: Istituto Geografico De Agostini Novara, 1998.

Cardinale, A.E. "Tra fumi acidi madame Curie scoprì il radio" ("How Mrs. Curie Discovered Radium in Acid Fumes"), in *Corriere della Sera*, March 15, 1998.

Catoni, M.L. "Cercando le Olimpiadi" ("Looking for the Olympics"), in *I Greci. Storia cultura arte società* (*The Greeks. History, Culture, Art, and Society*), edited by S. Settis, vol. 1, *Noi e i Greci* (*We and the Greeks*). Turin: Einaudi, 1996, pp. 539-609.

Cecchini E. "Il ponte aereo di Berlino" ("Berlin's Air Bridge"), in *Il libro dei ponti* (*The Book of Bridges*), edited by F. Dani. Pomezia: Sarin, 1988, pp. 216–219.

Chronique du XXème Siècle (*Chronicle of the 20th Century*). Bassilac éd., 1993.

Coen, F. *Israele: quarant'anni di storia* (*Israel: 40 Years of History*). Casale Monferrato: Marietti, 1985.

Cohen, B. et al. *Stato del mondo 1994* (*1994 Status of the World*) Milan: Il Saggiatore-Bruno Mondadori, 1994.

Corgnati, M. and Poli, F. *Dizionario d'arte contemporanea* (*Dictionary of Contemporary Art*). Milan: Feltrinelli, 1994.

Corliss, R. *Greta Garbo*. Milan: Milano Libri, 1993.

Cotroneo, R. "Nel bunker di Gates. Non ci spezzeranno come l'AT&T" ("In Gates's Bunker: We Will Not Be Broken-Up Like AT&T"), in *Corriere della Sera*, May 20, 1998.

Davis, A. *I Beatles superstar*. (Italian translation of *Quote Unquote: The Beatles*. Parragon Book Service, 1994). Rome: Gremese, 1997.

De Fornari, O. *Walt Disney*. Rome: Il castoro, L'Unità, 1995.

De Gaulle, C. *Le fil de l'épée et autres écrits* (*The Sword's Edge and Other Writings*), including "La discorde chez l'ennemi" ("Disagreement Within the Enemy"), "Vers l'armée de métier" ("Toward a Professional Army"), and "La France et son armée" ("France and Its Army"). 2nd ed. Paris, 1994.

Dineen, C. *Michael Jackson* (Italian translation of *Michael Jackson: In His Own Words*, Omnibus Press, NY, 1993). Milan: Kaos Edizioni, 1994.

Dizionario Larousse del cinema americano (Italian ed. of *Dictionnaire du cinéma américain* [*Dictionary of American Film*], Librairie Larousse, 1988, updated). Rome: Gremese, 1993.

Donadoni, S., ed. *L'uomo egiziano* (*The Egyptian*). 2d ed. Bari: Laterza, 1966.

Dorfles, Gillo. "I limiti del balletto 'sulle punte'" ("The Limits of Classical Ballet"), in *La danza a Milano nel Novecento* (*Dance in 20th Century Milan*), edited by Giorgio Taborelli. Milan: Amici della Scala, 1986.

Einstein, Albert. *Pensieri degli anni difficili* (*Thoughts During Difficult Years*). Turin: Boringhieri, 1965.

Enciclopedia della scienza e della tecnica EST (*EST Encyclopedia of Science and Technology*). 12 vols. Milan: EST Mondadori, 1974–76.

Enciclopedia della televisione Garzanti (*Garzanti Encyclopedia of Television*). Edited by Grasso, E. Milan: Garzanti, 1996.

Enciclopedia Europea (*European Encyclopedia*). 12 vols. Milan: Garzanti, 1976–84.

Enciclopedia Garzanti di filosofia (*Garzanti Encyclopedia of Philosophy*). 1st ed. 1993. Milan, Garzanti, 1996. Referred to as EGF for individual entries in this bibliography.

Enciclopedia Italiana (*Italian Encyclopedia*). 36 vols. Rome: Istituto Treccani per L'Enciclopedia Italiana, 1929-37; Appendix I, 1 vol., 1938; Appendix II, 2 vols., 1949; Appendix III, 2 vols., 1961; Appendix IV, 3 vols., 1979; Appendix V, 5 vols., 1993.

Encyclopaedia Britannica. 30 vols. and yearly supplements. 15th ed. Chicago-London, 1974.

Escobar, R. "Truman, sei tutti noi" ("Truman, You Are All of Us"), in *Il Sole-24 Ore*, October 4, 1998.

Foa, L., and Paolucci, S. *L'Europa* (*Europe*). Bologna, Zanichelli, 1976. For Paolucci's quote about Mr. Onassis.

Fornari, Franco. *Piscanalisi della guerra* (*Psychoanalysis of War*). Milan, Feltrinelli,1966.

Foucault, Michel. *Storia della follia nell'età classica* (Italian translation of *Histoire de la folie à l'âge classique* [*History of Madness in the Classical Age*], Paris, 1972). Milan: Rizzoli, 1976. The quotation used in the Introduction to this book is from the short second preface.

Frank, P. *Einstein la vita e il suo tempo* (*Einstein, His Life and Times*). Milan, 1949.

Freud, Sigmund. "Storia del movimento psicoanalitico" ("History of the Psychoanalytic Movement") (1914), in *Totem e tabù, Storia del movimento psicanalitico, L'interesse per la psicoanalisi* (*Totem and Taboo, History of the Psychoanalytic Movement, The Interest for Psychoanalysis*). Rome: Avanzini & Torraca, 1969.

Gamow, G. *Biografia della fisica* (*Biography of Physics*). Milan, 1974.

Gates, William. "L'informatica nella vita quotidiana" ("Computers in Everyday Life"), in *Ca' de Sass 139*, December 1997, pp. 20-23.

Gavi, P., Sartre, Jean-Paul, and Victor, P. *Ribellarsi è giusto* (Italian translation of *On a raison de se révolter* [*The Right to Rebel*], Paris, 1974). Turin: Einaudi, 1975.

Gavinelli, C. *Architettura contemporanea* (*Contemporary Architecture*). Milan: Jaca Book, 1995.

Gidal, P. *Andy Warhol: Films and Paintings, The Factory Years*. Da Capo, NY, 1991.

Guarracino, S. *Il Novecento e le sue storie* (*The 20th Century and Its Tales*). Milan: Bruno Mondadori, 1997.

Guinness Book of the 20th Century. London: Guinness, 1997.

Hobsbawm, E.J. *Il secolo breve. 1914– 1991: l'era dei grandi cataclismi* (Italian translation of *Ages of Extremes—The Short Twentieth Century 1914–1991*, 1994). 1st Ital. ed. 1995. 16th ed. Milan: Rizzoli, 1998.

Jordan, R. *Marlon Brando*, edited by T. Sennet (Italian translation of *Marlon Brando*, 1974). 2nd ed. Milan, 1985.

La religione degli europei (*The Religion of Europeans*). Turin: Einaudi, 1992.

Lapidus, I.M. *Storia delle società islamiche* (Italian translation of *A History of Islamic Societies*, Cambridge, Cambridge Univ. Press, 1988). Vol. III, *I popoli musulmani* (*The Moslems*). Milan, 1995.

Lawrence, Thomas E. *I sette pilastri della saggezza* (Italian translation of *The Seven Pillars of Wisdom*). Milan: Bompiani, 1949.

Lenore, V. *Madonna* (Italian translation of *Madonna*, Valencia, 1998). Fossalta (Modena): Logos, 1998.

Lewis, B. *Il Medio Oriente. Duemila anni di storia* (Italian translation of *The Middle East*, 1995). Milan: Mondadori, 1996.

Libro dell'anno 1998 (*1998 Book of the Year*). Novara: Istituto Geografico De Agostini Novara, 1998.

Ludgwig, E. *Guglielmo II* (Italian translation of *Wilhelm II*, Berlin 1926). Milan: Mondadori, 1927.

Lyotard, J.F. *La condition post-moderne* (*The Postmodern Condition*). Paris: Seuil, 1979.

MacDonald, D. "Masscult e Midcult" Italian translation of "Masscult & Midcult," in *Partisan Review* 4, 1960. Rome, 1997.

Madsen, A. *Chanel. Una vita, un'epoca* (Italian translation of *Chanel. A Woman of Her Own*, New York, 1990). Novara: Istituto Geografico De Agostini Novara, 1990.

Marhaba, S. "Psicoanalisi" ("Psychoanalysis") entry in *EGF*, op. cit.

Maria Callas alla Scala (*Maria Callas at La Scala*). Catalogue of the Teatro alla Scala Exibition. Milan: Ed. Teatro alla Scala, 1997.

Moreno, Paolo. "L'arte dei Greci" ("Greek Art") in *Arte. Storia universale* (Art. A Universal History), op. cit., pp. 52-79.

Moreno, Paolo. *I bronzi di Riace. Il maestro di Olimpia e i Sette a Tebe* (*The Riace Bronzes. The Master of Olympia and the Seven of Thebes*). Milan: Electa, 1998.

Morin, E. *I divi* (Italian translation of *Les stars* [*Stars*], Paris, 1963). Milan: Mondadori, 1963.

Morin, E. *Le Star* (Italian translation of *Les Star* [*Stars*]). Milan: Edizioni Olivares, 1995.

Nenarokov, A. *Storia illustrata della grande rivoluzione socialista. Il 1917 in Russia mese per mese* (Italian translation of the Russian work, *Illustrated History of the Great Socialist Revolution. 1917 in Russia, Month by Month, 1980*). Moscow: Progress, 1987.

Nevins, A. and Commager, H.S. *Storia degli Stati Uniti* (Italian translation of *A Pocket History of the United States*, 1991, mass mkt.). Turin: Einaudi, 1980.

Panikkar, K.M. *Storia della dominazione europea in Asia* (Italian translation of *Asian and Western Dominance*, London). 2nd ed. Turin: Einaudi, 1958.

Pansera, A. and Vitta, M. *Guida all'arte contemporanea* (*Guide to Contemporary Art*). Casale Monferrato: Mareitti, 1986.

Pelé (with Fish, R.L.). *La mia vita e il più bel gioco del mondo* (Italian translation of *My Life and the Beautiful Game*, 1977). Milan: Sperling & Kupfer, 1977.

Philolenko, A. *Storia della boxe* (Italian translation of: *Histoire de la boxe* [*History of Boxing*], Paris, 1991. Genoa: Il Melangolo, 1997.

Pianciola, C. "Esistenzialismo" ("Existentialism"), entry in *EFG*, op. cit.

Pianciola, C. "Jean-Paul Sartre," entry in *EFG*, op. cit.

Pleket, H.W. "L'agonismo sportivo" ("Competition in Sports"), in *I Greci* (*The Greeks*), op. cit., vol. I, op. cit., pp. 507-537.

Preve, Costanzo. "Verità e storicità del Novecento" ("Truth and Historicity in the 20th Century"), in Bontempelli, M. and Preve, Costanzo. *Nichilismo. Verità. Storia. Un manifesto filosofico alla fine del XX secolo* (*Nihilism. Truth. History. A Philosophical Manifesto at the close of the 20th Century*). Pistoia: CRT, 1997.

Riccardi, A. "Governo e 'profezia' nel pontificato di Pio XII" ("Government and 'Prophecy' in the Papacy of Pius XII"), in *Pio XII*, op. cit., pp. 31-92.

Riccardi, A., ed. *Pio XII* (*Pius XII*). Rome-Bari: Laterza, 1984.

Rivelli, M.A. *Le génocide occulté* (*The Hidden Genocide*). Lausanne, L'Age d'Homme, 1998.

Rivieccio, G. *Enciclopedia cronologica delle scoperte e delle invenzioni* (*Chronological Encyclopedia of Discoveries and Inventions*). Milan: Rusconi, 1995.

Rotha, P., and Griffth, R. *Storia del cinema* (Italian translation of *The Film Till Now*, 1960). Turin: Einaudi, 1964.

Roy, O. *L'échec de l'Islam politique* (*The Failure of Political Islam*). Paris, Seuil, 1992.

Rubinstein, Helena. *The Art of Feminine Beauty*. New York: H. Liveright, 1930. (Courtesy of Biblioteca Storia Unipro, Milan.)

Sadoul, G. *Storia del cinema mondiale* (Italian translation of *Histoire du Cinéma mondiale des origines à nos jours* [*World History of Film: From Its Origins to Today*]. Paris, 1964). 2nd ed. Milan: Feltrinelli, 1972.

Salvadori, Massimo L. *Storia dell'età contemporanea dalla restaurazione all'eurocomunismo* (*Contemporary History from the Restoration to Euro-Communism*). 3 vols. 1st ed. 1977. Turin: Loescher, 1988.

Sarin Editorial Committee, ed.. *Storia del computer. Dalle origini del calcolo all'intelligenza artificiale* (*History of the Computer. From the Origins of Calculus to Artificial Intelligence*). Pomezia: Sarin, 1984.

Sartre, Jean-Paul. *L'esistenzialismo è un umanesimo* (Italian translation of *L'existentialisme est un humanisme* [*Existentialism Is a Humanism*], Paris, 1946). Milan: Mursia, no date.

Sartre, Jean-Paul. *L'essere e il nulla* (Italian translation of *L'être et le néant* [*Being and Nothingness*], Paris, 1943). Milan: Il Saggiatore, 1965.

Savio, F. *Il tutto Chaplin* (*All about Chaplin*). Venice, 1972.

Schuller, G. *Il jazz classico* (Italian translation of *Early Jazz: Its Roots and Musical Development*, Oxford, NY, 1986). Milan: Arcobaleno, 1979.

Scienziati e tecnologi contemporanei (*Contemporary Scientists and Technologists*). 3 vols. Milan: Mondadori, 1975.

Segré, E. *Personaggi e scoperte nella fisica contemporanea* (*People and Discoveries in Contemporary Physics*). Milan, 1976.

Semi, A.A. "Psicoanalisi" ("Psychoanalysis"), entry in *EGF*, op. cit.

Stalin, Josef. *Questioni del Lenininsmo* (Italian translation of the Russian work, *Leninist Issues,* 11th ed 1939). Moscow: Foreign Language Editions, 1946.

Strachey, L. *La Regina Vittoria* (*Queen Victoria*). Milan, 1985.

Taborelli, Giorgio, scient. ed. *Arte. Storia universale* (*Art. A Universal History*). Milan: Leonardo Libri, 1997.

Taylor, A.J.P. *La monarchia asburgica* (*The Habsburg Monarchy*). Milan, 1985.

Townsend, W. and Townsend, L. *Biography of H.R.H. the Prince of Wales*. London, 1929.

Valentinetti, C.M. *Orson Welles*. Milan: Il castoro L'Unità, 1995.

Vercellin, G. *Iran e Afghanistan* (*Iran and Afghanistan*). Rome, 1986.

Vidal, Gore. *Hollywood* (Italian translation of *Hollywood*, New York-Toronto, 1990). Milan: Bompiani, 1990.

Vollard, Ambrose. *Paul Cézanne*. Paris, 1914.

Von Plufgk-Harttung, J., ed. *Storia Universale* (*Universal History*). 6 vols. Italian ed. Milan: Società Editrice Libraria, 1928, with no notation about the original edition.

Wahl, A. *Il calcio. Una storia mondiale* (Italian translation of *La balle au pied. Histoire du football* [*Kicking the Ball: A History of Soccer*], Paris, 1990-1993). Milan: Electa Gallimard, 1994.

Weisberg, H. *Chi ha ucciso Kennedy?* (Italian translation of *Whitewash. The Report on the Warren Report*, 1965). Milan: Feltrinelli, 1967.

Weiss, E. *Dizionario di concetti psicoanalitici fondamentali* (*Dictionary of Basic Psychoanalytic Concepts*), appendix to Freud, Sigmund. *Introduzione allo studio della psicoanalisi (1915–1917)* (*Introduction to the Study of Psychoanalysis 1915–1917*), 1932). Rome: Astrolabio, 1961.

Will, George. *Reagan's America*. New York: Penguin Books, 1988.

Zenni, S. *Louis Armstrong*. Rome: Nuovi Equilibri, 1995.

Zevi, B. *Storia dell'architettura moderna* (*History of Modern Architecture*). Turin: Einaudi, 1975.

Internet - Online Sources:
www.crimelibrary.com; May 1998.
www.foorester.com; June–July 1998.
www.gallup.com; June–July 1998.
www.ibm.com; June–July 1998.
www.idc.com; June–July 1998.
www.law.umkc.edu/ftrials/lindbergh; May 1998.
www.lindberghtrial.com; May 1998.
www.microsoft.com; June–July 1998.

Index of Names

(We selectively list the major individuals mentioned in the book. The names of the 100 leading figures are highlighted in bold).